SAS

SPEED   AGGRESSION   SURPRISE

TOM PETCH

SAS

SPEED   AGGRESSION   SURPRISE

THE SECRET ORIGINS OF THE SPECIAL AIR SERVICE

WH
ALLEN

I

WH Allen, an imprint of Ebury Publishing,
20 Vauxhall Bridge Road,
London SW1V 2SA

WH Allen is part of the Penguin Random House group of companies
whose addresses can be found at global.penguinrandomhouse.com

Penguin
Random House
UK

Copyright © Tom Petch 2022

Tom Petch has asserted his right to be identified as the author of this
Work in accordance with the Copyright, Designs and Patents Act 1988

The author and publisher gratefully acknowledge the permission granted
to reproduce the copyright material in this book. Every effort has been
made to trace copyright holders and to obtain their permission.
The publisher apologises for any errors or omissions and, if notified of any corrections,
will make suitable acknowledgement in future reprints or editions of this book.

First published in the United Kingdom by WH Allen in 2022
This edition published in the United Kingdom by WH Allen in 2023

Maps © Helen Stirling 2022
Original wings design by Johann Adam Rennebaum, Shepheard's architect. Courtesy of
Stromersche Kulturgut-Denkmal und Naturstiftung, Grünsberg Castle,
Altdorf by Nuremberg

www.penguin.co.uk

A CIP catalogue record for this book is available from the British Library

ISBN 9780753559406

Printed and bound in Great Britain by Clays Ltd, Elcograf S.p.A.

The authorised representative in the EEA is Penguin Random House Ireland,
Morrison Chambers, 32 Nassau Street, Dublin D02 YH68

MIX
Paper | Supporting
responsible forestry
FSC® C018179

Penguin Random House is committed to a sustainable future
for our business, our readers and our planet. This book is made
from Forest Stewardship Council® certified paper.

For Dave

Contents

Cast

Alexander, General. Appointed to take over Commander Middle East from the Auk by Churchill in Aug 1942.

Allenby, General Edmund, First World War General responsible for invasion of Palestine 1917.

Almásy, László. Member of Zerura Club who did not join LRDG because he was Hungarian, and in the German camp.

Arnold, Allan. Brigadier. British Military Attaché in Ankara, Turkey.

Auchinleck, Claude, *the Auk*, General from Indian Army who retook Narvik in Norway in Apr 1940, commander of South of England 1940, posted to India, Jan – May 1941, took over from General Wavell in Egypt, July 1941.

Bagnold, Ralph, British Officer and interwar desert explorer, who pioneered navigation beyond the 'Sand Sea' of Egypt. Founder of *Zerzura Club*. First CO of the LRDG.

Bayerlin, Fritz. Rommel's Chief of Staff in 1942.

Beresford-Pierce, Noel, General. Commander of 4th Indian Division to April 1941, then the Western Desert Force.

Bevan, John, Colonel. Appointed as Clarke's opposite number in deception in London as a result of Clarke's visit in Sept 1941.

Blaich, Theo. German pilot and Kommando hunter.

Bonnington, L Detachment, SAS Troop Commander.

Bourne, Alan. Royal Marines General who became the first commander of the commandos.

Brooke, Alan. Divisional Commander with Monty in British Expeditionary Force 1940. Appointed Chief of General Staff in Whitehall to replace Dill in Dec 1941.

Buck, Captain. German speaking British Officer who set up a special forces *Fifth Column* unit to pose as Germans.

Byng, Captain WHS. Officer sent to install RAF *Boys* telescope in Turkey to spy on Rhodes Harbour.

Byrne, Jack, British soldier. Signed on aged 17 to Gordon Highlanders, was wounded in France and volunteered for commandos in 1940.

Calvert, *Mad* Mike. British Officer responsible for demolitions training in early Commando. Would be last Brigadier to command SAS before they were disbanded.

Campbell, British Officer with 11 Commando.

Catroux, Georges Albert Julien, General. French intelligence officer in Rif War, Morocco, where he met Clarke in 1924. Free French Commander, Cairo, then commander of Syria-Lebanon after it was liberated in 1941.

Chambers, Jim. SAS Troop Leader in A Squadron with Fraser.

Cheyne, John. British regular soldier, Sergeant in Gordon Highlanders who joined 11 Scottish Commando in 1940. Became Fraser's sergeant.

Crichton-Stuart, Michael. Scots Guards, friend of David Stirling and commander of LRDG 'G' Guards patrol.

Churchill, Winston, First Lord of the Admiralty till May 1940, then British Prime Minster.

Clarke, Dudley Wrangel, joined the Royal Artillery 1916. British staff officer in 1939.

Clarke, *Tibby*. Dudley Clarke's younger brother who became a famous screenwriter.

Clayton, Pat. A desert surveyor and member of the Zerzura Club, commissioned into the British Army 1940 to lead an LRDG patrol.

Colvin, Felix. CO of 7 Commando.

Conningham, Arthur *Mary*. RAF officer from New Zealand appointed to 8th Army in July 1941. Instrumental in developing close air support for Allied ground forces.

Courtney, Roger, Commando Officer who pioneered the use of Folboat canoes for covert beach landing which led to the creation of the Special Boat Service (SBS).

Creagh, Michael O'Moore, replaced Hobo Hobart as commander of 7th Armoured Division in Egypt in Nov 1939.

Crüwell, Ludwig, General. Panzer General in Rommel's Afrika Korps.

Cumberlege, Cleland *Cle*, cousin of Mike. British Royal Artillery Officer working in GHQ Cairo in 1941 when recruited by Clarke to join his cousin.

Cumberlege, Michael *Mike* Bulstrode. Yacht captain, landing SOE agents in Mediterranean when recruited by Clarke.

Cunningham, Alan, General, brother of Admiral, fought the Italians in East Africa, then commanded 8th Army in 1941.

Cunningham, Browne, British Admiral commanding Mediterranean Fleet.

D'Arcy, Guardsman. Member of Jock Lewes' Commando Team.

D'Ornano, Colonel. Free French Corsican *méhariste* (camel cavalry) based in Chad who joined up with LRDG.

De Gaulle, Charles, General. Commander of Free French forces.

De Guingand, Freddie. British Officer; joint planning staff GHQ, Cairo from Dec 1940, Auk's intelligence officer Feb 1942, Monty's Chief of Staff, Aug 1942.

De Wiart, Carlton *Old Flamer.* British General, fought in Norway 1940, and responsible for recruiting many commando officers.

Deane-Drummond, Tony. British Officer in 2 Commando, which became 11 SAS.

Dill, John *Jack*, British General sent to Palestine in 1936 who Clarke served under. Replaced Ironside as Chief of the General Staff in Whitehall, May 1940. (Replaced by Alan Brooke in Dec 1941.)

Dillon, Brian Edevrain. British Tank officer recruited by David Stirling for Benghazi raid who then joined the SAS.

Donovan, US Colonel *Wild Bill.* President Roosevelt's envoy. Met Clarke in Jan 1941. Recommended creating US Rangers and OSS (CIA).

Dorman-Smith, Eric. Revolutionary British Officer and friend of Hemingway who worked with General Wavell between the wars.

Dorothy, Dudley Clarke's housekeeper at Stratton Street, Mayfair.

Drori, Palestinian interpreter working with 11 Commando.

Du Vivier, Jeff. Gordon Highlander, joined 11 Scottish Commando in 1940.

Easonsmith, Jake. LRDG Troop Commander.

Eden, Anthony. British Secretary of State.

Evetts, John 'Jack' Fullerton, Brigadier, General. British staff officer with Clarke in Palestine 1936, then commander of 6 Division in Egypt in 1940.

Fairbairn, William. First man outside Japan to earn a black belt. Former Shanghai policeman responsible for training commandos in unarmed combat.

Farmiloe, Robin. Adjutant of 11 Commando.

Fellers, Bonner. US Military Attaché to Cairo. US cipher code was broken by the Germans, Rommel nicknamed him *die gute Quelle* (the good source).

Fleming, Ian. British Naval Intelligence and writer, creator of James Bond.

Fleming, Peter. Friend of Clarke. Worked with commandos in 1940. Posted to Far East 1942.

Fraser, William, joined Gordon Highlanders in 1936, and was a corporal in 1939.

Freyberg, Bernard. New Zealand General, veteran of Gallipoli in the First War, and commander of New Zealand Division in the Second.

Galloway, *Sandy*. Scottish, British Staff Officer in Egypt.

Garnon-Williams, Captain, Royal Naval Officer in Whitehall assigned to commandos in 1940.

Gatehouse, Alexander. Royal Tank Regiment officer, friend of Dorman-Smith and armoured pioneer. Rose to General commanding a division at second Battle of El Alamein in Oct 1942. Sacked by Monty.

George VI, King of Britain during the Second World War.

Glennie, Ian. Troop Commander with 11 Commando.

Gort, Lord, commander of British Expeditionary Force in France until defeat in May 1940.

Gott, William *Strafer*. Colonel to General. Commander in O'Connor's *Army of the Nile*. Replaced Creagh as Commander 7th Armoured Division after BATTLEAXE, then became Corps commander.

Graziani, Marshall. Genocidal inter-war Italian commander of North Africa, and commander of Italian Forces at outbreak of Second World War.

Gubb, Pasha, Major General. British Officer with the Arab Legion. Met Clarke while Clarke was in Transjordan Frontier Force in 1930.

Guderian, Heinz. German General and architect of *Blitzkrieg*.

Gurdon, Robin. LRDG Troop Leader.

Gurmin, Trooper. Fake SAS man.

Hackett, John *Shan* Winthrop, British Officer appointed to provide liaison between GHQ and growing number of British special forces in 1942.

Halder, German Chief of General Staff, reporting directly to Hitler until sacked in Sept 1942.

Harding, John. British Officer, assistant to O'Connor, then Neame. Became commander of 7th Armoured Division in Sept 1941.

Haselden, John. British Captain and spy behind Axis lines in Egypt. Son to a British father and Egyptian mother. Fluent in Arabic, French and Italian.

Hemingway, Ernest. Writer and friend of Eric Dorman-Smith.

Hitler, Adolf, German fascist dictator from 1933.

Hobart, *Hobo*, British Officer, First War tank pioneer and innovator, then General commanding British Armoured Division in Egypt till Oct 1939.

Hoffman, Freddie, manager of Continental Hotel, Cairo during the war.

Ironside, Edmund, British General and Chief of General Staff (CIGS) at outbreak of war in 1939. (Replaced by Dill in May 1940.)

Ismay, *Pug*. British General and Winston Churchill's chief military advisor.

James, Edward Clifton. Monty's double in 1944 who wrote *I Was Monty's Double*.

Jellicoe, George. 8 Commando then Special Boat Service (SBS) officer.

Jones, Kenyon, $14^{th}/20^{th}$ Hussar Officer in Egypt, recruited into intelligence by Maunsell of SIME in 1940, joined Clarke in A-Force.

Keyes, Geoffrey. Troop Leader with 11 Commando. Son of Lord Admiral Keyes.

Keyes, Lord Admiral. Appointed first Commander of Combined Operations over Clarke and Alan Bourne in 1940. Father to Geoffrey.

Kléber, Jean-Baptiste. French General whom Napoleon deserted in Egypt in 1798. Assassinated in gardens of Shepheard's Hotel.

Lampson, Miles. British Ambassador to Cairo.

Lawrence, TE, *Lawrence of Arabia*. First World War instigator of guerrilla warfare, fought with Arab Revolt 1916 – 1918.

Laycock, Bob. Became Niven's uncle-in-law in 1940. Appointed commander 8 Commando by Clarke. Commander of Layforce: 7, 8 and 11 Commandos.

Leclerc, Philippe de Hauteclocque. French General commanding French forces in French West Africa.

Liddell Hart, Basil. First World War British Captain turned military theorist, whose book *The Strategy of the Indirect Approach* had a significant impact on both British and German military doctrine between the wars.

Lloyd-Owen, David. LRDG Troop Commander.

Lorenzini, Major. Italian officer Bagnold met in the desert before the war.

Lovatt, Lord. Cousin to David Stirling. Son of creator of 'Lovatt Scouts' in Boer War. Commando Officer.

Lumsden, General. Armoured Division Commander from Nov 1941. Commanded Gatehouse and Armoured Divisions at second battle of El Alamein. Sacked by Monty after the battle.

Maclean, Fitzroy. SAS Officer recruited by David Stirling in 1942.

Macpherson, Thomas. Troop Commander with 11 Commando.

Manstein, Von. German General who designed German plan for the invasion of France.

Marling, Buster, coordinated early commando raids in her car.

Marriot, Maud, *Momo*. Wife of Patrick, hostess to Cairo social life.

Marriot, Patrick Claude, Brigadier. Friend of David Stirling, commander of 29th Indian Brigade.

Mather, Carol. 8 Commando Officer. Shared cabin with David Stirling on boat out to Egypt. Joined SAS 1943.

Maunsell, Raymond. Head of Security Intelligence Middle East (SIME), friend of Clarke, they worked closely together in Cairo.

Mayne, Blair *Paddy*. Irishman recruited with McGonigall to 11 Scottish Commando, 1940.

McCreery, Richard. British Officer sent to Cairo by Brooke in March 1942 to advise the Auk on armoured warfare, and to reign in Dorman-Smith.

McGonigal, Eoin. Irishman and friend of Mayne, recruited to 11 Scottish Commando in 1940.

Melot, Bob. World War One fighter ace, Arabist and spy. Worked with the SAS then joined Special Raiding Squadron (SRS).

Mitford *Teddy*, Royal Tanks officer recruited to LRDG in 1940.

Montagu, Ewen. Royal Naval Intelligence Officer in London responsible for overseeing OPERATION MINCEMEAT. Wrote *The Man Who Never Was*.

Montgomery, Bernard, *Monty*. General, Commander with British Expeditionary Force in France 1940, then Divisional Commander south coast of Britain under the Auk. Appointed to take over 8th Army from the Auk by Churchill in Aug 1942.

Moore, Captain. Troop Commander with 11 Commando.

Morshead, Leslie, General. Australian Divisional Commander in Egypt.

Morgan, Brigadier, promoted General. Commander of *Sickle Force* in Norway, 1940.

Morris. LRDG Troop Leader.

Muirhead, Alex. Mortar Troop Commander with Special Raiding Squadron (SRS) in Italy 1943, then Fraser's A Squadron SAS in France 1944.

Mussolini, Benito. Italian fascist dictator from 1925.

Neame, General. Commander of Palestine at outbreak of war. Became Commander of the 'Army of the Nile' in Egypt in 1941 after O'Connor.

Newbold, Douglas. Member of Bagnold's Zerura Club, British Secretary of Sudan.

Nicossof, fictional Italian spy operating from Cairo, codename CHEESE.

Niven, David. Actor and British Officer, recruited by Clarke in 1940 to help run commando organisation MO9.

Olivey. LRDG Troop Leader.

Paget, Brigadier, acting General. In command of British Forces in Åndalsnes in Norway in 1940.

Pedder, Dick. CO of 11 Scottish Commando.

Phillips, Arthur. Birmingham boy soldier recruited to the Warwickshire Regiment before the war, and volunteered for the commandos in 1940.

Platt, Doreen. Clarke's friend; a South African heiress who married David Niven's brother Max.

Pleydell, Malcom. SAS doctor in 1942.

Prendergast, Guy. British Officer of the Royal Tank Regiment and flier. Member of the Zerzura Club, became second CO of LRDG.

Pritchard, Tag. Commander of X Troop, 11 SAS, parachuted into Italy.

Ranfurly, Aide-de-camp. General Neame's aide-de-camp.

Ranfurly, **Countess.** Wife of Aide-de-camp. Secretary at SOE office in Cairo in 1941. Friend of Clarke, Stirling and Wavell.

Reid, Denys Whitehorn, Brigadier. Commander of 'E Force' 1941.

Rice, *Atty*. Served with Clarke as an officer in Transjordan Frontier Force 1930, recruited to the commandos by Clarke in 1940.

Riley, Pat Sergeant. L Detachment SAS.

Ritchie, Neil, Brigadier then General. General Auchinleck's chief staff officer, before commanding 8th Army.

Rommel, Erwin. German General, commander of 7 Panzer Division in France then Afrika Korps in North Africa.

Roosevelt, President. US president during World War Two.

Ruge, Norwegian General, commanding Norwegian forces at time of German invasion in 1940.

Rumbold, Constantia. Used her father's house on Grosvenor Crescent as covert office for commandos in 1940. Her father, Sir Horace, the ambassador, met Clarke in Constantinople and Berlin.

Sadler, Mike. British, from West Country. Working in Africa at outbreak of war he joined the Rhodesian Artillery. Recruited to LRDG in Cairo, then joined the SAS.

Sansom, AW, Major. British counter intelligence officer Cairo, who stationed a man to watch *Joe-the-Swiss* to find out if he was a spy.

Scialom, *Joe-the-Swiss*, head barman of Shepheard's Hotel *Long Bar* (known as Joe's Parish).

Seekings, Reg. Tough boxer from the Fens who joined 7 Commando in 1940.

Shaw, Bill. An archaeologist and member of Bagnold's Zerzura Club, commissioned into the British Army 1940 and became LRDG Troop Commander, then intelligence officer.

Smith, Arthur, General. Head of GHQ Cairo.

Smith, Lance Corporal. Fake SAS man.

Stirling, Bill, brother of David. Scots Guards officer who was instrumental in setting up commandos training wing in 1940 then CO, 2 SAS.

Stirling, David. Joined Scots Guards at the outbreak of war, joined 8 Commando in 1940. Founded the real SAS with Clarke in 1941.

Stirling, Peter, brother of David. Worked at British Embassy and rented a flat in Cairo's *Garden City*.

Sykes, Eric. Former Shanghai policeman responsible for commandos' unarmed combat.

Tait, Bob. British regular soldier, Sergeant in Gordon Highlanders, who joined 11 Scottish Commando in 1940.

Tedder, Air Vice Marshall. RAF Commander in Egypt from June 1941. In Jan 1944 became Eisenhower's Deputy Supreme Commander.

Terry, Sergeant. 11 Commando.

Tevendale. Regimental Sergeant Major of 11 Commando.

Timpson, Alistair. Cambridge University and Scots Guards, friend of David Stirling recruited to LRDG 1941.

Todd, Ronnie, one of the first commando officers recruited by Clarke in 1940.

Waugh, Evelyn. Writer and British Officer. Joined Bob Laycock's 8 Commando in 1940. He became intelligence officer of 'Layforce'.

Wavell, Archibald, British General, worked with Clarke in Palestine 1937 (Wavell took over from General Dill), sent to command Egypt shortly after outbreak of war, August 1939.

Wilson, Maitland *Jumbo*. British Commander in Egypt and then a General in Second World War.

Wingate, Orde. Worked with Clarke in Palestine running 'night patrols' against Arab insurgents. Recruited by General Wavell and sent to Ethiopia to help Haile Selassie start an insurgency against the Italian occupation.

Wolfson, Vladimir, Commander. Royal Naval Intelligence Istanbul.

Schemes and Plans

6 Division – Commanded by General Evetts for planned invasion of Rhodes early 1941 which included commando force LAYFORCE.

7th Division – Clarke's fake British Division defending Cyprus created in June 1941.

8th Army – British Army created by the Auk to defeat Rommel in July 1942 (date of Dorman-Smith and the Auk's lunch).

12th Army – the fictional army produced by Clarke's fictional units based in the Eastern Mediterranean.

A-Force (*Airborne-Force*) – Dudley Clarke's fake SAS force. A-Force HQ provided the deception that there was an SAS HQ in Cairo from Apr 1941.

ABEAM – deception plan started in Jan 1941 that the British had an SAS parachute brigade, the first of Clarke's fictional units.

ABSTENTION – British operation to capture Kastellorizo, part of the Dodecanese Island chain.

Afrika Korps – two German panzer divisions deployed to Africa Feb 1941, redesignated *Panzergruppe Afrika* in August 1942.

ANTI-ROMMEL – deception plan to threaten Rommel's lines of communications in 1941 which relied on the existence of British special forces.

BASTION – Clarke's deception in 1942 to convince Rommel the Allies had 300 additional tanks using K Detachment dummies.

BATTLEAXE – operation in June 1941 to defeat Rommel which was a complete failure and led to General Wavell's dismissal by Churchill.

BREVITY – a short and unsuccessful attack on Rommel in May 1941 to stop his advance.

BYNG-BOYS – Clarke's scheme for Captain Byng to insert the 'Boys' long range telescope into Turkey to spy on Rhodes.

CAMILLA – operation devised by General Wavell to deceive Italians about troop movements from Egypt to East Africa in 1940 that Clarke implemented. Clarke's first strategic deception.

CASCADE – Mar 1942 deception plan expanding Clarke's fake forces after he realised the success of the SAS deception and K Detachment's fake tanks.

CHEESE – fictional Syrian named Paul Nicossof; an invented Axis spy operating from Cairo who was handled by Axis from Rome.

COLLECT – deception plan, June 1941, that Commandos and SAS would take Rommel's supply port of Tripoli.

COLOSSUS – First SAS operation, carried out by 11 SAS, on Italy. Used by Clarke to deceive Italians that Britain had a parachute capability in Egypt.

CRUSADER – operation launched in Nov 1941 to drive Rommel out of Cyrenaica and ultimately out of Africa.

E Force – British scout car unit commanded by Brigadier Reid that became key to threatening Rommel's lines of communications during CRUSADER in Nov/Dec 1941.

Eureka – Radio Set used to signal to Allied aircraft that it was safe to drop supplies and troops.

EXPORTER – Commando operation to land north of the Litani River in Lebanon to allow Allied forces to cross unopposed and advance into Syria.

Fifth Column – Ernest Hemingway's story of the name: the idea that forces can be concealed in the enemy camp ready to act at the right moment.

FLESHPOTS – two Axis spies driven through the Sand Sea to Cairo by László Almásy, the only member of Bagnold's *Zerzura Club* to join the Germans.

GAFF – 2 SAS operation to kill or capture Rommel in 1944 based on Fraser's intelligence.

GILBERT – French double agent operating from Tunis from Jun 1943.

GOODWOOD – operation for Allies to break out from the Normandy beachheads in 1944.

HOUNDSWORTH – operation to drop Fraser's A Squadron, 1 SAS into Morvan Forest, France, in 1944 in order to stop two panzer divisions reaching Rommel.

K Detachment, SAS – unit created in 1941 to simulate the existence of an SAS parachute Brigade using gliders and dummy parachutists. Expanded to fake aircraft, tanks and landing craft.

L Detachment, SAS – the real SAS parachute unit created in July 1941.

MANDEBILES – delayed, and ultimately abandoned operation in 1941 to take the Dodecanese Islands, specifically Rhodes, from the Italians to allow Allied ships free passage to Greece. See 6 Division.

Maquis – the French resistance.

Méhariste – French desert camel troops.

Mosquito Stings – term used by Clarke to describe special forces operations (see *Pin Pricks* and *Rapier Play*).

Neccanos – fake RAF bombers (as opposed to gliders) built by K Detachment, SAS.

Phantom – Radio team with long range communications to reach London from France.

Pin Pricks – term used by Lawrence of Arabia to describe special forces operations (see *Mosquito Stings* and *Rapier Play*).

Pintails – exploding dummy parachutists, similar to 'Saints.'

Rapier Play – term used by Lawrence of Arabia for fast, mobile action to deceive the enemy. Opposite of *Wood Chopping*.

RAYON, Clarke's deception plan in Aug 1942 to invade Crete, in order to prevent Rommel using troops stationed there to attack 8th Army.

Saints – dummy parachutists that explode on impact.

SICKLE FORCE – Two British Battalions sent to Norway in 1940 to help the Norwegians.

Sonderkommando Blaich – German aerial hunter killer unit based around a Heinkel 111 commanded by Luftwaffe pilot Theo Blaich.

Subliminal Methods – Clarke's concept of influencing enemy decisions without them realising.

TORCH – operation to land US troops in Morocco and Algeria, Nov 1942.

WATERFALL – Mar 1943 deception that Allied forces in Egypt capable of launching invasion of Peloponnese (Greece). Successor of CASCADE.

Wood Chopping – term used by Lawrence of Arabia to describe First World War tactics.

WORKSHOP – Commando operation, never carried out, to take the island of Pantelleria from the Italians in Dec 1940 / Jan 1941.

ZEPPELIN – Clarke's 1944 cover plan to divert German attention from Normandy landings to Mediterranean, specifically the Balkans. Successor to CASCADE and WATERFALL.

Introduction

The *Boy's Own* story of the formation of the Special Air Service is legendary: how David Stirling recruited a plucky group of renegades and forged a special forces unit in the cauldron of the Western Desert against the opposition of both the Germans and his own headquarters.

The story is also a myth.

In truth, no new unit can be formed within the hierarchy of the British Army from the bottom up. The SAS came from an idea. An idea born from the trenches of the First World War in the minds of mavericks who decided there was a better way of doing business. Those men were British, but their ideas were developed by Germans, who unleashed them on the world in 1940 in *Blitzkrieg*, the Lightning War.

The British response was unique, because it targeted the minds of men and women, rather than a country or army. This led to a revolutionary method of warfare which shapes the way the West fights today. The real story of the SAS's origins, told here, introduces two characters, Dudley Clarke and William Fraser, who have bit parts in the traditional narrative: Clarke was the mastermind of those ideas, Fraser, their most successful frontline operator. Without them there would never have been an SAS.

This is their story.

PART ONE

The Lightning War

I

On Assignment: 1939–1940

Dudley Clarke

Midnight, 31 August 1939 – Dudley Wrangel Clarke climbed the winding steps to his top-floor bachelor flat in a seventeenth-century townhouse on Stratton Street, Mayfair. The housekeeper, Dorothy, was used to his nocturnal arrivals, usually from the Café de Paris in Leicester Square. But tonight, Clarke was still in his work suit – there had been yet another flap in the office over Herr Hitler's demands of Poland.

Clarke opened the door to his flat. The visiting card of a German officer he knew lay on the doormat. He turned it over. On it were written two words:

'*Auf wiedersehen*'.[1]

Clarke, a 40-year-old staff officer working in the War Office on Whitehall, had got on well with the German officer. Recently, late at night in Clarke's flat, Clarke had asked him if he thought war inevitable.

'I don't know. It is probably too late to stop now.'

'Well, if we are going to war, I shall rely on you to send me a word of warning first,' Clarke had joked.

The German officer's parting note was innocuous enough on the surface. He had obviously left for Germany. But, for Clarke, the goodbye meant something he'd thought impossible was now inevitable – war in Europe, less than two decades after 'the war to end all wars'.[2]

Clarke walked across to the window and looked at the lights blazing over Piccadilly in the summer night. This time, he would not be left out of the action.

*

Like many of his generation, Clarke couldn't wait to fight in the First World War. The problem had been his age. Clarke had been at school cadet summer camp, aged just 15, the day war had been declared in 1914. As soon as he was old enough, in 1916, he signed up to the Royal Artillery, as the first silver Zeppelin appeared over his family home in Frinton-on-Sea, Essex. Later that year, as a cadet at the Royal Academy Woolwich, he wrote in desperation to his father, who was working for the Red Cross in France, asking him, 'to inquire about the possibility of getting posted to France . . . . . . <u>Do please try and fix things up</u>.'[3]

In 1917, while Britain reeled from the horrific death toll and the fateful name of the Somme burnt itself into the nation's psyche, a Zeppelin floated into Clarke's gunsights in Norfolk. To his frustration he was denied permission to engage for fear of destroying a village below the airship. He attempted to get to the frontline with artillery replacements crossing the Channel, only to be caught in France.

That year, America entered the war, and Clarke began fearing the question, 'What did you do in the Great War, Daddy?' He transferred to the Royal Flying Corps in a bid to get into the fight. He was 5 foot 7 and three-quarter inches tall, a three-quarters he keenly preserved on his application – and very bright: two requisites of a pilot.

He graded top, was selected as a fighter pilot, but the terrible winter of 1917–18 prevented flying training. He was disappointed to be ordered to the sunnier climes of Number 5 Aerial Fighting School, Egypt, to complete his course. He watched a torpedo from an Austrian U-boat pass astern his ship, and on arrival flew over the battle lines east of Suez, but the war in the Middle East had moved on. The Ottoman Empire's troops driven from Egypt by General Edmund Allenby, and now Allenby and TE Lawrence (later to be known as Lawrence of Arabia), had chased them north through Palestine, walking together through the Jaffa Gate, Jerusalem, in 1917.

Clarke went solo, completing his first flight without an instructor on dual controls in 1918. Clarke met Lawrence when he landed at their airfield on his way to Cairo for lunch. The most striking thing Clarke noticed about the untidy colonel was that he had lieutenant colonel's rank on one shoulder, and lowly lieutenant's pips on the other, displaying the promotions he had received in just three years for organising the most successful insurgency in British history.

Clarke dearly wanted to join Lawrence's X Flight, which fought over wide swathes of desert. The Bedouin ranged over the flanks of the Ottoman Army, watched over by this array of sunburnt antipodean pilots and their motley collection of aircraft. Back then, aged 19, Clarke had no idea what sort of education he was receiving. But when General Allenby's cavalry reached Damascus, a pilot from X Flight landed with news that Colonel Lawrence no longer needed recruits, and the door closed on Clarke's last chance to join the war.

That evening, he took a lonely walk beyond the boundary of the airfield, and there, lost to view in the surrounding desert, broke down and cried for the first time since childhood.

On the evening of 11 November 1918, Clarke's attempt to celebrate the armistice at Shepheard's Hotel in Cairo failed when the Royal Military Police closed the bar at 7.30pm – an unprecedented step, since Shepheard's bar never shut. Clarke was the only sober man at the party, as hotel guests ordered champagne to their rooms, and British and Australian officers fought with pillows up the wide staircase, choking the lobby with down. On the streets, Allied troops took their rioting more seriously. Clarke drove back to camp past a burning convalescent camp, an overturned fire engine, and troops looting Egyptian shops.[4]

Clarke left Egypt in peace, but there is an Egyptian saying that once you have drunk the waters of the Nile, you are bound to return. The country had entered his bloodstream.

Insurgents

Clarke's desire to go to war a second time was not glory hunting, but to avoid a repetition of bloodshed. Of his six friends in a 1914 photograph at cadet camp, two had been killed within the year, one had lost his leg at Zeebrugge, and their Sergeant Instructor had lost his life at Gallipoli.

Clarke had a qualified belief in ghosts, and when he returned from Egypt, he searched for them. At Blickling Park, Norfolk, where he lived with 500 trainee gunners, and at his flying school, London Colney, Hertfordshire, where he climbed the gate to see sheep grazing on what had once been runways, to try and find an echo of his fellow cadets who been posted to France. Clarke thought the second war in his lifetime could be so much better fought by something he called 'subliminal methods', rather than the physical carnage of the last war. Clarke wanted to place ideas in the mind of the enemy, without the knowledge of how they had come by those ideas, that would cause them to act in a way Clarke wanted. Clarke's subliminal methods were a product of both his unique mind, and his unique experience.

Dudley Clarke's first experience of insurgency warfare came as an infant. He was born in the Transvaal, South Africa, in 1899, where his father had worked for the goldmining firm Farrar Brothers. Clarke was just three when the British Army was outwitted by Boer *Kommandos* dispersed in the Transvaal, whose insurgency was only ended when the British introduced concentration camps. These events were burnt into his family's psyche, and his father returned to England to take a job in the City of London.

After the First World War, Clarke did ask his father for a job in the City, but was told that the Army was a higher calling. Clarke had returned from Egypt as a member of the Royal Air Force (which took over flying in 1919), not the Army, and so he returned to his first home, the Royal Artillery. And that, as Clarke said, was that. He would always be part of the Army, but became one of its most unorthodox officers.

Posted to Kurdistan in 1920, he escorted the contents of a British bank in Iraq down the Tigris from Amarah to Basra, escaping Sunni and Shia insurgents who had joined forces and attacked Mosul to throw out the British. He cursed the bankers who had written the amounts on the chests in both Arabic and English, as he ordered his men to open fire over the heads of an approaching crowd of Marsh Arabs. Convinced Arab interest in his cargo was commercial, not conspiratorial, he did not shoot to kill.

In 1922 he took leave for a tour of Europe but ran out of money, a common event for him, and remembered an Army regulation that any officer in the vicinity of a war should report for duty. He reported to British GHQ, Constantinople, where General Mustafa Kemal Atatürk (victor at Gallipoli over the Allies) was in the process of kicking the Allies out. The head of British intelligence saw through Clarke's ruse, but was amused and sanctioned an advance on salary.

Seconded to military intelligence, Clarke was sent undercover into a boarding house, whose landlord was a known spy for the Turkish nationalists. After a couple of late-night drinks, it transpired the spy was terrified of his double life. Clarke scared him further and turned the agent, after which Clarke then helped smuggle British anti-nationalist spies onto the waiting HMS *Trinidad*.

His unorthodox military education continued during his leave in 1926, when he took a job as war correspondent at the *Morning Post*, and travelled to Morocco to cover the Rif War. The leader of the Berber insurgents was Abd el Krim, whose strategy would influence Mao Zedong, Che Guevara, and General Võ Nguyên Giáp (later destroyer of American ambitions in Vietnam in the 1970s). Krim destroyed the Spanish Army in the Atlas in three days, killing fifteen thousand, and during his insurgency of 1921–26 his Berbers would inflict fifty thousand Spanish and fifteen thousand French casualties.

Krim would eventually yield – but he did so by allowing only the French into the mountains, vowing never to give in to Spain and General Franco's genocidal Spanish Foreign Legion in the north of the Atlas.

Clarke was a romantic, but his romances were always unrequited. In 1922 a Russian émigrée, Nina, persuaded him to carry money to a male refugee trapped in Sofia, Bulgaria, to allow them to escape to safety. On his way to deliver the cash on the *Orient Express* he passed through Yugoslavia and the Serbs misread his passport: *Clarke, Dudley Wrangel*, and assumed his surname was Wrangel, his first name Clarke. By chance the name of the commander of the White Russian (Tzarist) Army was General Baron Wrangel. And when the Yugo-Slav Serbs found Clarke was carrying a hidden pistol, they feared he was related to the general, and Clarke was arrested. The lesson he learnt was that in international circles he could use an alias: Wrangel.[5] He did hand over the cash but the love affair was less successful: Clarke surprised Nina in the French Riviera on his return only to find the man to whom he had handed the cash in her hotel bedroom.

In 1930 an Englishwoman who had 'meant everything in the world to him' turned down his proposal. When Clarke discovered he and her new fiancé were to be posted to Egypt, this propelled him further into his unorthodox career, transferring to the Transjordan Frontier Force: an isolated Arab mounted force officered by the British. Here he rode along the dynamite-blasted Hejaz railway, to Wadi Rum, and to remote desert oases to intercept Bedouin raiding parties – a pastime which had only been temporarily suspended while the Bedu fought the Ottomans with Colonel Lawrence.

With the frontier force, Clarke personally encountered little aggression, either between Arabs and Jewish people, or between either group and the British. He'd ridden into one Jewish settlement, Beit Alfa, and was promptly offered a glass of milk – not his usual tipple – and the settlers asked if his unit could test their defences. Clarke duly charged the kibbutz on horseback and swiftly reached the conclusion that the Jewish settlers had far more weapons and skills than they were displaying, and would be more than capable of holding off the Bedouin till his unit arrived.

In 1936, he was posted to Palestine, and his final insurgency of 'the peace', after which he wrote up a hundred-thousand-word report on lessons learnt from the Arab rebellion. Followed up by a further long piece on the lessons of Lawrence of Arabia.

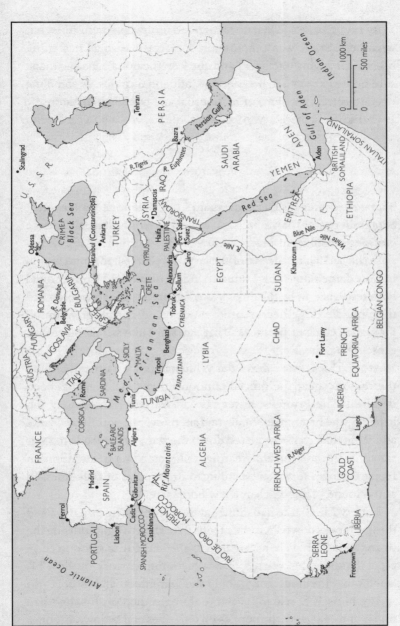

Europe, North Africa, and Southwest Asia, 1939.

By 1939, Clarke still had no recognised profession or position, but what he did have was a reputation. Described as small in stature, humorous, highly intelligent and quick on the uptake, he had made sure he was known, in a variety of influential circles, as someone open to certain missions of an unusual and confidential nature.[6]

Clarke, for generals who knew his talents, was a gun for hire.

War, 1939

Three days after his German friend's farewell note, on Sunday, 3 September 1939, Clarke walked to work across St James's Park in glorious sunshine. In deadly contrast to the excitement and enthusiasm he had felt on the eve of the last war, Clarke had found mobilisation depressing. The London Underground had been choked with reservists, lit by the dull glow of cigarettes of sad women and men, huddled together on their last ride before parting at Waterloo Station or Chelsea Barracks. That day the Tube would be empty, those men gone.

At 11 o'clock, everyone in the Whitehall office gathered around the radio to hear the official announcement that war had been declared. The Prime Minister's broadcast was immediately followed by the first scream of air-raid sirens over London, and Clarke and Whitehall staff thundered down the stairs and outside to their shelter, past the bearskin-wearing sentry standing to attention on Horse Guards. He was still standing to attention when they emerged at the sound of the all-clear a few hours later.

After work, Clarke had dinner at the Cavalry Club, then walked the few blocks down Piccadilly to his flat. The gas lights outside the In and Out Club were extinguished; ahead the Ritz stood in complete darkness. He started to put his mind to work on how his 'subliminal methods' might help the war effort, and in doing so secure himself a 'real job'. Clarke thought the Polish hadn't had much of a chance with enemies on two sides and Warsaw in ruins. But he saw this as a blessing in disguise – he was sure Russia and

Germany would be at each other's throats before long. With this in mind, he drafted a proposal for the Jewish Agency, with which he had worked in Palestine, to infiltrate the Balkans. He submitted his careful proposal first thing Monday morning.

It was rejected within the week.

Poland's collapse heralded the start of the 'Phoney War', and for Clarke, boredom. He was a cinephile, with a penchant for film noir (his idol was Marlene Dietrich) and he was delighted when cinemas reopened. He also indulged his other passion, entertaining beautiful and stylish women, and took his friend Doreen Platt, a fellow South African and heiress, out to dinner, followed by dancing at the Embassy Club on Bond Street.

In November, with the first of the winter smog adding to the general gloom of shortening nights and the discomfort of the blackout, a letter marked 'Secret' arrived. It was a summons from one of Clarke's former bosses in Palestine, General Archibald Percival Wavell, who had just been appointed commander of the Middle East. Wavell wanted Clarke to recce the 'overland route from Mombasa to Cairo as one of the means of maintaining and reinforcing Egypt should the Mediterranean and Red Seas become temporarily closed as a result of hostile action by Italy.'

With Egypt calling him, Clarke was given the weekend to pack, and went home to warn his housekeeper, Dorothy.

'I shall be away a few weeks,' he said, knowing the mission was four months. Dorothy was offended he didn't tell her where he was going, but Clarke knew the rules of the game better than most: friend or enemy, he only divulged what they needed to know.

Clarke then spent three difficult months navigating the headwaters of the Nile as a modern-day Dr Livingstone, even at one point travelling on a river boat bearing the good doctor's name. After a three-thousand-mile round trip he established that either keeping the Mediterranean open, or the long way round the Cape to Suez, were Britain's only options for supplying the Middle East.

It was March 1940 when Clarke returned to find Wavell in the new British HQ in the Semiramis Hotel. Its panoramic view over Cairo's Garden City reminded Clarke of his and Wavell's previous home in the King David Hotel, Jerusalem. The town was filling with Commonwealth troops and the Continental had given his room to General Bernard Freyberg, a Kiwi who was waiting for his division to arrive from New Zealand. Clarke didn't begrudge Freyberg; they had spent time together in London during the 1920s tracking both Bolsheviks and Irish nationalists who were interested in the contents of the Woolwich Armoury.

Clarke took a cab to Shepheard's Hotel, the scene of his thwarted armistice celebrations in 1918. Shepheard's was not the most expensive hotel in Cairo, but it was the most exclusive, its 550 rooms under so much pressure that guests were prepared to sleep in the lobby while they waited for an empty one. But Clarke knew the manager, and after checking in he sat with his back to the wall sipping a morning gin and tonic on the terrace.

For the British, Shepheard's terrace *was* Cairo – it was raised head-high above the street, its wicker tables and chairs sheltered from the sun by the balconies of the biggest suites directly above. The hotel staff wore white robes and tarboosh, the Egyptian fez. A pianist and viola played, and protection from the desert wind, the *khamaseen*, was provided by ornate rugs draped from the balcony's ironwork. The terrace was open to non-guests, and played host to officers and anyone of equivalent civilian rank, as well as any persons who could pass themselves off as such to the scarlet-clad, Montenegrin doormen armed with curved daggers. Successful interlopers often included prostitutes, pimps and spies.[7]

Clarke observed it would take a very discerning Rip Van Winkle to distinguish the street scene from 1918. Below in the bustle, Clarke saw a medley of regiments mixing together: the Sherwood Rangers, Britain's last mounted cavalry regiment on their way to Palestine; Australians, or Diggers, in their famous slouch hats; Indians in their turbans, early recruits to the regiments who would eventually supply over two million men to the largest volunteer army the world had seen.

Clarke wasn't the only talent Wavell was collecting for his

command, which stretched from Palestine to Iraq, through Egypt to Libya, and south to Ethiopia, across a fair chunk of the 3,600 square miles of North Africa's Greater Sahara. Wavell thought a desert explorer might have his uses, and across the terrace from Clarke sat Britain's greatest desert explorer.

Ralph Bagnold

Britain's greatest desert explorer, Ralph Bagnold, had arrived in Egypt by mistake. Posted to East Africa, his ship had zigged while her neighbouring vessel in the convoy zagged, forcing both to limp to Port Said for repair. Bagnold had taken the welcome opportunity to look up old friends in Cairo, where he was spotted at dinner in Shepheard's Hotel. The *Egyptian Gazette* announced his arrival with glee, pleased that the British were now putting 'square pegs into square holes', and a copy landed on General Wavell's desk.[8] Wavell swiftly poached Bagnold away from his East African posting – and sent him to their nascent armoured division out in the desert.

Exploration was in Bagnold's DNA. His earliest memories were of Jamaica, where he recalled a 'paradise for children' – mossy woods carpeted with wild strawberries, where he could pick an orange or a banana off a tree at will, or chew coffee berries, spitting out the beans.[9] His exploration was fuelled by H.G. Wells's; *The Time Machine* (1895), which draws heavily on the concept of the Fourth Dimension, and the idea that something could appear from another dimension would later have military application for Bagnold.

Bagnold had been in the Royal Signals in 1917, and was laying telephone wire when the British were the first to use tanks at the Battle of Cambrai, breaking the trench-war stalemate. He was posted to Egypt in 1926, where his father had served, and was drawn to a vast field for real exploration – the Eastern Sahara.[10]

The barrier to navigating west was the Sand Sea, an obstacle so intimidating that the Persian king Cambyses II had lost an entire army.

A wind arose from the south, strong and deadly, bringing with it vast columns of whirling sand, which entirely covered up the troops and caused them wholly to disappear.

Herodotus (425 BC)

A millennium and a half later nothing had changed.

Bagnold assaulted the first 400-foot dune of the Sand Sea in 1929, sitting alone in a stripped-down Model A Ford. Watched by a group of fellow pioneers, he hit the bottom at 40mph, stayed in a low gear, and contrary to everyone's expectations except his own, reached the top. But a sandstorm forced them back, one of their vehicles thrown to the bottom of a wind-scoured crater.

To Bagnold, this desert was a living, sentient being that resented his intrusion and was warning him it could do with him what it chose.[11] He would lie awake at night listening to the dunes booming to each other, as if communicating. In the desert he also felt there was a portal to the ancients; once, seeking refuge from a sandstorm, he crawled into a narrow cave and, lying down to rest, took off his watch and placed it on a rock ledge – to discover an ancient had done the same, and left a stone knife on the shelf.[12] Such was his affinity with the largest dune desert in the world that he did travel through time and into space in 2015, when NASA's rover *Curiosity* drove over the Bagnold Dunes on Mars.

In 1933, the Fascist Mussolini was building an African empire, and in the desert 800 miles south-west of Cairo, Bagnold encountered an Italian, Major Lorenzini, whose ideas filled Bagnold with anxiety. Over a 'sumptuous dinner' by the light of their headlights the Italian wondered aloud, 'If there is a war, what fun it would be to take a battalion to Aswan and seize the dam. What could you do?'[13]

The answer was nothing. The British had no capability in the desert, and the Aswan Dam, 600 miles upstream from Cairo, fed the whole Nile Delta with fresh water. Bagnold knew how easily such a long-distance raid could be done, and Lorenzini seemed just the man to do it.

Bagnold decided to buy American vehicles, more reliable than British, and train a group of officers in desert navigation; even if they only improved the maps it would be worthwhile. He took the proposal to his boss, 'Hobo' Hobart, who was renowned for his insubordination, his inability to follow orders he thought pointless, and his temper.

Hobo Hobart had a Military Cross from Flanders in 1915, and Distinguished Service Order from Iraq (then Mesopotamia). He was a tank pioneer who had embraced the concepts that would come to underpin the German *Blitzkrieg*,[14] and was one of a small group of iconoclasts who, between the wars, tried to reform the British Army. But, as war minister Leslie Hore-Belisha said, 'in all my experience as a Minister of the Crown, I never encountered such obstructionism as attended my wish to give the new armoured command to Hobart.' Hobart read and agreed with Bagnold's pitch, but predicted that it would be turned down.[15]

Not only did his commander, Henry Maitland 'Jumbo' Wilson, turn the idea down, but Hobo was fired. This was not due to Bagnold (Hobo already had many knives in his back, and had been sent to Egypt to get him out of the way) but because Hobo had gone on reforming in the desert. The Armoured Division he created would one day be known as 7th Armoured Division – or the 'Desert Rats'.

With Hobo sacked, Bagnold had tentatively shown his memo to his successor, General Michael O'Moore Creagh, 7th Hussars and son of a holder of the Victoria Cross. Creagh loved the idea and insisted on sending it to Jumbo Wilson for a second time and got an angrier response from HQ. Creagh suggested Bagnold should at least take him 'round his manor.' This he did – touring as far as the desert oasis of Siwa, and up to the Egyptian border to look at the Italian positions, poised to invade Egypt.

Bagnold had made a nuisance of himself, and marked his card with British HQ, but had got nowhere. He was at Shepheard's because he was being sent on a mission to Turkey to persuade the new republic to join the war. Clarke and Bagnold passed like ships in the night.

Subliminal Methods

Clarke's handwritten report was being typed up by his secretary, Miss Clarke (no relation), so he took some time to look up old acquaintances. Hanging out at the Continental Hotel Cabaret, he lunched with the hotel's manager, Freddie Hoffman. And with *New York Times* correspondent Joseph Levy. Levy thought Britain 'had lost her old cunning while the Germans had been learning from our experience of the last war.'

Before long Clarke found himself alone in the lift at GHQ with General Wavell. Wavell asked him what he would do when he finished his report.

'I have no idea,' Clarke confessed.

'Would you like a job out here?' Wavell asked. Clarke, on the spur of the moment – without the least idea what the job would be – said yes. Wavell then said nothing, which didn't surprise Clarke. When he had first met Wavell years earlier, a silent hour had passed mid-conversation while Clarke had escorted the general in a car to Haifa.

Wavell was a terrible communicator, but later, after discussing it with a colleague, Clarke reflected that Wavell might have meant an intelligence job. The prospect appealed to Clarke, since at that moment nothing was happening. Clarke flew back to London via Paris, a city he loved. There the street lights still shone, butter was on the menu, forgoing spirits meant switching to champagne, and Josephine Baker and Maurice Chevalier played the Casino de Paris.

In April, the Germans surprised everyone by invading Norway.

Clarke got back to London, and headed for the office at 10am on a Saturday expecting to find less than nothing to do. Instead, he discovered the War Office had been asking for him urgently. He was to carry orders as far as Rosyth, just north of Edinburgh to a force being despatched to Norway – and no further. The first thing he asked was if he could go to Norway too, but got 'no change out of this'. For Clarke, this simply meant he would have to find a way into the war through unofficial channels – something he had done many times before.

Part of his mission was to promote Brigadier Morgan to Major General in command of SICKLE FORCE, two battalions being sent to prop up the Norwegians. To do this, he would need a general's cloth sword shoulder badge, not available from the stores or a tailor at 7pm on a Saturday. Even his last resort, Archie Nathan's theatrical shop on Wardour Street was closed. He persuaded the Director of Military Intelligence, a general, to dash to his flat and pull them off his greatcoat. Before heading off, Clarke grabbed a hasty meal at the Berkeley Buttery, a café round the corner from his bachelor flat he referred to as his 'dining room', then caught a cab to Euston Station for the sleeper train to Edinburgh. He carried £10,000 in freshly printed bank notes, maps and intelligence summaries on Norway, all stuffed into eight large mail bags. Clarke was a small man, and the bags took up most of the cab.

Clarke spent the sleeper journey north with one hand on his pistol in his pocket after a last-minute addition to his charges, a Norwegian spy, seemed to know surprisingly little about Norway. He fell asleep dreaming of 'beautiful spies and villainous attacks' and woke up every time the man moved.

At Rosyth Port Office, Clarke delivered his mailbags, his Norwegian spy, and his message to Morgan. He looked out on the Firth of Forth, where the flagship cruiser HMS *Galatea* and her accompanying cruisers and destroyers were making steam; smoke was pouring over the water. The ships were getting ready to sail to Britain's first frontline of the war. Clarke suggested to Morgan that he should accompany SICKLE FORCE, then signalled London:

CONSIDER I CAN BE MORE USEFULLY EMPLOYED HERE THAN RETURNING TO LONDON. MORGAN AGREES. THEREFORE PROPOSE TO SAIL WITH HIS H.Q.

He didn't wait long enough for a reply, and took the pause to imply he was attached to SICKLE FORCE, though he probably did not tell Morgan he was a stowaway. Clarke understood how the British Army worked – if you wanted to get anything done, it was always better to beg forgiveness than ask for permission.

At 7am on Wednesday, 17 April 1940, and in his opinion 26 years late, Clarke sailed for the British frontline with Germany.[16]

Clarke arrived on the frontline at Lillehammer, with the brigade having lost all its artillery and transport to a U-boat. The first British battalion to get off the train at 3.30am, were 'sleepy' Sherwood Foresters, cheered up by being served coffee by Norwegian girls before being carted off. Clarke collapsed in his first bed on Norwegian soil in the Hotel Victoria in the early hours, only to be blasted awake by air-raid sirens a few hours later. He looked out to see the Luftwaffe Junkers 52s (the airliner he had flown to Germany in) pouring north to reinforce German airborne units at Trondheim. He gave up on sleep and ran a bath.

Clarke drove out to the frontline to watch the Sherwoods deploy. Men jumped down from their civilian trucks in good spirits. It was sunny and quiet – but Clarke heard the Norwegians say the Germans were at their most dangerous when they were quiet. The Sherwoods were sceptical the Germans would be able to challenge them now they had won the race to the high ground. Clarke even heard some say perhaps it was all still a huge game of bluff.

He stayed for a while, watching them move into position full of optimism, and drove on and pulled over at a Bren gun post. They had counted 70 Junkers 52s flying over to reinforce the German garrison at Trondheim. The Bren gunners had been willing them to fly lower and into range, but the pilots had been too wily for that. Each Junkers 52 could carry 18 fully armed men. Seventy planes would mean roughly 1,260 fresh reinforcements had touched down at Trondheim to their north. Trondheim lay between them and a larger British force landing under the command of General Adrian

'Old Flamer' Carton de Wiart (de Wiart had a blistering temper) – the men of SICKLE FORCE were being surrounded.

Clarke got back to Norwegian Commander General Ruge's HQ in a farm at 4pm, where it was immediately plain something was amiss. He had the same feeling of impending disaster he had had as a war correspondent for the *Morning Post* watching Spanish troops pinned to the Atlantic coast by the Berbers. Quiet confidence was gone, German panzers were pouring north from Oslo, the attack was expected within hours. Clarke watched the British brigade Commander, Morgan reassure Ruge that the British were committed, and whatever happened they would stand with the Norwegians.

But Ruge knew they were in trouble. He had been fighting the Germans for two weeks – he had prayed for bad weather, he had got sunshine, and he knew what came next. This was Clarke's – indeed any member of the British Army's – first experience of Blitzkrieg. They had no idea what was about to hit them.

Ruge had written an open letter to the British Chief of the Imperial General Staff, Edmund Ironside, begging him for help. He showed it to Clarke. Could he take it to London? It was written in English, and Ruge asked if he had expressed himself clearly enough. Clarke reassured him he had, and added that he would make a personal appeal to Ironside. Ruge took Clarke by the arm, into the snow and sunshine outside his HQ, and told him, 'You carry the fate of Norway in your hands, and I wish you a safe journey.'

That night, the full force of *Blitzkrieg* broke on Lillehammer: panzers, Stukas and heavy mortars. The young British territorials were no match for this – not in weapons, training, command, nor doctrine. It was an entirely new form of warfare and Clarke was among the first British officers to experience it. The frontline at Lillehammer collapsed that night.

Clarke left the HQ in a private car, hoping to reach the port of Åndalsnes before daylight, but at the first roadblock, owing to the car's Danish plates and its driver's civilian clothes, they were interned as suspected German agents. Frustratingly, they were fed coffee for half the night while waiting for Ruge's HQ to confirm their identity.

The next morning they pressed on, and by chance came across Brigadier Morgan and his two battalion commanders, drawn and tired from the night's fighting, grabbing lunch on the veranda of a wayside inn acting as a makeshift HQ. Morgan had lost contact with two companies of the Sherwoods. German troops kept out-flanking them in the snow, and the British didn't have any skis, making defence impossible. With a roar, a German plane swooped low overhead, and they dashed inside to get out of sight. Clarke could see German ski troops on the hills behind them. They had outflanked them again and were setting up a machine gun to shoot up the rear of the HQ. The HQ's only Bren gun went into action and, to the clatter of machine-gun fire, Clarke tried to cram his secret documents into the wood burner of the inn, while the Brigade Major fed the flames with crisp banknotes. They made a run for it, Morgan's overloaded staff car wheel-spinning out of the sludge in the yard as German rounds cracked overhead.

Morgan gave Clarke his car and driver, and Clarke fled Norway pursued by German skiers and parachute troops, personally order-ing bridges to be blown to hinder their advance. Morgan's driver, a heavyweight boxer, helped, because he had a 'wonderful ear for a Stuka', announcing their arrival by shouting 'Fly!', his acute hearing giving them time to dive for cover before the bullets arrived.

They made it to Åndalsnes, where Clarke collapsed in the ruined hotel being used as HQ with a welcome tin mug of champagne. But he was soon told there was no way he was getting out of Norway by flying boat, as the Luftwaffe had complete air superior-ity. He escaped at 3am on 25 April 1940 on the HMS *Galatea*, heading back to Rosyth.

He got into Euston Station at 9am on Friday, 26 April, wolfed down a breakfast of eggs and bacon, stripped off the clothes he'd worn for two weeks and lay in the bath at Stratton Street, wonder-ing if he was to be the sole survivor of an ill-fated expedition.

*

Back at the office in fresh uniform, Clarke found he was an 'object of interest' in Whitehall. He was the first British officer to have experience of the new German military in action, and Ironside greeted him cheerfully. Clarke had checked, and it turned out Ironside had been highly amused when Clarke's wire from Rosyth had been shown to him. Clarke was good at reading people. Ironside would be the first to admit he was completely unsuited to Whitehall, and would be far better off on the frontline himself. He had no problem with his subordinate volunteering to put himself in harm's way. Clarke also understood that in the British Army initiative is welcome if it goes well, and Clarke's unofficial posting had brought more good than harm.

Clarke showed Ironside Ruge's personal appeal, but he was too late – General Ruge's Norwegian Army had been destroyed, and Ironside wanted to pull forces out of the wreck, not reinforce. Ironside, a big man, dismissed Clarke with a friendly slap on the back, and told him to get some rest and come back the next morning.

Clarke tried to relax, and had dinner at the Ritz before collapsing into clean sheets. The following morning, his forty-first birthday, he reported to Ironside, who greeted him with, 'Communications with SICKLE FORCE have all gone to hell! Somebody will have to go and get the troops out of Åndalsnes before it's too late.'

Ironside thumped Clarke on the chest. 'And *you* seem to be the only one who knows his way around there!'

Clarke hoped his face did not betray his feelings; no orders could have been more unexpected, or less welcome. Becoming an expert on Blitzkrieg had its risks, and he had been lucky to get out of Norway alive. Since then, things had got considerably worse.

Back in Scotland on the evening of Sunday, 28 April, the bar of the Royal Hotel, Invergordon, was filled with bedraggled naval pilots who had ditched in the sea next to their overcrowded aircraft carrier. The landing deck had been too full of aircraft being evacuated from Norway for them to land onboard. As each one returned to the bar, changed into borrowed clothes, a cheer went up and someone at the piano struck up 'A life on the ocean wave'. The pilot was handed a beer and told his survival story, which got more hair-raising the more beer got consumed.

Stories of ditching in the North Sea didn't help Clarke's confidence when, at 11pm, his RAF contact stuck his head round the door and gave him the nod. Clarke left the warmth of the bar and drunk pilots to stand on a shivering jetty waiting for a motor launch to his Sunderland flying boat: a wartime conversion of the old Empire flying boats he had flown home from Egypt for the coronation of George VI and Elizabeth in 1937. The fuselage was bare of luxury chairs, white table cloths, waiters and fine dining, replaced by a crew uncovering their guns as they lifted off.

Once airborne, an aircrew brought back cups of coffee, and the top gunner dropped down from his turret to tell Clarke, 'I've got a hunch we're going to have a bit of fun on this trip.' Eventually, Clarke got to sleep, but it seemed only moments later he was being shaken awake by the gunner, and his watch read 3.30am:

'The captain is asking for you on the intercom. He wants you to go forward.'

Clarke clambered up to the flight deck of the throbbing aircraft. The morning sun streamed into the cockpit and the co-pilot gave up his seat. The captain asked Clarke if he could pick out which fjord led to Åndalsnes. Clarke looked at the panorama of sparkling fjords and snow-capped mountains, and confessed he hadn't a clue.

Circling, the navigator recognised a lighthouse and orientated himself, and the buzzer went for action stations. They dropped into the fjord towards Åndalsnes and Clarke realised something was amiss. The town was ablaze, smoke billowing over the water. They circled over the town. There were no boats on the quay, and no sign of life below. This was no place to land a cumbersome flying boat, so they aborted.

Clarke and the captain consulted in the cockpit. The captain's concern was the safety of his aircraft and crew. Even the slowest Luftwaffe aircraft could shoot a Sunderland to pieces, and being caught on the water would mean immediate destruction. Clarke's primary focus was to get British troops out of Norway. It was decided to put Clarke ashore in a rubber boat at the head of the fjord, hopefully far enough away from the Luftwaffe and German ground troops to protect the plane, while still giving him a fighting chance of making contact with the British. They needed to get it done quickly.

It did not start well.

The gunner reported distant Luftwaffe aircraft over the intercom as they splashed down, and while inflating the dinghy the flying boat was a sitting duck. The captain, desperate to get Clarke ashore, told him to get clear of the flying boat as fast as possible so he could take off. But the situation turned farcical. They'd overinflated the rubber dinghy and couldn't get it through the door – it took ages to deflate, all the while the rising sun silhouetted Luftwaffe planes circling over Åndalsnes. They chucked the dinghy out, where it floated, just. Clarke judged it 'a flabby and pitiful apology for a boat', and started to blow it up again.

At 4am on the Norwegian fjord Clarke was freezing. He had many talents, none of them maritime. He got into the boat the wrong way round with 'toy' oars and, blasted by the flying boat's four 1,000-horse power engines, spun hopelessly on the water.

The spinning stopped with a bump when he was pinned against the hull. The door opened and one of the crew grabbed him with a boat hook, then shouted inaudible instructions at him drowned out by the roar of the engines, and pushed him towards the shore. This time he made better progress and as he watched the flying boat lift off, felt desperately alone bobbing in her wake, watching her bank to safety over the North Sea.

It took him an hour to struggle to shore in the bitter cold, not helped by having his suitcase wedged on his lap up to his nose. He reached the bank and waded, carrying his suitcase still labelled with *Ritz Hotel, Paris*. Floundering through rushes, he dragged the dinghy behind him before reaching dry land and fortifying himself with a tot of whisky from his flask.

He hit a road and flagged down a passing Red Cross vehicle, which gave him a lift but would not take part in any of his 'dark projects' – the Red Cross are neutral, and cannot assist combatants. The Red Cross dropped him close to the town where he found the British HQ in a hotel. He reported to a brigadier, who told him all comms had broken down and SICKLE FORCE had probably been overrun.

The brigadier called a conference at 8.15am to organise the British last stand. Morgan showed up, looking more haggard and tired than when Clarke had last seen him, and broke the news that his force had been practically wiped out. When the conference finished, an argument started about who was in command – the British Army is a gerontocracy, not a meritocracy, and seniority is based on a calculation of age and time served as recorded in the Army List. As Morgan and Clarke left the crowded room a plaintive voice asked if anybody had an Army List to hand.

Clarke and Morgan headed inland, Morgan to round up any survivors of his brigade, and Clarke to find General Paget, the overall British commander, to tell him to get the hell out of Norway. The cratered road made progress painfully slow; it was littered with hundreds of vehicles, abandoned, blown up, with no sign of life.

The reason became apparent when there was a loud roar behind them and bullets whipped up the snow down the middle of the road straight in front of the radiator. They ran from the car, careful to shut the doors to make it look like the other derelicts, and hid in a cowshed while the German aircraft made two more passes.

As they drove on they were attacked every 15 minutes – they never heard the aircraft, the first indication was plumes of snow from cannon or machine gun. Luckily, the first pass missed every time, and then the race was on to get to cover before the aircraft could circle for another go. They would slam the doors and plough through the snow to the nearest tree or wall, or into a drain for cover. It was exhausting. Not to say terrifying. Once the hum of the aircraft disappeared they continued up the road to hell.

With the Norwegian spring providing 18 hours of daylight, the onslaught was relentless and the carnage all around them demonstrated what had happened to SICKLE FORCE. Their luck held and they pulled over outside the next town to watch Stukas dive-bomb it before they entered, but beyond that the road was blocked by two craters and an unexploded bomb, its fins sticking out of the snow.

Clarke took over from the driver, and drove, alone, in an effort to negotiate the obstacle, while everyone sheltered in case he hit the bomb. Slipping in the debris and snow the car became stuck, and no amount of revving the engine would free it. Rocking, and close to the bomb, his driver shouted, 'Leave it!'

Everyone emerged with relief as Clarke picked his way on foot back through the Luftwaffe-delivered minefield.

Luckily, a motorcycle dispatch rider turned up on the other side of the obstacle carrying a letter from Paget for Clarke. Clarke jumped on and rode pillion the remaining 25 miles to HQ, dodging eight entirely personal low-flying attacks.

He was pleased to find Paget's HQ calm, with no trace of the chaos and pessimism he'd found in Åndalsnes, but was disappointed when the general told him there was no way he could get his troops back down the road Clarke had travelled unless the RAF was sent to cover the withdrawal. Clarke prepared for the return trip to Whitehall and Paget wired the signal:

CLARKE SHOULD SEE YOU EARLY REF. AIR SUPPORT. PLEASE ENSURE AIRCRAFT AT AANDALSNES TO-NIGHT 29/30 APRIL

Clarke doubted the wire ever got through.

Before he left, Clarke was asked by Paget to accompany him personally to explain to his Norwegian friend, General Ruge, why he was being abandoned, scarcely a task Clarke relished. He watched Paget deliver the news that Clarke hadn't returned with what Ruge had asked for.

Ruge looked at Clarke.

'So, Norway must go the way of Czechoslovakia and Poland. But why? Why withdraw when your troops are still unbeaten?'

He had staked all his hopes on Britain. On Clarke. Clarke saw him shudder, as though to rid himself of a painful memory, before turning back to Paget.

'But these things are not for us to decide, General. We are soldiers, and we have to obey.'

The tension was over, without hint of bitterness, and they talked about the best way out. Clarke arranged for Ruge to be shipped to the far north to continue his fight from Narvik, where British forces were now landing under command of General Claude 'the Auk' Auchinleck to retake the town and stage a belated British rescue attempt. Ruge made ready to head for the coast and Clarke went looking for some transport himself.

He got back to the coast with the help of an elderly Norwegian taxi driver. They pulled into the evacuation point, the town of Molde at the far end of the fjord from Åndalsnes, where half of SICKLE FORCE had come ashore back when this war still seemed unreal. He found the town destroyed and the one remaining jetty on fire.

Clarke tried to persuade the taxi driver to escape German occupation, but he wanted to go back to Oslo and his wife and kids. Clarke thrust 30 quid into his hand, then with Ruge and his staff, and around a hundred men he stood next to the burning jetty, peering into the blackness for sign of a ship. The hours dragged on. Just before midnight, an English voice shouted from the darkness and the liner *Ulster Prince* and a destroyer emerged from the gloom. They hosed down the flaming jetty and ran out a gangplank.

One by one the men sprinted up the gangplank past the flames, but onboard Ruge discovered the ship was bound for Scapa Flow in Orkney rather than Narvik and General Auchinleck, and no amount of persuasion could get him to remain on the ship. Clarke tragically watched him and his whole staff, so desperately close to safety, retrieve their bundles from the cabins and file down the gangway in the glow of the flames to await the bombs and German panzers.

*

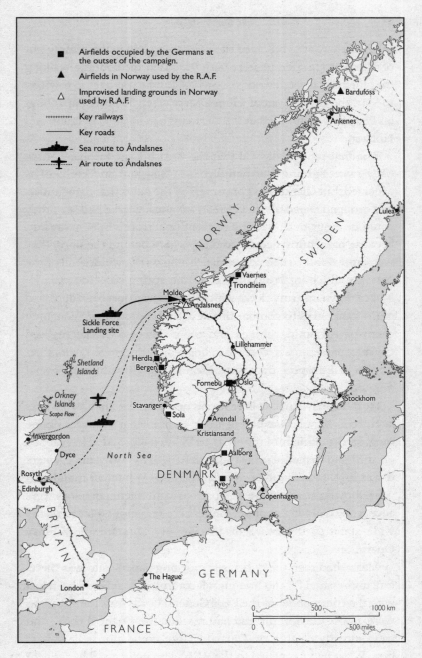

Legend:
- ■ Airfields occupied by the Germans at the outset of the campaign.
- ▲ Airfields in Norway used by the R.A.F.
- △ Improvised landing grounds in Norway used by R.A.F.
- ┈┈┈ Key railways
- ──── Key roads
- ⬥ Sea route to Åndalsnes
- ✈ Air route to Åndalsnes

Norway, 1940.

In London, Clarke followed the continuing bad news coming out of Norway. He tried to relax with friends in the country, walking the bluebell-carpeted woods of Sussex. But he was back in town on 10 May, and coming out of a lunch party when he heard paper boys on Piccadilly shouting that the Germans had invaded Belgium and Holland.

The first reports flashed that the British Expeditionary Force (BEF) was fighting German forces in Belgium and Holland as expected, but Clarke was concerned by the news that parachutists had dropped ahead of the German advance. Clarke had seen they could be easily dealt with by conventional troops in Norway but, because parachutists could land anywhere behind the lines, they were impossible to defend against. Sitting on the windowsill of the Norway office in Eaton Square in the spring sunshine, Clarke looked down on army clerks with rifles who had just been deployed in London parks to combat this new parachute threat. Watching them patrol amid nannies and their charges, Clarke realised German parachutists were spreading fear in Britain, far from their targets in Europe – they were ideal material for his subliminal methods.

He didn't have to wait long for his next job. Less than two weeks later, on 23 May, he was eating breakfast at the flat when the phone rang, summoning him to report to Whitehall ASAP. He grabbed his stuff and dashed across St James's Park to the War Office, where it was immediately obvious *a flap* was on. Whitehall mandarins were moving at above-average pace, usually silent corridors were alive with slamming doors and urgent conversations. He ran up the wide stairs to the office of the Deputy Director of Military Operations.

Clarke had seen the optimistic morning papers, and was therefore unprepared for this briefing: all communications had been lost with the commander of the BEF, General Lord Gort, the Germans were across the Somme and had reached the Channel coast, and were already closing on Calais. Clarke could not believe it at first. What had happened to the BEF? The Belgians? The French?

They had been fighting less than two weeks! He felt dazed and bewildered, hardly knowing where to begin.

But Clarke had known this could happen. In 1933 he'd been in Munich, and watched Hitler arrive, along with crowds marching to the Nuremberg rally, ranks of women singing, 'We lost husbands and fathers in the last war. We are ready to lose sons and brothers in the next!' And the previous year in Berlin, just before the war, the head of British intelligence in Germany had confided in him, 'Those panzers will go in one end of France and out the other in six weeks.'

Blitzkrieg had been unleashed on a massive scale – the Germans had torn through the French in a weak sector opposite the Ardennes forest, then swung north to the coast, cutting communications with the BEF, whose fate was still unknown. The BEF *was* the British Army: 400,000 men.

Clarke was briefed on his second rescue mission of the war. The plan was for Brigadier Claude Nicholson and the 30th Infantry Brigade to hold Calais – they would have to prepare to be besieged until Ironside could send the Canadian division over to get the BEF out of France. Clarke was one of two staff officers he had selected to work on the problem.

Shell-shocked, Clarke walked down the corridor to the other officer's room. Alan Hornby wasn't there; he had been planning Norway and his maps were still on the wall. Clarke looked at the maps, which minutes before had seemed vital, and ordered up some maps of Calais. He picked up Hornby's file and started to brief himself. Then the phone rang. The Air Ministry read out a report from a pilot who'd just flown over Calais; it was an inferno.

Clarke hung up. He picked up the red phone on the desk, the secure line to the Admiralty. Someone had to tell Nicholson. He read out his instruction to the brigadier, thinking it was dreadful to sit in a Whitehall office and tell men fighting an overwhelming enemy that there was to be no withdrawal.

The signal flashed from the roof of Horse Guards to a destroyer off the French coast. The reply was swift: 'Received and understood.'

Permission was requested to evacuate a few hundred 'useless mouths', the wounded and non-combatants, that night – they asked nothing else.

Inside the British perimeter in Calais, straggling columns of refugees choked every road. Led by their priests, they wandered like a forlorn crusade while the British Army – voluntary soldiers and conscripts of His Majesty – stood expecting to die with only a few anti-tank rifles to meet the might of Rommel's panzers.[17] Second Lieutenant Airey Neave was on the ground and saw Clarke's instruction carried out. 'The last stand was made among the Wagons-Lits and in the sand dunes. A man shot himself with his own rifle in an archway which housed the regimental aid post; beside me a young soldier was crying quietly.'[18]

Clarke thought if there was ever a moment for his subliminal methods, then this was it.

2

The Shadow: 1940–1941

Pitchforks

When Alan Hornby walked back into his Whitehall office, Clarke took the opportunity to grab a quick lunch, and returned to find the Director of Operations, General Dewing, wanted to see him. He went to Dewing's office, to be greeted with, 'I've got a job for you.' Clarke protested that he was in the middle of this 'Calais business', but Dewing told him that he was needed for some other 'tricky business': Ireland. The director explained that the Irish police had raided a house belonging to an Irish businessman of German parentage. The raid found traces of a German parachutist, a file containing military details on Irish harbours, airfields, bridges, roads, and drop zones for parachutists, and the distribution of the Irish defence force, along with a radio transmitter, a code book, and a safe full of bank notes.[1] The Irish were terrified the Germans were about to carry out a Norway-style takeover, using parachute troops and shock troops concealed in merchant ships – so terrified that they had secretly sent two agents to London to see if Britain would help.

Once again selected for a mission of an unusual and confidential nature, Clarke was to coordinate the defence of Ireland with 'our friends over there' who, at that very moment, were in a meeting in the Dominions Office. Clarke was to join the meeting immediately, and set up a working relationship with them.

Clarke's mind span as he walked across Whitehall – it wasn't so long ago he had been hunting Irish Republicans. The meeting at the Dominions Office on Downing Street was in full session when he arrived. The chair, a distinguished civil servant, seemed completely out of his depth, and Clarke got the impression that his entry was being hailed with welcome relief. There were six representatives of civil departments, a puzzled young man from the Air Ministry, and two 'gentlemen of Eire'.

Clarke was introduced to 'Sean' and another man, who he was told was from the Irish Army. Sean, a not uncommon name in Ireland, was, as Clarke guessed, an alias – 'Sean' was Joe Walshe, Minister for External Affairs, and about as influential a man as the Irish head of state. The other man was Colonel Liam Archer, Irish Director of Military Intelligence, who had been wounded in the Easter Rising.[2]

Sean explained the nature of their visit. They were painfully aware how helpless their country would be should the Germans choose to invade, but there was no time to convince their people of the sense of getting Britain's help. What they needed was an undercover plan. The man from the Irish Army stressed the need for secrecy – only the Irish Prime Minister, Éamon de Valera knew of their trip.

Clarke seized the opportunity, as per his brief, to 'summon a little drama to my aid', and proceeded to describe the German threat in hair-raising detail, finishing: 'I have an aeroplane standing by at Hendon and, if our friends here agree, I think we ought to continue our discussions on the spot as quickly as we can get there.'

The Irish delegation were only too glad to have a man with first-hand experience of German parachute operations to help and the civil servants were clearly relieved – Clarke had grasped the situation, so they could dodge the responsibility. This was now a matter for the military and Irish authorities.

Sean arranged to meet Clarke at the staff entrance to the Ritz. Would he please not come in a staff car, and in civilian clothes that didn't bear the obvious stamp of a British officer. An hour later, at the back door to the Ritz, his disguise met with approval, and he was paid the dubious compliment of being assured that he might be taken for almost anyone but an officer of the British Army.

Their taxi was waved through at Hendon without formalities to a twin-engine De Havilland Flamingo that General Dewing had put at his disposal. Clarke was prodding at the large ashtray by his seat when he was told it was Churchill's; the new prime minister was on shuttle runs over the Channel to prop up French resolve and keep them in the war, and this was his aircraft. Clarke was left in no doubt just how important his mission was. Not that he needed the reminder – if Ireland entered the war, Britain could close the gap in air cover over the Atlantic, and dramatically improve the turnaround time for corvettes and destroyers protecting her convoys, which were currently being torn to pieces by U-boats. Conversely, if the Germans conquered Ireland, it would finish the war – the stakes could not be higher.

He landed shortly before dusk at Belfast airport, chosen both for secrecy and because Clarke could see the Commander of Northern Ireland, General Huddleson, who would have to implement any plan Clarke formed. Sean and his compatriot parted with no words of goodbye, and vanished from the airport as strangers, as had been agreed.

Clarke briefed General Huddleson on what he needed – a mobile force that could travel over the border – and he reached Dublin by train the following day in time for a late lunch at the Shelbourne Hotel, where he was to wait for someone to make contact.

The hours passed. Clarke felt he was learning the first lesson of the secret agent – how to get through the long and tedious hours of inaction without appearing to be waiting for anything at all. At dusk, his vigil ended when Sean arrived driving a small car with an 'anonymous and shadowy figure'. Clarke was given his second lesson in the secret agent business when *The Shadow* asked for his room keys, and Sean asked him to get into the car.

The Shadow went to Clarke's room and removed everything that could identify him, even down to laundry marks on his clothes. When the bundle was returned to him he was astonished to discover the thoroughness with which the job had been done. What Clarke may not have fully appreciated is that from the moment he left the hotel his presence in Ireland became deniable by both the Irish and his own government – should, of course, anything happen to him.

In the centre of Dublin, Sean pulled over at an engineering yard. Clarke was taken into the dark yard, between the silhouetted skeletons of machinery, through a door and down a flight of steps, and then along a maze of corridors. Clarke wasn't to know, but this was three minutes from his hotel, and he'd been driven around to disguise its location.[3] If Clarke was nervous he had a right to be – he was a British officer walking into the HQ of the Irish Army. Clarke was stopped by two armed policemen while Sean disappeared deeper into the underground labyrinth, before returning to lead him to a conference room.

In the Irish operations centre, the men, all in civilian clothes, probably had mixed feelings about his presence – none shook his hand. The atmosphere was distinctly chilly. Sean, however, was enthusiastic, and explained who Clarke was and what he had seen. He introduced Clarke, without names, to the General Staff of the Irish army.

Clarke was asked to speak first. He tried his best to paint a vivid picture of German capabilities; of parachutists, panzers, and the *Blitzkrieg*. He then went on to describe the help Britain could offer: a mobile force was being assembled right now in Ulster, and British aircraft were ready to fly in on invitation. He did not mention the massive strategic implications of all this. He was here to scare, not persuade. His frankness went down well, and soon he felt like a travelling salesman, drawing up a shopping list of military assets the Irish were short on. The meeting closed in far more cordial spirit, and afterwards men drew him aside to quiz him on German parachutists in Norway. Clarke didn't hold back. He didn't have to.

Still minus his ID, Clarke was dropped back at the hotel, a rendezvous set for ten the following morning in the National Museum of Ireland, just behind his hotel, which, not by chance, adjoins the Dáil Éireann – the Irish Parliament.

There were few visitors at the museum the following morning, and Clarke was pretending to examine Irish antiquities when Sean appeared at his side. Sean led him into the curator's storeroom, from where a staircase led underground. Clarke was learning his third secret agent lesson; insurgency operations have always made good use of tunnels. A few turns of the corridor and Sean explained they were directly below the Dáil Éireann.

Sean asked if he would like to see the parliament of Ireland, and so for a short time their mission was suspended while Clarke stood in the empty chamber. Then they were back underground, past the same armed police, and into the same conference room. Their confidence in him must have improved, because now he knew, roughly, where this room was.

The principle of British intervention had been accepted; the problem was that it could only occur after the Germans landed. What Clarke couldn't know was that Éamon de Valera was wary of any pre-emptive move, for fear of German retaliation.[4] Clarke repeated his tales of Norway, but with the political wind against him the general staff stood firm, the Irish commander in chief, summing up stiffly: 'The Irish are better suited than any others in the world for guerrilla fighting. [. . .] Where we haven't the weapons people will fight them in the fields with spades and pitchforks.'

Clarke felt a wave of despair. He explained that *all* German parachutists carried automatic weapons. For him, this was the same talk he had heard before Norway. Before Poland. No one was getting it. His one success was to get a British staff officer posted to Dublin for liaison, provided, of course, he came in civilian clothes. When the meeting wound up they asked if Clarke would do them a favour – could he go and recce Phoenix Park and see if it was a likely site for landing parachutists in Dublin?

Sean and Clarke drove out to Phoenix Park on a peaceful spring evening. Clarke thought it would be difficult to find a more convenient site for an airborne invasion, and his suggestions on how to defend it went down so well he was asked if he could consult on another site – a military airfield – the following morning before he left.

That night, Sean invited him to a covert dinner with someone he was told was the minister for defence, who was eccentric and clearly not neutral in regard to the Germans. The minister dashed to and fro as host, pouring out sherry and whisky, but Clarke couldn't get him to budge on allowing British forces to deploy south of the border. And the minister repeated the morning's pitchfork argument. Clarke had to admire the Irish conviction that their guerrillas could take on German paratroopers. It turned out the minister was an amateur inventor, and Clarke was treated to designs, drawn on the tablecloth, for everything from magnetic mines to tanks. He left with a dozen new ideas for the mechanical improvement of war, but few for the better defence of Ireland.

Sean dropped him back at the hotel, said it had gone well, and Clarke was back in the conference room the next day with a bigger crowd. This time the minster for defence was there, and Clarke had brought Max Tyler with him, the promised British Liaison Officer. Clarke assumed others present in the room were from the Irish government. It was still all civilian clothes and no introductions, it was cordial, but no one budged on the after-invasion issue. He introduced the British officer and it was time to make his exit. Churchill would go on to offer de Valera 'a declaration [. . .] accepting the principle of a United Ireland' in return for joining the war. The Taoiseach declined.[5]

Clarke had a picnic, the cover for his recce, overlooking the military airfield with Sean. Then, as he came out of the hotel for the taxi to the train, a burly figure sidled up to him and slipped a parcel into his hand. The Shadow was returning his identity. Whether Clarke realised it or not, all that talk of guerrilla war had planted a seed of an idea. He would, of course, never be able to mention the trip – a secret he kept to the grave – nor that some of his inspiration for his subliminal methods came from Ireland.

'A Real Job'

Clarke was soon back at the Whitehall office, only to be told his boss, Ironside, had been sacked. Ironside had travelled to the front in France to try and persuade the Allies to counterattack, but wound up in an argument with French generals, grabbing one, Gaston

Billotte, and shaking him. For his part, the French commander, General Maxime Weygand, had wanted to punch Ironside in the head. Ironside got his way, but the subsequent counterattack at Arras ran into General Johannes Erwin Eugen Rommel and his 7th Panzer Division, and Churchill felt 'as the adverse battle drew to its climax I and my colleagues greatly desired that Sir John Dill should become CIGS'.[6]

General Dill took over, and Clarke found himself working directly for another Palestine veteran – it was with Dill he had witnessed the start of the Arab–Jewish conflict in 1936.

Clarke had reported for duty in Jerusalem in 1936, looking forward to a peaceful overseas posting to his favourite country in the world. He pulled into the soft pink-stone portico of the brand-new King David Hotel in a two-seater Delage tourer nicknamed the 'Ghost Train', bought from Jack Barclay for his tour. The next morning he started work in the very small peacetime British HQ for Brigadier John 'Jack' Fullerton Evetts – who, when asked how he got on with Dudley Clarke, answered, 'Splendidly, I work all day, he works all night.'

A few weeks into the job, on Sunday, 16 April 1936, Clarke was taking siesta when the phone rang at his bedside. Clarke had been looking forward to a lazy game of polo, but the duty officer said, 'I am afraid there is a situation, and I think you should come over here at once.'

Clarke grabbed his clothes and ran over the road to HQ. Two nights previously, Arab highwaymen had robbed several cars on the Jaffa Road, and then singled out three Jewish passengers and shot them dead in cold blood. In retaliation, two Jewish people had entered an isolated hut the previous night and shot dead the two Arab occupants. Now, as a result of wild rumours circulating of widespread Jewish reprisals, the Arabs had risen up, and Jaffa was strewn with overturned cars and burning buses. The city's streets ran with blood. Clarke grabbed the phone to start coordinating the response of the meagre British forces.

During this first intifada, the Arabs went to work using the skills

TE Lawrence had taught them, blowing up trains and hitting convoys while Clarke fought the insurgency with the small number of infantry and aircraft the British possessed. On one occasion, he adjusted mortar fire himself because the infantry were unfamiliar with the new weapon and dropping the rounds short. Clarke, the artillery officer, showed them how to site the weapon properly and hit the insurgents. On another occasion, he was following the infantry on horseback with his orderly – he hated walking – and jumped a barricade the Arabs were erecting in a village behind the advance. His orderly fell off, and the Arabs quickly made for him. Clarke, for the first and only time in his life, drew his sword in anger and charged them, determined to stick any who came in range, but they fled, fearing the cold steel of his *arme blanche*.

General Jack Dill then arrived with a troop surge to get a lid on the situation, and HQ expanded into the King David Hotel, after which Dill saved Clarke's life twice. First, while they were on air reconnaissance. Clarke had undone his seatbelt to lean out to get a better look at a feature in the battle they were fighting when the plane hit turbulence and fell away below him. Dill grabbed Clarke's ankles as Clarke flew over his head – there were no parachutes in those days. Then, as Clarke's counter-insurgency operations started to bite, Dill summoned Clarke into his office:

'I thought I told you to move your quarters into the King David,' said Dill harshly.

Clarke had a flat nearby, with a garage for the Ghost Train below it. Dill insisted that Clarke move immediately, without going back for his belongings. Clarke was flabbergasted. His boss seemed more embarrassed than angry, but he didn't understand the cause. Until he later asked a friend who was security officer, who revealed that Clarke's success in counter-insurgency had placed him in the top three of the Arab hit list.

From then on, Clarke followed simple rules: varying his routine; reversing his car to park at night with headlights on full to blind a gunman, his pistol visibly in his hand; never sitting in a public place; and always sitting with his back to the wall, a practice he never gave up. Clarke was mildly disappointed six weeks later to be bumped off the list of top targets, and was allowed to return to his flat. But he never lost the skills nor stopped doing the drills. Others weren't so thorough – the district commissioner of Galilee, Lewis Andrews, returned to his habit of walking to evensong at the Anglican Church on Sundays, and was shot dead on the road to Galilee.

The close relationship between Dill and Clarke led, in 1940, to Dill asking Clarke to be his Military Assistant. The new head of the British military, Jack Dill, was a man Clarke knew well as an impulsive Irishman, whose kindness was only occasionally interrupted by massive bursts of temper. During their long walks across the Judean hills he had come to learn a good deal about his hopes and ambitions. This would be Clarke's first opportunity to unveil his subliminal methods on the world.

With Dill in charge at the War Office, Clarke set out with him for his first meeting with Winston Churchill. Churchill was about to shuttle over the Channel in his Flamingo, and the security-conscious Clarke stared in disbelief when Churchill picked up an insecure telephone and started, 'I am going to fly with CIGS to—'

Clarke hit the receiver. Talk about a flight to France could cost both Churchill and Dill's lives at the hands of the Luftwaffe.

There was a tense silence. Hanging up on Churchill was never done.

Clarke had introduced himself to the most powerful man in Britain.

On the afternoon of Tuesday, 4 June 1940, Clarke listened in Whitehall as Churchill updated the Commons on the Dunkirk evacuation, and how some 338,000 Allied troops had been carried 'out of the jaws of death and shame, to their native land and to the tasks which lie immediately ahead'. For Clarke, the oratory could not hide the truth that, for the first time since the seventeenth century, the British Army had been driven from the Continent with the loss of all its transport and munitions.[7]

Churchill finished, 'We must be careful not to assign to this deliverance the attributes of a victory. Wars are not won by evacuation.'

On the way home across St James's, Clarke put his irregular mind to work. He ran through historical comparisons – Spanish guerrillas against Napoleon, the tribesmen of the Indian Frontier fighting the British – to find a military precedent for the defeated British Army. But, more importantly, he drew on his own memories. Clarke's experience was as unique as his mind. He thought of the Rif War and the Berbers he had seen fight the Spanish and French, those Arab insurgents on dusty roads and across the railways of Palestine and, something he would never publicly credit, a truculent Irishman in a Dublin bunker.

His idea needed a brand. Clarke remembered the Boers of his birth, and the Boer Army – beaten and scattered to the four winds – who formed small, mobile bands, living off the land, hitting and running. They were called *Kommandos*. It was a great name for a handful of ill-armed fanatics who, on native ground of their own choosing, could dissipate the strength of far greater numbers of regular troops.[8]

He climbed to his top-floor flat and started to jot his one-page pitch on his Stratton Street letterhead: 'Britain might still have something to learn from the past tactics of Spaniard, Boer and Arab [. . .] To aim mosquito stings with telling effect upon the ponderous bulk of the German Army.'[9] TE Lawrence had called them 'pin pricks'. Clarke looked at the page. This was the best pitch for his subliminal methods so far, but would it get him the job?

The next day brought a fine summer's evening – the Germans stood on Dunkirk beach surveying the wreckage the British Army had left behind, and Clarke followed Dill into their marble-floored Whitehall office. Dill looked out of the window. It was quiet. Silver barrage balloons rode in the sky. One appeared to be emerging from the top of Lord Nelson's pigeon-shit encrusted hat on Trafalgar Square.

Dill turned from the window. 'Somehow, we must find a way of helping the Army exercise its offensive spirit again.'[10]

Clarke hit him with the *Kommando* concept.

Dill was seeing the chiefs of staff in the morning – could Clarke rough out the scheme on paper for him? Dill knew Churchill would love it. Churchill was an ideas man: in the First World War the then prime minister, Lloyd George, said Churchill, as First Sea Lord, produced a new paper on strategy or tactics every day, and finding a new one on his desk every morning was like a hen laying eggs.[11]

That night, Clarke marshalled his thoughts on paper in the form of a few short notes. Clarke burnt oil, refining the pitch. He knew he had the two crucial items for success: a brilliant idea, and a sympathetic audience. He would not be in the room when Dill pitched it, but he knew Dill well, and they had shared time on the receiving end of what he was talking about. Churchill would jump at it, but his right-hand man would have to green-light the plan. That man was General 'Pug' Ismay, who Clarke had shared a long journey back from Aden with, sharing thoughts on subjects such as Mussolini's ambitions in Africa.[12]

Clarke hurried over St James's Park in the morning to hand in his pitch – Dill took it to the chiefs of staff, and sent for Clarke before lunch.

'Your Commando scheme is approved.'

Clarke was to set up the Commandos, and a raid across the English Channel was to be mounted at the first conceivable opportunity.[13] Clarke and his subliminal methods were in business.

Clarke felt mobility was key to his vision – the Boers had their horses, the Arabs their ability to melt into the hills – what did the British have? Britain was an island, its defence, and offence, had always relied on the sea.

Clarke crossed the road to the Admiralty. The Royal Navy, having been hammered at Dunkirk, were now attempting to evacuate troops from a small port called Saint-Valery-en-Caux in France. He was prepared to be rebuffed – the Army's stock with the Navy did not stand high just then. He pitched his idea to an admiral on duty, and the man leapt out of his chair.

'What?! The Army want to get back in the fight already! That's the best news I've heard for days. For that you can have anything you like from the Navy.'

Clarke asked him if he had anyone that could set up an *irregular* Navy. The admiral sent him down the corridor to the Second Sea Lord. You only had to scratch a naval officer to find the pirate, Clarke thought.

He repeated his pitch: Arabs, Berbers, Boers, mosquito stings = Commandos.

The Second Sea Lord rubbed his hands with glee. 'I've got the very man you need.'

It was agreed that the man in question, Captain Garnons-Williams, should report to Clarke as soon as he hit port. Provided he survived his current mission: sinking two old hulks in the entrance to Zeebrugge harbour under fire, to prevent U-boats using it as a base.

Clarke had secured transport. His next problem was men; but Dill told him no existing unit was to be diverted to the commandos from home defence. Otto Marling Lund, Deputy Director of Operations at the War Office, who found Clarke three rooms next to his for his new secret organisation MO9, suggested he recruit from the Independent Companies. These were territorial (part-time) units that had been put together for operations in Norway – where resistance had collapsed.

Clarke visited the Independent Companies, who were licking their wounds in the hills outside Glasgow, and listened to their sad accounts of disappointment and frustration. General 'Auk' Auchinleck, who had commanded them in Norway, said 'in this wild, undeveloped country where we, with all our wealth of experience, should be at our best, we are out-manoeuvred and outfought every time. It makes me *sick* with shame.'[14] The Auk learnt his soldiering on the North-West Frontier of India, fighting against some of the insurgents who had inspired Clarke. He said of the Independent Companies, 'They give the impression of being callow and undeveloped, which is not reassuring for the future unless our methods of man-mastership and training for war can be made more realistic.'[15]

The Auk was right: the men of the Independent Companies lacked training. As one recruit said, 'imagine how we felt when we saw a towering ice-capped mountain in front of us standing about 2,000 feet high, we South London boys who had never seen a mountain before, most of us had never been to sea before. [. . .] This was the first time I had ever done a speed march, it was really hectic, it was desperate. I mean we were sort of fighting for our lives.'[16]

But this is what he had been offered, and Clarke looked for likely Commando recruits. In the Independent Companies' mess tent, he was overjoyed to find Atty Rice, a brother officer from the Transjordan Frontier Force 10 years earlier. They had ridden together over the same trails as TE Lawrence, camped at Petra and Wadi Rum while chasing Bedouin raiders. He also found Ronnie Todd from the Argyll and Southern Highlanders. Clarke's Commando scheme renewed the two officers' enthusiasm, and over lunch they agreed they would hand-pick their 100 best men and be ready for the first Commando raid in two weeks.

Back in London, Clarke recruited an all-female staff for MO9 HQ, calling them the Operations Directive. The first was his friend Constantia Rumbold, daughter of former ambassador to Berlin Sir Horace Rumbold. Clarke first met her father, the far-sighted ambassador, in Istanbul, then again in Berlin during the early days of Hitler's power in 1933, when the ambassador warned: 'The Jewish community in this country [Germany] are faced with a much more serious danger than mere bodily maltreatment or petty persecution.'[17]

To keep from the prying eyes and leaks of Whitehall, they convened in Rumbold's living room, a short walk across St James's Park on Grosvenor Crescent. Sir Horace had retired to the country with ill health, and Miss Rumbold issued instructions for Commando officers to report to her butler for 'charity committee' meetings wearing civilian clothes, a precedent for future special forces.

Another recruit was Buster Marling, a young relation of Otto

Marling Lund, who found Clarke offices. Marling owned her own car, and was therefore able to drive to the coast to liaise with the commandos before their mission. According to Clarke, she had a 'disarming cheerfulness which never failed to send a commando off into the night with a light heart'. And then there was Joan Bright, 'a lady of unusual personality', who is rumoured to be Ian Fleming's model for Miss Moneypenny.

As well as not recruiting from active units, another of Dill's stipulations was economy in armament. This was not surprising, given that most of the BEF's had been left on the Dunkirk beach – there were only 40 Tommy guns in Britain. Clarke evaded the G.1098, a form the Army still uses today which stipulates what equipment a unit and individual should be issued, and set up a central store in London where commandos would be able to sign out what weapons and equipment they needed for a specific operation. Clarke described it as a cross between the warehouse of a theatrical costumier and the property room of a film studio. It was presided over by a genial custodian who acquired a flexibility unparalleled among the quartermasters of the regular Army, whose most frequent refrain is, 'stores are for storing'. If Joan Bright was Miss Moneypenny, the commandos' sympathetic quartermaster was Q.

This formidable team was augmented beyond the dismal corridors of Whitehall by actor David Niven, whom Clarke said he recruited because he was without the least trace of the rigidity of the professional soldier.

Clarke had learnt from experience that military operations and theatrical production are closely related. Clarke acted himself – in 1923 he'd revived the Officers Dramatic Society, producing and playing the lead in Cyril Maude's *The Flag Lieutenant* at Woolwich Theatre. This was not his only army production. Shortly after the success of *The Flag Lieutenant*, an impressed general had asked him to stage a Royal Artillery pageant for the next year's Royal Tournament. It featured 300 animals, including elephants and camels, and had a human cast, augmented by the books of a Soho casting agent, of

650. The show told the story of British Artillery through the ages, and ran at the Olympia for 30 performances, 2 a day, beating all records for attendance.

Clarke's next major production was in 1935 in Aden, where he was appointed to arrange King George V's Silver Jubilee celebrations. The site he chose was Holkat Bay, which had a natural amphitheatre created by the mountainside overlooking the sea; Clarke once again went to town. At 6.50pm on the night of 6 May, the audience, mostly local, covered the mountainside in their thousands as massed bands and local dancers covered the sand below, while the sun set behind the fort on the hill behind them. Darkness fell, and the audience turned from the bay to watch the moving ceremony of a floodlit Union Jack being lowered to the strains of the Last Post, while the guard marched away, leaving a single sentry.

All of which was a distraction for what Clarke had planned next.

He had unwisely called his production 'Invasion' at a time when the threat of Mussolini's forces invading East Africa were high – the locals were nervous, the British less so. (The locals were right – Italy would invade Abyssinia [Ethiopia] just three months later.) The audience were looking over their shoulders at the lowering Union Jack, while a British destroyer silently crept into the bay under cover of darkness. The stage lights blasted back on, and a flight of aircraft zoomed across the sky in support of landing forces pouring onto the beach. The destroyer, HMS *Penzance*, opened fire with blank ammunition while pre-buried explosives blew sand into the air to simulate shelling, and Rolls-Royce armoured cars sped onto the beach, firing at the 'invaders'.

Just as Clarke had hoped, the mock battle proved wonderfully exciting and realistic. He was thoroughly pleased, until a sudden cry went up from the hillside: 'The Italians are here! The Italians are here!'

Blind panic ensued, the audience falling over each other to get clear. There wasn't much the police could do to restore calm and, when the band returned at the end of the performance for 'God Save the King', the hillsides were bare – his entire audience had fled for their lives. Placing fear in the minds of this audience was a successful demonstration of his subliminal methods, albeit unintentional.

Once back in Britain, Clarke accompanied his younger brother Tibby, a copywriter whose client was the British cinema sound system, to early talking films. This became his main passion. If he hadn't been in the Army, Dudley Clarke would definitely have been in the film industry. Film would provide much of the inspiration for his subliminal methods, but for now, Clarke the cinephile was happy to recruit a real-life film star. The way Niven tells it, he was recruited to the commandos by accident – but perhaps not.

Niven's star was flying high in Hollywood before the war. He had just starred in *The Dawn Patrol* (1938) with Errol Flynn, and was under contract with MGM for further films. But while on board Dougie Fairbanks Jr's yacht off Catalina island, California, he was awoken at six o'clock in the morning, along with fellow guests Laurence Olivier and Vivien Leigh, by an American bumping alongside to wish them luck because Britain had declared war on Germany.[18]

Niven had military experience: at 18 he had briefly joined the Highland Light Infantry (nicknamed Hell's Last Resort), following his father, whom he never knew, because he was gunned down in the waters of Suvla Bay, Gallipoli, in 1915. In 1939, at the outbreak of war, he had his brother Max fake a call-up telegram to enable him to break his contract with MGM and get back to Britain. Max Niven was dating, and would soon marry, Clarke's best friend Doreen Platt.

Niven's face was on every billboard around London as a fighter ace in *The Dawn Patrol* and when asked which service he was going to join, he unwisely replied the RAF. The press had a field day, and his subsequent interview with the RAF went spectacularly badly.

The Group Captain opened the interview by telling Niven that the only other actor he had taken on had had a drink problem, and they didn't encourage actors to join *this service*.

Niven's response? 'Then fuck you!'

They were toe to toe when an inner door opened, and a higher-ranking officer appeared. Rather than appealing to this higher power, Niven turned to him and snapped, 'And fuck you too!' The Guards turned him down, and so did the Royal Navy, unless he wanted to be stoker. He was seeking solace over dinner at the Café de Paris when he noticed a beautiful WAAF[19], and had a funny feeling that he would never forget her. It was here that he was recruited to the Army by a lieutenant colonel of the Rifle Brigade, who had heard about his visit to the RAF. Niven was then at his club, Boodle's, when a ruddy faced naval lieutenant commander saved him from a paper-waving member of the old guard, who was affronted that the man on the front of his newspaper was a member of his club. The lieutenant commander was none other than Ian Fleming. The naval intelligence community, Fleming and the M's (which included Clarke), were a tight knit bunch and now Niven was definitely on Clarke's radar.

The 1st Battalion, The Rifles had been wiped out at Dunkirk by the time Niven reported to their depot in Tidworth. He'd been recommissioned as a lieutenant, and moved into a nearby cottage with his Danish girlfriend. He was invited to dinner with friends one night, with Foreign Secretary Anthony Eden and Churchill.

'Young man, you did a very fine thing to give up a most promising career to fight for your country,' the prime minister told Niven. 'Mark you, had you not done so – it would have been despicable!'

Soon enough, Niven was shown a very interesting document by his adjutant calling for volunteers for an elite force of a highly secret nature, with questions about qualifications, age, air and seasickness.

'I think it must be parachuting,' the adjutant said. 'I heard rumours that they were forming something like that.'

'Jesus! I don't want to be any part of that,' Niven replied.

But the boredom of chasing non-existent parachutists round Salisbury Plain beat him into submission, and he found himself in an interview with Colonel Dudley Clarke. Clarke explained the whole concept of quick cut-and-thrust raids on the enemy coastline, and hinted that he had some other special ideas which he might disclose later. Niven wanted in.

Clarke perhaps had second thoughts about Niven's lack of rigidity on a Sunday night soon afterwards, when he was woken by a phone call. Apparently a man claiming to be a 'well known film star' had been caught in West Sussex changing into the uniform of a British officer and arrested as a suspected German agent. Niven had been driving back from a picnic with friends in Godalming. The light was failing, meaning they would have to stop because of the blackout rules and be marooned in the countryside. Niven realised he had his uniform in the trunk, which would mean they could continue their journey. He pulled into a convenient gateway on Hogs Back to change out of his tweeds, where he was promptly overpowered by two members of the Sussex Home Guard who were clearly not cinema-goers, and believed he was a German parachutist. Clarke had to bail him out.

Wrangled by Buster Marling the first commando team, 11 Commando, assembled in Southampton, and Clarke and Niven drove down to watch the rehearsal for the first attack. Meeting Garnons-Williams at the Household Brigade Yacht Club on the Hamble at Warsash they set sail into the Solent on a rakish cream motor yacht. Against the setting sun, they met the Commando flotilla in craft of varying seaworthiness, many of which didn't make it to the target due to engine trouble. This might have worked getting the Army off at Dunkirk, but they needed something more reliable for their return trip.

They overnighted in Southampton, and set out early for London to find the streets crammed with French sailors – French resistance was over, and the French Navy had run for British ports.

Back in the office, Garnons-Williams appeared, beaming.

'I've got them! RAF "crash boats", fast, reliable and seaworthy. They're small and they won't take the whole lot, but the Air Ministry have promised me six and we ought to manage thirty men apiece.'

Clarke wrapped up the final 'Charity Meeting' at the Rumbolds' residence, chaired by the dark-haired Miss Rumbold.[20] She had just finished distributing instructions to some young and athletic-looking men, when, on the steps of the Grosvenor Crescent house, Ronnie Todd turned to Clarke and said, 'I hope that you'll come with us.'

Clarke thought about it, but not for long – he felt that under the circumstances, he had to back his own judgement and go to France as well.

Just three weeks after Dunkirk, on the afternoon of 24 June, a flotilla of 6 RAF crash boats slipped their moorings and headed into the Channel. Based on interwar powerboat racers, they were the best craft for the job. The six speed boats opened their throttles and the commandos clung on as they sped over the sea at over 30 knots. Dusk fell, and they were buzzed by a flight of Spitfires, who recognised them as friendly, and they throttled back approaching the French coast. Running silently to their assault beaches, the commandos blackened their faces with greasepaint Clarke had obtained from his costumier on Wardour Street.[21]

The team assaulted Le Touquet. Todd's team hit the town, lobbing grenades into a hotel full of Germans. Clarke watched the ensuing firefight from the water: the flash then thump of explosions, and tracer arcing into the night sky, one of the crew next to him exclaiming, 'Here we go! The party's started.'

The men on the boats almost came to grief when two sentries cycling on the hard sand spotted them, after the onshore commando lookout cocked his Tommy gun and his magazine fell off with a clatter.[22] The enemy got the drop on them and opened fire. Bullets cracked overhead, and Clarke flung himself into the bottom of the boat, thumping his ear as he landed. The Germans pedalled off for reinforcements but Clarke and his crew made themselves scarce before their return; Todd's assault team also got away without casualties.

The first British special forces raid wasn't much of a strike, but as *The Times* reported, 'the point is that this incident shows the offensive spirit, which is exactly what the public wants, and which, if it had pervaded to a greater extent in the general strategy of the war, might have materially changed for better the course of events.'[23]

It was clear, what with recruits having to be warned off eating snow and Tommy-gun magazines falling off during raids, that this subliminal force needed special training. The solution came from an unlikely source. One of the Independent Companies – the 5th Scots Guards – was a ski battalion, and there had been only one place from which to recruit proficient skiers for the British Army: the aristocracy.

Skiing was a pastime of wealthy Brits: the Flemings, Ian and Peter, learnt at Kitzbühel in Austria; 8mm family film shows a young David Stirling performing proficient parallels.[24] His elder brother, Bill Stirling, and Brian Mayfield joined 5th Scots Guards, along with Freddy Spencer Chapman, who was recruited because he'd twice driven reindeer across Lapland.[25] The unit wasn't solely made up of skiers – many were proficient climbers and mountaineers, including Jim Gavin, who would later climb Everest.

The battalion went to Chamonix in March 1940 to carry out intensive training, and were on top of Mont Blanc on 10 May when Germany invaded France. They caught the train to Paris, and from there flew back to Croydon. Frustrated and eager for action, Brian Mayfield, Jim Gavin and Bill Stirling 'chartered' a submarine – HMS *Truant* – to land them in Norway. The plan was to ski in from the coast and blow the Bergen–Oslo railway. But the *Truant* hit a magnetic mine six hours out of the Firth of Forth, and only just managed to limp back to Scapa Flow.

Retiring to the Stirlings' family home, Keir House in Perthshire, they were joined by Bill's cousin Simon Fraser, Lord Lovat, who had just been recruited by General Adrian 'Old Flamer' Carton de Wiart, the man Clarke had been sent to Norway to save, who conducted interviews from his bath, eyepatch over his missing eye and his body crisscrossed with battle scars.

The presence of Lovat was fortuitous: in 1900, his father had formed the first new regiment in the British Army since 1700, the Lovat Scouts – an irregular force recruited from Highland ghillies. The ghillies were experts in concealment, tracking and shooting, and were recruited to combat the threat posed by the same Boer commandos who had inspired Clarke. The Lovats' principle was that deer were a harder quarry than humans, and they would go on to become the British Army's first sniper unit.

At Keir House, the friends shared whisky around the fire and Bill Stirling came up with the idea that the six of them, reinforced by a few selected officers and NCOs, should form the nucleus of a new training school.[26] It would be based in the Highlands, and prepare soldiers for smash and grab raids on targets in enemy-occupied territory, an approach which, after Dunkirk, seemed the only possible form of offensive warfare.[27]

It was an idea which dovetailed spectacularly with Clarke's need for specialist Commando training.

Inverailort House, a Victorian shooting lodge near Lochailort in the Western Highlands, was requisitioned to train Commando troop leaders. The midges were bad, there were insufficient tents, and they were short on cooks, rations and transport. All of which the instructors made up for with their enthusiasm. Clarke's first students arrived in June – twenty-five puzzled subalterns, among them Second Lieutenant David Stirling.[28]

David Niven was ordered to report too, but before he left he made a quick and fruitless reconnaissance of the Café de Paris in the hopes of seeing the WAAF who had captured his imagination. Unsuccessful, he settled for a late-night rendezvous with his Danish girlfriend before jumping on the train for the Western Highlands.

At Lochailort, Mayfield commanded, Bill Stirling was chief instructor, and Lord Lovat and his ghillies took care of fieldcraft. Fieldcraft training was based on the traditional lore of the Lovat Scouts: stalking and using long-range telescopes. There was also practical map reading and direction finding, especially by night, and a detailed study of ambush techniques, assisted by live fire demonstrations.

Alongside fieldcraft, former 5th Scots Guards man and sapper 'Mad' Mike Calvert ran a demolitions wing with tremendous originality and enthusiasm, continually devising and trying out new gadgets.[29]

Close combat training was taught by two former Shanghai police officers, William Fairbairn and Eric Sykes. Fairbairn was the first man outside Japan to have a black belt,[30] and the two had gained fame, or notoriety, after breaking up a Comintern group in Shanghai using their 'methods'. They set up a 'killing house' in a derelict cottage, where students, armed with pistols, learnt to engage targets appearing in the half-light from any position, with only a split second to identify if their target were friend or foe.[31] Recruits learnt to use instinctive fire – raising and firing a weapon from muscle memory, without conscious thought.

A new troop leader from 2 Commando, Tony Deane-Drummond, described Fairbairn and Sykes as looking like benign businessmen, except their mantra was: 'remember, balls, ears and eyes – go for them!'[32] The two men also designed a fighting knife: a dagger that was easy to stick into and pull out of the body. The Fairbairn–Sykes knife became synonymous with the Commandos, and later the SAS.

Each course ended with a gruelling 48-hour survival exercise over the punishing Highland terrain called a 'perisher'. The country was tough, midges ate you alive, and you were always wet, either from sweat or rain, but if you passed you had earned your dagger.

Niven, after two months running up and down the mountains of the Western Highlands, crawling up streams at night and swimming in the loch with full equipment, felt he was 'unbearably fit', his code for his raging libido. He spoke with the chief instructor, Bill Stirling, about the problem, who relented and gave him a 48-hour pass – just enough time to get to London and back. He went to the general store in the village and sent a telegram to his girlfriend:

*ARRIVING WEDNESDAY MORNING WILL COME STRAIGHT
TO FLAT WITH SECRET WEAPON*

He didn't make the rendezvous – he was picked up by two Royal
Military Police on arrival and taken straight to an office in St James's,
where a man in a suit asked why he was sending coded messages
to a spy.

'Sir . . . that's not code – that's fucking.'

Clarke had more patching up to do, but he promoted Niven to
captain, and the film-star-turned-soldier became MO9's liaison
officer.

The *Le Touquet* raid highlighted that RAF crash boats could only be
a stopgap; they could not get close to the beach and commandos
had to cross-load into rubber dinghies to actually get ashore. The
RAF also badly needed them to rescue downed pilots, leaving very
few for the newly created commandos. The craft were, bizarrely,
an invention of TE Lawrence, who had come up with the idea
after watching an aircrew drown while they were waiting to be
picked up.

Clarke was having a late dinner at the Berkeley Buttery when he
found the solution. One of the regulars, Mr Dodds, was intrigued
by Clarke's injured ear, which was still bandaged after his dive for
cover on the Le Touquet raid. Mr Dodds suspected Clarke may have
been roaming further than across St James's Park, and gently
quizzed him. Clarke knew that Mr Dodds owned an oil tanker fleet,
and discretely outlined his problem.

'Is it urgent?' Dodds asked.

It was.

He got up from the table, telling Clarke he had some plans that
might be of use. Dodds took a taxi to the City and woke his office
watchman. After a search through some files, he returned to Clarke
with the plans for the Eureka boat, a craft designed by an American
named Andrew Higgins.

Andrew Higgins's lumber yard in the Mississippi Delta was

bankrupt in the 1930s when he turned to making boats, founding the Eureka Tug-Boat Company. The Eureka was first designed for trappers and other tradespeople navigating the shallow, marshy waterways of the delta. It was a fast, flat-bottomed boat that had its propellers partially mounted in a tunnel, meaning it could force its way through mud and reeds, or run over an alligator or submerged log, without suffering damage. Crucially, the Eureka was also designed so that it could beach itself and rapidly relaunch.

The Eureka found an obvious market among the rum-runners of the prohibition-era Mississippi Delta, and Higgins's fortunes soared. Prohibition was repealed in 1933, and his gangster market collapsed, but luckily the US Navy saw the boat's potential as a landing craft, and had ordered some. It was the plans for this militarised version, stripped back with two machine guns up front, which Dodds and Clarke inspected in the War Office in the early hours.

It looked ideal.

Clarke went over the road to the Admiralty in the morning. They agreed, and placed a substantial order with a British dockyard. Clarke had ordered Britain's first purpose-built raiding craft.

Just as Clarke's vision for his Commando initiative seemed on the verge of being realised, it was subsumed by the prime minister's own vision for the project – the first raid had not been well received in high quarters. First, Churchill didn't like 'pin pricks' or 'mosquito stings': he wanted Commando units in their thousands executing huge raids – but what he really didn't like was that members of the Cabinet arrived with coverage of the raid in the evening papers when he knew nothing about it.[33] Clarke had the press release ready to go before they hit port – that was the point of the operation. The impact of his subliminal methods was not physical, but in the minds of the enemy.

Unfortunately, 'displeasure was shown at the extent of publicity that followed', and Churchill foisted a full general of the Royal Marines, Alan Bourne, on Clarke and Niven as commander.[34]

Clarke would have liked the first few raids to be humble affairs carried out with a degree of obscurity and carefully curated press coverage, and feared that the advent of this high-powered CO might attract 'limelight to the scene before the stage had been properly set'.

Clarke's fears appeared fully justified when Churchill sent a memo to Pug Ismay on 2 July:

> *If it be true a few hundred German troops have landed on Jersey or Guernsey by troop-carriers plans should be studied to land secretly at night on the Islands and kill or capture the invaders. This is exactly one of the exploits for which the Commandos would be suited . . . Pray let me have a plan.*[35]

A much bigger raid needed a bigger team: 3 Commando was added to 11 and rapidly established in Plymouth. On 11 July, Buster Marling commenced work, and on the fourteenth she waved them goodbye from the quay.[36] There had been insufficient time for proper training, or reconnaissance of the target. In thick fog, one destroyer invaded the Isle of Sark by mistake, which the Germans hadn't invaded, and the other hit the Jerbourg peninsula on Guernsey. The peninsula's rocky cliffs were unsuitable for beach landings, and the commandos got soaked getting ashore. They investigated a position where a machine gun was reputed to be mounted and found no gun, they then searched a nearby house to find it occupied by a strange, possibly mentally ill, man, and promptly fell back to the evacuation beach with his nonsensical words echoing in their ears.[37]

Guernsey has one of the largest tidal ranges in the world, and back at the beach the tide had risen by 33 feet, the surf was heavy, and the raid came apart. The crash boats couldn't get ashore; a dinghy carrying machine guns capsized, drowning a gunner. At 2.40am, orders were issued to the remaining men to swim out to the crash boats – at which point it transpired three of the commandos couldn't swim. The remainder struggled out to sea, Lieutenant Grant of the Royal Naval Reserve repeatedly diving in to rescue more men from drowning before finally, dripping wet, they returned to their destroyer.

On 15 July, MO9 made their sheepish report to Whitehall; Churchill was furious.

> It would be most unwise to disturb the coasts of any of these [occupied] countries by the kind of silly fiascos which were perpetrated at Boulogne and Guernsey. The idea of working all these coasts up against us by pin-prick raids . . . is one to be strictly avoided.[38]

Clarke's boss Dill may have disagreed, but Churchill's chief staff officer and military adviser, Pug Ismay followed his lead: 'Our policy has been against anything in the nature of pinpricks'.[39]

Clarke and Niven could only have felt dismay when a full Admiral of the Fleet, the 67-year-old legend Lord Roger Keyes, was appointed as their first Director of Combined Operations. Keyes had been Chief of Naval Staff during Churchill's outing as First Sea Lord in the disastrous Gallipoli campaign of 1915, and been commander of a 1918 raid to the same port as Garnons-Williams had just block-aded, Zeebrugge. Keyes's operation had been notably less success-ful; it not only failed to stop U-boats using the port, but was an action so bloody it occasioned eight Victoria Crosses, one given to an entire battalion of marines. Keyes had been appointed for big things, and was studying the feasibility of supposedly 'medium-sized' raids using between five and ten thousand men.[40]

Clarke's subliminal methods looked dead in the water. He believed that 'neither the War Office nor the Admiralty ever felt again that same personal interest in the evolution of the Commandos . . . [and] their management found the difficulties increasing in propor-tion'. The commandos had outgrown Clarke's concept, and ceased, by definition, to be a special force. Planned raids were ambitious, but none materialised, and the Army was earning nothing from the four thousand commandos they had trained. By October, MO9 was under threat, and Clarke felt the bailiffs closing in.

In November 1940, he received a second summons: Wavell wanted him for a special job on his staff in Cairo. No more detail than that, but it sounded like an 'intelligence' role. Europe had been where the action was, but now, with Italy in the war, Africa was more tempting. The decision was taken out of his hands in any case. Dill announced he wanted Clarke in Africa, and that he was to hand over MO9 in 48 hours and report to Wavell as soon as possible.

11 *SAS*

Before he left Britain, Clarke's vision took wing. Clarke had, as Niven's Rifles adjutant had guessed, always wanted parachutists. Clarke had seen their impact first hand; again, not only the military impact – but the constant threat that they could be dropped anywhere, which generated anxiety.

The first meeting about parachutists occurred in June 1940, and Clarke pushed his parachute project again after the arrival of Admiral Keyes, viewing it as a means to continue his small raids in line with his subliminal methods. Unfortunately, before he could get a raid off the ground, Churchill again became ambitious, wanting a corps of at least five thousand parachute troops and airborne tanks – 'pray let me have a plan'. The resulting design for a glider carrying an 8-ton tank never flew; instead, Clarke sent Admiral Keyes a more realistic paper on his assessment of the 'Air Needs of Irregular Forces'.[41]

With scant resources in both personnel and parachutes, the reality was volunteers from 2 Commando fell to earth from the belly of a few obsolete Whitley bombers at RAF Ringway outside Manchester – which was exceedingly unpleasant and dangerous. Lieutenant Tony Deane-Drummond, who had been kicked in the balls at Lochailort by Fairbairn and Sykes, weighed an impressive 26olbs (118kg), when the weight for a parachutist, including their equipment, was supposed to be 25olbs (113kg). He landed heavily on the drop zone at Ringway. Clarke became haunted by the thought of what could go wrong, and decided he could hardly continue to accept responsibility for this new enterprise without trying at least one jump himself. He got on the train to Manchester to collect his second set of wings.

He was put through a series of 'dreadful' acrobatics on mats, encouraged by parachute instructors; then he was suspended from the roof of a hangar by a harness, where he was swung and twisted in all directions, before jumping off a scaffold, all the while the voices of instructors yelling incomprehensible instructions at him. Finally, fitted with his chute, which pulls the body forward once the four straps are clipped into the rotating buckle on the chest, he hobbled out onto the tarmac where a twin-engine Whitley was running up its motors. But an RAF officer stopped him. The wind had risen too much for the jump to take place.

The wind speed continued to increase, and on the train home Clarke found himself oddly disappointed. He had died a hundred deaths training and felt cheated. Soon after his return to Whitehall, the RAF ruled no one over the age of 35 could jump. Clarke was too old; he would never get his parachute wings.

At Ringway, 2 Commando went on training, one troop leader trying to make parachuting less scary by turning it into a competition to clock up as many jumps as you could. One night he even did a jump from a balloon in full mess kit, complete with spurs – he was going to a formal dinner but had to fit his balloon jump in. It raised a laugh and perhaps helped make parachuting seem a bit less intimidating to recruits.[42]

But parachutes did fail. Driver Ralph Evans was killed on 25 July and Trooper Stanley Watts on 27 August.[43] The parachutes failed for a number of reasons, and Clarke realised the Whitley, with its hole-in-the-floor exit, was unsuitable for dropping parachutists.[44] A common failure was 'somersaulting', where the parachutist falling through the hole went head over heels in a spin, tangling his lines as the chute deployed, preventing it from opening properly. Most lethal was a static line failure – the line, which pulled the chute from its pack as the trooper jumped, was attached inside the fuselage by an O ring that wasn't sufficiently strong. When things went wrong, parachutists would plummet towards earth in full view of their waiting comrades, powerless to help. Refusals were common, and training stopped.

Clarke stressed that from both a psychological and an operational point of view, an aircraft with a side exit was required.[45] Another obsolete bomber, the Bombay, had a side door and showed more promise, but too few were available. Instead, the deadlock with the Air Ministry was eased by the War Office consenting to soldiers being dropped from Whitleys after they were modified – including with stronger O rings – but morale was understandably unpredictable as jump training recommenced. Refusals were still common.

The difficulties in training large numbers of parachutists, and finding aircraft for them, led to gliders, which could be towed by aircraft before being released. Clarke had been interested in gliders from the day he had heard the Germans had landed them on a Belgian fort and taken it with flamethrowers. But in 1940, the battle for air resources was dominated by the needs of the Battle of Britain, and no gliders were built.

Then, on 12 October 1940, the whole airborne programme was pulled from Clarke and Combined Operations. The problem was the scale of the planned operations; as Churchill's ambitions increased, discussion between the War Office and Air Ministry led to the conclusion that there was no way of evacuating so many parachutists from hostile territory, and this severely limited their employment in raiding operations.[46] This would not have been the case with Clarke's smaller raids; his vision had been to drop in by air, raid, then get out by boat.

Now airborne special forces looked grounded, but five hundred officers and men of 2 Commando had already been trained. One of the biggest difficulties in Whitehall for the Commandos had been the name. Staff officers thought that 'commando' was 'scarcely the appropriate term, given it referred to one of their most successful enemies, and insisted that Special Service (SS) should be used.[47] Clarke had parried with the 'sinister parallel' of including the abbreviation SS on British documents, and it had taken Dill's intervention for him to be allowed to use 'commando'. But many officers found it difficult to use in conversation, and on written documents they continued to use SS, without trace of irony, for all irregular forces other than the Commandos. And now, as 2 Commando were removed from the Commandos, they reverted to being Special Service troops. On 21 November 1940, perhaps with glee, a staff officer added 'Air' in parentheses – and three extra strokes of a typewriter, and the S(A)S was born.

On 3 December 1940, with Clarke's departure to Cairo imminent, the first SAS demonstration was given on Salisbury Plain. Clarke was pleased, it was a popular event. General 'Auk' Auchinleck and his Brigade Major, Neil Ritchie, arrived in their staff cars along with other dignitaries, including Crown Prince Olaf of Norway. The Auk was now in command of the defence of the south coast, and was here to watch his troops being tested by 11th Special (Air) Service Battalion, posing as German parachutists.[48]

Approaching the drop zone (DZ) that dawn, the 38 SAS parachutists could see a vast mass of cars and spectators below the hole in the floor of their Whitleys. They dropped in four troops, each group falling as a 'stick' from a single aircraft. Landing amidst the throng of spectators, they struggled with their chutes on the drop zone, while fighting off enquiries in a 'comic opera' to get on with their mission.

The umpires told one stick they were pinned down by machine-gun fire from a Bren carrier. The SAS NCO asked where it was and staff officers, ten deep, parted so he could see his British enemy. But the SAS took advantage of the chaos. The defenders assumed the paratroopers, moving on foot, would be slow to reach the objective, the village of Shrewton. But B Troop, SAS threaded through the crowd, unobserved by the Auk's troops, and headed for the staff officers' car park.

Staff chauffeurs were surprised when the troop, armed with Tommy guns, arrived and stole the biggest car they could find at gunpoint – which belonged to the Crown Prince of Norway.[49] The troop also took a motorbike and, riding shotgun on the overloaded car, sped off. Back on the drop zone, the other SAS troops recovered their weapons from their parachute containers and ran towards their objective, the bridges over the River Till west of Stonehenge, to cheers from the onlookers.

Ahead of them, and the defenders, B Troop screeched into Shrewton and took the main bridge over the Till.[50] The defenders fell back in disarray, and the remaining SAS troops seized the other crossings with ease. The speed and complete surprise had unhinged the defenders – the Auk was impressed.

Two days later, Clarke shut the door to his bachelor pad at 12 Stratton Street. It would soon be blown to pieces by a stick of bombs from a Heinkel He 111, with women tearing their dresses to make tourniquets for the maimed and dying in the Ritz brasserie across the road. He flew out of Poole Harbour in disguise on an Imperial Airways flying boat. His passport listed him as Clarke, Dudley Wrangel, a British subject of South African birth, his profession as journalist, his height as 5 foot 7-and-three-quarter inches.[51] Clarke was undercover, heading to Egypt knowing more than any person in Britain about the uniquely British response to the *Blitzkrieg*: special forces.

3

Kommandos: 1940–1941

William Fraser

Twenty-three-year-old William Fraser was not obvious material for the sharp end of Clarke's subliminal methods. He was 5 foot 11-and-three-quarter inches tall, weighed 140lbs (63kg), had brown eyes and dark brown hair. The man of few words from Aberdeen, Scotland, was handsome, but never left an impression. When he had signed to the Army from school in 1936, aged 19, the doctor recorded he had slight dorsal kyphosis, an imperceptible rounding of the shoulders, a defect so trivial as not to be relevant. But sometimes in Army records it is the subtext that is important – in this case, young Fraser wasn't standing up straight, and there was something about him this doctor did not like. In fact Fraser was hiding a 'defect' in the eyes of the British Army, indeed British society of the day – he was gay.[1]

Being gay could not only have precluded him from his family career (both his father and grandfather had served in the ranks of the prestigious Gordon Highlanders), it could also have landed him in jail. British prisons were full of gay men who had been handed in by friends, neighbours and countrymen. However perhaps the fact that Fraser was good at deception made him the ideal operator for Clarke's methods.

Fraser was not only military born and bred, he excelled at everything military. Despite his humble beginnings Fraser received the best education a young man without family means could achieve: first, at Aberdeen Grammar, founded in 1257, one of the oldest grammar schools in the country; then, after the death of his father and his mother's remarriage, at Woking County Grammar School. The school was known for its Cadet Force and its sport; Fraser made the football team, which won the Surrey Secondary School Championship.

If Fraser was born to the Army, he was bred to it by his stepfather, Major John Joseph Heath MC DCM MM, a war hero. Like his father, Fraser's stepfather made captain having risen through the ranks before his commission. When Fraser was 11, in 1929, Heath was commissioned an officer, having served as the Warwickshire's Regimental Sergeant Major, the highest non-commissioned rank and most prestigious position in the British Army. You can make General in less time and with less ability.

In the Gordons depot at Aberdeen in 1937, Fraser the cadet made the football team, the bayonet fencing team and the depot gymnastics demonstration squad. And, when posted to the First Battalion, Gordons, he was immediately promoted to lance corporal in March 1937, where he received 'distinguished' on his non-commissioned officer's course. The Gordons' regimental magazine recorded, 'we congratulate [Lance Corporals] Lillie and Fraser on their promotion and hope they will keep their eye on the baton'. (The highest rank in the British Army carry batons on their shoulders – generals wear one, field marshals two.)[2] Fraser had recognisable talent – he was fit, had quietly spoken confidence, was an excellent shot, and vital for any future officer, was very good at navigation.

With war declared, in September 1939 Corporal Fraser deployed to France with the BEF. The Gordon Highlanders formed part of one of Britain's best divisions – the Highland Division, of twelve thousand soldiers – and were first into the line. Fraser spent the coldest winter of the century in a mud-filled barn just outside Lille, with two inches of ice on the telephone wires, and temperatures well below freezing. Telephone poles and trees snapped like matchsticks and, whenever Hitler threatened to invade, he and the battalion had to light fires under the Ford V8 engines of their Bren Carriers to crash out to their positions on the Belgium border.[3]

The British Army was expanding rapidly for war, and, desperately short of officers, scoured its ranks for talented young non-commissioned officers. Fraser celebrated Christmas in the muddy barn, then on 29 December 1939 got the boat back to Britain – posted to 165 Officer Cadet Training Unit, Dunbar, Scotland. It was the first example of the war of what would become known as 'Fraser luck', because very few Gordons made it home.

After Fraser had left for Britain, on 10 January 1940 a disoriented Messerschmitt Bf 108 had crashed in fog north of Maastricht, carrying the German plans for the invasion of France. The maps revealed the German route through Belgium into France – *Fall Gelb* (Case Yellow) – which the British Expeditionary Force were well placed to resist. But Allied command worried they were a plant, and the British had all their eggs in one basket: a thrust into Belgium to meet the German advance. To their south lay the Maginot Line – a supposedly impregnable fortified line that ran the length of the German–French border from Switzerland, but it had run out of funds, and concrete, at the Ardennes forest. Realising the Germans could drive through the Maginot Line at its weakest point, British Command decided to detach the whole Highland Division, and with it the Gordons, to bolster French forces further south.

The German plans were not in fact fake, but the compromised plan gave the progressives, led by the architect of *Blitzkrieg*, General Heinz Guderian, the chance to execute a better plan. He and the leading lights in the celebrity generation of German generals like Erwin Rommel now gathered the highest density of armour that the world had ever seen, hidden under the canopy of the Ardennes forest, just north of the section of Maginot Line that the Gordons and Highland Division occupied.

These men were disciples of the type of warfare espoused by British revolutionaries such as Hobo Hobart, and First World War captain turned military theorist Basil Henry Liddell Hart. Guderian translated Liddell Hart's *The Strategy of the Indirect Approach* and distributed it to his panzer officers. Fighting his own Luddites in Germany, he told them, 'that's the old school, and already it is old history. I put my faith in Hobart, the new man.' But it wasn't the tank, or panzer, that was the decisive factor in *Blitzkrieg* – it was how it would be used.

The British theorist Captain Liddell Hart had been concussed by a shell in 1915, and then returned to the line in time for the Somme offensive of 1 July 1916. His whole battalion was wiped out on the first day and he was hit three times, blown up and gassed before being evacuated on 19 July. Like Clarke, the First War had inspired him to wonder if there wasn't better way of doing business. He made the stunning, though obvious, observation that war was a part-time profession. No commander was likely to have ever fought a battle before, therefore war fighting could not be learnt by experience. He set about studying campaigns from the Romans to the present day, searching for commonality in success, and came up with a second stunning observation: in every battle, success was most likely to come from those who dared to take the *indirect approach*.

On the night of 3 May 1940, the first German patrols probed the Gordons' defences 50 miles south of the Ardennes forest. Nineteen-year-old Jack Byrne's C Company came into contact, and the company drove them off, but in the firefight Byrne caught a load of shrapnel in his right thigh.

An Englishman, Byrne had heard that he'd be kissed by a duchess with a golden guinea between her lips if he enlisted with the regiment – the lure the Duke of Gordon had offered for his first recruitment drive in 1794. Within an hour he'd walked into the nearest recruiting office and demanded to join the Gordon Highlanders. After 'a very long day', the desk sergeant was persuaded to change Byrne's age from 17 to 18 and his religion to Presbyterian, and waved him onto a train to Aberdeen. As for the tryst with the duchess, he was taken to the Officers' Mess to admire her portrait and touch her bonnet.

Carrying Byrne from the battlefield, his comrades took the opportunity to remind him of his date with the duchess. One piece of shrapnel was so deep the surgeon couldn't remove it and Byrne would fight the war with a piece of German metal wedged in his leg. Byrne was evacuated, and joined in Fraser's luck, though not before being left for dead in fighting outside the Dunkirk beachhead: a German bayoneted him in the groin to make sure he was dead. 'During this unhappy period in our history,' Byrne said later, 'many isolated groups of soldiers, cut off during the retreat, fought on to the bitter end without hope of life or victory, determined not to shame the land from which they came.' But French villagers found him and carried him to the British lines. His injuries had saved him from captivity, or worse.[4]

The full force of the German Blitzkrieg broke on 10 May. Among the lead units, soon to be *Blitzkrieg's* poster boy, General Rommel sliced into the Allied rear. The panzer cohorts broke through the Allied line north of the Gordons, severing them and the Highland Division from the BEF, and any chance of making Dunkirk. While the BEF fell back to Dunkirk, over the next two weeks, the Gordons and Highland Division fled 300 miles to their rear, via a route that took them south of Champagne, through Sezanne, then Paris, then north of the French capital, hoping to make it out of France via Le Havre.

Once unshackled from Dunkirk, Rommel blasted across country and cut them off from Le Havre, encircling them in a small fishing village called Saint-Valery-en-Caux. The Gordons' last stand was made at St Valery – it had a mole, a pier, running to water deep enough to bring a destroyer alongside, and the Highland Division hoped the Royal Navy would be able to pull off the same stunt it had at Dunkirk. (The small boats story was great PR for Churchill, the new prime minster, but 70 per cent of the 338,000 men who escaped Dunkirk did so via the mole.) But whereas Dunkirk was protected by canals and not overlooked, St Valery is an inlet surrounded by cliffs – and Rommel arrived on those cliffs on 11 June, the day Clarke walked into the Admiralty to ask if they could help form the Commando.

Rommel's panzers and 88mm guns rained fire on the port and evacuation vessels, and his dive bombers attacked Royal Navy destroyers. Evacuation was abandoned. That night the Navy hoped to bring in the two hundred vessels under cover of darkness, but fog closed on the port, preventing the Highlanders' last chance of escape. The BBC announced that the BEF had been successfully evacuated from Dunkirk – as one Highlander put it, 'I still remember it: "This is the BBC . . ." you know, the old toffee-nosed way of talking ". . . The BEF have been successfully evacuated from Dunkirk". I thought, *what a load of old bollocks*.'[5]

At 10.30am, the bugle sounded the ceasefire. Proud Highland Troops were so depressed they felt like shooting themselves. Most of the Gordons were wiped out defending the perimeter; a few made Veules, a nearby village with a wooden jetty where the Navy managed to pull off six hundred men. Survivors would break the news to Fraser of what had happened.[6]

Before the Gordons were captured, on 16 February 1940, Fraser and other officer cadets had been greeted on the parade square at Dunbar by the Regimental Sergeant Major, Andy Drummond, saying, 'I knew that things in France were not going that well but Jesus they cannot be this bad.'[7]

Officer training was an incredibly proud moment for Fraser. Though he was Army born and bred, his stepfather had only been commissioned late in his career, because before the Second World War young officers were recruited solely from aristocracy, which he definitely was not. Commissions used to be purchased from the Army – the more prestigious the regiment, the higher the price, and though this system was officially abolished in 1871 the practice still underpinned the nature of all British regiments. The Gordons had been reassuringly expensive.

Fraser passed out with elan on 25 May 1940 (he graded 'A' at the weapons training school), proudly wearing his second lieutenant's pips sewn onto his dress uniform, his Gordons tartan kilt and glengarry. He was ready to get into the fight. But the following day the scale of what had befallen the BEF in France became apparent, when the British Army started evacuating from Dunkirk.

Fraser reported for duty at the Gordons barracks in Aberdeen on the last day of the Dunkirk evacuation, 4 June, and discovered that his battalion hadn't made it. Listening for the fate of his comrades on the BBC, he heard Churchill's legendary broadcast: 'We shall fight on the beaches, we shall fight on the landing grounds . . .'.

Knowing that the fate of his friends, and that of more than twelve thousand men of the Highland Division, was being airbrushed from history to spin Dunkirk as a victory was galling.

On 12 June, St Valery fell to Rommel – no amount of bravery and tradition had been able to compensate for the British Army's failure to modernise. For Fraser, the Gordons was his family, and when he found out, his enemy got a face and a name – Johannes Erwin Eugen Rommel. The Scots might have hated the English, but they hated Rommel more.

Natural Selection

Clarke's request for Commando recruits – 'the man who is quick in thought and quick on his feet' – had just reached Fraser's commanding officer.[8] Fraser, smarting from the loss of his battalion, volunteered immediately.

Fraser was interviewed by Captain Ian Glennie, as one of two potential section commanders for his troop. Fraser's record spoke for itself, but a huge advantage over other officers was that because he had served in the ranks, he knew his men intimately, and Glennie needed to select men for his troop. Fraser recommended Byrne, who was recovering from his wounds – anyone who would lie about their age, get wounded twice in combat and then volunteer for unspecified duties of a dangerous and hazardous nature had more than proved themselves. Among others Fraser knew was a tough, nononsense NCO, Bob Tait, his best friend, Jeff Du Vivier, a man so grey that no one else knew him. Then there was a man called Dougie Keith, and finally a hard-bitten Scottish sergeant called John Cheyne.[9] The Gordons flooded to the Commandos, and the troop – 8 Troop of 11 (Scottish) Commando – unsurprisingly became known as 'Gordons Troop'. Fraser was B Section commander. They were arguably the most motivated of the first commandos. The Scottish Commando would adopt a black hackle – a black feather – in its headdress, the Scots symbol of an unresolved quarrel.

Fraser and his recruits marched into their temporary home, the disused Netherdale tweed mill, a Victorian structure in Galashiels in the Scottish Borders. It was draughty, cold and the food appalling. The officers promptly moved into a local hotel, while the troops made the best of the spartan conditions, which did not include running water. As soon as he arrived at their new base, Fraser's troop leader, Ian Glennie, was packed off to the training wing at Lochailort, along with all the other 11 Commando troop leaders, to learn the ways of this new warfare. On arrival there, Glennie was met by two 'extraordinary' ex-Shanghai policemen – Fairbairn and Sykes. One of the other new Scottish troop leaders, Thomas Macpherson, thought it polite to introduce himself, and tried to shake Sykes's hand – next thing he knew he was flat on his back.

'That's your first lesson,' Sykes said. 'You've got to be ready for anything all the time.'[10]

Back at the mill, Fraser's new CO, Lieutenant Colonel Dick Pedder, relished the hardship as a way to challenge his recruits. He had been recruited by Clarke from the Highland Light Infantry – or 'Hell's Last Issue', which was Niven's old outfit, and Niven likely had a hand in his recruitment. Pedder would stand no nonsense: he knew exactly what he wanted, and he ruthlessly culled and returned to unit those he found lacking. Some said he was an unlikeable man, that he was a loner and an extreme authoritarian with a quick temper. When the commandos were ordered to report for training in Ayr, more than a hundred miles away, Pedder turned it into a selection march. Another new 11 Commando troop commander, Geoffrey Keyes, son of the admiral, described it as rather a shock.[11]

Geoffrey Keyes had done a stint in Norway as a liaison officer, and watched General Auchinleck retake Narvik. Days before his father was appointed over Clarke by Churchill, Geoffrey had applied to the Commandos, and wrote to tell his parents. His father replied he had been made Director of Combined Operations and had already given instruction that his son be offered a job.

Keyes the younger would never live down the accusation of nepotism, which sat particularly uncomfortably with Robert Blair

'Paddy' Mayne, one of two Irish officers 11 Commando had picked up. Mayne and Eoin McGonigal had signed on in Ireland, but were attached to the Cameron Highlanders in Ayrshire when the shout for volunteers went out.

Mayne was a boxer and had played second row for Ireland; McGonigal also boxed. Many of the men who had transferred from the regular infantry had just done a stint of marching through France, but Keyes was not terribly well equipped for the physical side of soldiering. Though tall, he was not strong, and his contemporaries described him as weedy. Worse, he sounded like Bertie Wooster. Keyes was the son of a military legend, and other commandos suspected he had a chip on his shoulder and was trying to prove himself.[12]

Pedder set a cracking pace on the march to Ayr. For those like Fraser, who (unlike Keyes) had served in the infantry, this was no problem. They covered the first 11 miles in three hours, carrying 40lbs (20kg) of kit. Then Pedder upped the pace. Keyes finished lame, as did most of his cavalrymen.

Fraser and his men watched with amusement as 'Geoffrey's Cavaliers' finally struggled into their bivouac that night on the banks of the Tweed before throwing themselves into the river to cool off. Keyes had strained his Achilles tendon, which stiffened overnight, and in the morning Pedder sent him ahead with their transport to recce that night's bivouac. Keyes protested – it wasn't so far and he thought he could do it, but Pedder refused. The display of favouritism further marked Keyes's card in the eyes of Paddy Mayne.

Fraser and his men awoke in the open on the banks of the Tweed. The men picked up their packs and set out to march the rest of the width of Scotland. They slept rough in the hedgerows under their blankets, using packs as headrests. The pipes and drums that accompany any Scottish regiment could be heard coming from miles away. The column passed through towns and villages haunted by the ghosts of missing husbands and sons, and the locals rushed out to hand them bannock, the traditional hard cake that had fuelled many a Scottish Army. With their arms swinging to the music, they felt proud: 'The people were gems, especially the girls. It was a wonderful feeling marching through Ayr behind the pipes.'[13]

This wasn't a regular army – they were prepared to do and die – they were out for revenge.

Fraser and the men of 11 Commando crossed to the Isle of Arran to complete their training. The island had a laird, a small fishing fleet and a Victorian shooting lodge called the *White House*. Otherwise the houses of the main town, Lamlash, were small and squat, known as bothies, where commandos billeted without bathrooms or running water. The seafront had an old wooden pier, which had been built to carry a tourist trade that had never arrived. It rained constantly, but when it could be seen from the mainland it had a high point in the centre called Goat Fell, and suited Dick Pedder's purposes splendidly.[14] He set about further thinning the ranks of 11 Commando in endurance runs over Goat Fell – 2,867ft (874m) above sea level – a vicious climb in full kit. For those that made it over Goat Fell and back, amphibious operations awaited.

Fraser swam in boots and full kit in the Firth of Clyde, which was freezing. When one new recruit, a piper from the Gordons, arrived, he watched a troop march up the old pier blowing up their life jackets, before jumping off and swimming ashore. He was convinced he had entered a 'mad house'.[15] But they got fitter, and more able.

Then, on 7 September 1940, codeword *Cromwell* was issued; the invasion was imminent. On 11 September the commandos were switched to home defence.[16] 11 Commando were asked to test the defences on the mainland. Just across the Firth of Clyde was the busy Fleet Air Arm base at Bute. On the southern tip of the Kintyre peninsula, surrounded by sea on three sides, it was the ideal target for the commandos' new skills. On the night of the test, Fraser and his men blackened their faces. The airfield had been warned and should have easily resisted the Commando force, had the commandos used a direct approach.

At the entrance to the airfield later that night, a strange major arrived at the gate in a staff car. He was an 11 Commando sergeant and, using a very old blag, he criticised the sentry's turnout and ordered the guard be inspected. The airfield's troops filed out, to find themselves immediately surrounded by men with blackened faces wielding guns. Meanwhile, a 'WAAF officer' sauntered into camp, a Tommy gun hidden under her coat. Her escort, also in WAAF kit, was carrying a bag of grenades. These, too, were both Commando officers.

With the sentry disarmed and locked up, a truckload of workers – more commandos – drove through the gate, and simultaneously Keyes's troop cut the wire and occupied the airfield's defence trenches. One plane took off before belatedly realising the airfield was being overrun and turning to attack. The umpire subsequently ruled it would have been shot down by Keyes' men in a live oper- ation. The 'WAAFs' lobbed grenades through windows, the work- ers dropped from their truck, uncovering their weapons, and the defenders, running to the trenches, found them occupied by commandos.

There was jubilation among 11 Commando. Their small group had taken the forewarned airfield in less than 30 minutes – although they can seldom have been more unpopular. For the traditionalists, this simply wasn't how the British Army ran exercises. That was the attitude that had seen Hobo Hobart's tanks ruled unfair in train- ing exercises in the 1930s, but unfortunately, no such umpires had been present to rule out Rommel's panzers in France.

After months of training on moorland, the worst ground a sol- dier has to cover, while carrying full kit, the weight significantly increased by ammunition and weapons including heavier machine guns, Fraser and 11 Commando were undoubtedly fitter than the rest of the British Army.

And then 8 Commando landed.

The soldiers of 8 Commando were a product of their CO, Bob Laycock, who had been recruited by David Niven in London. Niven had finally found the WAAF he had seen in the Café de Paris at a free lunchtime concert in the Tate, organised to take people's minds off the Blitz. They were married three weeks later. Bob Laycock was her uncle.

After the publicity of the Le Touquet raid, British officers beat a path to Clarke's MO9 door asking to be Commando COs, and the standard proved extraordinarily high. When Bob Laycock showed up, Niven felt duty-bound to intervene. Laycock had a master-mariners certificate, a good qualification for a Commando CO, but was about to be posted as Anti-Gas Staff Officer, Africa, and was due to leave for Cairo in 48 hours. Clarke claims Niven and Laycock found a replacement for the Anti-Gas job, Niven claims Clarke disappeared into the corridors of Whitehall and pulled some strings. The latter seems more likely.

Laycock was given a list of potential officers to recruit from, but as it was going to be a long war, he decided to recruit his friends.[17] Laycock's young friends were members of the London club White's, and they 'rallied to him'. They included Randolph Churchill (son of the prime minister), Evelyn Waugh, George Jellicoe, Carol Mather and David Stirling. Unsurprisingly, 8 Commando was nicknamed the Blue Bloods.

The first practice landing with 8 Commando was a disaster. Most of the officers, having been left in the mess on their ship too long, had become paralytically drunk, and the officers of 3 Commando, attached for the raid, overslept in their bunks and hit the beach late and disorganised.[18] Fraser looked sceptically at this, but not much surprised him. However, he might have raised an eyebrow when Laycock was then given command of the whole brigade. As per Churchill's ambition, the assault force grew to more than fifteen hundred men.

A practice assault on 7 January 1941 fared better. Troop Commander Roger Courtney's men rowed silently ashore in folboats, two-person fold-up canoes that could be dropped by submarine to provide lights to guide landing craft ashore at night.[19] This was the nascent Special Boat Service (SBS), but the davits of Fraser's covert assault ship, *Glenroy*, could be heard on land from 4 miles offshore. When Fraser and his men landed and marched inland to take their objectives amid a huge formation, they nicknamed themselves the 'Bumbling Herd'.

Commandos were no longer Clarke's mobile forces carrying out pin-prick raids; under Churchill and Admiral Keyes, they were a reimagining of the two men's first seaborne operation at Gallipoli. In Whitehall, Churchill was making suggestions such as, 'why don't you take Calais and hold it for 24 hours?'[20]

The officers of 8 and 11 Commandos found they had little in common; 8 Commando described Fraser and his cohort as very young, quiet, and overdisciplined, which could be seen as attributes in special forces.[21] But Fraser would become closer with some of the 8 Commando ranks. In their net they'd caught Arthur Phillips, a stocky and handsome 23-year-old from the tough streets and gangs of Birmingham, from which he'd been sent to the Army at 16 for his own good. The difference between a great soldier and a successful criminal has always simply been a matter of how they are employed.

He'd been in trouble on and off with his regiment since enlisting, and they'd been happy to release him to the Commandos when he volunteered – Commandos were a good route for COs to get rid of troublemakers. When Phillips had reported to Commando HQ at the Suffolk port of Felixstowe in November 1940, he'd met another agitator, a tough boxer from the Fens called Reg Seekings, whose nose was squashed across his handsome face.

Warned they were going on operations overseas, Fraser was given leave, and reported back on 28 January 1941. The loading of the Commando Brigade was a mess; each Commando should have been on a single ship with the requisite landing craft to launch an assault, but Fraser discovered that they were to be split; half under Dick Pedder on *Glenroy* – the 8 Commando ship – and the other half with Keyes and Fraser on *Glengyle*, the 7 Commando ship. A third Commando ship, *Glenearn*, was added at the last minute.

Rumour had been they would be capturing the island of Pantelleria, in the Mediterranean, for which the moors of Arran had been marked out on their practice landings. But as they weighed anchor at 11pm in haste to meet their escort, the whole brigade would have to be docked and cross-loaded before they could carry out an assault – even if Admiral Keyes had wanted to launch the assault he would not be able to without finding somewhere to reload the vessels. He was furious.

This plan – called WORKSHOP – had few adherents, least of all the Commander in Chief of the Mediterranean Fleet, Admiral Browne Cunningham. Without Royal Navy support it was scuppered. The politicking became academic when the Luftwaffe arrived in the Mediterranean and even trying to get to Pantelleria, through the Mediterranean, from Gibraltar, became too dicey. Part of Wavell's worry for which he had sent Clarke up the Nile had come true, the three Glen ships – *Glenroy*, *Glenearn* and *Glengyle* – were rerouted round the Cape of Good Hope, much to Admiral Keyes's chagrin. In this chaos, on 31 January 1941, Bob Laycock's Commando Brigade, all three Commandos, was renamed 'Layforce'.

On 3 February, Fraser was issued his tropical kit and a tetanus shot, and as they steamed south the long way round to Suez, Hitler eyed the Balkans, Greece and North Africa. On board, the Commando troop leaders published the *Glengyle News*, with editorship likely by Randolph Churchill and contributions from Evelyn Waugh. Besides drinking and high stakes gambling, the Blue Bloods had found a way to amuse themselves in transit.

On Sunday, 16 February, Fraser was at sea when he read in the *Glengyle News* of the first SAS raid of the war: 'The exploit of British parachutists . . . must be rated as the most thrilling in a long list of audacious strokes carried out against Mussolini'.[22] It had been seven months since the last commando raid, and Fraser knew that some of 2 Commando had been parachute training. What he now found out was this was the first raid by an entirely new force – the Special Air Service.

4

Pirates: 1941

The Desert Commandos

Ahead of Fraser, en route to Cairo in December 1940, Clarke gambled in the bright lights of Estoril on the Portuguese Riviera, before his flying boat landed at Las Palmas, Bathurst, Freetown and finally Lagos, Nigeria. Here, in the sweltering heat, his shirt sticking to his back, the unacclimatised Clarke carried out his last task as outgoing head of MO9. He held a series of conferences in the steamy heat with officers of General Philippe de Hauteclocque's Free French force, exploring whether his Commando raiding principles could be extended to Africa.

Hauteclocque had adopted the nom de guerre 'Leclerc' to protect his family in Nazi-occupied France, but the fake name was the only thing that wasn't straightforward about him and he inspired both confidence and adoration among his own men.[1] Clarke's talk with those men ran to sand seas and Citroen Kegresses (French halftracks with good sand-crossing capabilities) and camel troops – the *méharistes*. The distances involved in any raid seemed daunting to Clarke, and carried a tang of the 1924 adventure novel *Beau Geste* rather than a realistic special forces operation. But the *méharistes* assured him the Sahara held no barriers, and before they parted foundations had been laid for operations which would have startling possibilities.

On 18 December 1940, Clarke's flying boat finally splashed down on the Nile, but when the tender docked at the pontoon at Rod-el-Farag, the officer sent to pick him up struggled to pick him out among the disembarking passengers. Until he spotted that a man he had assumed was American – wearing black-and-white plus fours, check golfing cap and dark glasses – was in fact Clarke, travelling under the alias of the war correspondent, Wrangel.[2]

Clarke found Wavell in a new HQ nicknamed 'Grey Pillars' – a grey art-deco building, with pillars in front of it. The war with the Axis was ramping up, and the building echoed with workers redeveloping the space as Army departments grew and moved. The whole Qasr el-Dubara (Quarter of Palaces), which included the British Embassy, had become a military zone enclosed by wire and guarded by the Royal Military Police, and requiring a pass to enter. The caves south of the city, from which stone for the pyramids had been excavated, were now filled with ammunition. The Egyptians remained neutral but the British Army did itself no favours with the locals, with racist slurs not being banned by the Army until 1944, and that rule not then being enforced.[3]

Clarke studied the map board in Grey Pillars with Wavell, thinking that the distances were immense and the going some of the worst in the world. But Wavell explained he had created a force called the Long Range Desert Group (LRDG), commanded by Ralph Bagnold which could operate over this area. The startling possibilities Clarke had envisaged with Leclerc's officers suddenly seemed plausible, and Clarke realised his Commando principles could be applied across thousands of miles of uncharted desert.

As Clarke stared at the map, distances shrank, far oases became near and impassable tracts of desert morphed into routes of attack. Clarke traced the route from the far side of the desert, and Leclerc and his *méharistes*, to the Kufra Oasis. Inside Libya, it was occupied by the Italians, who had kicked the Senussi out. Refugees died in their hundreds in the surrounding desert, in a genocide that had pushed them into the arms of the British. Kufra, fed by fossilised water, was the jewel of the desert. Whoever controlled Kufra, controlled the desert. Here, thought Clarke, was an opportunity.

Since Clarke had last seen Bagnold, the great explorer had become desperate. He had first pitched his idea in September 1939, with Hobo Hobart's blessing, and again in January 1940. In June

1940, and with Mussolini seized by a frenzied desire not to be absent from the victors' banquet,[4] Bagnold cut out the middlemen and went straight to the Commander in Chief, Middle East. Convinced that Major Lorenzini's earlier threat to blow the Aswan Dam could become a reality, he gave his memo about his desert special force to his friend, Brigadier Dick Baker, operations officer at Grey Pillars, who placed it on Wavell's desk.

Bagnold was in Wavell's office within the hour. Knowing Wavell had served on Allenby's staff in Egypt during the last war, Bagnold mentioned the present lack of anything corresponding to the Light Car Patrols that had proved so effective against the Senussi insurgency. In 1917 these units had chased the Senussi into the desert after they had risen against the British to the call of Jihad from the Ottoman Caliph of Islam. A similar unit could give advance warning of attacks from the Italians crossing the desert to Aswan. What, Wavell asked him, if he found nothing?

'How about some piracy on the high desert?'

Wavell grinned. 'Can you be ready in six weeks?'

Wavell pressed a bell. Bagnold expected a clerk, but in walked Wavell's second in command, 50-year-old General Arthur Smith.

'I wish any request by Major Bagnold in person to be granted immediately and without question.'

In the corridor outside Wavell's office, Bagnold remembered that Wavell was the leading exponent of strategic deception, and that clearly the impact of his proposal wasn't going to be military, but rather what it would do in the minds of Italian Commanders.

Bagnold contacted his old exploring hands, known as the Zerzura Club, after the mythical 'Oasis of the Birds', the Holy Grail for desert explorers. The call went out to Pat Clayton (surveyor), Bill Shaw (archaeologist), and Guy Lenox Prendergast (Royal Tanks). Of the three, Clayton and Shaw were picked up, commissioned and fitted for their uniforms by an Egyptian tailor within 48 hours. Only Prendergast, a flyer serving with the Army in England, couldn't be spared. Another member of the Zerzura Club, Douglas Newbold, was serving as the British Secretary of Sudan, so he recruited another Royal Tanks officer, Edward 'Teddy' Cecil Osbaldeston Mitford. At 32, Teddy substantially lowered the average age of these proto special forces commanders.

The member Bagnold didn't invite was their Hungarian friend László Almásy, for the simple reason that Hungary was on the other side. In 1932, Almásy, another flyer, and Pat Clayton had been based at Kufra, and, when flying over the massive plateau of Gilf Kebir in a Gypsy Moth, had glimpsed a valley full of vegetation. Their subsequent attempts to find the entrance to this fertile valley by car failed, but it was the closest anyone in the club came to solving the mystery of Zerzura. Almásy knew his way across the desert as well as anyone – most likely he would offer his services to the Germans, and could be a real threat.

The team bought fifteen 1.5-tonne commercial Chevrolet trucks through a dealer in Cairo and borrowed another fifteen from the Egyptian Army. They cut off their cabs, fitted sand tyres, and put racks on the side for sand channels. They armed the vehicles using the light, drum-fed Vickers GO machine guns designed for aircraft they found in the Cairo stores. Now they needed personnel.

Jumbo Wilson had been talked to, possibly over sundowners at his and Wavell's shared house on the Nile, and offered the new LRDG a force of ANZAC troops. His rationale being that they were responsible, self-reliant sheep farmers at home, and thus accustomed to great open spaces. The Aussies said no to seconding some of their best men to a 40-year-old civilian boffin in uniform who wanted to set off into the desert. Bagnold then pitched Clarke's old colleague, New Zealander General Bernard Freyberg – who had done his share of unusual soldering, including swimming to be first ashore at Gallipoli. He consulted his government, who gave him the nod.

The request went out for men for 'an important but dangerous mission', and half the Kiwi division promptly volunteered. But when they arrived to start training, the two young troop leaders and 150 men were disappointed to be met by three relatively old commanders. This was not the special force they envisaged – it looked more like an outing of Oxbridge dons. But the desert knowledge of the Zerzura Club won them over, and they were ready for deployment in six weeks. Ten days later, they were parked 150 miles into the impassable Sand Sea facing Libya, waiting for the Italians to enter the war.[5]

Mussolini had timed his invasion of Egypt to coincide with Hitler's invasion of Britain, and declared war on 10 June. But when Hitler choked, his huge, cumbersome force, lacking transport, with largely obsolete equipment, finally lumbered across the Egyptian border on 13 September. A hundred miles to the south, Clayton and Shaw's LRDG patrols sped in the opposite direction, west into the desert. Shaw's patrol hit the Palificata – the north–south road that led to Kufra.

In piratical mood, they burnt unguarded aircraft at an Italian airfield, and took out two 6-ton lorries on the fortnightly Italian supply convoy to Kufra.[6] The other patrol, led by Clayton, sped south past Kufra, undetected by the Italians, and headed 300 miles away to the isolated French airfield of Tekro, just over the border with Chad. French colonies were undecided which way to go – Vichy or Free French. It was only two months since the British had blown the French Navy to pieces at the Algerian port of Mers-el-Kébir, killing thirteen hundred French to stop their ships falling to the Germans. The sudden appearance of this strange force from the desert – bearded, wearing *chapli* (open-toe sandals), shorts, Palestinian police *shemaghs* and armed to the teeth – was more than alarming.

A week later, the two patrols rendezvoused back at the southern tip of the massive plateau of Gilf Kebir, their survival now measured in the distance between refuelling stations, just as Lawrence's had been measured on days a camel could travel between oases. In the desert, Bagnold's pre-war rules now became lore for the LRDG:

Never travel with only one vehicle beyond walking distance from help.

Never leave anyone alone out of sight of a landmark not clearly visible from far away.

*Never use water for any purpose other than drinking or topping up
car cooling systems.*[7]

The plateau had ancient ochre paintings showing people swimming
in a time when water was plentiful and the region was temperate.
Travelling in the footprints of these people and amid their stone
circles before the war, Bagnold and Shaw had once met their
descendants, people who were the last remnants of a long-vanished
civilisation. Now, from the top of the plateau, Bagnold watched his
patrols' trucks roll into view – the LRDG was in business – this was
now Bagnold's desert.

The day after his arrival in Cairo, Clarke woke and breakfasted at
Shepheard's to the cry of a kite overhead and the gentle chink of
china. Not only the weather but the atmosphere of victory could
not be further from the depressed, besieged feeling that had pervaded the corridors of Whitehall. Wavell had doubled the number
of Bagnold's Patrols with British Guards and Rhodesians, and now
that they had been reinforced, the British seemed to be everywhere
behind Italian lines. Marshal Graziani began to doubt his own intelligence reports of British weakness, and the invading Italian Army
ground to a halt.[8]

A huge strategic deception had started, one based on placing a
subliminal fear in the mind of the enemy commander. Just a week
before Clarke had landed, on 9 December 1940, the morning haze
over the Italian front line had been split by a sound no Italian or
German (and few Americans) had ever expected to hear again – the
opening salvo of a British offensive.[9] Marshal Graziani's huge, cumbersome force had fallen back in disarray.

It was in this unfamiliar atmosphere of victory that Clarke
reported to Wavell at Grey Pillars to be briefed on his latest mission.
In addition to Clarke and Bagnold, another of Wavell's recruits was
Orde Wingate. Wingate, a Zionist, had run night patrols in Jerusalem on Clarke's watch until his extreme methods had seen him sent
home. Wavell thought that if Wingate had fought an insurgency,

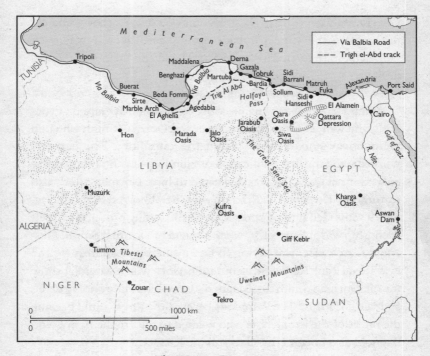

The Western Desert, 1940.

he should be good at starting one. And sent him to Ethiopia to raise a force to support Haile Selassie in overthrowing the Italian occupation.

Another recruit was 45-year-old Eric Dorman-Smith. Dorman-Smith was a man so unorthodox HQ staff described him as an 'evil genius'. Wavell and Dorman-Smith were firm friends; Wavell had lost an eye at Ypres and Dorman-Smith had won an MC. Wavell thought he could control his ideas by sorting the good from the bad and keeping him on practical lines.[10]

At the end of that war, and suffering from shellshock, Dorman-Smith was in a café in Italy on Armistice Day, 1918 when he saw a man a few years younger than himself enter on crutches and was piqued by the fact that he was a civilian but had the Croce di

Guerra, Italy's second highest decoration. Sudden cheers and car horns from the streets outside announced the war was over, Dorman-Smith turned to the man, and said, 'So that's that. Have a drink!'

That man was Ernest Hemingway.

When Hemingway's manuscripts were stolen at Gare de Lyon, Paris, and writer's block threatened, it was Dorman-Smith who told Hemingway not to obsess about the causalities. The pep talk worked – and the first publication of Hemingway's first short-story collection, *In Our Time* was dedicated to him. Dorman-Smith also featured in *The Sun Also Rises*, though he abhorred bull fighting, which reminded him of Ypres. One of the lasting products of their friendship was at Sandhurst, when a friend of Dorman-Smith, Alexander Gatehouse, was trying to find a suitable headdress for the new Royal Tank Regiment – something soft, which wouldn't show the oil. Dorman-Smith tossed him his Pamplona bull-running beret, and said, 'Try this.' The Pamplona beret of the Royal Tanks became the motif of the iconoclasts who wanted to reform the Army, who Bagnold also now recruited to run the LRDG.[11]

Now, in 1940, Wavell drafted in Dorman-Smith from his official posting as Commandant of Haifa Staff College and sent him up to analyse the situation in the desert. He teamed up with another friend, his old Sandhurst instructor, General Richard Nugent O'Connor, commander of what Churchill called the Army of the Nile. Probably Britain's most talented general, O'Connor had won one of the first MCs in 1914, and a second MC in Italy in 1918, along with the Italian Silver Medal of Military Valour.

Wavell had given O'Connor 'very sketchy instructions' on what to do about the Italians, which O'Connor didn't mind as he liked being left on his own.[12] Consequently, on 9 December the British 'indirect approach' went into action for the first time. Described by Dorman-Smith as a 'round the back of the arse attack', the Italians had realised too late the attack was coming from their rear.[13] Gatehouse's tanks wiped out their armour and the Italian camp commander went down firing his machine gun in his pyjamas. The iconoclasts punched a hole in the Italian front line and, with Bagnold's special force and now this British *Blitzkrieg*, rather than attending a banquet Mussolini looked as though he was on the menu.

In Wavell's office in Grey Pillars the morning after his arrival, Clarke realised that although his freelancing days had been good while they'd lasted, they were now over. Wavell wanted a special section of intelligence for deception of the enemy – a permanent position in a role that did not officially exist in the British Army.[14] Clarke's office was a converted bathroom, and he shared a secretary with Wavell's second in command, General Arthur Smith – an arrangement that had a definite shelf life.

Clarke's first task was to dream up means to disguise the movement of an Indian division from O'Connor's desert army to attack the Italians in Eritrea. Wavell had thought this through, and the deception was made up of real air and sea raids on the wrong country – Somalia. Bogus logistics were deployed, wrong maps were issued, there was dummy wireless traffic and 'leakages' to known spies in Egypt, Aden, India and South Africa. The Japanese consul – a direct conduit to the Axis – was informed, private telegrams were sent uncoded, and rumours were started in the bars and nightclubs of Cairo. The resulting plan, OPERATION CAMILLA, would become Clarke's playbook, and was a stunning success.

The plan also had an unanticipated benefit: thinking the British were about to land in Somalia, the Italians started to evacuate. Orde Wingate went to work with his guerrilla force in neighbouring Ethiopia, and the Italian conquests in East Africa fell like dominos as fast as their campaign in the North African desert blew away.

While Shepheard's Hotel prepared its legendary New Year's Eve party, which usually culminated with a partially clothed woman emerging from something, an interesting memo arrived on Clarke's desk. It was from British Intelligence and dated 30 December. Intelligence had picked up the diary of an Italian officer captured during

O'Connor's advance; he had written 'Late in the night, the group informed us that enemy parachutists landed near our area.'[15] Clarke knew there were no parachutists, but clearly the Italians were jumpy. Intelligence suggested that some use might be made of the Italian preoccupation – perhaps dummy parachutists. How the Italians had reached the conclusion that the British had parachutists in the Middle East at a time when there were none is not hard to guess. With Bagnold's men seemingly appearing out of nowhere, it is likely they had jumped to the wrong conclusion about how the LRDG operated.

Clarke started toying with the idea of fanning the Italian suspicions. Remembering the nannies being protected by clerks in Eaton Square, and the worries of the Irish, he thought that fake airborne troops would not only add to British strength, but would make the Italians dissipate some of theirs in protecting lines of communication, rear areas and airfields against possible airborne attack.[16]

The hangovers from Shepheard's were subsiding when, on 2 January 1941, the Army of the Nile, led by O'Connor, still wearing his Italian medal for valour, outfought and destroyed two Italian corps with numbers ten times their own. He captured Sidi Barani with 38,000 prisoners, including four generals, seizing 73 tanks and 237 guns, at the cost of only 624 Allied killed, wounded or missing. Mussolini was in serious trouble.

Even more startling news reached Clarke: not only did the Italians think the British had some parachutists, but the British *were* planning to drop some real ones on Italy. He should not have known this. But because 2 Commando (who were now called 11 SAS Battalion) had been under MO9, in London MO9 was copied in. Even the draft operation would be sent to them by mistake. Officers at RAF Ringway received a severe dressing-down from RAF command for the error.[17] For Clarke this was gold dust. It mattered less what the plan was, only that the SAS were going to drop on Italy. A parachute operation mounted on Italy could, very easily, have come from Egypt.

Abeam

The target for the SAS was identified by a Mr Ardley – an engineer at George Kent and Sons in London, who had studied the plans for the recently completed Apulian aqueduct in Puglia. Destroying the aqueduct would deprive some two million inhabitants of parched southern Italy of their primary water source, and the cities of Bari and Brindisi, which were the main staging ports for the flagging Italian campaign against the Greeks in Albania. Since the Italians were now losing in both Albania and Africa, Whitehall thought it possible that the Italian government might be dubious of the advisability of continuing an unsuccessful campaign on two fronts.[18]

It was a brilliant identification of a strategic target.

After Ardley had presented his case to the War Office on 12 December 1940, on 2 January 1941 a meeting was convened to work out how to hit it. Sabotage was ruled out – intelligence suggested the operation could not be carried out by inserting agents to work with the local anti-fascist resistance forces. Bombing was also ruled out, as at the time the RAF were struggling to hit a barn door, and had nothing that could deliver ordnance with the required accuracy. But the SAS were still training under RAF command at Ringway.

Things moved very fast. The next full moon, when pilots would be able to see the aqueduct and carry out the night drop, was on 12 February, and there was enough light either side of this date for an attack from 7 to 19 February. The chiefs of staff, led by Pug Ismay, approved the plan OPERATION COLOSSUS on 8 January 1941. That day Churchill was sent a memo which mentioned both the idea of a cover force inserted by submarine and a parachute unit made up of sappers, but he never read the detail. Ringway were instructed to get on with it. It evolved solely into a parachute operation, with a submarine being sent to pick up the team.

Two thousand miles away, in a converted bathroom in Grey Pillars, Clarke began work on his first order of battle deception plan, though he didn't realise it at the time.[19] The order of battle (ORBAT) is how an Army describes its organisation from the biggest to the smallest: the division, down to brigade, to regiment or battalion, then the troop or platoon. Clarke wanted to create an entirely fictitious parachute brigade in North Africa, around two thousand men, and started to sketch out 'The Scenario for "ABEAM" ', the name for his deception plan.

Clarke would later describe his deceptions in terms of 'story', 'scenario' and 'treatment' – the terms of cinema and film. Clarke sat down to write the story of the SAS. This wasn't a one-liner – if he was to convince the Italians the British had a parachute capability in North Africa it needed to be a detailed description of an entirely fictional unit: what equipment it had, how it trained, who was in it, what aircraft it used, and a backstory covering its development.

The *treatment* of this story would be how he passed it off to the Italians. There would be a cast, and he'd give them the story and character motivations, just as any film director does. He never described the rest of his production in these terms, but there would be *props*, things he needed made. There would be *production design*: papers, stamps and signals. And there would be spies, who were actors, spying on his fiction, and telling the Italians it was real. Clarke's last production had been 'Invasion' – this was a lot more ambitious.

One of the first things he had to do in his scenario for ABEAM was create a backstory: a plausible logistics trail and order of battle for his fictitious special force. He started by sketching out how such a troop deployment might look in reality, something his prior experience made him uniquely positioned to do. In Clarke's scenario, the 1st Special Air Service Brigade, two thousand men, had arrived in Egypt on 30 December 1940; he chose the date he had received the memo from intelligence and it tied in with the preparation of the genuine SAS operation. For Axis agents the dates would all seem to align. The SAS came aboard the ships *Strathnaver* and *Reina Del Pacifico* and landed at Suez – again, both of these ships were real liners, converted into troopships, which had recently berthed at Suez. The first had been part of a convoy that had sailed from the Clyde, the second had landed ANZACs; although neither had contained any parachutists, both had unloaded troops, which Axis spies monitoring the port would already have reported.

He'd got his fictional brigade to North Africa – now he needed an ORBAT. ABEAM's non-existent troops would consist of HQ 1st SAS Brigade, commanded by a brigadier; a brigadier with an HQ, and some liaison staff, some of whom would appear in Cairo. Clarke loved dressing up, and would get parachute badges made for himself and others. It would need a brigade signals section (radios are very important for isolated parachutists), and radios create traffic that the enemy can listen to. He broke the SAS into three battalions – 1st Special Air Service Battalion made up of para-chutists, and 2nd and 3rd SAS Battalions in gliders. He had been instrumental in guiding Britain's glider programme – although none had been built, he knew what they should look like, and would get some fake gliders made.

Underlying this fiction was the fact that Clarke was himself a pilot. He had crash landed in the desert on three occasions when his engine conked out, and looking down from his Bristol Scout cockpit in 1918 he had seen nothing but desert for miles and miles. He'd thought then that the whole place was a huge aerodrome where you could land anywhere quite easily. Gliders and parachut-ists would work well in North Africa, and be a terrifying possibility for the enemy.[20]

In his story, 1 SAS battalion was five-hundred-strong, carrying Smith & Wesson automatics, specially designed hand guns, Brens, anti-tank guns, demolition stores and 2-inch mortars dropped in special containers. All the ranks were trained in demolition work, particularly in sabotaging Armoured Fighting Vehicles.[21] They were going to be able to knock out the key to the enemy's strength.

The two glider battalions were bigger – 750-strong – and although Clarke didn't give them Churchill's airborne tanks, he did give them a couple of two-seater Morris armoured cars and some Bren Car-riers, each of which was carried in a specially designed, entirely fictional glider. He then outlined the real events at RAF Ringway, including the difficulty in parachuting from Whitleys, and described the SAS demonstration on Salisbury Plain – all of which would be potentially verifiable for Axis intelligence.

Clarke even added helicopters to his fake SAS. He gave them a reconnaissance platoon carried in helicopters to recce targets and landing places for the gliders, and also some helicopters for the HQ element to use. Clarke appeared to have borrowed Ralph Bagnold's time machine – but while at MO9, he'd been presented the design for the twelve-seater prototype helicopter developed by a shipbuilder called James Weir. The Air Ministry had originally taken an interest, and Air Vice Marshal Tedder had been shown a prototype, but Tedder 'didn't know anything about soldiering at all'[22] – nor, does it appear, did he want to. Development had stalled and then been abandoned as the RAF focused on the Battle of Britain.

The RAF had failed to spot the enormous potential of the prototypes for carrying troops, something an Army pilot, such as Clarke, jumped at. For the Navy, too, having a vertical-lift aircraft to combat the U-boat threat would have completely changed the Battle of the Atlantic. But Clarke put a red line through the section on SAS helicopters, conjured in his bathroom office in Grey Pillars. While he could pass ANZAC infantry off as SAS, find some flesh-and-blood parachutists to put on the ground and fake some gliders, there was little chance of him getting one of Weir's prototypes to Egypt.

Nevertheless, extra layers were added to his ABEAM scheme. A two-thousand-man brigade is a big unit – so Clarke 'hid' his fictional brigade in Jordan. In his scenario, after 1 SAS Brigade had disembarked at Suez they then travelled by rail to Lydda in Palestine – the route he had taken in 1930. From there, he created a breadcrumb trail of their movement until they reached a camp far out in the desert. His first idea for this desert base was Al Jafr, 180 miles east of Amman. He knew it did have a base, so initially seemed plausible, but it also had a small population; it was therefore not a great place to hide two thousand men, fictional or otherwise.

Needing somewhere more remote, he crossed out 'JAFR' in his draft scenario and wrote: 'advance parties have gone on to a camp out in the desert further east. This is somewhere near BAIR.' He chose the Bair Wells because they are in the middle of nowhere – a flat feature which gives excellent vantage in every direction – and has a couple of ancient wells used by the Bedouin. Here Clarke was nodding to his knowledge of Lawrence of Arabia and the Arab Revolt. Because it was from Bair, Lawrence used his 'rapier play', rather the First War tactics he called 'wood chopping', carrying out a raid to deceive the Turks he was heading north to Damascus rather than south to the port of Aqaba. Once the Turks had sent their troops north he took the port with little resistance, though Lawrence shot his camel in the back of the head by mistake in a charge against Turkish infantry and sailed over its head.[23]

With the creation of dummy paperwork and memos tracing the movements and equipment of his fake SAS brigade, the bones for Clarke's grand deception were in place. But he knew he needed to flesh them out with more activity on the ground, and went to town, literally.

Dressed as a staff officer of the fictional SAS Brigade, he wandered round his usual Cairo haunts, wearing the armband of 'HQ Airborne Division' – a red band with the 'authorised' parachute badge on it. Presumably, since there was no British Airborne Division and no official badge existed, Clarke designed this himself, most likely with help from local tailor John Jones who would go on to produce far more stylish badges for the real SAS.

The details of the cover story were important. The British Embassy tipped Clarke off that the Japanese *chargé d'affaires*, a known spy, was travelling to Turkey, and had been granted an entry visa to Palestine on 14 January. Clarke booked himself on the same sleeper train. After putting himself in sight of any Axis agents in Cairo, Clarke boarded the train for Lydda, Palestine, following the route of the fictional SAS. The ruse was that he had come to Cairo in advance of the rest of the Airborne division with the 1st SAS Brigade, to advise GHQ and make preliminary arrangements for the reception of the division in the spring. Clarke proceeded to be as indiscreet as he could without blowing the deception – giving the Japanese spy the opportunity to see his red armlet of Airborne Division with parachute badge, and leaving an envelope in the carriage addressed to 'Colonel Clarke, HQ Airborne Division, Old Sarum House, Salisbury', which had been redirected to 'GHQ. Middle East'.

If Clarke's choice of Bair Wells was plausible, now he was having fun at the enemy's expense – *Sarum House* is a ruined stone-age fort dating to 400 BC, nothing more than a mound of earth and a deep ditch, something the Japanese and Germans would have discovered if they'd checked. It is also adjacent to Stonehenge, and the river crossings over the Till that 11 SAS had captured on their first demonstration drop.

When Clarke got to Palestine, he briefed the local commander of British forces General Philip Neame. Clarke told him they must give the impression the utmost secrecy was being maintained regarding the arrival of an SAS brigade, and that elaborate precautions were in force around Bair. Neame promptly contacted Lieutenant-General John Glubb, better known as Glubb Pasha, who commanded the Arab Legion. Clarke had first met Glubb after flying into his tented camp in 1930. He recalled how instead of the flamboyant fancy-dress favoured by Lawrence, Glubb looked like he'd stepped out of the pages of H.G. Wells's' *Mr Kipps*, wearing a dark four-button suit of Edwardian cut, a stiff collar and tie, and a fedora in the desert.

The two had remained friends and he assured Clarke he needn't fear, and that no one would get anywhere near the Bair Wells. From then on in the North African campaign, any Axis spies attempting to penetrate the fictitious SAS base were given rough treatment and sent on their way, which only served to confirm that the British were hiding a parachute force there.

Before he left, Neame also agreed to send two soldiers to Cairo for Clarke to coach and then let loose, posing as SAS convalescents from Alexandria Hospital injured in parachute training. Like Clarke, the men would wear parachute badges and act with 'guarded indiscretion'. Meanwhile, back in Cairo, Raymond Maunsell, head of Security Intelligence Middle East (SIME) and Clarke's partner in crime, carelessly discarded receipts for the 'SAS Xmas Fund Subscription' on an Egyptian train. Clarke had also briefed the RAF, who issued secret instructions to all pilots to give wide berth to aircraft towing gliders or operating parachute troops.

Clarke started looking for a way of producing fake gliders and real parachutists to be dropped near Cairo – his vision was that specially designed folding dummy gliders could be moved on lorries and simulate the presence of the SAS anywhere in the theatre. One plan was to stage a drop and base the gliders at Siwa aerodrome, the oasis from which Ralph Bagnold's LRDG operated. Clarke scored it out in his notes, for now. But he was clearly thinking of the best way to create a confluence of his deception, the SAS, and the existing special force, the LRDG. Clarke didn't need a time machine – he had a crystal ball.

Clarke summed up ABEAM with the words, 'finally, the usual whispers and indiscretions could be employed', which meant staged careless talk at the bar at Shepheard's and anywhere else the Axis got their information. And so in early 1941, the SAS had entered the Axis, if not the British, order of battle.

But Clarke had one last, brilliant idea that had nothing to do with the ORBAT, and was aimed at the mind of one man – Mussolini. Mussolini's fascist policies had meant genocide for the African countries he occupied. Both Shaw and Clayton had picked up refugees in the desert when the Italians took Kufra in 1931, Senussi families choosing to flee to almost certain death, rather than face rape, torture and mutilation. Throughout Mussolini's new African empire his troops raped and killed civilians on a massive scale, and individual crimes were horrific. Clarke wondered whether he could convince Mussolini that the SAS were training these people as insurgents, and planning to drop them on Italy. Mussolini was hated by everyone from the Senussi to the Abyssinians, which made the ruse believable.

After his meeting with Neame, Clarke left the Windsor Hotel in Haifa on 18 January, leaving behind receipts for maps of British Somaliland and Haar; a remote region used by Wingate to train insurgents, signed and acknowledged by the stamp of the Adjutant of Battalion HQ, 1st Special Air Service Battalion. Clarke had made one for all his SAS documents. The British were, of course, not universally popular in Palestine, and Clarke knew the receipts would find their way to the prying Axis eyes.

The question of what the SAS were doing in East Africa appeared for Mussolini in terrifying black and white when a photograph was printed in *Parade*, a magazine for Allied soldiers, which was avidly read by Axis spies. In the picture, an Abyssinian parachutist stood in front of a Bombay bomber on a desert airstrip, the crew ready to climb aboard, and the plane protected by security policemen from Glubb's Arab Legion. The caption read –

READY TO DESCEND ON ITALY!
One of the Abyssinian parachutists training with British units.

Clarke, of course, had arranged for the photoshoot, staged at Heliopolis airfield outside Cairo. The Abyssinian parachutist was in fact a Cairo laundryman cast by Clarke. The Bombay bomber – Clarke's preferred parachute aircraft – was real, as were the airmen, the uniforms of the field security police officer, and the distinctive headdress of the Arab Legion. It all indicated that the photo had been taken in the secure SAS base at Bair, which had been sealed off to outsiders.

The reality was that Abyssinian insurgents parachuted into southern Italy wouldn't last very long. But that didn't matter – Clarke knew his enemy, and his subliminal play only needed to work on the mind of one man – Mussolini.

The Cauldron

The results of Clarke's meeting with Leclerc's men now came to fruition. The LRDG picked up the Corsican *méhariste* D'Ornano, a tall man in Arab dress who wore a monocle, his blue-grey hair covered in dust, who had crossed the Tibesti mountains of northern Chad by donkey with his men. He was welcomed into the war a thousand miles from Cairo with a salute from the bearded guardsmen of Captain Michael Crichton-Stuart's LRDG patrol, coming to attention in the sand wearing flip-flops, after which they toasted with Pernod.[24]

It transpired that Bagnold, without authority, had flown to see Douglas Newbold, member of Zerzura Club serving as the British Secretary of Sudan, and with his advice had flown to Chad, who were wavering on which side to join in the war. Persuaded, Chad had entered the war with the Allies. Bagnold had even crossed over on the airfield in Sudan with Britain's foreign secretary, Anthony Eden, without telling him what he was doing. The iconoclasts were so far out on a limb they were barely referring to their own HQ let alone Whitehall.

The following day, D'Ornano became the first Free Frenchman to die in the war, during a raid on the isolated Italian outpost of Muzurk.[25] But the raid on 11 January 1941 was a success. Muzurk was closer to Algeria than Egypt and proved to the Italians just how far behind Italian lines the British could project forces, though not how they were doing it.

As the patrol pulled out, the LRDG men were massively impressed to watch a French captain called Massu, who had been shot through the calf, cauterise his own wound with a lit cigarette. At the escarpment above Muzurk, they buried a popular Kiwi sergeant called Hewson alongside D'Ornano, the Italians still firing at ghosts in the distance serving as a last salute.

After Muzurk, the LRDG patrol headed south for Chad and Tummo, a mountain well that lay on the ancient caravan route from Lake Chad to Tripoli. After days in the wilderness, they wound up through the mountains along the stony road built by the *méharistes* and reached a green and sheltered valley at dusk, where they could see the ancient fort of Zouar, surrounded by a cluster of native huts. Bugles rang out from the fort, the Union Jack and Tricolore flying side by side, as Senegalese guards saluted their entry. It was day 24 of their operation, and would have heralded a talk at the Royal Geographical Society in peacetime for both endurance and navigation. The team washed in unlimited water, ate roast mutton, drank wine and brandy, and the officers were treated to a seven-course dinner in the mess. Clayton opened a signal from Bagnold sent from GHQ: How many trucks were fit to join the French for an immediate assault on Kufra?[26]

Clarke's Commandos had moved onto land.

Leclerc's motley force of a hundred French and three hundred locals had enough fuel to get to Kufra but not to return. The force battled their way north through the ghibli wind, Kiwi and Guards LRDG patrols providing a vanguard. However, the Italians picked up Clayton's patrol, and with aircraft and superior firepower soon forced them to make their last stand at Gebel Sherif – a low feature in the desert where the remains of their Chevrolet wrecks still lie in the sand. Two New Zealanders, Moore and Tighe, and Guardsmen Easton and Winchester walked 200 miles to safety, a remarkable feat of endurance. Clayton, their elderly patrol leader, who had never been a soldier, but whose drive and leadership had been vital to establishing the LRDG, entered captivity.[27]

Leclerc sent Crichton-Stuart and the rest of the LRDG back to Cairo, sparing them the coming siege of Kufra. This was no special forces operation, and would last a month before the oasis finally fell to Leclerc on 1 March 1940.

Clarke relished their achievement. Wresting the distant oasis of Kufra from the Italians meant the Allies had a base for activities against the open Libyan flank of the enemy. And with the LRDG striking and melting back into the desert, the idea of a fictional SAS brigade became easier to sell. On the ground, the operation had required some very special real soldiers.

The Army of the Nile was closing on Benghazi, Churchill and Wavell's final objective for it. But O'Connor, Dorman-Smith and 7th Armoured Commander Michael Creagh saw a far bigger prize than the 'mediocre results' desired by their masters.

Cyrenaica protrudes into the Mediterranean in the same way that north-west France of Calais and Dunkirk bulge into the Channel. And, huddled in a bleak, windblown hut on an airfield, surrounded by derelict Italian aircraft on Cyrenaican coast, fuelled by bully beef, captured parmesan and Chianti, O'Connor and Dorman-Smith saw the opportunity to slice across the bottom of the bulge along an old trade route, the Trigh el-Abd, and cut the retreating Italians from their base of Tripoli. The Germans called it the *Kesselschlacht*, the 'cauldron battle' – once you shut the lid, you could boil your enemy. If they did this, they would end the war with the Italians. But if they didn't shut the lid, O'Connor's smaller force would be isolated in the desert, on a long line of supply, and probably get destroyed. Dorman-Smith flew to Cairo to get Wavell's permission to take the gamble.

In Grey Pillars, all expression drained from Wavell's face as Dorman-Smith explained the idea. Wavell said nothing, quietly arranging pencils on his desk, taking them up in handfuls before first forming them into fours, then threes, pushing them into close order, and then in open order. Eventually, as Dorman-Smith drew a breath, Wavell interrupted, 'Tell Dick [O'Connor] he can go on, and wish him luck from me. He has done well.'[28]

At 10.45am on 5 February the lead elements of 7th Armoured Division – the 11th Hussars in Rolls-Royce armoured cars – hit the coast road at Beda Fomm. Thirty minutes later, the first retreating Italian trucks appeared; they had shut the lid on the cauldron with half an hour to spare. With wave after wave of Italian attack, the British and Commonwealth forces were reduced to 15 tanks, their reserve had run out of fuel, and the Italians still possessed 50. But with every attempt by the Italians to break out in the pouring rain, their resolve weakened. Just as at Agincourt, the rain proved lethal for armour, and their tanks and troops slid around in the mud, the British Artillery able to fire on their positions. The Italian tanks nearly made it; the closest being knocked out just short of the Rifle Brigades' mess tent.

On the cold, clear dawn of 7 February, O'Connor and Dorman-Smith drove up to the battlefield. They arrived at the 'collapsed elephant' of the Italian tank outside the mess tent, where inside a hasty celebration was underway. The sun came out and they could smell the sea across the veldt, which was flowering with asphodel and covered with herds of gazelle and flocks of great, slow-flying bustards.

The wreckage of the Italian Army stretched for 15 miles: trucks; tanks blown to pieces; upturned field guns; prisoners huddled, cold, damp and dejected; abandoned command trailers, their ornate wood and Romanesque carving reminiscent of fairground rides. A priest bowed to them, and there were bodies everywhere. It was a battle of total annihilation – Italian forces in North Africa had ceased to exist.

Dorman-Smith mused 'that the same dawn and the same quiet antelope that owned the plains had seen the passage and end of other armies'. He was right, they stood on the edge of ancient Carthage. O'Connor asked him what they should do next.

'Go all out for as far as we can get.'[29]

Nothing stood between them and Tripoli. The Army of the Nile advanced, reaching the Libyan border on the 9 February 1941. And as if Mussolini's troubles couldn't get any worse, the following day the SAS dropped on Italy.

Operation Colossus

Admiral Keyes waved off X Troop, 11 SAS from RAF Mildenhall in six Whitley special forces conversions. The RAF had fitted long-range fuel tanks and they were crammed with 30 containers of explosives and equipment. Accompanied by two Whitley bombers that would fly a diversion raid, the air flotilla disappeared into the fading light to dodge the Luftwaffe in its flight through France. And Keyes penned a missive to his old friend Churchill.

The team touched down in Malta at 9am on 8 February. To meet them was the well-built man whom Fairbairn and Sykes had poked in the eye – Troop Leader Deane-Drummond, who had flown out on a Sunderland flying boat to prepare their arrival. The whole mission was nearly wrecked by an Axis bombing raid, but on 10 February the SAS crammed into the fuselages of their Whitleys. Sitting alternately on the floor, knees bent, parachute packs wedged into their backs, feet pressed against the opposite hull amid the explosive and equipment at 5.40pm, they rumbled off the airstrip into the sunset.

The six assault Whitleys set course for the south of Italy in radio silence, along with the two diversion bombers. The diversion bombers aimed for Foggia, 50 miles north of the true target, which provided a good enough explanation to the Italian defenders as to where the air flotilla was headed.

Over Sicily, they climbed over sporadic flak, but between Sicily and the mainland one of the diversion bombers developed engine trouble. The pilot scanned his map for somewhere he and his crew could meet a British sub, and having ordered his crew to bail out, broke radio silence, sending the message in the Syko code saying he was 'out of action'. Unwittingly he chose the exact location of the real rendezvous in the Sele Estuary, which only the SAS Commanders knew, and compromised it. The submarine, HMS *Triumph*, aborted.

In the aircraft the SAS did not know this was now a one-way ticket. But they had always known the chance of getting out of this operation were slim to none – the rendezvous in the Sele Estuary was 55 miles from the target, through country which would be crawling with enemy after the raid. And the rendezvous was a farmhouse whose owner, Giovanni Zanotti, was reputed to be anti-fascist and pro-British, but no one knew if he was at the farm-house or interned.[30]

Deane-Drummond was asleep, and was awoken by the intercom:

'Fifteen minutes to target.'[31]

His team roused themselves and began to prepare, but the intercom was silent when from the rear of the aircraft the tail gunner rushed in, 'Get cracking, you're due to drop in one minute.'

The intercom had failed and pandemonium ensued. The troop wrestled the door hatch open, lining up their containers to the roar of engines and deafening rush of freezing air outside.

At 9.42pm, with the drop light above him still glowing red, Deane-Drummond swung his legs over the hole and looked down on Italy, briefly wondering what he was doing. The light above him went green, his men shoved four containers quickly through the hole, and he dropped after them. His chute deployed almost immediately, the white silk pulsing over his head, and he noticed the silence away from the aircraft. He'd dropped at 500 feet and had 15 seconds to landing, but thought he made his best landing yet, rolling into a ploughed field about 100 metres above the aqueduct.

He had seen the aqueduct immediately when his chute opened, and now as they approached in the light of the moon he saw it was not guarded. It stretched across the steep ravine of the Torrente Tragino, the bottom of which was covered with scrub and small trees, and then led up to a small hill beyond. Over the brow of this was a second aqueduct crossing another stream, the Fosse della Ginestra. The mountain rose steeply to his left to a group of barns, and perched high on the mountaintop, beyond the aqueduct, the lights of Calitri twinkled – a labyrinth of ancient houses built on the mountainside to take advantage of any breeze; the landmark the pilots had used to mark their drop run over the ravine.

His section gathered round him, and they searched for their containers, only to discover the lights on them – initiated when they hit the ground – hadn't worked. In the moonlight they found some, and were recovering their weapons when X Troop's Commander

Tag Pritchard and his team came jogging up the hill, followed by the junior sapper officer, Second Lieutenant Paterson. The men weren't to know but the RAF had tipped the senior sapper with all their engineers into the wrong gorge, and the faulty drop lights inside their aircraft meant their explosives were scattered over the mountains.

Paterson improvised, while Deane-Drummond encouraged some farmers they'd captured to help look for more explosive. At first this was done at gunpoint, but several of the Italians agreed to work willingly, saying that it would give them something to talk about for the rest of their lives in a part of Italy where very little happened.

At quarter past midnight all the charges were set, and five minutes later Paterson signalled they were pulling out, lit the fuses and ran for cover. On hearing the warning signal, Deane-Drummond fired a small charge he had placed on a bridge nearby. At 12.30am the aqueduct blew, followed 30 seconds later by Deane-Drummond's bridge. The explosion at the aqueduct echoed round the mountains, but Deane-Drummond's exploding bridge surprised everyone. It showered X Troop with lumps of concrete and rail, and some shrapnel hit the barn where the prisoners had been shut for their own safety. Thankfully the barn roof held and none were hurt. Sheepishly, Deane-Drummond confessed he had forgotten all about them when he decided to blow the bridge.

Tag Pritchard ran back to check the damage – the aqueduct was a wreck and water was flooding down the ravine. Soon they heard the sound of a great waterfall – they'd done it, and they cheered and cheered. Deane-Drummond thought the hollering wasn't very tactical, but then again, they had just made a huge explosion.

Operation COLOSSUS was a resounding success.

The team never made it out. Two mornings later, and just over 20 miles from the target, Deane-Drummond woke with his teeth chattering and every bone in his body aching, and saw a peasant a hundred metres in front of him. His section's tracks were clearly visible in the mud and snow – their Italian interpreter went to speak with the peasant, but Deane-Drummond knew in his heart the game was up.

The sound of dogs followed, then below them children running back to the village in excitement. Beyond the children were the villagers, including a semi-circle of armed men closing on them. Deane-Drummond realised he couldn't kill these people for a few hours more freedom, and his section surrendered.

X Troop, SAS had always known the odds were against them, but Britain's first special forces parachute operation was still a stunning success. Less than a year after Clarke had walked into Dill's office with his Commandos concept, they had achieved force projection into an enemy country using long-range fuel tanks, navigated and dropped on an isolated target, and improvised to destroy it. It stunned the Italians, and the Germans, who wondered where on earth this capability had come from. A smiling King George VI went to Ringway to congratulate 11 S(A)S on their comrades' operation. It should have led to the birth of the SAS as a fully fledged unit.

Instead, the shit hit the fan.

'I do not remember having been consulted in any way upon the proposal to land parachute troops in Italy. [. . .] Let me have a report as soon as possible upon the preparation and execution of this plan, showing exactly what authorities were consulted. Make sure that for the future my initial is obtained to all projects of this character.'[32]

This bomb from Churchill landed on Pug Ismay's desk on 15 February, just as Mussolini went public with the raid and news agency wires burnt round the world.

Ismay scampered into the corridors of Whitehall with damage limitation on his mind. In the ensuing enquiry, his get out of jail card was that Churchill *had* been sent the initial idea, then titled PROJECT 'T', which mentioned 'dropping parachutists to destroy the Apulian Aqueduct', on 28 January, and was then sent details of the operation itself, which also mentioned landing parachutists, on

9 February. Churchill was a busy man, running a war, and it might be suggested Pug could have done more to draw the prime minister's attention to the documents, given their import. But it was still all there, with photos – Churchill just hadn't read it.

Clarke had come up with a brilliant riposte to *Blitzkrieg*. Special forces are not just special because of selection, training, weapons or methods – they are special because their impact is strategic. The aqueduct was swiftly repaired, but the damage to Italian confidence never was. On a mud-covered Italian mountainside, a few infantrymen had blown up a bridge but the repercussions went round the world.

But this view found little favour in the upper echelons of the British command, and the SAS were soon rebranded again, becoming the 1st Parachute Battalion. And were re-envisaged, as one of their 'originals' put it, 'as highly disciplined, superbly trained, attacking infantry [. . .] The new intakes were rather more regular, infantry-minded people.'

The SAS in Britain ceased to exist as fast as it had been created.

But the Italians didn't know that. The very real arrival of the SAS in southern Italy, coupled with Clarke's elaborate deception orchestrated from Cairo, destroyed the fragile confidence of Hitler's main ally. The Italian response to this new aerial threat, seemingly based just over the Mediterranean, was focused on civil defence.

The fear of British parachutists and airborne Abyssinian insurgents led to the closing of roads throughout the country, and the redeployment of troops and Carabinieri to scour the hillsides. It made little sense to the Luftwaffe and the German ground units who were driving through the country on their way to the Mediterranean, but Clarke had planted a fear in Mussolini and the Italian high command that would last the rest of the war. Italy would never again completely commit to overseas operations knowing that there was a threat closer to home, which would have dramatic consequences for the Germans in North Africa and, later, Europe.

As for the SAS, far from Whitehall and British High Command, working from his converted bathroom inside General Wavell's HQ in Cairo, Dudley Clarke kept the flame alive. As the ghost of Lawrence might have had it, the SAS was 'an idea, a thing intangible, invulnerable, without front or back, drifting about like gas . . . we might be a vapour, blowing where we listed. Our kingdoms lay in each man's mind.'[33]

PART TWO

The Indirect Approach

5

The Bumbling Herd: 1941

Greece

On 10 February, Fraser read in the *Glengyle News* about the first British victory of the war: 'The Army of the Nile has asked and it was given. They have sought and they have found. They knocked and it was opened unto them.'[1]

At 11.30am the ship's anchor rattled into the tropical waters off Freetown and leaning on the crowded rail Fraser, sweat beaded on his forehead, got his first glimpse of Africa. The heat was oppressive and the hot smell of tropical decomposition hit him. In the distance he could see the white sandy beaches backed with tropical rainforest stretching to the low shanties of Freetown. This was the furthest Fraser had been from home. Unlike Clarke's, Fraser's journey had been measured in weeks not days, and their convoy was now surrounded by massive grey armoured Navy cruisers required to shepherd them past German pocket battleships operating in the South Atlantic. It looked like the war with the Italians would be over by the time he got to Egypt.[2]

The following morning, in a Cairo suburb on the other side of Africa, the sun blasted Eric Dorman-Smith awake in his staff car. His mouth parched, he had ground to a halt at 4am when his rear right tyre blew, having driven 730 miles from the frontline to get permission from Wavell for O'Connor to advance into Libya on Tripoli.[3]

He flagged a passing cab, headed for Shepheard's, bathed, changed, and was in Wavell's map room by 10 o'clock, prepared to be at his most persuasive. Wavell greeted him cheerfully, then waved at the wall, saying sarcastically, 'You find me busy with my spring campaign.'[4]

Dorman-Smith had to do a double take – to his horror, the map of North Africa was gone, replaced by *Greece*.

Churchill had been reading the Germans' mail – highly sensitive intelligence called ULTRA – and knew the Germans planned to invade Greece. Inspired by the Greeks' Sparta-like stand against Mussolini in Albania, Churchill prepared to send British and Commonwealth troops onto the shores of the Balkans for the second time in the century. Describing his experience of the Gallipoli disaster as being like a sea beast fished from the depths and exploding at the loss of pressure,[5] which propelled him into the political wilderness, here was his chance to put it right. The Greeks did not want rescuing and British resources were far too meagre to stop the panzer divisions, but Churchill was going to do it anyway. This meant there would be no advance on Tripoli, and the Army of the Nile would be further depleted to supply forces to support Greece.

The following day, 12 February, Clarke was feeling ill. He had not been feeling himself for a couple of weeks and decided to get a check-up. The doctor took one look at his yellowing eyes and pallor, immediately diagnosed jaundice, and admitted him to 15th (Scottish) General Hospital in Cairo.[6] Clarke's one-man operation shut down, and would remain shut for a month, depriving Wavell of Clarke's skills at the critical moment Wavell started to spin plates in the eastern Mediterranean.

While Clarke was at his check-up, Wavell's Greek plate wobbled, as the long-range Heinkel He 111 carrying Rommel flew low over the Mediterranean from Sicily towards Tripoli. Streams of Junkers 52s flew in the opposite direction over Rommel's head, having just dropped Luftwaffe ground crew in North Africa.[7] Hitler had briefed Rommel at Berchtesgaden in front of the red marble fireplace presented by Mussolini – he wasn't going to let his fascist ally fold. But Rommel landed in Tripoli at midday to find Italian officers with their bags packed, ready to leave.

Sitting in the glass-domed nose of his Heinkel, Rommel had a panoramic view of his battlefield as he flew towards the British. Hitler had wanted him to deploy to defend Tripoli; instead Rommel flew on, 350 miles east, to ground that was flat and hard, and looked ideal for panzers. He was only 200 miles from lead British units, sitting stationary, expecting the order to advance. For Rommel, this was never going to be about defence.[8]

The Mandibles

The key to Greece for the British was the Dodecanese island chain. In Italian hands, 150 islands stretched from Rhodes in the east to the tiny, isolated Island of Kastellorizo in the far west, cutting Greece off from Egypt. It was imperative the Allies invade these, to gain control of airfields that could otherwise destroy the vessels heading to Greece through the Aegean. OPERATION MANDIBLES, named by Churchill, the intention was to bite off German forces in Greece. But the jaw could work both ways. If the Allies didn't get control of the Dodecanese, the Royal Navy could be eaten alive by dive bombers. In GHQ Cairo, the unofficial name for this scenario was the 'Mediterranean Dunkirk'.

The Greek war engulfed Fraser and the Commandos. Commandos were lightly equipped, with no heavy weapons or mortars, because their original purpose had been raiding, not conquering and holding ground. But Wavell was out of troops, and desperate. The three Glen ships, Fraser and fresh troops sitting in an estuary off the African coast, were an easy target. Wavell signalled Whitehall: 'We are urgently considering "Mandibles" but must await arrival Glen ships before major operation.'[9]

There was no run ashore for Fraser at Freetown. His ship's screws span, carrying them over the equator at nine o'clock on 13 February. When Churchill found out about the mess in the loading of the commandos, he was angry, told them to sort it out in Cape Town and dispatched the foreign secretary, Anthony Eden, to Cairo, to make sure there was no backsliding on his wishes.

Dill and Foreign Secretary Eden touched down in Cairo on 19 February, the day Fraser's ship finally nosed into Cape Town. But the commandos were so slow, Wavell couldn't wait for their arrival. The Middle East had commandos, raised from Middle East units at the same time as Fraser and the others in Britain – but with none of the advantages in selection, training or equipment. Fraser was still in the Indian Ocean two days later when Wavell fed the Middle East commandos to the mandibles. At 2am on 25 February, 4 miles south-west of Kastellorizo, two hundred men of 50 (Middle East) Commando split off from their covering cruisers and started the run into their target. The weather was good, the sky clear, the vessels lit in bright starlight, with a gentle breeze blowing across a smooth sea. The operation had been billed as a walk in the park.

Kastellorizo, codename ABSTENTION, was 4.5 miles square, had a population of fifteen hundred and was a mile off the (neutral) Turkish coast. Admiral Cunningham was keen on this island because he found its deep-water port attractive, but he had a blind spot for airpower. The island had no airfield and counterattack had been considered 'unlikely'; in the event of air attack, the idea was for the commandos to disperse and take cover.[10] The only person who seemed to foresee this could go wrong was Brigadier General Staff (BGS) in GHQ, Alexander 'Sandy' Galloway. A veteran of Gallipoli, he added two hundred regular troops from Cyprus to reinforce the commandos once they were ashore.

The Italians counterattacked in force with aircraft from nearby Rhodes. The commandos lost their fire support and only means of communication when their gunboat, HMS *Ladybird*, was hit and limped back to Cyprus. After which Italian gunboats and German E-boats shot up the harbour and the Italians landed in force. The commandos fell back to their landing beach.

Having had no contact with the troops ashore, the Royal Navy destroyer *Decoy* arrived two nights later with reinforcement troops, only to be greeted with two signals flashed in quick succession:

EMBARKATION NOW OR NEVER . . .
SUICIDE TO LAND ANY MORE MEN HERE.[11]

Eastern Mediterranean, 1941.

The seasick company of Sherwood Foresters launched into the maelstrom to pull the commandos out, but left behind 41 commandos, including 11 wounded and 3 dead. It did not bode well for Fraser and the commandos approaching Suez.

Axis aircraft had dropped acoustic mines blocking the Suez Canal, and after five days sitting in the Red Sea, on 10 March 1941, Fraser and the Glen ships finally made it to Egypt. General Jack Evetts, commander of MANDIBLES, came aboard to brief them. Evetts, who worked with Clarke in Palestine, was a tough Scotsman, a former Cameronian (Scottish Rifles), and was pleased by the arrival of 11 Scottish Commando to join his operation, promising them, 'A bellyful of fighting.'[12]

Docking at Ferara Wharf at six the following evening, Fraser and his men marched two dusty miles to Genifa Camp. Here they were welcomed by Wavell (the highest-ranking officer in country) and Dill (the highest-ranking officer in the British Army), reinforcing the importance of their mission. Both generals said that great things were expected of Layforce.

Commando Troop Leader Jock Lewes said when they achieved this amazing feat of arms, the most amazed would be themselves. In 8 Commando he was an anomaly: good-looking and often mistaken for Douglas Fairbanks Junior, Niven's 'Dougie', the former Oxford Rowing Blue described himself as the fittest man on the boat.[13] He had signed on in Bow, East London, to the Tower Hamlet Rifles, and was only recruited to 8 Commando because Bill Stirling had seen his marksmanship at the rifle ranges at Bisley. He wasn't a Blue Blood at all. He came from Australia.

The following day the *khamaseen* blew – the hot springtime wind that brings orange sand up from the desert – knocking over their tents, giving Fraser his first taste of Egypt.[14] The battered remnants of the Middle East Commando marched into camp to join them, prepared to go into the breach again as Layforce's 'fourth battalion' (the term commando had been banned again, and they were called SS battalions).

Churchill sent Fraser and the commandos help in an unlikely form: 'what about flying out some of this for the storm troops of MANDIBLES.'[15] The *this* was amphetamines. Churchill had taken a personal interest in capsules found on downed Luftwaffe pilots nicknamed Stuka Tablets. The assumption was that they helped Stuka pilots pull out of their vertical dives.

Physiologist Sir Henry Dale was called in and identified the capsules as methamphetamine. The amphetamine patent was held by US firm Smith Kline French, which sold the drug under the brand name *Benzedrine*, which was marketed as a nasal decongestant and a treatment for mild depression. To avoid breaching the patent, German firm Temmler synthesised methamphetamine by adding a carbon molecule. Before the war, Temmler had marketed the new drug for its medicinal benefits, in a campaign copied from *Coca Cola*, and it helped power the National Socialist economic miracle and was sold to German women in a brand of chocolates to help with housework and the children.

German troops exhausted by the tempo of *Blitzkrieg* asked their families to send them the sugar-coated pills as they marched into Poland. German High Command were reluctant to admit its Army had a drug problem, despite the fact that German troops consumed 35 million tablets in France.[16]

The British trialled Benzedrine (bought from the US) on two Commando Troops training in Scotland. On a 66-mile march in full kit, 64 men of Squad B powered by amphetamines started, and 45 finished. Squad A received a placebo and only 26 finished.[17] It was conclusive that the drugs worked. But it wouldn't end there – the Second World War would become further chemically enhanced.

On his release from hospital, Clarke decided to take sick leave in Cyprus: the spring sunshine would be ideal for his jaundice. He took a room in the *Castellis Hotel*, Kyrenia – a beautiful fishing port in northern Cyprus, framed by Kyrenian mountains. Spring is the best in Cyprus, the country covered in flowers, and oranges and bitter lemons are harvested. He laid back and enjoyed the sea view, fresh air, and fresh fish. He did not, perhaps, partake in any very good Cypriot wine, to give his liver a chance to recover.

In the sunshine, Clarke's muse spoke to him. Dudley Clarke was a career soldier, but one for whom creativity and writing were passions. Clarke's younger brother Tibby's first novel, *Go South – Go West*, had been published in 1932.[18] Perhaps inspired by what he perceived to be his younger brother's success, Clarke started to fill the hotel letterhead with an account of his time in Norway. By the time he picked up the message at the front desk from Wavell for him to report back to Grey Pillars *immediately*, he had filled 40 pages of Castellis Hotel foolscap.

Clarke flew into Cairo for a short interview with Wavell. General Evetts was preparing to take the largest isle of the Mandibles,

Rhodes, had analysed the Kastellorizo cock-up and identified a complete lack of intelligence. He pushed for more on Rhodes from Grey Pillars, who produced nothing. Rhodes was a heavily defended island, the Italians fully expected an attack, and Evetts badly needed to deceive them about his intentions. [19]

Clarke took a cab to Evetts's 6 Division, in their new headquarters on the Qasr-el-Nil and entered a building thronging with divisional officers. He was pleased to be reunited with Evetts, the two of them had held a very thin line in Jerusalem together in 1936 before Dill's troop surge arrived. David Niven's uncle, Bob Laycock, was also there, finally in the Middle East with the most advanced iteration of Clarke's Commando initiative. From the moment Clarke crossed that threshold, he and Fraser were in the same command: Clarke, the innovative staff officer dreaming up deceits with a guiding hand in special forces development and Fraser, the frontline operator.

For their operation to crack Rhodes, the divisional staff had been reinforced by naval and air elements, to form a miniature Combined Operations HQ. The division, in addition to Commandos, was to have regular forces, even tanks, for the operation. But in the bustle, Clarke took to his desk feeling it was a rather bewildering commitment for him, a single officer, with no staff or organisation of any sort at his disposal, to recce the island, and deceive the enemy as to their intentions. But being Clarke, he set to it with his usual ingenuity.[20]

First, he had to work out a cover plan for the operation. The scale of the operation, a full division with the Glen ships' commandos, would be obvious to spies and air reconnaissance. Rather than try and hide an invasion, he led the Axis to believe that they planned to invade Karpathos first, the second largest of the Dodecanese. Invading Karpathos was believable, even logical, as it was a stepping stone to Rhodes. It had actually been part of Evetts's original plan, but the late arrival of the Commandos meant he didn't have time to execute it. Clarke's deceits were usually better than the real plan, and swallowed for that reason.

He then needed to draw attention away from the real assault beaches in the north of Rhodes. He already had the SAS Brigade in his back pocket, confirmed by the 11 SAS drop on Italy, so he planned a fake drop by the SAS to take the airfield at the south end of Rhodes – a prelude to pretending the invasion force would hit beaches in the south. To do this he proposed to move his fictional 1 SAS Brigade from Transjordan to Crete, near enough to strike Rhodes, in April.

He still desperately needed some flesh-and-blood SAS soldiers to back up his fiction. General Neame in Palestine, who had promised him two soldiers when he had visited him, had been moved to replace O'Connor in the desert while he was on sick leave. The first thing Clarke did was signal Palestine and remind them of General Neame's promise – their reply was swift: the Staffordshire Yeomanry would supply Lance Corporal Smith and Trooper Gurmin. The first real actors in Clarke's SAS fiction.

Having decided to parachute the SAS on Rhodes, Clarke then set to work on the problem of getting more information on the target. He came up with the DOLPHIN and the BYNG BOYS Schemes.

The *Dolphin* was a sailing ketch owned by Lieutenant Claude Michael Bulstrode Cumberlege, a Royal Naval Volunteer Reserve who had been called up and was now landing Secret Agents around the Mediterranean for the Special Operations Executive (SOE). Mike Cumberlege had been raised on board his father's yacht in the south of France. His father was a former admiral, and Cumberlege worked running yachts for American millionaires between the wars. He was as useful with his fists as a boat, and the closest he came to settling down was marrying a beautiful Canadian and setting up home in Antibes. Even then he spent most of his time at sea. With a gold earring and a thick beard to disguise his good looks he was the perfect pirate for the job.

Clarke knew all this because pirate Mike's cousin, Cleland 'Cle' Alexander Martin Cumberlege, was in the Royal Artillery and, like Clarke, a staff officer with GHQ. Clarke spoke to Cle about his roguish cousin, and they decided they should borrow the ketch, and the two cousins do a close-target recce of the shoreline of northern Rhodes, posing as a local vessel. Needing a crew that could pass as local, Clarke enlisted Mr Zazlani, his contact at the Jewish Agency in Palestine, who recruited three Jewish crew to whom Clarke gave the rank of gunners.

The Dolphin sailed for Athens to practice getting close inshore and landing their recce parties on an isolated part of the Greek coast. After which Clarke would meet the Dolphin, incognito, in Piraeus, to brief them on their first run on the target.

The BYNG BOYS scheme was a reference to Clarke's love of Vaudeville. As a young flying officer in 1917 he used to crowd round the piano in the Ship Hotel, Reading, with other cadets and bang out the latest hits, of which the Byng Boys' 'If You Were the Only Girl in the World' was one.[21]

Now the 'BYNG' of BYNG BOYS, was Captain WHS Byng, and the 'BOYS', the RAF's long-range telescope. Clarke also got hold of an ex-Italian super-long-range camera, the only one of its kind in the world, and a Flight Lieutenant Henser, an RAF photographer who knew how to operate it. The Boys telescope was 1m long, around 60cm in diameter, and had to be flown out from England. Clarke needed Captain Byng to get it into position on the Turkish coast, facing Rhodes, then Henser could start taking pictures of the most vital part of the objective – Rhodes harbour.

It was Fraser and the Commandos' job to take Rhodes harbour, at the northernmost tip. The Turkish coast was just 16 miles north of Rhodes harbour. Here the coast is bleak and inhospitable, cliffs provide no inlets for ports, and the closest town, the tiny fishing village of Bozburun, lies on the north side of the Marmaris Isthmus, from where no roads lead to the views on Rhodes harbour. This made it an ideal location to establish an observation post.

Understandably, the neutral Turks didn't want Captain Byng spying on Rhodes from their cliffs. Even dressed in Clarke's cover story as a 'meteorological party'. But the Turkish British Military Attaché, Brigadier Arnold, persuaded them to let Byng train a Turkish crew to do the job. Byng flew to Adana, Turkey with the gigantic telescope, which he carried by pack mule on a hazardous journey to a rocky crag overlooking Rhodes. Here he installed his Turkish mercenary unit and intelligence began flowing.

The Castle of String

It was clear to Clarke he could no longer operate single-handedly: he needed his own organisation.[22] In addition to his deception work and intelligence gathering, he was running MI9. MI9's job was to secure information from British prisoners of war in enemy hands and assist them to escape. Clarke felt it was one of those undefined secret activities which fell to him as personal intelligence officer for special duties to the commander in chief. Although Clarke was drowning in the volume of work, his reach was extraordinary because lifting Allied prisoners of war from all over the Mediterranean increased his burgeoning intelligence network.

In Grey Pillars, Wavell's right-hand man General Arthur Smith agreed. Their shared secretary didn't have time to do Smith's work. There was an endless number of visitors to Clarke's bathroom, some of whom did not look like they should be allowed in a British HQ. And everywhere he went, it seemed that everyone in GHQ did work for Clarke in some capacity. Smith was happy to wave goodbye to Clarke, authorising him to set up his new outfit under the title ADVANCED HEADQUARTERS 'A FORCE'. The 'A' stood for 'Airborne', because Clarke would use his new HQ to double as the fake, forward HQ of 1 SAS Brigade as it moved from Transjordan to join 6 Division's assault on Rhodes.

The fake SAS now merged with the future, real SAS. Clarke's A-Force HQ planning fake SAS parachute drops on Rhodes was working with Fraser, Stirling, Mayne and Lewes, and all the future members of the real SAS. Clarke had moved from H.G. Wells and the Time Machine, into Quantum Physics and the theory of *Retro-causality*. The idea that future events impact the present.

There was another reason Clarke needed his own place: General Smith was right. He was using a large number of double agents and contacts of varying reliability to run his deceptions – and had this range of contacts been allowed in 6 Division's HQ, it would have soon become plain to 'the curious international circles of Cairo' what the British were planning. A dedicated HQ meant visitors of all types could be admitted discreetly and interviewed under conditions of secrecy, without need for passes. And without them seeing anything they might then leak to the Italians and Germans.

Clarke opened shop in the building opposite 6 Division which was named the Castle of String – harems for Egyptian palaces were often protected by a resident eunuch, who held string instead of keys for the locks. Now the Castle of String was protected by an Egyptian, with legs so crumpled and twisted beneath him as to be useless, and who propelled himself on a wooden trolley. He lived in the basement room, and came and went through the windows in which he had contrived an ingenious form of entrance. The only thing that offended him was the offer of money, though he would accept small packets of tea for his services.[23] He was the ideal sentry for Clarke, whose main visitors were spies, both invited and uninvited.

In preparation for SAS's arrival in Egypt, Clarke ramped up his fictions – documents leaving the building were stamped A FORCE ADVANCED HQ and many, additionally, BATTALION HQ, 1st Special Air Service Battalion. Operating from the Castle of String as one of his many aliases, from Wrangel the war correspondent, to brigade staff officer of the mysterious SAS, Clarke was known to all as The Colonel.

Flat 19, The Castle of String, consisted of three rooms: one for Clarke's secretaries, one for his staff, and his own office, in which he installed a large safe he had ordered for his files of deceptions and contacts. The centre of his room was filled by an even larger mahogany bureau, and largest of all, an air-conditioning unit, which looked like an enormous radio set, and emitted the same metallic hot smell as the London Underground.

At the bureau he covered sheets of foolscap with some of the best and most workmanlike prose that his first official recruit, Kenyon Jones, said he had ever seen. Kenyon Jones quickly recognised how widely read Clarke was, but his key observation was that The Colonel could literally get anything done – the whole apparatus of GHQ seemed to be at his disposal.[24]

Kenyon Jones was a Welsh rugby international, Oxford Blue and an officer in the 14th/20th Hussars. Jones had originally been recruited into intelligence work by Clarke's friend, Maunsell, who had been scattering SAS Xmas receipts on the Egyptian trains. Because Jones was fluent in German, Maunsell thought he could come in handy running double agents, and he was the first officer he recruited in 1940 to SIME. Kenyon Jones's red face had become an unusual sight running around Gezira Island before breakfast, where British staff had an aversion to physical exercise.

Later in 1940, MI6 in London notified them an Italian spy, Renato Levy, was being sent to Cairo by Italian intelligence, but had reached out to British diplomats in Italy and wanted to come over. Kenyon met Levy in Cairo; he was around thirty-five and spoke reasonable English, having spent time in Australia. Kenyon set Levy up in a pension, and discovered his primary concern in life was women. Levy waited on a radio from his masters that never showed, so Kenyon got him one. Then Kenyon sent him back, with the radio, to Italy, with a code he had invented. Levy would pretend to the Italians he had set up a spy ring in Cairo. The spymaster was an entirely fictional Syrian called Paul Nicossof, codename CHEESE, with a backstory and character to match. In Rome, Levy would hand over the radio and code to Italian intelligence to operate themselves.

At the allotted call time, in Abbassia Barracks, Kenyon Jones and an operator sat by their set, and tapped out a greeting from CHEESE to his new masters. From Rome, a reply came. For Kenyon Jones it was undoubtedly the biggest thrill he had in the war.[25] He floated back to his room. When he told Maunsell, Maunsell was overjoyed and said they had to tell Clarke.

Jones joined Clarke, and the traffic was handed on to another full time handler. Typical of Nicossof's traffic would be 'I am alone and without funds. I cannot hire agents.' Nicossof was moody and mercurial, always in debt, and sank into the depths of despair when no money came his way. But he would revive with every specious promise of cash from his Axis masters. Sometimes he would threaten to pawn his radio set for funds, he knew nothing about the military, and most of his transmissions contained chicken shit. But, occasionally, he would send the Axis a stunning revelation. This fictional agent, CHEESE, was arguably Britain's most important channel for deception in the Second World War because it gave Dudley Clarke a direct line to the heart of the Axis camp.

While Clarke set up shop, and attended the final conferences for the assault on Rhodes with Laycock and Evetts in 6 Division HQ, out in the Western Desert the first of Wavell's plates came crashing down – Erwin Rommel was on the move. On arrival in Tripoli, Deutsche Afrika Korps radiated the complete assurance of victory in Rommel's eyes.[26] First contact came on 24 February when his lead units blew away two British scout cars, a lorry and staff car. Rommel sensed weakness. By 30 March, the British were in full retreat, and O'Connor's former right-hand man in the desert, John Harding (now assistant to General Neame), took Wavell to one side to personally beg him to send O'Connor back out to replace Neame.[27] In Cairo, General Arthur Smith rang O'Connor, who was less than happy 'at the thought of taking over command in the middle of a battle which was already lost'.[28]

That evening Wavell summoned Clarke to Grey Pillars. Clarke was getting used to being the go-to for any British crisis. Wavell wanted Clarke to slow Rommel down. The only way to do it was to threaten his rear areas, forcing him to leave troops to protect them, giving him fewer in the front line. Wavell wanted Clarke to simulate preparations for an attack on Rommel's lines of communication through Libya from Tripoli.[29] These supply lines followed a long and winding road along the coast to the frontline. The lines' proximity to the sea gave Clarke an idea for a plan to meet Wavell's needs, and who could carry it out. The most obvious way to threaten the supply lines was an amphibious assault by the Commandos. Clarke was constantly in and out of 6 Division HQ, supplying them with information and updating his deception plans. What if they put the Commandos to sea, and he leaked that they were after Rommel, rather than Rhodes?[30] He called it PLAN ANTI-ROMMEL.

While Clarke worked on PLAN ANTI-ROMMEL, General O'Connor flew up to the mud-splattered British HQ near the frontline in Barce on 3 April, to attempt to save the Army of the Nile. On arrival it was clear to O'Connor the situation was already more serious than his chief believed. By 6 April, Rommel was relishing his dazzling successes and sensed victory.[31]

That morning, Clarke ran up the steps into Grey Pillars to present PLAN ANTI-ROMMEL. He arrived a bit late for the 10 o'clock commander in chief's conference and found Wavell, his old boss Jack Dill, and Anthony Eden all waiting for him with glum faces.

The Germans had invaded Greece.

Everyone recognised the importance of the operation to capture the Dodecanese islands, but now, with the Luftwaffe pounding Piraeus harbour in Greece, and dominating the Aegean, there seemed no point sending Fraser, the Commandos and 6 Division into Rhodes. MANDIBLES was working for the Germans and British forces would be trapped in Greece. With Rommel breaking through in the Western Desert, they needed to do everything they could in Egypt to stop him. The plate-spinning was over and they were looking at a load of smashed crockery.

The depressing conference dragged on, the slowly turning fans above the long table doing little to dispel the atmosphere. Everything except the commandos would be sent to the desert: 6 Division were to be broken up. The Commandos were useless, they had no heavy weapons and four vehicles – what were they good for?

Then Clarke lightened the mood by presenting his plan. He outlined his idea to the chiefs and Wavell, Dill and Eden approved it immediately.

Bob Laycock arrived in Cairo to attend the divisional training conference at 6 Division, only to find that the division was being broken up. Rhodes would be postponed until 6 Division was reformed. He went back to Genifa to break the news to Fraser and the Commandos.

At dusk that evening, British HQ at Barce on the frontline was about to be overrun by Rommel's troops. One of the last to leave that night was O'Connor, who jumped with Neame into his Lincoln Zephyr, four-door saloon. Behind him, Neame's aide de camp, Lord Ranfurly, climbed into a Ford Utility. The small convoy hammered through the desert and O'Connor mentioned the moon seemed to be in the wrong place. There were, ominously, no other vehicles from their retreating HQ on the track – because they were on the wrong track.

O'Connor had fallen asleep when Ranfurly whispered through the window they had just driven into the vanguard of Rommel's forces, and hoped they would crawl out of the car and get away. It was too late. The Germans emptied the staff car at gunpoint – and Britain lost its best armoured commander at the moment it needed him most. British resistance was over, and Rommel was on his way to Tobruk.

At 3.30pm the following day, at Genifa camp, Fraser and his men received the warning order they were to prepare for an assault. At dawn they picked up their packs, weapons and ammunition, marched the 2 miles back to the dock and were all aboard the *Glenearn* by 7.20am.[32] Clarke was pleased. For once he had a real force to back up his deception. Laycock arrived in Port Said and came aboard the *Glenearn* to set up his HQ. Fraser and 11 Commando were going to war – or at least give the appearance of it.

The Battle for Tobruk

Everything now hinged on whether Rommel could take Tobruk. If he could run supply ships there, and be resupplied so close to Egypt, little would stop him reaching Suez.

Dorman-Smith flew into Tobruk through a ghibli.[33] The few battered palms were being blown flat outside the cave which was HQ for General Leslie Morshead, Commander 1st Australian Division, and John Harding. The two were confident – this battle was in their DNA, similar to what their fathers had fought at Gallipoli. Rommel attempted to batter his way on 10, 13 and 14 April. The Aussies earned his respect as Axis casualties climbed to 1,200: the same number Rommel had lost in the entire French campaign with 7th Panzer.

Meanwhile, Fraser with 11 Commando, and 7 Commando put to sea, their target now Bardia which had been captured by Rommel. The commandos' orders were to hit the port on the night of 16/17 April, destroying all enemy vehicles encountered and capturing a few prisoners.[34] It was a hit-and-run, to add some flesh to Clarke's deception as much as to cause physical damage.

On board their assault transport, HMS *Glenearn*, Fraser made sure his section went through their final checks. They were to travel light – canvas shoes, steel helmets, no respirators, only 15 magazines per Bren gun, 200 rounds per Tommy gun. The convoy sailed at 4am on 16 April on a calm sea, the wind rose in the afternoon heat from Force Two to Force Five, and all afternoon the air-raid warnings sounded, but the Luftwaffe failed to materialise. The sun set, and Fraser, Tait, Byrne, Du Vivier and the rest of 11 Commando blacked their faces and prepared for action.

The CO, Pedder, gathered his officers to issue his orders. Fraser and the troop commanders huddled with their notebooks, the ship pitching heavily. Fraser went through the detailed loading plans and routes for his landing craft to the beach, and peered at the map of the target, with an indication of where they thought a coastal gun was.

But as they huddled in the gloom, the roll meant ahead of them a heavy surf was running onto Bardia beach. The same surf had prevented the submarine from launching Captain Courtney's fragile two-man folboats. And, as the ship closed inshore, the violent roll aboard made it apparent launching their landing craft was going to be hazardous. Just ahead, the destroyer HMS *Decoy* radioed she had a 15-degree roll from bow to stern in Bardia bay. When she ran aground, the operation was called off.

Clarke was not entirely disappointed. Having real troops to back up his falsehoods had 'paid well'. He found out that the Japanese consul in Port Said had reported to his minister the moment the Glen ships had sailed. Clarke's deception was now in play.[35]

With the Commandos at sea, Clarke thought he could do better. He had planted the move of the SAS to Egypt in preparation for the assault on Rhodes – now he could use them to scare Rommel. Kenyon Jones was made Commander of K Detachment, 1 SAS: Clarke's dummy glider detachment. The plan had been that these dummy gliders be deployed on airfields in Crete, a short hop to the islands of Karpathos and Rhodes. To support Clarke's fiction the SAS Brigade were going to drop on the MANDIBLES. Now they got new orders: for an airborne operation against the enemy's lines of communication in Libya.[36]

K Detachment, SAS's base was at the Qasr-el-Nil barracks at the roundabout at the end of the road. This housed the NAAFI[37] (the Army supermarket for British goods), an outdoor cinema, and a football and cricket ground. It also had workshops and was cut off from the outside world by high-sided barrack blocks. Just the place for K Detachment to build balsa-wood gliders before crating them to Crete, where Kenyon Jones was to recce airfields for them to deploy.[38]

On 11 April, Lance Corporal Smith and Trooper Gurmin, Clarke's first flesh-and-blood SAS soldiers, had arrived by train in Cairo. Clarke had ordered them to report to the barracks of the Field Security Police, where they were to be accommodated, and ordered them not to leave until he had briefed them. In the morning they would be transformed into Lance Bombardier Smith and Gunner Gurmin, Royal Artillery, of the First Special Air Service Battalion.

Bombardier and Gunner are ranks of the Artillery, and were chosen by Clarke because the Artillery was huge, consisting of 96 regiments and over a million men. It would be entirely possible that Smith and Gurmin, meeting fellow Artillery soldiers in Cairo, could plausibly explain how they had never met, and how their outfit, the SAS, had never been heard of.

The devil was in Clarke's detail. He gave them a 'get out of jail' pass to show to the Royal Military Police if they were picked up for wearing badges of the non-existent SAS. He also gave them as detailed an SAS backstory as an actor might expect in accepting a role: after Dunkirk they had volunteered for parachute work and ended up at Ringway. Clarke gave them a breakdown of the real trials and tribulations of parachute training.

He named Lieutenant Colonel Jackson (the CO of 11 SAS) as commander of 1 SAS. He even told them he was from the Pamplona-beret-wearing Royal Tank Regiment, because after Operation COLOSSUS the Italians would have tried to establish who, and what, had hit them. To support their act, Clarke himself was to become part of SAS Brigade Headquarters. On 7 April Smith and Gurmin had been told they were likely to go on operation immediately. He had their posting order typed and up and signed by 'the Captain and Adjutant of 1 SAS', and had given it to Maunsell to lose. Clarke didn't specify where, but Maunsell was good at getting Clarke's documents into the wrong hands.

After their briefing Smith and Gurmin removed all their real Yeomanry badges, and attached their Royal Artillery badges. They attached small metal wings on their shoulder straps, where normally the name of their regiment would go. Finally, Clarke handed them parachute wings in packets – instructing them to get them sewn on the sleeve in the same position as the Tank Corps wear their white tank badges.

The SAS men set out into Cairo, to be discreetly indiscreet.

The real pressure on Tobruk from Rommel required a real response. No sooner had Fraser and the Commandos docked in Alexandria, he had to tell his men that there was no shore leave for security reasons. It was hoped that the operation would take place as soon as the weather improved.[39] But eventually it was 7 Commando who got the job. Fraser could only watch as *Glengyle* set out for the port, now codenamed PIG, and wonder about whether 7 Commando were up to it.

The short answer was that they were not. At the root of 7 Commando's problems was their CO, Felix Colvin (Waugh would immortalise him as Colonel Fido Hound), who, like many men, found the battlefield a frightening and confusing place.

Once they got ashore, Clarke's deception compounded their problems – repeated Commando scares meant Rommel's men and the Italians were alert to Commando raids and reacted accordingly. In the barracks they found a half-eaten slice of bed and butter, and the floor of one of the rooms was still wet from recent scrubbing. The motor park, which should have been full of vehicles, had recently been emptied. They burnt a stack of tyres anyway and 'completely destroyed it'.[40]

The commandos failed to stop two cars from speeding away, and the hard rock of the road proved impervious to their explosives. Their next target was a bridge, but they only managed to blow a 3-foot hole in the middle. To finish it off, they soaked the timber trestles with petrol and lit it, hoping for some more damage, but it was time to head for the boats. A team sent after the coastal guns stole the firing pins and blew their breaches, which was a small success.

Back on the beach the weather had freshened considerably. One landing craft was beached in the swell and couldn't be moved, and they tried to destroy it with grenades. The remaining landing craft struggled back to the *Glengyle*, their cooling systems clogged with windblown sand, but some craft got lost. Eighty-seven men were unable to find the beach, and this party was left ashore with orders to make it to Solum on the Egyptian frontier on foot – they were captured.[41]

At sea, while recovering the landing craft, *Glengyle*'s lifting equipment broke. Finally, at 5am, the *Glengyle* had to put some distance between herself and the Luftwaffe before daylight arrived. In addition to the missing 87, she left one landing craft, which never made it alongside. One officer was shot dead by a sentry for failing to give the correct passcode.

Jock Lewes had been right: the Commandos had astonished no one. Now, as far as Grey Pillars was concerned, they were troops to plug the dyke of Wavell's collapsing empire.

Odyssey

Three days later, on 24 April, the *Mediterranean Dunkirk* got underway. And in Cairo, a GHQ desperate for troops started to dismantle Layforce.

In Alexandria, Fraser finally got shore leave from *Glenearn*, only to return to find 11 Commando being shipped to an unknown destination with orders to act independently.[42] He and his men unloaded their kit from the ship and entrained to the transit camp at Amariya, 40 miles south of the port.

Fraser crossed the Suez Canal that night, and at 9.30am crossed the frontier into Palestine. Fraser had no idea what was going on. He and his men marched through the town of Haifa and onto a sports ground they were told was their bivouac area. They were all starving – they had no logistic support, no vehicles, no cooks, and only what they were carrying. Luckily the local, 1st Battalion Essex Regiment, laid on a tea.

On 28 April they marched to the dock and boarded a ship, only to be ordered off. Fraser had little idea of the chaos ensuing out in the Mediterranean. With the Dodecanese still in Axis hands, including Rhodes, Royal Navy and Allied shipping was being sunk at an alarming rate. They got on another ship, this time helping to load 13 armoured Bren Carriers. Fraser and his men were familiar enough with this British Army workhorse to drive it, but it made it no clearer where they were headed. Finally, on 29 April, they sailed.[43]

The following day, Fraser stood on the rail and watched a low, orange island on the horizon coming out of the haze, before they docked at Famagusta. He was in Cyprus.

Crete was a more likely immediate target for the Germans than Cyprus, but unlike Crete, Cyprus was virtually undefended: 11 Commando had been rushed to protect it. Fraser and 8 Troop went down the gangplank and marched 7 miles north in full kit to Salamis. His troop pitched tents amid the long-abandoned Roman ruins of the harbour. The next day they marched 12 miles inland to Lefkonik, on the broad Mesaoria Plain. The plain, 60 miles long, lies between the Troodos mountains to the south and the Kyrenia mountains to the north. Much of it is covered with *Kafkalla*, a compacted soil that forms a hard pan – virtually a runway.

The Germans had ten thousand airborne troops. It was unclear what Fraser and the 50 men of 8 Troop equipped with rifles, Tommy guns, a few anti-tank rifles, and Bren guns were supposed to do on this vast airfield if any of this number landed. But Pedder would not be deterred and set his men to sighting defences to combat an overwhelming parachute operation. In desperation, 11 Commando started training locals to help with their mission.

To keep them on their toes, Pedder rotated the troops between their outposts in remote towns and ports. Fraser's troop had one truck for their equipment, otherwise they moved on foot. But the biggest problem for any British garrison on the ancient island was alcohol. The worst offence among many was carried out by an officer, Mayne. He and his best friend McGonigal had been drinking in a Nicosia night club and were the last men standing when Mayne called for the bill. Mayne, suspecting that he had been overcharged, called for the manager. When the manager was rude, McGonigal was unable to stop Mayne standing him in the middle of the wooden dance floor and firing into the floor around his feet to make him dance. Mayne was arrested, and placed under the supervision of another troop leader.

But 11 Commando's salvation would arrive from the usual source – Dudley Clarke.

6

The Lebanon: 1941

Undercover

Wavell called in Clarke for a briefing. He was concerned that he had left 14,600 troops in Greece, and he wanted Clarke to open more escape routes for MI9 via Turkey and the Dodecanese. Clarke was enthusiastic. He anticipated this visit to Istanbul would also allow him to expand PLAN ANTI-ROMMEL, by planting it on the Abwehr in Istanbul. That should enable him to set up a network of agents for future deceits.

But as Clarke was about to leave Wavell stopped him. He warned him he thought Iraq was about to blow up in his face. Former Iraqi Prime Minister, Rashid Ali el Gailani, who the British had deposed for his Axis sympathies, encouraged by Axis spies and one million Lire had seized the opportunity of collapsing British power to install himself in Baghdad. Iraq fell uncomfortably between General Wavell's Middle East Command and India where the Auk had been posted. The Auk had airlifted 350 men of the 1st Kings Own Royal Regiment into Basra on 17 April to secure the Basra oilfields (Britain's interest in the region), and was reinforcing them by sea. But in Wavell's sphere the British were holed up in an airfield outside Baghdad. With the Germans in Greece, it was only a short flight to Aleppo, Syria, then on to Mosul and Baghdad. Wavell told Clarke that if he saw any evidence of the Vichy French allowing the Germans to support the Iraqi *Golden Square* insurgency via the Vichy French Lebanon-Syria mandate he intended to move north from Palestine and take out the threat.

Clarke left the office with the clear understanding that if things in the Levant went south, Wavell expected him to do something about it.

Clarke had been prepared for undercover work by 'The Shadow' in Dublin. He checked his shirt and double-breasted suit for laundry marks, emptied his pockets of all but his Letts appointments diary, placed his passport, with occupation 'journalist', in his suit pocket. Finally, he secreted the letter from Wavell to the British Ambassador in Turkey, his only genuine credentials.[1]

Clarke landed in Cyprus on the same evening that Fraser left for it, 26 April. He had dinner with the governor, Sir William Battershill, at his house in Nicosia. The governor worried about his lack of forces to defend against parachutists. Clarke reassured him that the Commandos were being sent, and had some ideas about setting up guerrilla units in the Troodos mountains if the island was over-run. Orde Wingate had returned to Cairo victorious having installed Haile Selassie on the throne in Addis Ababa, and had given Clarke an interesting paper called 'Guerrilla Force Theory'.

In the morning, Clarke boarded the Egyptian civil airliner from Nicosia. He landed in Adana, southern Turkey, presented his fake credentials and boarded the Ankara express. Once at the capital he dropped in on the military attaché, Brigadier Allan C. Arnold, to thank him personally for allowing Captain Byng to train a Turkish crew and install the Boys telescope on the cliff opposite Rhodes harbour. The telescope was now supplying excellent intelligence on Axis shipping in and out of Rhodes.

Clarke appraised Arnold of PLAN ANTI-ROMMEL, and Arnold thought he knew a good contact in the German embassy who might prove profitable. Afterwards, Clarke took the overnight sleeper to Istanbul, crossed the Bosphorus and checked into the Park Hotel, next door to the German Embassy. Here he kept an unobtrusive rendezvous with Commander Vladimir Wolfson, the assistant Royal Naval attaché, and a British spy.

In three weeks undercover, Clarke, with Wolfson's help, succeeded in getting most of the Anti-Rommel story to sources in direct contact with the enemy. Best of all, for Clarke, they established nine channels in Istanbul for future deception, which could be triggered remotely by Clarke from Cairo.

On the MI9 side, they set up an organisation under Commander Wolfson through which hundreds of Allied fighting men were recovered from hostile territory, a scheme that could continue if Germany invaded Turkey, which everyone in Istanbul thought was imminent.[2]

Clarke arrived back in Ankara, on his way to Cairo, to the news the RAF had hit the Luftwaffe on three Syrian airbases. Wavell's fears had been confirmed; the Luftwaffe were staging through Syria to Iraq. Clarke didn't need a codeword from Wavell to divert to the warzone. The Vichy French were flying in more fighter aircraft and troops from France, via newly captured German airfields in Greece, and it looked as though open hostilities with Vichy France were imminent.

Clarke took the *Taurus Express* from Ankara for Tripoli, in Lebanon, on the night of 17 May. At noon the following day the express pulled into Adana. The border was closed and all British and Allied passengers ordered off. The platform filled with confusion, groups who had left the train gathered round their baggage on the steaming platform, where the wildest rumours flew around: Britain has declared war with France! Wavell has marched into Syria! The RAF have bombed Beirut!

Clarke couldn't get any better information from the British Consul on the platform, but his disguise held. Unlike his countrymen, he was allowed to continue south into the warzone as a war correspondent. He boarded the train with the few remaining passengers.

In the morning the sleeper rattled into Tripoli, just inside Lebanon, part of the Syrian-Lebanon French mandate, and inside the enemy camp. With the morning sun bleaching the wayside platform, Clarke got off the train and rented a car and driver for the two-hour journey down the coast road to Beirut. He spent the night in Beirut and found the atmosphere 'very tense indeed'. The country was on the verge of war, the RAF had launched more strikes on Syrian airfields, French troops had mobilised and filled the streets, and Clarke felt it was not a time to linger longer than was absolutely necessary.

Clarke knew that it was Wavell's intention to send an Allied force from Palestine into Lebanon and march north into Syria. But as Dewoitine D.520 Vichy French fighter aircraft toughed it out with RAF Hawker Hurricanes, which were marginally outclassed, there was every possibility the Vichy French would be able to block the advance at the biggest natural obstacle: the Litani River.

The Litani stretches 20 miles inland from the coast before swinging north to meet the foothills of Mount Hermon, the highest point on the Lebanese–Syria border, cutting the country between the sea and the mountains. It now became the target for Clarke's covert reconnaissance. Fraser and 11 Commando were just over a hundred miles from this coast. If they could land north of the Litani and take the river crossings from the Vichy on the French bank, then Wavell's force could cross unopposed.

Clarke inveigled his way into the confidence of a Jewish refugee family, fleeing Hitler for Palestine, using his honest love of Palestine. And, on the morning of 20 May, they drove along the coast road in the sunshine as it wound south from Beirut, the family unaware they were enabling their passenger to observe the troop movements and defence preparations along the route.[3]

Clarke claimed to have a photographic memory. He could record images in detail – though they faded after a few days. Now he 'photographed' the beaches of Lebanon, and Vichy defences, as he approached the Litani River.

The family were none the wiser when, having driven 30 miles to a brighter future, their passenger persuaded them to stop the car. Clarke used 'a lucky stratagem' to successfully manipulate a halt at the key point of the Litani River crossing. He wandered about the main crossing over the Litani River to look at the French positions.

There was a fortified redoubt above the bridge, and Vichy French troops were heavily dug in on the orchards and rocky terrain on the north bank – an opposed river crossing was going to be tough. He had passed beaches to the north that had looked suitable for a landing, bar one which was heavily defended and needed to be avoided.

Satisfied with his reconnaissance, Clarke and the family pressed on for Jerusalem, stopped repeatedly by troops and police as they approached the Palestine border, and Clarke had some anxious moments. But his fake passport and disguise held good, and they crossed into Palestine, and into British territory, and Clarke breathed a sigh of relief.[4]

Clarke waved goodbye to the family in Jerusalem, waited until after dark, then headed for the British HQ. The sentry at the gate may not, initially, have believed he was working for them, but he showed his paperwork and eventually was granted an audience with General Jumbo Wilson. Jumbo had just been evicted from Greece, having left behind many of his troops, and was now in charge of the invasion force Wavell had scraped together, made up of Australians, Free French and Indian Artillery. Jumbo Wilson may not have had the idea that the invasion should include a sea-borne landing by 11 Commando until Clarke arrived.

On arrival in Jerusalem, Clarke discovered German paratroops had started landing on the island of Crete, in the largest airborne assault the world had ever seen. Dorman-Smith had flown to warn General Freyberg, who was defending the island. An initiate of ULTRA, Dorman-Smith could sometimes appear as a soothsayer to those who didn't know where the information was coming from. Freyberg looked at his watch as the first parachute appeared from a Junkers 52, and proclaimed at least they were on time.

The following morning, Clarke flew out of Palestine for a long and urgent interview with his chief in Grey Pillars. Clarke downloaded all he knew on Lebanon, supplying intelligence on the river crossing, assault bridgehead and all he had seen on the coast. Wavell told Clarke that the invasion of Lebanon wasn't scheduled until 7 June, which, to Clarke's joy, gave him two weeks to attempt to assist with a deception plan. Clarke's focus remained reducing casualties through his subliminal methods.

Dorman-Smith, back from Crete, flew out to Jerusalem the next day to explain to Jumbo how 11 Commando would be used north of the Litani River to allow his forces to cross unopposed. And Clarke started to think about how to deceive the French.

In Crete, poor communications, a lack of understanding of the aerial dimension of the battle, and a lack of self-belief on the part of the defenders had lost the island. The evacuation shamed everyone, and CO Colvin was found hiding under a table sitting hunched on the floor: 7 Commando was lost. Laycock and Waugh escaped on a motor launch.

Despite the loss of Crete, Clarke still needed to ramp up PLAN ANTI-ROMMEL to support what he was feeding double agents. The Germans looked to be dominant across the whole Levant, and in the Western Desert a short, appropriately named OPERATION BREVITY had failed to stop Rommel. The few K Detachment, SAS gliders that shipped to Crete had been destroyed before the Germans landed. If the Germans had found fake gliders on Crete, Clarke's house of cards would have collapsed.

With the RAF stretched very thin, Clarke had transformed some of his gliders to twin-engine bombers. And, while he was on his mission across the Levant, Kenyon Jones had set up a forward operating base for K Detachment, 1 SAS Brigade, at Fuka – three unused airfields on the coast in front of Rommel's advance. Sixteen gliders, diverted from Crete and hastily converted to RAF bombers, had been shipped from Qasr-el-Nil barracks with Lieutenant Robertson and a team of 20 sappers on 10 May. Nicknamed 'Neccanos', these were in place and attracting the attention of the Luftwaffe.

But the main play of Anti-Rommel remained the SAS – and K Detachment, SAS now started constructing balsa gliders on Helwan airfield, just south of Cairo. By the time Crete fell on 1 June, Clarke had 27 gliders; this was a big airborne force – 27 gliders could lift

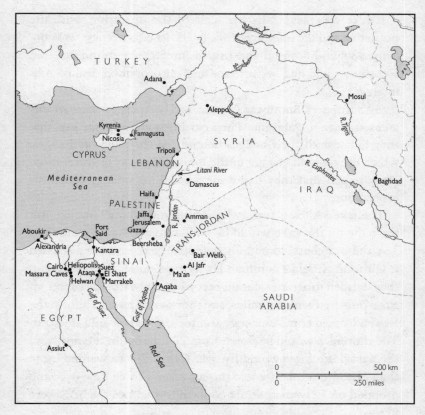

Eastern Desert, Levant and Southwest Asia, 1941.

five hundred men – meaning he could get the whole of the (fictional) 1st SAS Battalion airborne. To back this up Clarke stationed a number of 'SAS troops' at the airfield – K Detachment's sappers, presumably having sewn wings on their uniform. Clarke's team: A-Force HQ in the Castle of String, the sappers based at Qasr-el-Nil barracks at the end of his road, from where they travelled to and from Helwan airfield, made a convincing representation of the advance party of the Special Air Service Brigade arriving from Transjordan.[5]

Clarke was pleased by the scale of the operation, both the personnel and the huge array of gliders. Its effectiveness was confirmed when Maunsell and British Intelligence found out that Helwan airfield had become the subject of a good deal of Axis interest.[6]

'SAS troopers' Smith and Gurmin had been issued rail warrants and sent back to Palestine. Their parting note to Clarke said that they had left all their badges behind, except their cap badges, which they would change in the taxi on the way to the station. They hoped that they had done a good job and exceeded his expectations.

The fake SAS was rapidly becoming something tangible. But the icing on the cake would be parachutists. Clarke wanted to give the 'watchers' something definitive to report. He discussed it with the airfield's commander, Wing Commander Rees, and they decided to arrange dummy drops on Helwan. The parachutists would be visible for miles, and they would have to inform the Egyptian police, in itself a guarantee the Axis would find out. The dummies would be flown from Heliopolis, in the north, so the parachute force would fly over Cairo. Clarke wanted more than one aircraft, and when this air assault force flew over and dropped on Helwan it would confirm to the Axis the SAS were in town.

At Helwan, the dummies would be quickly recycled back up to Heliopolis, and ideally there would be three intensive days of SAS training drops over Cairo. Clarke knew all these airfields from his days in his Bristol Scout over Cairo in 1918 and he knew how all this would appear to the enemy. He ordered some RAF reconnaissance, and their pictures look completely convincing – an air armada ready to fly behind Rommel's lines.

He asked Freddie De Guingand, an Army officer in the Joint Planning Staff if he could organise this parachuting with the RAF. Clarke would arrange the details of the reception with Wing Commander Rees 'to give the whole thing an air of reality'.[7] De Guingand set off into Grey Pillars to find some parachutes.

Shepheard's Hotel

The cover plan Clarke developed for OPERATION EXPORTER, the invasion of Lebanon and Syria, centred on Shepheard's Hotel. As spring turned to the summer of 1941, Clarke felt guilty going upstairs to his room at night past the young, sleeping officers littering the foyer, clutching their 48-hour leave passes. Shepheard's had always been tolerant of guests without rooms – they would be woken before paying guests arose and offered coffee or something stronger on the terrace, to the call of the first kites circling overhead.

The hotel was founded in 1850 by Samuel Shepheard, a ship's officer, who washed up in Cairo aged 26 after taking his crew's side in a mutiny. The building had been residence to Napoleon's most talented general, Jean-Baptiste Kléber, whom Napoleon deserted in 1798 after the Royal Navy blew the French Navy off the Nile. Kléber fought on, with no hope of bringing his army back, and only his stunning generalship saved them. He was assassinated by a man posing as a beggar, while walking under one of the trees in the garden – Kléber's Sycamore still stood in the grounds. After working late on how to deceive the French, Clarke took his morning gin and tonic on the terrace, after which his driver took him to 'morning prayers', Wavell's briefing at Grey Pillars, for which he was usually 30 minutes late.

He returned after work to the happy-hour crush at the Long Bar, nicknamed The Short Range Shepheard's Group; the standing joke was that getting served at Shepheard's was the only thing that would slow Rommel down. Presided over by a head barman, the eight-language-speaking white tuxedo and bow-tie-wearing 'Joe-the-Swiss' Scialom, the bar was known as *Joe's Parish*. Joe never forgot a face nor their drink. His date of birth escaped him, a descendant of Samuel Shepheard's original banker, he claimed no nationality since he was born on a ship.[8] Counter Intelligence Officer Major AW Sansom had one of his NCOs stationed permanently incognito at the Long Bar to work out if Joe was a spy. If he was, he was brilliant; Sansom, who watched him several times himself, never saw him budge when one of his officer customers dropped his voice to tell his drinking companion a secret.[9]

Clarke didn't hang out at Shepheard's just for its name. In Cairo, spying was a national pastime. In spite of Churchill's directive to Eden to lock up Axis nationals, the Egyptian government still allowed thousands of Italians and hundreds of Germans to walk around freely. Sansom found the summer of 1941 pretty trying. With Rommel poised on the Egyptian frontier, and a constant stream of officers coming in from the desert for a brief spell of leave, time and again he would stumble on two officers swapping information over a glass of beer. And have to remind them that careless talk in Cairo, especially in Joe's Parish, definitely cost lives.[10]

Then he discovered a potentially worse racket run from the bottom of the terrace steps. The red-light district was opposite Shepheard's, and he was having a drink at the Long Bar one evening with a young infantry subaltern when the subaltern's friend didn't show. Leaving Shepheard's after dinner, he had been taken to the most beautiful prostitute he had seen in his life, and, after paying her five pounds, was led to a courtyard where the last thing he remembered was a blow to the head. Embarrassed, the young man didn't report the incident.

Sansom realised the racket could do more damage than broken skulls and lost cash and shut it down in a sting operation. His fears were justified: the woman was Romanian – in the Axis camp. No one ever knew if a British officer had been blackmailed for information.

If Axis spies weren't the problem, the Egyptian Moslem Brotherhood, including disaffected Egyptian Army officers, Nasser and Anwar el-Sadat were. But, amid the crush of spies in the bar was Rommel's greatest asset, one whom no one, not Clarke, nor the man himself, knew was a spy. *Die gute Quelle* – the good source – as Rommel named him, was the outspoken US military attaché

Bonner Frank Fellers. The US code had been compromised, and anything Bonner Fellers sent to Washington went straight to Rommel. Which, with the British courting US entry into the war, was pretty much everything.

For Clarke, sitting on the terrace sipping his gin, Shepheard's was perfect. Careless talk was his stock in trade.

Clarke's cover plan for OPERATION EXPORTER was tricky given the obvious troop movement in northern Palestine, RAF strikes against Syrian airbases and the very public arrival of Free French leader, General Charles de Gaulle in Cairo. Clarke spent two weeks working on lowering Vichy French vigilance on the Lebanon border, again focusing on misleading about the timing of the invasion, rather than persuading the Vichy French it wasn't going to happen. The scenario was an Anglo-French diplomatic bust-up – an entirely believable event in any era of history.[11]

When Clarke had arrived in Cairo in 1940 to recce the route up the Nile he worked out of an office with a cheerful little French group, which was headed by a young major and his flamboyant Basque assistant known as 'French Bob'. The major was now chief of staff to General Georges Albert Julien Catroux who commanded Free French forces in the Levant. Clarke first met Catroux in 1924, as a *Morning Post* war correspondent in Morocco, when Catroux was chief of intelligence at French HQ in Fez. They met again in 1936, when Catroux (now a general and commander of Syria-Lebanon) helped him with the Palestinian insurgency. With this personal relationship, his deception for the Lebanon invasion centred on the story of a quarrel between General Wavell and General Catroux, following Catroux's failure to persuade Wavell to attack Syria.

Clarke thickened his plot by leaking that General de Gaulle was actually in town to mediate in this dispute. De Gaulle was staying at Shepheard's, and with his buy-in, Clarke then warned Shepheard's Hotel staff de Gaulle was leaving early because mediation had broken down. He intended to give up his rooms: his luggage was packed and a special aircraft ordered, could they arrange everything for his departure immediately? In Khartoum, Sudan, they were warned he would land on 6 June on his way to Fort Lammy in Chad. He was on his way home two days before the real invasion – which was now 8 June.

In Shepheard's, Axis spies took note.

Clarke didn't just rely on the Axis supplying the Vichy French with this plausible breakdown in Anglo-French working relations. He flew to Jerusalem, and, with the assistance of Palestinian police, detectives ran an Arab spy over the border into Lebanon. The spy gave the French outposts news that General de Gaulle was that day, 6 June, flying to Khartoum, and for the moment the planned Allied operation was off.

The French secret service swallowed it whole. On 8 June, Australian, Indian, British and Free French troops crossed the border virtually unopposed. Jumbo's force sped north towards the Litani where, if things went according to plan, 11 Commando would take the far bank to allow them to cross.[12]

First Contact

At 11.50pm on the night of 8 June 1941, huddled in the darkness on board their assault transport, Fraser and the men of 8 Troop stood ready for battle, feeling the roll of the ship as she approached the Lebanese coast. Which meant they were up against the enemy of all Commando operations: ground swell.

Groundswell from distant storms gets bigger the further it travels. The irony was that, on a calm and windless night, the swell running into the Levant was so big the captain had to swing broadside to protect the landing craft as they were lowered.

Fraser and his section struggled with heavy packs, weapons and bandoliers of ammunition across the gangplank to their landing craft, which was swinging dangerously on its davits. Tait wrestled with the additional burden of the troop's 5-foot-long 14mm Boys anti-tank rifle, aptly nicknamed the Elephant Gun. All the while their landing craft threatened to smack into the hull. Finally, the order went to lower boats, and they bounced with relief into the chasm of dark, foaming water below them.

The engines revved, and at 12.30am, eleven landing craft of 11 Commando started to slip their moorings and form up around HMS *Glengyle* ready to head for the unlit Lebanese coast. In the darkness Fraser, aboard the rocking landing craft, wrestled with his fear. This was his first time into combat. He had been a soldier all his life, but that didn't mean he would know how he would react as the first rounds went over his head.

The captain of *Glengyle* was hailed by the patrol launch below. It was their Royal Naval adviser Lieutenant Potter, and Palestinian policeman, Sub-Lieutenant Colenut. The latter had been attached for his local knowledge of the coast, and thought the surf was so bad that the boats would be rolled over if they attempted to land. The captain had to make a call. There was no way they could get the majority of the force onto the assault beaches, and at 1.30am the operation was cancelled. To Fraser's relief they came alongside, and were winched back to the pitching deck. But while the *Glengyle* struggled to recover her craft, from the darkened coast they were being watched.

At 3pm that afternoon they docked at Port Said. With the Australian advance closing on the Litani, the CO, Pedder, assuming they would be sent on a different mission, immediately set out for GHQ Cairo for new orders. He was diverted aboard their flagship HMS *Ilex* for a conference – there was to be no change of plan: they would go straight back and land in daylight. At 4pm he was back on *Glengyle*, fifteen minutes later they sailed.

There was a full moon and no swell when *Glengyle* lowered her landing craft again off the mouth of the Litani at 3am on 9 June. Fraser and his men went through the same drill, aware that this, their second visit, was unlikely to be a surprise, and cast off for the coast.

The Commando craft formed three convoys: Keyes would hit the beach just north of the Litani River and take the main crossing. Troops with Eoin McGonigal would land a mile further north and take Kafr Bridge, where the main road south crossed a dried river bed and cut off the French from reinforcing the Litani to the south. And the main party, landing between them, would stop the French interfering with the first two assaults and secure the route north from Litani for the Australians. This group would be led by Pedder, with Mayne's 7 Troop and 8 Troop, with Fraser and his B section. Their orders were to seize and hold the enemy position long enough for the Australian Brigade to cross the river.

The French had woken up after Clarke's initial deceit, and were now fighting hard. The main bridge across the Litani River was probably destroyed, and the 21st Australian Infantry Brigade was attempting to cross the river: a rapid passage with only light casualties was vital to the overall success of the operation.

Clarke's intelligence was sound, but the subsequent RAF photographic reconnaissance did not show either the mouth of the river, or any part of the crucial coastline – the reconnaissance aircraft had overflown the target and started photographing too far north. On Keyes's landing craft, heading to secure the vital river crossing, they struggled to make sense of the shoreline. The RAF photographs missed the beach by quarter of a mile; worse, the mouth of the Litani was obscured by a sandbank.

With the sky growing lighter, they aimed for one of the whitewashed houses they had seen as a landmark from the bridge of *Glengyle*. Keyes and his men hit the beach; one officer, the keenest of all, jumped into water and sank up to his tin hat. The remainder waded ashore knee-deep and the landing craft pulled off. The commandos advanced to the dunes and dropped their packs. Keyes looked around – it was light enough to see the masts of feluccas, sailing dhows, in the river mouth to his north, and to his horror he realised they had landed south of the river.

Keyes set out to start the river assault they'd been sent to avoid, walking into the back of C Company, 2/16th Australian Battalion,

'Diggers', who were waiting to support their attack on the north of the river. Their company commander was very surprised to see them, but said he would lend Keyes some of his seven boats.

Keyes advanced to the river through the Australian troops, but as they approached the Litani a red light went up from the redoubt on the far bank. Immediately, the whole beach – from where they landed to within 100 metres of the river – was raked by heavy and accurate fire from 75mm guns, mortars, heavy mortars and heavy machine guns. They took cover looking across to the area where Clarke had stopped the car and walked about the French positions. Clarke had thought an opposed river crossing was going to be tough, and now it was. Pinned to the ground, they started to take casualties from very accurate sniping.[13]

An early casualty was Keyes's radio, which took a bullet – now he couldn't communicate with Pedder north of the river. The plan hadn't survived contact with the water, let alone the enemy.

McGonigal and commandos to the north closed on their beach. One craft hit a reef; the drill on grounding was to get out immediately, a stationary landing craft is a sitting duck, and commandos in full kit disappeared beneath the waves. But their training jumping off the jetty in Arran kicked in, and they formed a chain to make it ashore. With enemy fire cracking overhead, the rest of McGonigal's troop was dropped deep, and waded ashore in a heavy sea, over rocks, each wave breaking over their heads and shoulders. They covered the last 40 metres to shore under machine-gun fire, and advanced 150 metres inland to discard their lifebelts and haversacks as they had planned.[14]

Now they were off the beach they realised that not only were the French expecting them, they were also in the wrong place – they were *south* of their wadi and French positions facing over it, not north. They were in front of the French instead of behind them, and paying the price.

In between the two other landings, Fraser was with Pedder's group. Vichy French fire hit the water around the landing craft, and tracer snaked overhead. To enable a quick getaway coxswains hit reverse to stop the craft beaching, and any hope that Vichy French resistance would be token vanished.

To Fraser's left, 1 Troop disembarked and their troop leader raced up the beach and threw himself into cover behind a sand dune. The men behind were still scrambling out of the landing craft, rounds cracking overhead, while they dashed over the 20 metres of open beach. He was beside a dry stream bed and so started to walk along it, at the same time trying to untie the lifebelt attached to his rifle. Colonel Pedder was shouting to push on as quickly as possible.[15]

Over Fraser's head he could hear the crack of bullets, but they seemed fairly high. The Navy were keen to get off the beach, so keen that as soon as the firing started the landing craft made back to sea, which resulted in about 70 per cent of the men having to swim ashore.

Fraser waded ashore and sighted mortar fire exploded on the beach in front of him while tracer ripped overhead. The Commandos took casualties immediately. Fraser might have had pause to consider this was just the type of regular soldiering he, and Byrne, had been striving to avoid.

Into the dunes, he gathered his men in the scrub. He was separated from the rest of 8 Troop, who were some way off to his left with Pedder and 1 Troop. He found himself with Mayne and his troop, so followed them off the beach.

Ahead of Fraser, Mayne tried to cross the road, took casualties and became pinned down. Fraser took his section to the flank, to provide fire support and covered Mayne and his troop across the road, their rounds keeping French heads down, then headed inland after Mayne. In rough country, Fraser couldn't see the rest of 8 Troop, and his troop leader, but he didn't worry too much about losing contact with A Section and Troop HQ, because he expected that contact would be again made in the hills at their objective.

Fraser was not part of Mayne's troop or mission, and split from them to take his hill. With no orders, Fraser pushed eastward into the hills, gaining the crest with no opposition. This was *Auftragstaktik*, a doctrine that would later be called 'Mission Command'. He knew what Pedder wanted, and he was getting on with it with just half a troop.[16]

In heavy fighting, 11 Commando made their way inland. The Vichy French adopted a tactic of allowing them to advance then hitting them from the rear with snipers hidden in the rough Lebanese terrain.

Pedder's radio took a bullet and when the French started shelling them they had no means to call their own artillery. They didn't have their own mortars, but having just captured a 75mm artillery gun intact, the commandos improvised.

The gun was pointing away from the French battery, so they grabbed the tailpiece and heaved it round so it was pointing towards the nearest French gun. With their mixture of cap badges, the commandos had almost every military skill in their ranks – including artillery. The commandos shoved a shell in and fired. The result was amazing: there was one hell of an explosion and the French gun flew up in the air like a toy. They must have hit the ammo.

Quickly, they traversed onto the next French gun, sighted, and fired. There was a pause. Nothing happened. Commandos looked round the Lebanese hills. Where had the shell gone? Then there was a flash and a puff of smoke in the dome of a chapel about half a mile up the hillside. A thick Scottish voice said, 'That'll make the buggers pray!'[17] Lowering their elevation, they took out the two remaining French guns. And in case anyone was under an illusion there is chivalry in war, machine-gunned down the escaping crew with their Bren gun.

Commandos had a high number of officers because Clarke envisaged special forces would need dynamic leadership at the lowest level. Young officers have always been counted on to provide high-risk solutions in the British Army; Fraser's role, a section commander, would normally be an NCO: a sergeant or corporal. But in this struggle with the French, that risk-taking leadership started to pay a high price. Pedder's party, pinned down by snipers and surrounded, tried to fight back. Suddenly a section officer, 23-year-old Lieutenant Alistair Coode, said he had spotted the sniper and grabbed a rifle, but as he was taking aim he went down, shot in the chest. Then his sergeant was shot in the shoulder, from a different direction.[18]

Pedder decided to fall back – back down the gulley they'd come from, towards the sea. The HQ party: Pedder; the adjutant, Robin Farmiloe; and their regimental sergeant major, Tevendale, ran for the gulley. As they broke cover, sniper rounds cracked past them. Tevendale was about 20 metres to the right of Pedder when he heard him shout, 'Tevendale, Farmiloe, I'm shot.'[19]

Pedder span, and took the second bullet in the chest. By the time Tevendale reached him he was dead.[20]

A young lieutenant, Bryan, heard Farmiloe shout the CO was dead and they were pulling back. He shouted for his men to make for some scrub about a hundred metres away and started to crawl for it himself. All the time bullets were cracking past much too close for comfort and he kept very low. Bryan's sergeant had been wounded and decided to stand up and run to catch them, but a machine gun caught him and he fell, his face covered with blood.[21]

As his sergeant died, Bryan felt a tremendous bang on the head and knew he'd been hit. However, when he opened his eyes he saw that it was in his legs. He decided not to die and dragged himself into a bit of a dip, but every time he moved, the French opened up on him. He could hear one of his NCOs yelling to keep down or he would be killed. He kept down. When the French overran them, he was captured. And his leg was amputated by guillotine in the French Military Hospital, Beirut.[22]

RSM Tevendale then got word that Farmiloe, who had assumed command after Pedder's death, had been hit. Tevendale ran to him. Farmiloe had been shot in the head, his temple smashed in, and died instantly. Tevendale was the last man standing; 11 Commando's HQ had been wiped out. Yet, when they got to the bottom of the gully, back at the beach, they regrouped to try again.

To the south, the sun rose higher and to the growing chorus of cicadas, Fraser and his men pressed inland in the heat. They had made it over the first crest when the French opened up on them. Fraser hit the dirt and assessed the opposition. The French cavalry had dismounted and, lacking heavy weapons, had taken up positions in the trees ahead.

The operation had become a series of disconnected little battles, whose success depended on their leader. Fraser led his section into the trees, hurling grenades, shooting it out with the cavalry, and quickly overcame them. The French were no match for Fraser and his determined band of Scots. They paused to check their ammunition. Fraser was concerned: they didn't have enough for this prolonged battle. They had cleared the French north of the river, and now needed to link up with the Australians.

Fraser turned south along the ridge towards the Litani. His team marched quickly, met no more resistance, and reached a crest from where they looked down on the river. There was gunfire in the distance, but they couldn't know it was Keyes and his men trying to cross the river. Then they took some incoming fire from the south side of the river; worse, the Australians started shelling them, thinking they were French.

With no means to communicate with the Aussies, Fraser had to avoid a blue-on-blue, and withdrew his section behind the hill. When they dropped down into cover they found they weren't alone. Another unit, Lieutenant Richards and a section from 4 Troop, had found themselves similarly out of touch and were unsure what to do. Fraser decided they should work together and form an ad hoc troop to carry on with the mission. His men in cover, Fraser climbed back up to carry out a recce. He saw that heavy fire was being directed on the bridge area, which Keyes was trying to cross, from the hill to his right. He clambered back down and issued his orders for the ad hoc team made up of his men and Richards's section of 4 Troop, to attack the French from the rear.

Fraser's section worked its way along the forward slope, facing the river, near the area where Clarke had seen the French digging in, dealing in turn with three machine-gun posts. The French infantry were in strength in the woods on the ridge, and in tough fighting Fraser and his team shot it out, killed and wounded many, and took prisoners. Fraser, without orders, but with *Auftragstaktik*, was cutting a swathe through the French defence. By the end of the assault he had captured in excess of sixty prisoners, and removed any opposition to the Australian advance.

But leading from the front is risky. Fraser was ducking and weaving in the scrub and rocky terrain, working his way along the ridge towards the bridge, when he felt a smack in the head. Next thing he knew he was on the ground. The round, most probably a ricochet, had struck his helmet chinstrap, another example of 'Fraser luck'. Dazed, suffering from concussion and 'a graze to the head', he handed over the section to Sergeant Cheyne.

He'd left instruction that once they cleared the hill they should strike out north. The commandos of neighbouring Captain Moore's troop should have been to their north, between them and Pedder's party, and Fraser was puzzled about the lack of troops in that area.

It is telling that of the subsequent sketch maps produced by 11 Commando's officers, Fraser's is by far the most accurate. Understanding the battlefield, discerning where your troops are, and where the enemy are, is the third dimension of combat. Fraser shared this skill with Rommel, who also not only understood what was happening, but produced incredibly detailed sketches of his battles from memory.[23]

Meanwhile, Mayne, after taking the position across the road with Fraser's help, regrouped on the objective. From there he could see soldiers to his north, towards McGonigal and the northern team, firing towards Kafr Bridge, the road that McGonigal and the others should have secured to cut off French reinforcement. He crawled close enough to them to hear them speaking French, grouped his men before 'whaling' grenades into a gun pit, while his men took the position from the rear. The Vichy French surrendered.

Mayne sent a runner to find CO Pedder to tell him he'd cleared out the immediate area of the beach. He came back unable to find him. Like Fraser, Mayne climbed inland planning to turn south to the Litani. He surprised twenty French soldiers of a headquarters party and shot one of them dead. The rest immediately threw away their weapons and raised their hands.

They'd 'bagged' some food and beer, and after six hours of solid fighting, took a break. While they were dining, the phone rang and Mayne realised there were more Vichy French nearby. Mayne took the section's Bren gun, renowned for its accuracy, and laid out the rest of his men to a flank. Following the phone wire, he crept through the scrub and came up behind the Vichy French company. His accurate machine-gun fire coming from their rear caused the Vichy French to panic and surrender. Mayne captured 50 prisoners, mortars and machine guns – by anyone's reckoning it was an outstanding performance. [24]

Like Fraser, he arrived on the crest above the Litani, to be fired on by the Australians. By 11am 11 Commando had captured all its objectives in individual actions. But no one, including the Australians, knew this.

The French had time to regroup. And then they counterattacked.

At 5.30pm, Fraser's men linked up with the commandos around Kafr Bridge. Fraser was still in pain and concussed. His men found the reason Captain Moore hadn't linked up with them: he had spent the day trying to hold his position together, with no comms, and having one captured motorbike shot out from under him trying to rally the troops.

He and his men had spent most of that afternoon shooting it out with French armoured cars. Armed with 35mm cannon, and a coaxially mounted machine gun, the vehicles outgunned anything the Allies had. The French had moved up machine guns and mortars, and a French reconnaissance aircraft had flown overhead. Two French Navy destroyers fired at them – their six-inch shells sounded like trucks flying overhead. They missed, but the ships sailed on to inflict casualties on the Australians, in their densely packed jumping-off points south of the river.

One by one, the French identified commandos' positions and pounded them with 75mm artillery and mortars. The commandos, pinned down by machine-gun fire, were unable to respond. With French artillery finding their range, 35mm cannon fire hitting the rocks around them, as the afternoon progressed the situation became increasingly desperate.

Sergeant Cheyne spread Fraser's men in a thin line in the rock and scrub in time to see six more armoured cars attack from their right. McGonigal's 6 Troop, defending the right flank, had abandoned their position without warning, and the whole defensive position started to collapse.

With the perimeter collapsing they fell back towards the sea. At dusk they defended a ridge which they held until 7.45pm. By this time, the number of armoured cars had increased to 20, and pinned them down from the left, while enemy infantry was advancing on high ground to their immediate right and their machine guns still covered their front. The commandos were surrounded – with their backs to the sea.

At eight o'clock, thankfully, night fell, and all the troops were ordered to retreat to the Litani. The order: every unit, and man, for themselves.

Cheyne led Fraser and the section back on the route they had come. They knew it well enough, and knew they had cleared the French out of the area. Fraser's section made the river at 12.30am. At 3.30am, Cheyne and another sergeant, Nicol, swam the river with a line. The men helped Fraser across while B Section, 8 Troop held on to the line to cross the torrent to the home bank.

Mayne was already across on the home bank. He had never gone back to link up with the rest of the commandos, and had lost one man to another blue-on-blue with the Aussies. But with no knowledge of the terrain to the Litani, the other troops headed for the coast. They hit the beach and hid in a forest waiting for the moon to set. Once it was fully dark, at 12.30am, they headed south down the beach for the mouth of the Litani.

At 1am they reached the village of Aite Niye. This was the fortified outpost north of the river, and they crossed through barbed wire on the beach, past the village, and were spotted. Tracer fire ripped into them from a machine gun at point-blank range, cutting down yet another young officer, Lieutenant Parnacott. Trapped between the wire, sea and village, four men were killed in the firefight and three wounded. The situation was hopeless. When they had expended their last grenades, Captain Moore ordered they surrender.

Tait refused. Earlier that day he had single-handedly taken out a French scout car with his elephant gun; now he threw it away, stripped off his uniform, and dived into the sea. He swam south, in open water, round the mouth of the Litani, and onto the home bank.[25]

South of the river, Keyes had fought all day to try and reach them, crossing the river with his troops. He had established a toehold on the far bank and captured a French 25mm anti-tank gun. He used it to take out the redoubt covering the river crossing, which allowed the Australian company to cross in their wake. But the Aussies had orders not to move on till nightfall, so Keyes, in the absence of orders, decided to hold on where he was.

The rest of 11 Commando had disrupted the French defence to the Kafr Bridge a mile north. Fraser and Mayne were just on the other side of the ridge to his front. But, with the absence of communications, or any senior Allied commander on the spot, the attack froze.

That night the Australians moved on, but walked into the wire on the south side of the fortified village of Aite Niye, and in a heavy firefight fell back with one casualty. The remnants of 11 Commando filtered into Keyes's lines. In the morning Keyes followed the Australian advance as far Aite Niye. The French had surrendered to their prisoner, Captain Moore, and he was waiting for them. Keyes gathered Moore, McGonigal and their 16 remaining men, and ordered the whole Commando to withdraw.

The advancing Australians, passing the commandos gathered at their RV at the Australian Artillery south of the Litani, felt pity. The unit had made their job easier, but had obviously taken 'a real bashing'. The strain of battle was etched on their dehydrated, dust-caked faces.

Men from 11 Commando went to collect the dead and wounded's weapons and haversacks that had been dropped south of the river, but the Australians had removed most of them already. The next day, Keyes sent out a salvage party north of the Litani to scour the beaches where Fraser and the rest of the Commando had come ashore and dropped their packs, but they found only empty haversacks on the beaches. The commandos were unable to recover any of their Brens, Boys anti-tank rifles or Tommy guns either.[26]

The Bag of Wind

The troops of 11 Commando were sent straight back to defend Cyprus. The survivors marched back to their tents at ancient Salamis on 15 June. Five officers had been killed, including their CO; one wounded, and Lieutenant Bryan was a prisoner in Beirut Hospital having lost a leg. In total they suffered 128 casualties out of 500: a heavy cost. There was resentment that while the Germans had gone through the French 'like a knife through butter', when fighting the British the French had fought like tigers.[27]

Clarke had been in Jerusalem on the eve of the invasion, and, having just finished deceiving the Vichy French, received an urgent signal from Wavell, worried the Germans were about to drop on Cyprus. He wanted a deception plan, quickly, to delay the German attack by two weeks to allow 11 Commando to get back to the island along with reinforcements.

Clarke's solution was genius: he signalled Wavell the same day suggesting an outbreak of *plague* in Cyprus. Plague, caused by the bacteria *Yersinia pestis,* is transmitted by flea bites from rats and caused mass death in the Middle Ages. Although by the 1940s it was treatable with antibiotics, these weren't always available. A recent real outbreak in Haifa, on Jumbo Wilson's patch, was a case in point. Clarke thought it believable it had been transmitted to Cyprus, and medical officers he consulted thought that fears of plague might lead to German doctors insisting on inoculation of the invading force, which might postpone the invasion by one or two weeks.

Wavell approved it, and signals flashed on a compromised cipher about a plague outbreak. And, as Fraser landed back on the island, one of Clarke's operatives, Captain Ogilvie-Grant, of A-Force, flew in to coordinate plague and other deception measures on the ground.

Aside from 11 Commando, the island's defences were meagre. Clarke decided to pretend they had a complete British division with attached local troops, raising the total strength from around 3,500 to something like 20,000.[28] With memories of his first trip to Norway and his theatrical costumier on Wardour Street, he immediately promoted the island's commander, Brigadier Rodwell, to major general. Brigadiers command brigades; major generals, divisions. It was a simple deceit for the *Abwehr*, who liked to have everything in the right place, and for whom giving a man a rank for a formation he did not command was probably an anathema, though probably one that pleased Rodwell.

Rodwell's command became the fictional 7th Division, allegedly consisting of three infantry brigades, four squadrons of tanks and an 'SS Battalion' – British staff officers still struggled to call 11 Commando by their real name. Clarke had Rodwell draft a completely fake defence plan for Cyprus using his bogus units. The plan raised the estimate to thirty thousand troops defending Cyprus, with a map of where the units were. The plan was dropped on one of Clarke's Cairo double agents, who gave it to a German agent they knew was loose in Cairo. The plan worked – later they would find out that all of the intelligence was reproduced in a briefing issued from Rome.[29]

It was the next 'order of battle' deception plan that started with the SAS. In the eyes of the Axis, Clarke was rapidly increasing the size of Allied forces in the Mediterranean – which would, eventually, lead to one of the greatest deceptions of the war.

But no sooner had 11 Commando got back to garrisoning Cyprus than Mayne returned to being his own worst enemy. On 20 June, the new CO, Keyes, went to have dinner with the governor, and 11 Commando had an Officers' Mess night to blow off steam. Mayne got drunk and out of control. Since guests were present, he was asked to leave by Major Napier, the senior officer present. Napier had been left behind in the rear party, and not fought with the rest of the Commando, and Mayne may have resented this. Having said good night to their guests, Napier was making his way back to his tent through their unlit camp, when he was jumped by an unknown assailant and beaten up. In the morning, Keyes arrived back to uproar in the camp. Napier pointed the finger at Mayne; Keyes did his best to remain impartial and investigated, but there was no proof.[30]

The next day it transpired that the risk-averse Hitler, who had lost 3,600 out of 20,000 parachutists in Crete, had other reasons not to move on the island – from his lair, pumped on steroids by his personal physician, he had been busy planning his biggest mistake of the war.[31] ULTRA picked it up, Churchill signalled Stalin, and on 22 June 1941, to cheers from the Commando, the Germans invaded Russia. Britain was no longer alone.

On the 23 June, Laycock flew in to congratulate them on their mission, and by now Keyes felt sure enough Mayne was guilty to produce him before their commander. Laycock gave him a rocket and 'returned him to unit' – sacked him from 11 Commando. Mayne left the island for Genifa camp, a Special Service holding pen for the those who had been removed due to injury or bad behaviour, where he came down with a bout of malaria and was hospitalised.[32]

Laycock spoke to the unit about its future: 7 Commando had been destroyed, 8 Commando was generally in disgrace; 11 had fought their Trojan War, and some had returned, but all the Commandos were to be disbanded. Laycock flew out, and, while Fraser and his men were drafted in to help unload vessels in the docks due to the shortage in personnel, Keyes did the rounds to find out what everyone wanted to do.[33]

He got quite a response for the 'Burma show' – an initiative to form guerrilla units in the Far East to counter Japanese expansion. Of the men, 80 wanted to remain with Special Service; 33 to join Burmese guerrillas; 90 wanted out of the Army, to join the Navy or RAF; 10 wanted to become officers; 20 to go home; leaving 100 wanting to join other units.

But the breakdown among the officers was very different. The majority wanted to stay in Special Service, and the next largest number wanted to join the new parachute unit they heard was forming. Fraser said he wanted to join the parachutists, if possible. His troop leader, Glennie, and Mayne's friend McGonigal also volunteered. In the ranks only 10 of the men volunteered; however all of Fraser's, Gordon's team, decided to follow their boss. Including Byrne, Du Vivier, and Tait.[34]

7

The Game: 1941

Operation Battleaxe

The creation of a new parachute unit, the real SAS, occurred because Clarke had a problem deceiving Rommel. Rommel's success was incomprehensible to Churchill: Wavell's forces outnumbered Rommel's close to ten to one. Rommel was supposed to defend Libya, instead he had reached the Egyptian border. But German Chief of the General Staff Halder said that by overstepping his orders Rommel had brought about a supply situation the Axis couldn't cope with. Halder dispatched Rommel's friend General Paulus to rein him in: 'he is perhaps the only man with enough personal influence to head off this soldier who has gone stark mad'.[1]

Churchill, reading this in ULTRA, telegraphed Wavell informing him the Germans were exhausted, and in fearful difficulties: 'a victory in the Western Desert to destroy Rommel's Army . . . would at least save our situation in Egypt from wreck'.[2]

Clarke had got back from his covert recce of Lebanon on 21 May, to be told that in addition to deceiving the French, Wavell urgently needed him to do something to deceive Rommel. Wavell had no faith in the attack, called OPERATION BATTLEAXE. He told Dill in Whitehall: 'I think it right to inform you that the measure of success which will attend this operation is in my opinion doubtful.'[3][4]

Churchill had sent him 300 tanks that had broken down because their cooling system did not work in the desert. And even if they ran, they would be outgunned by panzers. The RAF couldn't get him any recce pictures due to a shortage of cameras. And his own recce scout cars were shot to pieces by superior German ones, meaning his force would go blind into the enemy.

But Wavell had tied Clarke's hands. The attack on Rommel would start on 15 June, but Clarke was not even allowed to run a deception until British forces crossed into Lebanon on 8 June, in order not to jeopardise that invasion. That would give any plan he came up with just six days to deceive Rommel.

Clarke came up with the only plan he could think of – the story that the British were moving tanks forward to protect their forward supply dumps in Egypt, while their main forces were advancing in Syria-Lebanon. This was approved by Wavell on 6 June. It was a very long shot that Rommel would buy this as anything other than what it was: the buildup to a British offensive. Clarke knew it was a weak plan, which had to reach the enemy within six days of its start, so he held out no great hope for its success.[5]

And, thanks to the compromised US code of attaché Bonner Fellers, Rommel's 'Good Source', he was right. Rommel said that 'at the beginning of June there were many signs that a major British attack on our Tobruk front was to be expected.'[6]

Although he wasn't allowed to launch a new deception plan, Clarke still had a working plan in his pocket – his PLAN ANTI-ROMMEL – the idea the British would launch raids on Rommel's lines of communication. He fell back on PLAN ANTI-ROMMEL, which produced a startling and surprising result.

One pillar for Clarke's PLAN ANTI-ROMMEL was the Free French troops in Kufra preparing for long-range raids on Rommel's Libyan lines of communication. But having taken Kufra Oasis it was impossible for Leclerc to supply his garrison out of Chad via the Tibesti mountains and across 400 miles of desert. Starving, he abandoned the oasis, leaving a garrison of 250 Chadian troops with no transport, living on captured Italian rations. There was no chance they could mount long-range raids; as Bagnold put it – the whole oasis group consequently became a liability.[7]

Rescue was mounted by Bagnold and the LRDG, the only troops capable of operating in that arena, speeding 750 miles from Cairo with supplies. To mount raids, they needed both fuel and an air bridge to Cairo. Guy Prendergast, the missing member of the Zerzura Club, was finally released by the Army and became Bagnold's second in command. In Cairo he approached the RAF to help establish an airbridge, who refused. He bought two WACO biplanes[8] from a Cairo pasha, painted them with roundels to prevent the RAF shooting them down, and set out for Kufra, flying low, below Luftwaffe fighters.

The WACO had a range of only three hundred miles so he had to set out a series of aviation gas drops for the WACOs to cover the 750 miles. It was hair raising – dodging the Luftwaffe and ghibli wind ripping through the desert, both of which could be lethal. Reunited with Bagnold, they found one of their New Zealand soldiers could also fly and also recruited a French pilot from Leclerc's departing garrison, establishing a private air force and air bridge to Bagnold's kingdom. The RAF refused to service their aircraft, but the Egyptian mechanics at the Cairo airport kept them in excellent condition.

The real problem at Kufra was fuel. With the supply lines so long, and GHQ unwilling to spare a tanker, they were able to do little more than protect themselves. The operation did expand. With the high-frequency aerials over Kufra they pushed patrols north to protect the oasis and set up a permanent observation post on Rommel's line of communication called 'Road Watch'. This observation post supplied details of all the traffic travelling to and from Rommel's front line to Tripoli. From this moment, GHQ Cairo got a daily, minute-by-minute breakdown of eastbound and westbound traffic on the coast road, the sort of human intelligence that only the LRDG special force could produce. And they set new records – no westerner had travelled into the deep desert in spring and summer. Temperatures hit 50°C in the shade and patrols were constantly blasted by ghiblis.

Bagnold was exhausted. He was 45 and suspected his adrenal gland had been overtaxed. It was likely a recurrence of malaria or dengue, the diseases that had caused him to leave the Army in the 1930s. With Prendergast in place, Bagnold flew out of his kingdom for the last time in a WACO, passing over his desert, the Sand Sea, and all he had discovered. He entered Grey Pillars for a well-earned desk job.

The LRDG were doing their best, but Rommel did not regard them as a threat – yet.

Through May and June, Clarke leant heavily into his SAS 'story' to support his plan anti-Rommel: that the SAS Brigade had moved to Egypt in May. He hid the 2,000-strong fictional force carefully, at a place called Kantara. Kantara had been a busy railway crossing of the Suez Canal during the First World War but had long since had a population in single figures. Clarke based the SAS in a place where nothing ever happens, with acres of empty warehouses, where strangers stick out. With the airborne SAS in Kantara, they could either drop behind Rommel's lines in Egypt or fly into Cyprus at short notice.

And they had been parachuting. De Guingand had found Clarke some parachutes for his dummies to drop on 6 June.[9] The Egyptian police in Cairo were warned to look out for parachutists on the very visible route to Helwan airfield. And did indeed see them jump from planes. The dummies were swept up by K Detachment, SAS, and no one was any the wiser.

It worked: intelligence picked up from one of their sources on Sharia Qasr-el-Nil – 'the street of spies', a few blocks from Clarke's office – on 9 June a British soldier visiting a local electrician's shop had been heard to say that if people saw parachutists coming down over Cairo, they should not be alarmed or shoot them down, because they would be British. Kenyon Jones told them that this information might interest Clarke. It did: he scribbled back, 'would you tack this down a bit'. He wasn't just deceiving the Germans – even British soldiers thought they had a parachute force. Now, Wavell was muttering about wanting to set up a parachute unit – the confluence of Clarke's fiction and Fraser's reality was moving closer.

Then he met some people who really wanted to jump out of planes.

The Game

It was inevitable that, at Shepheard's, Clarke would meet 8 Commando Officer David Stirling. But what happened next couldn't be foreseen.

Bob Laycock had kept his Blue Blood friends out of Wavell's fires and in role – hoping to strike behind Rommel's lines. He had written to General Arthur Smith in Grey Pillars, 'unless we are actively employed soon I anticipate a serious falling off in morale'. Laycock had offered Bagnold to convert two Commandos into four LRDG squadrons, which would definitely up the ante in raiding behind Rommel's lines. [10, 11]

The meeting to discuss this at 10am on 22 May in Grey Pillars, the day after Clarke flew in from Jerusalem was almost certainly attended by Clarke. While Laycock could see himself as a future desert raider, and Clarke might have concurred, even encouraged him, across the table sat Ralph Bagnold – remote, austere and something of a mystic. The divide between him and aristocratic Bob Laycock seemed unassailable; they might as well have been from different planets. Bagnold turned him down flat, stating his strong preference for the formation of new groups exclusively from armoured fighting vehicle units and motorised units, especially New Zealanders. [12]

Laycock moved 8 Commando closer to the front, at Mersa Matruh, and aimed several raids at Gazala, a couple of airfields near a small inlet west of Tobruk where Rommel could bring in limited supplies. But an attempt to hit this aboard HMS *Aphis* had only resulted in a running battle between the Luftwaffe and commandos from which anyone was lucky to emerge alive. The next attempt to strike out from besieged Tobruk in Clarke's Eureka boats also failed, because their captain kept getting lost. And Randolph Churchill's attempt to allow the RAF to parachute him and a team in got nowhere. [13]

The only success Laycock had was persuading the Australian General Morshead to use them in Tobruk alongside his troops. But Morshead said he would require them to have ordinary infantry company equipment – Morshead wanted heavily armed men in his trenches, not daggers and Tommy guns.[14]

The result was that Stirling and the other Blue Bloods spent more and more time in Cairo, and trouble was bound to happen. Stirling punched a cab driver, who he thought had ripped him off. Another troop leader shot a pigeon on his windowsill at Shepheard's that was annoying him; the bullet went into the building opposite. The adjutant of 8 Commando used the Egyptian Railway Telegraph, rather than British cipher, as the fastest means to communicate with his troops partying in Cairo, meaning the Egyptians gave the information to the Germans. Shepheard's also had a message board in the foyer, meaning at a glance a spy could tell who was in town.[15]

Grey Pillars had reached the point where it simply wanted shot of this problem.

Stirling could see the writing was on the wall, and he would be compelled to return to regular soldiering, for which he was patently unsuitable. He became very keen to make the acquaintance of Dudley Clarke.[16]

No one knows who introduced Stirling to Clarke. What is clear is that Stirling sought Clarke out. Clarke would subsequently scrawl 'Stirling' in his Letts appointments diary. But, for reasons that shall become apparent, his 1941 diary vanished. While temperatures soared, the kites circled overhead, and jacaranda trees wept purple petals into the street, Stirling must have appeared as an unlikely blessing for Clarke in the shade of rugs flapping in the *khamaseen* on Shepheard's terrace.[17, 18]

Clarke had been putting out fires all over Wavell's empire, but the BATTLEAXE operation was going to be exactly what it was: a double-handed blunt swing at a man who would certainly dodge it. Clarke wasn't even able to deceive Rommel when the blow would fall.

Clarke was a careful man, but his currency was people, and knowing who to trust was his job. Everyone underestimated the 25-year-old David Stirling. Fellow troop leaders had nicknamed him the Giant Sloth and his cabin mate, Carol Mather, had been concerned about his health on the ship out. Stirling talked quietly. He had been unable to speak until age four, at which point surgery had removed a tongue restriction. He spoke very precisely, but quietly, and Clarke had to lean in to hear him.

Stirling knew about the 11 SAS raid carried out on a railway bridge in southern Italy – it was an aqueduct, but Clarke could let that pass. And Stirling thought that parachuting was the logical way to get behind Rommel's lines. Stirling told Clarke he was confident he could argue the case for a parachute unit to a general. While Stirling appeared confident and persuasive, Clarke had done his homework: Stirling's reputation preceded him, and Clarke wasn't going to put him in front of Wavell straight away. What Clarke needed to know was could Stirling get this thing to fly? But he told Stirling that Wavell was already thinking about creating a parachute force, and, more to the point, Clarke could see the potential of a real parachute unit to threaten Rommel.

Stirling hadn't told many people about his idea because if it was intercepted at a lower level, it would be sent upstairs with a very negative opinion attached. He was right. But Stirling was talking to the man who could get anything done in GHQ. Someone who knew more about Special Force operations than anyone else in the British Army.

Clarke wanted real men jumping from real aircraft. He was less interested in what they actually did. But, as Stirling said, Clarke had a great influence on him. [19]

Brigade Major Neil Ritchie never forgot David Stirling walking into his office in Grey Pillars. Ritchie, who had watched 11 SAS drop on Salisbury Plain with the Auk, had just joined GHQ and was about to take over as Deputy Director of Operations.

His office was in the same corridor as another new man: Air Vice

Marshal Tedder, who had rejected Clarke's helicopters. Tedder was second choice for Commander of the RAF in Cairo, the original RAF commander's aircraft had got lost and run out of fuel over Sicily; he was currently a prisoner of war. Ritchie was already finding his new counterpart trying. He was a consummate staff officer, and, like all good staff officers, kept a record of his activity, knowing he was not irreplaceable. Something Tedder's enormous ego seemed to preclude.[20]

Ritchie was very busy at his desk when the door opened, and in came this chap he had never seen before. The man was dressed in the regimental kit of the Scots Guards. When asked who he was, he told Ritchie:

'My name is David Stirling. And I came out here with the Commandos and they've been disbanded and I think that I could start a parachute organisation out here which could be very useful in doing things.'

Ritchie asked him what he knew about parachuting.

'Nothing.'

Had he ever jumped out of an aeroplane? No. But he'd soon learn.

Wavell had that morning discussed the parachute unit with both Arthur Tedder and Ritchie. Which Stirling knew, because Clarke knew. Ritchie took him down to see Arthur Tedder before it dawned on him to ask how Stirling had got into the building.

'I got the sentry to look in the other direction and I got past him and got in here.'

It struck Ritchie that this was the sort of chap who might be quite useful. He decided he would look after him and his interest in a parachute unit. Stirling had a sponsor, and the SAS was about to take wing.[21]

Parachuting

Clarke had another parachute request, from Bob Laycock. Jock Lewes, fittest man off the boat, had reached the same conclusion as Stirling, and also decided to go by air. Lewes went to see Bob Laycock, back from Crete, who had been discussing the future role for Layforce. Clarke was only too happy to help Niven's uncle, Bob Laycock get his force airborne; and Lewes got permission to conduct informal parachute experiments in early June. OPERATION BATTLEAXE was on 15 June, and neither Lewes nor Laycock might have attached the significance to the date of the first parachute drop in the Middle East that Clarke did.[22]

Lewes took his small party and reported to Fuka airfield where K Detachment, SAS, showed them what they had been doing for Clarke. Fuka was the site Kenyon Jones had recce-ed for dummy gliders for 1 SAS Brigade, which had subsequently been converted to bombers, the *Neccanos,* for PLAN ANTI-ROMMEL. On the night of 12th June, their efforts were rewarded when the Luftwaffe hit the airfield with 60 bombs, to K Detachment's delight, while very real anti-aircraft gunners shot down one attacker for their trouble.[23]

Lewes arrived with Guardsmen Davies, Evans, and D'Arcy, and discussed the details of the jump with an RAF officer, who was most helpful although none of them had jumped before.[24] By now K Detachment had done three dummy SAS drops on Helwan Airfield in Cairo.[25] The RAF officer showed them the chutes that they had been using. But, when Lewes and his men inspected the log books, they saw the last periodical examination had been omitted. Checking the chutes had been less important for their dummy packages, but Lewes decided they were (probably) OK.[26] They settled in for the night, planning to drop the following day.

In the morning, as Lewes and his men got their kit ready, David Stirling and Sergeant Storie showed up from Mersa Matruh. Stirling told Lewes he was doing a job in Syria and had been cleared to jump. And Lewes got annoyed. What job in Syria? Lewes had been working on this for a while, and Stirling was interfering. Somehow he had got in on it at the last moment.[27]

It is not hard to fathom that Clarke tipped Stirling off. Clarke was giving enthusiastic support to any Commando who wanted to jump out of an aeroplane.

The method for deploying dummies and real parachutists was the same in the RAF's view. In an ageing *Vickers Valencia* biplane, belonging to 216 Squadron, the RAF flew up to demonstrate to Lewes, Stirling and the men, how they had been faking drops for Clarke. 216 Squadron were a transport squadron operating these old Valencia biplanes, known as *string bags*, and they threw out a dummy made from sandbags and tent poles. The parachute opened OK, but when they landed they found the tent poles smashed.

Then they tried jumping off the top wing of the Valencia, a height of about 3 metres off the ground, then a little parachute control.[28] There were no parachute instructors in the Middle East, and no one knew what they were doing. The RAF gave them the terrible advice to dive out as though they were going into water. The chute deploys when the *static line*, hooked up to the inside of the fuselage, is pulled taut by the exiting parachutist falling in the slipstream. This static line is attached to the chute folded carefully in the parachutist's pack, which it pulls out, and, once taut, a weak cord tied to the top of the chute snaps. The parachutist falls free and the chute fills, and the parachutist descends to earth with a canopy billowing above him.

The correct exit is to propel from the door, feet first and together, and cross your arms across the chest. Which allows the chute to deploy in the manner described. But, with slipstream ripping past at 70 mph, if the parachutist's arms or legs stick out, he spins. Which can result in any of the disasters experienced at Ringway. The parachute catching part of the aircraft, *somersaulting,* or producing a *candle*, where the spinning twists the parachute lines tight, like a candle, preventing the chute opening properly. Without this knowledge, they flew inland in their Valencia *string bag,* which was also doing a mail run.

The setting sun threw shadows into the Qattara Depression to their left: the huge feature, over one mile deep, strewn with broken rock and salt marsh runs from the coast at El Alamein all the way inland to Siwa Oasis. It was getting dark, when their mail run biplane reached the Siwa desert, where they touched down.[29]

If the date of the drop didn't show Clarke's hand, the location does. The men didn't know where they were. It was odd they had not just circled up over Fuka, and dropped into the nearby desert, normal practice for parachute training. Instead, they had flown for over an hour, south and inland. There is not much in the desert an hour inland from Fuka until Siwa Oasis. The forward operating base of Britain's other special force, the LRDG. It was from here Prendergast controlled LRDG patrols ranging out hundreds of miles behind Rommel, from high-frequency antenna among the Berber huts.

Siwa was the original location of Clarke's SAS deception. He had wanted to simulate the presence of SAS gliders on Siwa aerodrome, but had crossed out ~~Siwa~~, and put aerodromes, plural, any one might do. Reading the intelligence from the captured Italian diary in December 1940, he had thought Siwa the logical place to fake a parachute unit. An oasis on the edge of the desert, a desert Clarke had flown over and knew as a giant airfield, from where an airborne force could range for hundreds of miles into the enemy's rear.

Retro-causality, or a plan – here were special forces, airborne, dropping on the site of his original location for the SAS. Jock Lewes and David Stirling touched down on the remote desert landing field at dusk, just before Wavell's tanks rolled on Rommel. Hard to believe this wasn't Clarke's doing.

The parachute team, unaware they were part of anything other than a parachute experiment, hooked their static lines to the inside of the aircraft, and circled up over the desert airfield. They jumped in pairs: Lewes first in the door, and at the signal from the RAF dispatcher, he dived out, followed by Davies. The RAF dispatcher watched them fall clear, the aircraft circled back over the airfield and, on the next pass, D'Arcy threw himself out, followed by Stirling.

D'Arcy went clear, but the terrible parachuting advice meant the six foot seven Stirling had no chance of making a good exit. The slipstream caught him, ripping him down the side of the fuselage. The static line pulled taut, broke, but instead of falling free his parachute caught on the tail. Next thing he knew he was spinning, dragged behind the aircraft. He had no way of looking up, his head being pushed down, then he broke clear and fell.

D'Arcy was surprised when Stirling fell past him. Stirling's chute had been torn. The calculation was simple. Stirling's parachute had a hole, so provided less drag, so he overtook D'Arcy. He would hit the desert faster, and therefore harder.

On the drop zone, Lewes had made a perfect landing, Davies had come in hard and a little shaken, but Stirling cratered into the ground. The team ran over to him. He couldn't see, and was in pain from a spinal injury. D'Arcy landed shaken, and had a few scratches, and behind him Storie landed OK.

Guardsman Evans was spared the ordeal. The pilot decided it had got too dark to parachute, and landed. It took Stirling an hour to recover his sight, he could also walk, but there was no way he could parachute.

The injury did not improve Stirling's standing with Lewes, who waved him goodbye, on his way back to Cairo. The others slept on the airfield, and jumped again the following day. This time pushing out a container and the four jumping after it. The previous drop they had worn their short-sleeve shirts and shorts, but now, covered in cuts and bruises, they decided to put on pullovers. They didn't have any helmets.

This time Lewes was injured. It is very hard to steer a static-line chute, even if trained. It has four web straps from which the lines attach to the round canopy overhead. By pulling hard on the straps on one side you can spin the chute, and steer a little. But, in the process, air is spilt from the canopy, and you fall faster. Trying to avoid some oil barrels on the airfield, Lewes went in hard. Now Lewes also had a spinal injury and Evans similarly damaged his ankle. These men were on trial and error, not instruction.

According to the report on the experiment the intended operation was eventually cancelled, chiefly because the parties were too badly shaken. They underestimated the tenacity of both Lewes and Stirling. And Clarke's desire to create a real parachute force.[30]

The day British tanks rolled on Rommel, Stirling checked himself into hospital in Cairo with a back injury. The 15 June attack in Halfaya 'Hellfire' Pass broke down and Rommel was waiting. The tanks ran into a battery of four 88mm guns. At one point in the chaos, General Noel Beresford-Peirse – whom Dorman-Smith had nicknamed 'no Napoleon' – ordered Gatehouse to 'rally forward'.

Gatehouse stared at his radio. Then asked him to repeat the order.

He assumed Beresford-Peirse, who was not a tank man, had screwed up and was just using the wrong language, and had meant 'forward rally' – which is the opposite, and correct command, which means put your tanks out of harm's way behind the infantry and guns.

Beresford-Peirse screamed down the radio, 'You have your orders, Gatehouse – carry them out!'[31]

Gatehouse lost 99 out of his 104 tanks.

Rommel, having dodged the blow, counterattacked. He cut into Creagh's 7th Armoured Division, taking them completely by surprise. And was overjoyed when he intercepted a message from Creagh asking Wavell to urgently get up to the desert. The chief flew up, but the battle was lost.

Rommel had become superhuman; like a comic book character, the British named him the 'Desert Fox' – he seemed to use a reality distortion field to drive his tiny army to achieve the impossible. Churchill needed a scapegoat, so Wavell was fired.[32] Instead, Churchill put his trust in the Auk – whose swift reaction in Iraq had impressed the prime minister – surely here was a man he could do business with, a man who could beat Rommel. Auchinleck was told to proceed forthwith to Cairo and relieve General Wavell.[33]

To Clarke's surprise Rommel didn't immediately move on Suez.

Rommel's moves were dictated by the fuel gauge on his panzers, not tactics.[34] Desperately short on fuel, Rommel was on the end of a long supply chain, over a sea owned by the Royal Navy, through an unenthusiastic ally, Italy. And his boss was more interested in Russia. Rommel's predicament had started to reassemble Kléber's, the General, Napoleon left behind in Africa.

Real parachuting injuries were a boon to Clarke. He told Maunsell, his friend and the head of Middle East intelligence, to leak that a British parachutist was in Agusa Hospital, Cairo, recovering from a broken ankle, which he got on the 11 June, practicing jumps at Helwan. The injured parachutist said the new parachutes specially produced for the east were not very satisfactory, and one man in his battalion was killed the same week he broke his ankle.

Clarke himself set off to talk to his real parachute casualty – who was in Heliopolis Hospital, not Agusa. Clarke kept some things secret. Stirling had deceived Evelyn Waugh into thinking he'd broken his back, then gave it away by wiggling his toes. Countess Ranfurly (wife of O'Connor's recently captured aide de camp) and Bill Stirling went to see him. Bill Stirling had arrived in Cairo looking for work, and Ranfurly may well have been David Stirling's introduction to Clarke, who was one of her favourite people. She had recently been spending every night at the Stirlings' flat. Working as secretary at the SOE office Cairo she had discovered their rampant corruption and lack of security, and at Arthur Smith's request she removed documents at night and typed copies at the Stirlings' for Bill Stirling to give to Smith the next day. Then she had to rush them back, to what Cairo cab drivers called the 'secret office', in the SOE flat on Gezira island in the morning before anyone noticed. She asked David Stirling what he would do when he was better, and he told her that he belonged to Bob Laycock's Commandos but they were being disbanded shortly. Stirling, in his quiet voice, told her that when he was recovered, he had a scheme to put to HQ.[35]

Crichton-Stuart, veteran LRDG officer and friend of Stirling, visited.[36] He had been a regular visitor to Stirling's tent behind the front at Mersa Matruh, on his way behind Rommel's lines. He listened to Stirling talk about his idea, and offered to introduce him to the new LRDG Commander, Prendergast.

But Stirling's most frequent visitor was Clarke. If Stirling had wanted to prove to Clarke he was serious, then cratering the Siwa desert had done it. Clarke and Stirling started work on the pitch for the real SAS. They called it L Detachment, because L comes after Kenyon Jones's K Detachment, Clarke's deception outfit based in Qasr-el-Nil barracks.

Clarke needed Stirling to physically create this new force. Stirling knew he would have to recruit the best of the Commando officers and of those he knew best, the top two were his cabin mate, Carol Mather, and fittest man off the boat, Jock Lewes. Both were men who were prepared to do anything to get into the action.

When Lewes arrived at his bedside, he pitched him the idea.

Stirling knew Lewes wouldn't want to get involved if it was going to be a short-term flight of fancy. Stirling thought Lewes was a serious sort of chap and Stirling supposed he'd come across to him in the past as a bit of a good time Charlie. Lewes quizzed him on the details of the plan. Then turned him down flat. To get into the action he had signed up for Laycock's other initiative, and was on his way to join the Aussies in Tobruk. But he had asked Stirling a load of questions for which Stirling didn't have answers. Stirling was not a details man, and realised anyone in GHQ would be going to ask him the same questions. He realised he needed to refine his pitch if was going to succeed.[37]

Back on his feet, Stirling headed to Shepheard's to accost Mather. This was another tough audience. But with the Commandos being disbanded, Mather was wondering what to do. Stirling pitched him in the lobby, both of them lying on chaises longues below the stone pillars reaching to the frieze of Egyptian Eagles, which spanned the vaulted ceiling. Mather was too jaundiced to accept, even though he felt he was ratting on his closest companion of the last 12 months. He really could not give the idea credence, and knew Stirling too well to think it would work. Another fiasco was the last thing that he could take. Like most officers from 8 Commando, he turned it down.[38] Stirling had a credibility problem.

But while recruiting was going badly, Clarke helped Stirling develop his pitch. Stirling realised Clarke was an influential chap, and Clarke promised to give him all the help he could – provided they use the name the Special Air Service, the SAS. Stirling agreed.[39] Clarke filed Stirling's pitch, 'Case for the retention of a limited number of Special Service troops, for employment as parachutist', in his secret PLAN ABEAM file.

The introduction of this pitch was the cornerstone of PLAN ANTI-ROMMEL: an organisation for raiding the lines of communication, aerodromes, oil dumps or any other enemy dispositions. Now the Commandos were disbanded, to continue ANTI-ROMMEL Clarke needed a unit that could at least give the appearance of providing this threat. Stirling and Clarke added that the parachutists could be evacuated from their targets by submarine – the original concept for Clarke's cross-channel parachutists.

While this was largely a cut and paste, the argument that followed wasn't. The document highlighted the inability of Commandos to operate in the Mediterranean due to inadequate RAF fighter protection. And that although things went wrong for German parachutists in Crete, small units, like Clarke and Stirling were proposing, had worked for the Germans in Greece.

Group Captain Guest, RAF, was of the opinion that the project was sound. Clarke had been working closely with Wing Commander Rees on K Detachment drops for the SAS in Helwan, and Guest was Rees's boss.

The plan then broke down into two phases. First, a small training centre would be established which would be both instructional and operational. Second, this would be expanded to a parachute unit that might night drop 15 to 20 parties at the same time. This was an expansion into something approaching Clarke's 1 SAS Battalion. The pitch stressed men should be available from 8 Commando, and already trained for their special forces role, apart from the parachuting. This took the burden of resourcing the plan off GHQ. The unit would go after enemy aircraft, tanks and armoured cars. Just as Clarke's fictional 1 SAS had been 'trained' to do.

To seal the deal, this proposed force was economical in manpower and required no additional troops, and gained the maximum effect from surprise. Parachuting added speed. Some aggression could be added later.

It was an excellent piece of staff work. The pitch offered to use redundant troops and obsolete aircraft to reinforce the existing SAS Brigade fiction. It would be difficult for a hard-pressed general to turn down.

On 17 July, the Auk summoned Clarke to Grey Pillars. Clarke took his car from Shepheard's to the Qasr-el-Dubara, not knowing what to expect. He had never worked for the Auk, and when he walked in, the tall, freckled, rugged-looking soldier could not have been further from the scholarly Wavell.

Clarke immediately discovered the Auk was far more worried by the situation on the Middle East's northern front – the borders of Syria and Iraq – than by Rommel and the Western Desert. The Russian Army had collapsed, the Germans now held the whole Black Sea coast of Bulgaria and Romania, and their lead panzer units were across the Dnister towards Odessa in south Ukraine. From Churchill's perspective in Whitehall, it might look like Rommel was the wolf closest to the sled, but from the Auk's perspective in Cairo, the huge German army rumbling through Ukraine, threatening Turkey and the Syrian border looked more dangerous.[40]

He needed Clarke to come up with something fictional, and armoured, to send north to stop panzers carrying out a pincer movement from Russia in the north, to meet Rommel's panzers coming from the west. Clarke's fake army would get bigger, and Kenyon Jones busier.

Then they turned to Rommel.

The Auk knew he would have to attack Rommel. Churchill had already told him to, but the Auk wanted Clarke to buy him some breathing space by keeping Rommel on the defensive. Particularly since fresh troops were due to arrive via the 12,000-mile route Fraser had taken. Clarke explained PLAN ANTI-ROMMEL, the threat to his lines of communication, and an attack on his base in Tripoli, originally designed back in April. This consisted both of the seaborne threat of landing commandos behind his lines, and the existence the SAS Brigade with their ability to drop anywhere in his rear. The Auk agreed to continue the artificial threat.[41]

With the Auk signed up to PLAN ANTI-ROMMEL, and the continuation of the SAS threat, the Auk told Clarke he thought that Rommel would not be in any mood to mount a serious attack for some time. They decided the best way to upset his plans in the coming weeks would be to force him into urgent and premature defensive preparation for a supposed British offensive in August. It was now July – so they set the date of the first fake offensive as 9 August, three weeks away. Then they planned to issue a plausible reason for why it was cancelled at the last minute. By repeatedly crying wolf, by the time they really attacked in the autumn, they might have lulled him into a sense of false security.[42]

The SAS would be very useful. Clarke needed to keep Rommel on his toes for three months with repeated scares. He may or may not have mentioned Stirling's initiative, but he clearly pre-framed what was to come.

That lunchtime, Dorman-Smith's Ford, covered with dust from the fast drive from Haifa, and the Auk's open-top staff car arrived separately at Mena House Hotel.

The Auk had asked for Dorman-Smith for his command but it had been blocked by Whitehall. Mena House, a 30-minute drive west of Cairo, with its view of the pyramids, is both tranquil and discreet. Used by Army officers and dignitaries, and their mistresses, it was far enough away from Cairo, and from the intrigue of Grey Pillars and General Arthur Smith, for the meeting.[43]

The two men had become close in India in 1938, sharing long walks in the Simla Hills beyond the Auk's HQ before breakfast. Both men were convinced Britain would win the war. Hitler's Army was zig-zagging into Russia and the former corporal appeared to have shot himself in the foot.[44] But how to win?

The conversation can be traced by its results: the Army of the Nile needed to become a proper army. A month later it would become the 8th Army. They also needed a commander who understood mobile warfare. There wasn't one, but General Alan Cunningham had made swift work of the Italians in East Africa alongside Wingate's Ethiopian campaign. He would take command of the 8th Army two months later.

British special forces reminded Dorman-Smith of Hemingway's guerrillas in *For Whom the Bell Tolls*, which he had just read. They were going to get their biggest role yet for the forthcoming autumn offensive.

The next day, Clarke was waiting for Lieutenant David Stirling at Grey Pillars. Stirling took a taxi to the military zone, Qasr-el-Dubara, heading for GHQ. In the Auk's office were Ritchie, General Arthur Smith, Clarke and possibly Dorman-Smith. Stirling, the youngest by miles, might have been nervous. But the Auk was an entirely sympathetic audience.

The Auk's rugged, square jaw and good looks made him look younger than his 55 years. He had left his young wife, Jessie, behind in India, as he wanted to share the hardship of his men. His first contact with modern war had been down the road, on the Suez Canal, between milestones 49 and 50, in 1915, when the two machine guns of his redoubt had opened fire on Turks trying to cross the canal on pontoons.

There were reasons for Stirling to be optimistic; the Auk's theory was that 'if you give a man a job to do, let him do it. You don't interfere with him.'[45] The *Auk* leant in to hear Stirling as he talked quietly.

In many ways Mather, Lewes, Jellicoe or his larger, athletic brother, Bill, would have been odds-on to create a new regiment in the British Army. But that was the point. From Clarke to Bagnold and on, special forces were the domain of *l'étranger*. The Auk liked what he heard, and stood to shake Stirling's hand 'Whatever comes of your project,' he said, 'your presence will greatly relieve Clarke's burden.'[46]

8

Special Forces: 1941

L Detachment

Two weeks later, Clarke finished up on Shepheard's terrace and headed for Qasr-el-Dubara militarised zone for a 10 o'clock meeting with Stirling. Clarke had collected representatives of all the departments in Grey Pillars that could make L Detachment, SAS a reality.[1]

The meeting was chaired by the Deputy Director of Military Training, Colonel Baillon, and Stirling opened by outlining the purpose of the new unit. Firstly, to train parachutists, secondly, to be used in operations. The Adjutant General, Colonel Butterfield, who was responsible for personnel, replied that out of the disbanded commandos only 250 had volunteered to stay in special forces. He had another 120 undecided, the rest were allocated to return to their own unit, go to Tobruk or become Burmese guerrillas.

This didn't go down well with Stirling. He said he had been given the understanding he had around 1,600 men to select from. And he had been doing the rounds recruiting and had already provisionally selected 21 men from the Scots Guards, 18 from the wider Commando and hoped to get another 11. But to get the best possible personnel he wanted to recruit from some specially trained men now present at Tobruk. He said his problem was he had very few to select from, as the best officers had already accepted positions. In reality, those officers were in 8 Commando and had turned him down. He was talking specifically about recruiting Jock Lewes and his team of guardsmen in Tobruk.

Baillon pointed out Stirling needed to go through the formal channels and refer to Adjutant General Butterfield. Stirling felt the weeds cloying around his ankles – he knew the adjutant general's branch was going to be unfailingly uncooperative.[2]

Things got worse.

The RAF waded in. Wing Commander Selway, who had not been in on the original RAF research Clarke had done, said he had not been given any previous information about this new SS Unit, but would take the matter up and report fully on possible cooperation with the RAF. Stirling had never been in a meeting at this level, and pointed out that it was essential to know if the RAF were prepared to cooperate, or they wouldn't have a parachute unit. This was a strategic error: the Wing Commander responded by digging his heels in.

In the ensuing argument it was 'agreed' – at least it got written down – that training would not start until the role of the RAF was defined and a parachute instructor from Britain had arrived. This was a disaster for both Clarke and Stirling – waiting for a parachute instructor from Ringway meant a delay of months. By now the assembled staff officers could be pretty confident they had killed this plan. They had a war to run and the last thing they needed was an initiative that would be a drain on both their resources and time. At which point Clarke, who knew this game better than anyone in the room, changed the subject, and poured some oil on the waters of the troubled meeting.

Clarke pointed out from his experience gained in England it was very important pilots and parachutists should be trained in aircraft that would be used on actual operations. He knew 216 Squadron had Bombays and these were what he was after. This seemed to be approved. And, of course, he also pointed out it would be impossible to hide the formation of this parachute unit once they started training. After all, he had no intention of hiding it. The point of the whole thing was, for Clarke, that he would be able to publicise the SAS.

While Stirling might be anxious that the unit should have a 'special badge' and that it was essential this should be looked on as a highly specialised force – the only thing they all agreed on was that

L Detachment, 1 SAS could be based at Kabrit. Subject, of course, to RAF confirmation.

Clarke may have reached up to Stirling's shoulder after they left the room to reassure him. Stirling thought it was personal – that it was because an officer who worked for Ritchie, who he referred to as 'that little shit Smith', was out to get him. He referred to GHQ as layer upon layer of fossilised shit. But the British military is less likely to be malicious than obstructive – and obstructive in proportion to how hard you push it to change. Stirling was learning the rules of the game, but Clarke already knew there would be ways round the problem.

After the meeting, and the reassurance from Clarke, Stirling set out for the siege of Tobruk to solve his biggest problem – persuading Jock Lewes to join the SAS.

Fraser's CO, Keyes, had forwarded his request to Laycock to join the parachutists, but when 11 Commando left Cyprus, Fraser was left behind to organise the 'baggage party'. This is the lowliest and worst job in any battalion, which falls to the most junior officer. While the rest of the officers enjoyed sundowners on the terrace at Shepheard's, at 7.30 on the night of 6 August, Fraser finally left Famagusta having loaded their baggage. While he stood on the rail watching Cyprus slip into the darkness, this probably reinforced the feeling he did not want re-join the regular British Army.[3,4]

The day he arrived in dusty Genifa camp he found the commandos in chaos. Churchill had got wind they were being disbanded and was furious. He ordered that no SS personnel were to be sent home unless already sailing.[5] Churchill wanted them reconstituted immediately, was sending Laycock back out and placing them under command of Admiral Cunningham. No one had the least idea what to do next. Disillusioned troops gathered in the dump of Genifa camp were doing what soldiers refer to as 'getting on and off the bus' – in his case boat – the physical manifestation of a command chaos. This proved a fertile recruiting ground when it was posted on orders that all ranks wishing to volunteer for duty with a Special

Service unit could forward applications. Clarke had sorted this recruitment via GHQ and Stirling turned up a couple of days later.[6] Most of these men from 7, 11 and Middle East Commando had never met Stirling – who was utterly convincing in his pitch.

Stirling gathered everyone in 11 Commando in their mess tent, explained the purpose of this new unit, and then interviewed the prospective troop leaders, Fraser and McGonigal. Fraser had something Stirling liked: his surname. Stirling's uncle, the man who had founded the Lovat Scouts, was Simon Fraser; William Fraser was from 1st Battalion the Gordons, which made him an ideal candidate.

In the sweltering August heat, Fraser sat down opposite Stirling, who was about as posh as anyone Fraser had ever met. The bare wood table between them, Stirling quickly guessed that Fraser was less a Highland stag-shooting, reel-dancing Fraser, and more a streets of Aberdeen Fraser. Fraser may have dodged questions on education, and being from the ranks, but he was clearly not an aristocrat. Stirling may have thought him completely different from any of the other officers he had seen, but he had a good report from Keyes and combat experience in Lebanon.

Stirling was more at home with university-educated Irishman Eoin McGonigal, and McGonigal got posted to L Detachment three days before Fraser on 15 August. But Stirling couldn't afford to be choosy, and Fraser got his posting on 18 August.[7] Ten days later, 12 of his men followed him, including Tait, Byrne and Du Vivier.

Mayne was no longer part of 11 Commando, and had no one to recommend him for his Burmese guerrillas. Those volunteering needed recommendations from both their CO (Keyes, who had sacked him) and Bob Laycock, who knew what he'd done. He was out of options. Keyes's second in command in 11 Commando wrote that several good officers, and some not so good, had gone off with Stirling's SAS and some with Courtney's Special Boat Service.[8]

L Detachment attracted other troublemakers: Seekings, wounded at Bardia which spared him being captured on Crete; and Phillips, the Birmingham gangster. Phillips had been in trouble since he got off the boat. His record was more white space than writing, due to his many redacted offences. Having come ashore with 8 Commando in March, he never made it any further than Genifa camp, getting into trouble and receiving five days' detention on his first run into Cairo. On return he immediately got in trouble again, was sacked from 8 Commando and sent to GHQ, who awarded him another eight days' detention and posted him to work in the Officer Training Unit in Cairo to get him out of the way.

The Officer Training Unit was in Qasr-el-Nil barracks and while Phillips was stacking officers' blankets, he watched Kenyon Jones's K Detachment build fake gliders. It may have struck him that they did not have many rules and looked like a unit he could work with. When the shout went out for volunteers for L Detachment, he volunteered. A man with a record as long as his arm, who had witnessed the comings and goings of K Detachment, he was posted to Kabrit (1SS Unit), and four days later he was with L Detachment, SAS Brigade.[9]

The SAS was self-selecting – it attracted the outcasts and misfits for whom regular military life was anathema.

Fact and fiction finally merged when Fraser bounced down the dirt track that led to Kabrit camp. Fraser dropped his kit on the ground and looked at the camp on the bleak peninsular at the southern entrance to the Great Bitter Lake. It wasn't by chance that at the first meeting of the SAS it was decided that they should be based there at Kabrit, 90 miles west of Cairo. The naval base there, HMS Saunders, was also the Combined Training Centre, Middle East, the Egyptian equivalent of the original Commando training base at Inveraray, Scotland. It was here that Middle East Commando had practised getting on and off their whalers before landing craft arrived in the Mediterranean.

In the Pharaohs' day, the lake was open to canal traffic to what is now Cairo. The lake had then dried out until its salt-caked basin was flooded by waters of the Mediterranean and Red Sea meeting three years after the death of Samuel Shepheard in 1869. Its high salinity gave it its name. Fraser looked at the Royal Navy parked up on the lake: grey warships ready to go south to combat *Kriegsmarine* U-boats and surface raiders in the Indian Ocean. Or north, to fight in the Mediterranean through Suez – the reason the *Luftwaffe* and *Regia Aeronautica* visited regularly, lobbing acoustic mines like those that had prevented MANDIBLES, and bombing the nearby RAF base.

By the time Fraser arrived, the ambition for a combined training base at Kabrit had faltered along with Churchill's ambitions for the Commando. Just a few battered landing craft were moored at the point, depleted by Greece and then Crete, and few of those that remained in running order. Instead there were whalers, the row-boat Clarke's landing craft had replaced. The Navy had no facilities ashore. The repair shop was an ex-Danube river tug, *Princess Elizabeth*, moored near the landing craft. The high salinity made the shore of the man-made lake barren, accommodation was tents, and the camp office was a Suez Canal Company houseboat moored alongside the sea wall at the end of the point. Other offices had been improvised from packing cases scrounged from the RAF. The comfort in which individuals lived depended entirely upon their skill as carpenters and their success in 'procuring' wood.[10]

None of this mattered to Clarke. L Detachment were now located just 25 miles south of the fictional SAS Brigade at Kantara. And, as the Auk had said, once L Detachment started jumping out of aircraft at Kabrit airfield, Clarke's burden of keeping Rommel looking over his shoulder would be relieved. In addition, Clarke's new PLAN COLLECT – to deceive Rommel they may hit his base in Tripoli to divert his forces – was doing well. On 28 July, the *Oceania convoy* of three ships rushed from Italy to Tripoli to drop infantry troops of Italian 2 Corps into the port, showing they thought the British were about to attack it.[11]

But in Kabrit the real SAS recruits went scrounging, their camp becoming the envy of the Navy. Most of Freyberg's Kiwis had been left behind in Crete, and would have no further use for their tents and supplies. L Detachment spread the net wide, dropping in on other units stationed along the Suez road by night in their Morris truck. What they didn't need they fenced at Egyptian roadside kiosks, flogging the Army stores for cigarettes and stuff they couldn't get easily.[12] But training did not progress as fast. Fraser saw a wit had scrawled, under the 'L Detachment SAS' sign propped on sandbags at the entrance, 'Stirling's rest camp'. Stirling needed Lewes.

The reason he wanted him so badly was because he was one of the best coaches in the world, a skill for which he was legend. If anyone could get L Detachment, SAS off the ground, it was Lewes.

Lewes was a legend because after arriving at Oxford University in 1933 his athleticism quickly earned him a rowing Blue, he became the club's president and, in 1937, faced the monumental task of breaking their arch rival, Cambridge University's unbroken 13-year run of victories in the Boat Race. He designed their training schedule, hid training and selection from even his own university, and finally gave up his place in the boat when he realised there was a better rower. He won, using the strategy of the tortoise over the hare. In the final lengths his crew blew Cambridge off the water in what sporting press described as the greatest struggle in history. He celebrated by climbing onto the statue of Eros in Piccadilly Circus before thousands of adoring fans while police shut down the streets.[13]

With his tour of duty over, Lewes was due to rotate out of Tobruk. But the dock at Alexandria from where the destroyers ran to Tobruk was nicknamed 'the condemned cell', and the Luftwaffe sunk the Australian fast supply destroyer that night. The following night, 25 August, Lewes waited on the wrecked quay in Tobruk hoping the supply destroyer's replacement would make it.

He had had his first taste of combat charging over an Italian position, emptying his magazine into the embrasures which honeycombed the hill, as Italians, dressed only in trousers, fled for their lives. Or fell screaming, brought down by his fire. Some knelt with raised hands, crying pitifully, or just whimpered as they grovelled underfoot.[14]

He had nearly been killed on a patrol when one of his team triggered an S-mine, which flew up into the air before exploding, releasing hundreds of lethal ball bearings. Lewes hit the deck just before it blew, the ball bearings whizzing overhead at chest height like angry bees. But he'd felt abandoned – with no unit, they were attached for rations here, then there, and then on to the next position. It was like going from home to home, the work was dangerous, with little to take pride in. Three times Stirling had travelled on the night boat and crawled into Lewes's troglodyte existence to try and get him to join the SAS. Each time he turned him down. But Stirling's words started to eat away at him: 'Jock, are you happy with the state of things?'[15, 16]

The destroyer sped out of the gloom, threw her supplies onto the dock, and Lewes rushed up the gangplank. The air-raid warning sounded, and the vessel immediately cast off and powered out of the harbour for open sea.

Lewes got off the boat in Alexandria the following day, Tuesday, and checked into the Hotel Cecil, on the front. Skinny and covered in desert sores, he sat at the bar and ordered a John Collins. He spent the rest of the week in the Cecil decompressing, before heading to Shepheard's for a blowout. And, no surprise, Stirling showed up. Stirling had the opportunity, but not the means, to create a radical new force in the British Army and was at his most persuasive. Lewes said he would think about it. Stirling said he would be back in the morning.

Lewes read his bible that night in his hotel room. With the heat of Cairo through his window, to the laughter of those on leave below, he read Jeremiah: 'And seekest thou great things for thyself? Seek them not: for behold. I will bring evil upon all flesh.'[17] In return, God promises Jeremiah he will look after him in battle. The next morning, Stirling showed up. The three Egyptian Eagles rose on the roof of the lobby above Lewes, and Stirling asked him for his decision; Lewes said yes, but he didn't know why.[18]

The SAS was about to take wing.

*

Fraser watched Lewes, the tall, tanned Australian native, arrive at Kabrit and figured things were going to change. He was right. Whoever had scrawled 'rest camp' had to eat their words. Physical training got very, very tough: route marches started at 20 miles, and worked up.[19] These 'Lewes marches' became the cornerstone of L Detachment training. They replicated what they would have to do walking into and out of their targets, with little water, while navigating in the barren desert.

Fraser filled his pack with sand for weight. It didn't take Lewes long to twig some men were emptying the sand in the desert, then filling the packs back up before the final checkpoint. He issued bricks, counting them into and out of their packs.[20]

Lewes did all the marches himself. And water was similarly checked at the end of each march. When one recruit suggested that Lewes had drunk his, he emptied his bottle in front of him. In everything, Lewes was a perfectionist. No one had trained like this before. Fraser excelled. His navigation was excellent and Lewes put him in charge of navigation training. He was fit. And as a former regular, was above average with all the weapons they were trained to use, including captured Italian and German ones.

But Lewes didn't just require brawn: he needed them to *think*. Some, like Seekings, struggled. He was dyslexic, with little education, and was out of his depth with a notebook. Coupled with the appalling rations, the situation blew up in their mess tent. Seekings, a big man, was starving after a night march and could have eaten a donkey. At breakfast, he came in and wanted some jam on his bread, but there wasn't any. Frustrated, he banged the table. Fraser was on duty as the orderly officer and spoke to the cook, then went over to calm Seekings, telling him that there would be jam roll that night.

That night Seekings went up to get his jam roll. There was only a bit left. Seekings looked at the end of the jam roll and lost it, shoving it in an orderly's face. Hell broke loose. Fraser rushed over, got hold of Seekings, and marched him outside. Seekings was sure he was for the high jump; it was a chargeable offence. But Fraser marched Seekings straight into the cookhouse, and told staff, 'Give this man a meal.'[21]

Even if Fraser understood his men, no one understood Fraser. Always proud of his regiment, he started wearing his Gordons kilt, and adopted a stray dog, a dachshund he named Withers, which he decked up in a naval coat. It followed him everywhere, with deep and soulful eyes.[22]

Fraser's men nicknamed him 'skin', slang for gay. But type was important to Mayne. The Royal Navy mess at the lakeside had plenty of alcohol and the other L Detachment troop leaders, Mayne, McGonigal, and Bonnington, found good company with naval officers. But Fraser became a target for the huge second row and boxer Mayne, who gave him a hell of time. The others described him as cruel.

Fraser might have spent more time with his dog than his fellow officers, but he levelled the playfield with his navigation. Navigation, as Bagnold recognised, was the difference between life and death in the desert. Recognition of features on the poor maps, coupled with accurate bearing and pacing, were essential to get a patrol on target.

With Lewes's arrival, L Detachment mutinied. Fed up with poor rations, digging in their own tents and trenches, and a lack of soldier fuel – beer – they wanted out. They could see no method to the madness, were fed up, so held a meeting in the lecture tent and decided to return to their units.

Lewes faced it down; many were surprised he made it out of the tent alive. The tent was in uproar, with Lewes shouting, 'The trouble with you people you've all got a bloody yellow streak a yard wide down your backs! You just can't take it! That's your problem! Unless you can prove otherwise.'

Fraser may have flinched, since among the one hundred recruits, many had been wounded, lost friends, and fought in the disastrous early campaigns. Lewes's reverse psychology worked though. He challenged them to do what he could do: in the SAS, officers would lead by example.

Operation Crusader

On 16 August, Clarke was back in the Auk's office in Grey Pillars. The Auk's offensive to defeat Rommel, now called CRUSADER, was set for the end of the year. Clarke needed to ramp up the cover plan for this: COLLECT. This consisted of the threat of SAS and Commandos taking Tripoli, and giving the Germans the new notional date for the offensive as 15 September. The real thing would be around November.

The following morning, Clarke was at the pontoon at Rod-el-Farag, waiting for the launch out to the Imperial Airways flying boat to Lisbon. The staff at Rod-el-Farag may have thought this small figure looked familiar, though he never wore military uniform and his passport listed him as a journalist. Clarke stood in the launch to the flying boat swinging on its mooring, clambered out into the hull, and took his seat. It was hot waiting to lift off, but he may have reflected this one had comfortable seats, two abreast, and he could hear the stewards preparing food in the galley – a far cry from his mission to the war in Norway.

After looping through Freetown, he touched down in Lisbon. Clarke headed here, rather than Istanbul, because German panzers were approaching the Crimea in Ukraine. Only Odessa held out on the Black Sea coast, and it was only a matter when that would fold. Then everyone expected Germany to invade Turkey, shutting down Clarke's Istanbul operation.

Clarke moved into the Lisbon suburb of Estoril. The bright lights, casino and gambling suited his purpose. At the time, it was an overnight stop for air passengers between the Middle East and Britain, and therefore a valuable centre for the collection of information from careless or 'venal' travellers. Those who liked, or needed, money would always be an easy target for Clarke. Casinos would, of course, become a popular haunt of Ian Fleming's 007.

Clarke's opposite in Estoril was Baron Von Rheinbaben, head of the local *Abwehr*. Clarke discovered that, as a spy centre, Lisbon turned out to be more prolific than Istanbul. Clarke picked up 16 agents: three transmitting direct to Germany and four who were in daily contact with Von Rheinbaben. Down the wire from Lisbon, Rommel started getting warning the British would attack in September – and prepared accordingly.

Clarke flew on to London to advise on creating an equivalent to his Cairo 'A-Force HQ' in Britain. Whitehall didn't do deception, and Clarke was also worried that A-Force in Cairo, knowing nothing of plans in Britain, would innocently compromise a real plan. His fictions were far ahead of Whitehall, and Clarke knew this was a real risk, one that could result in loss of life. Clarke's presentation resulted in the creation of the 'London Controlling Section' for deception – Clarke really could get anything done.²³

Clarke's subliminal methods now reached the US. Back in January he had given US Colonel 'Wild Bill' Donovan his brief on Commandos. Clarke had sent the proposal up through official channels at Grey Pillars, in August 1941, presumably in response to a request. They wrote on the covering memo: 'You may care to see the enclosed correspondence from Dudley Clarke . . . We feel that it would probably be unwise to let the Americans have the paper . . . as they may feel that we are trying to teach our grandmother to suck eggs.' Which was perhaps a reference to the American War of Independence, when Americans sniped at Redcoats from the bush, leading to the argument that the Americans invented special forces. The British military only passed on Clarke's record of the Commando, not all of his proposal.²⁴ But Clarke had already given Donovan his notes before Donovan left Cairo in January, and now, anticipating obstruction from GHQ, had left the full proposal with US Military Attaché Bonner Fellers, who put it in his diplomatic bag. Clarke, having just seen the Spencer Tracy vehicle *Northwest Passage*, in which Tracy led a band of *Rogers' Rangers* suggested that would be a good name – US Rangers.[25]

Donovan had not just been interested in Clarke's Commandos. He wrote a few lines about the fear spread by British parachutists (11 SAS) in Italy. There is no record of how much Clarke told him of his methods, but when Roosevelt asked him to draft a proposal for the creation of a new agency similar to the British Secret Service, Donovan came back with a different proposal – to carry out five functions: open, or white, propaganda; secret, or black, psychological-political warfare, sabotage and guerrilla warfare; special intelligence; and strategic planning – sounding a lot like Clarke's A-Force playbook.[26]

Donovan was also receiving advice at home from Ian Fleming. In July, Donovan was appointed head of the Office of Strategic Services (OSS) which had far more in common with Clarke's A-Force than intelligence. Whereas intelligence gathers just that, Clarke's A-Force was a far more active participant. Clarke's subliminal methods included intelligence and deception, but also active operations. There seems to have been some inspiration from Clarke in the activities of the OSS, which would one day become the CIA.

With Clarke out of Cairo, he wasn't around to help Stirling with the proposal for the L Detachment, SAS's first operation.

Stirling's pitch was the second part of the original SAS pitch: to knock out German and Italian aircraft on the ground. It was what the British Army term a 'back of the fag packet' plan – big on ambition, short on details. But, with most of Rommel's airfields miles from the sea, one detail Stirling did need was how to get the force back after having destroyed the aircraft. A submarine wasn't going to work.

Prendergast was in town to interview prospective new troop leaders for the LRDG. Alastair Timpson had an appointment with him at Shepheard's, but knocked on his door in the afternoon to find him asleep.[27] He found out that Prendergast had just touched down from dodging Messerschmitt 109 fighters and Italian Macchis flying above him, having been at Kufra the day before, then break-fasted in Siwa and lunched at 8th Army Headquarters near Bagush – a 1,200-mile round trip. There was nothing short-range about Prendergast.

The interview went well and Prendergast invited Timpson to have dinner with him. Timpson was yet another Scots Guards officer, like Stirling and LRDG veteran Crichton-Stuart, and Timpson had known Stirling since his Cambridge days. It was a warm night, and they sat out in Shepheard's garden, beneath palms and Kléber's Sycamore, when Stirling joined them to out-line his plans for his new SAS Detachment.[28] If this was by chance, or Crichton-Stuart's doing or Timpson's, neither one recorded.

Stirling told Prendergast of the plan for his newly formed para-chute unit, which he intended to use in the forthcoming offensive, and which would require LRDG cooperation. They talked late into the night. Elegant food and ice-cold wine disappeared in a mirage of dust and rock and camel thorn, of thirst and heat and violence. Amid the coloured lights and palms that night the seeds were sown of a partnership between the LRDG and SAS.[29]

When Ritchie showed the plan to the Auk, he sent it straight to the 8th Army. They jumped at it. The 8th Army was now commanded by Admiral Cunningham's younger brother, Alan Gordon Cun-ningham. He found himself out of his depth and lacking confi-dence, having never commanded an armoured unit, and having quit smoking at doctor's orders and deprived himself of the sol-dier's solace of tobacco. But his Brigade General Staff, Brigadier Sandy Galloway, veteran of many of Wavell's operations, was the most enthusiastic fan of the real SAS so far. He was worried they would be hammered by the Luftwaffe again, and here was a para-chute force offering to take out their aircraft on their airfields on the eve of his attack.

Galloway got straight on the phone to Grey Pillars to ask how they could get more SAS parachutists. What was the bottleneck? Recruitment? Or aircraft? He wanted them under his command in

8th Army. And, while Laycock was back in town, Stirling was now in charge.[30]

The fag-packet plan had some problems, the biggest of which was explosives. The gun cotton 11 SAS had dropped into Italy with is heavy, designed to blow holes in things – meaning a lot would be required to blow an aircraft to pieces.

Jock Lewes was obsessed with explosives. He had spent his youth riding with his siblings up to Mount Jellore, close to his family's estate, bathed in the pools of Jellore Creek with views over the blue mountains, wreathed in blue eucalyptus mist in the early mornings. It was when navigating and living in the wilderness that Lewes learnt to shoot like a sniper, hunting small marsupials at long distances. He experimented mixing potassium chloride, sulphur and making detonators from his .303 rifle cartridges. Eventually, he blew shrapnel into his brother's leg, and reduced his own hand to a tangled mess of blood and finger. After surgery, the pyromaniacal Lewes had one short finger, but a sounder understanding of chemical mixing and use of detonators in explosives.[31]

After L Detachment finished training for the day, Fraser went to his tent, fed Withers and changed. Shortly, the sound of explosions echoed from the lakeside. The experimentation went on for weeks, until one evening Lewes came running up to the camp, clearly excited, shouting, 'I've got it, I've got it!'

Fraser and the others walked down to the shore to see what he had got.

The RAF at the neighbouring airfield had told Lewes most aircraft fuel tanks are in the wing. Using old aircraft wings and fuselage skins, propping them between oil drums and putting fuel below them, Lewes had been trying to get a bomb to blow through the aircraft skin and ignite the fuel, like it would on a real aircraft wing.

Lewes set a squishy-looking large black sausage atop the wing and stuck in the pencil detonator. Then he cracked the glass phial, which allowed the acid to melt the wire that held the plunger. In turn this would make a connection inside the detonator. Lewes then ran to where Fraser and the others nursed their beers.

There was a flash, followed by a bang, in front of the lake. The wing was blown clear and the smouldering tray on the sand between oil drums showed it had ignited the fuel. The Lewes bomb – one part plastic explosive to one-quarter thermite, rolled in engine oil – was an incendiary explosive device. To Fraser, it looked like L Detachment were in business.[32]

Without a parachute instructor, Fraser and the men jumped off towers they had built themselves from scrounged wood. They built a trolley on rails from which they launched themselves, which was then abandoned due to some broken bones. They jumped off the tailgate of trucks speeding across the desert. Lewes jumped first, but as speeds increased – 15mph, 20mph, 25mph – by the time Lewes did it at 35mph, injuries were inevitable.

Mayne jumped and everyone heard his head hit the deck. Fraser and Du Vivier jumped and were both injured, and sent to hospital to have their injuries checked. Fraser had fractured his arm, but played down the injury when he got back to camp that night.[33]

Everyone's ambition was to get their wings – in SAS parlance, to get 'badged'. This motivational tool was designed by Lewes. Once they had completed training, and the qualifying parachute jumps – set as four daylight jumps, two night jumps, and one into the Suez Canal (which later got scrapped) – they could sew the wings onto their sleeve. Then, after their first combat drop, move it onto their chest, above their breast pocket.

Lewes drew his inspiration for the design from Shepheard's. In 1890, the architect of Shepheard's, Rennebaum, sketched Egyptian motifs, including the lotus flower and versions of the winged sun god, Ra.[34] These wings appeared all over the hotel, in their largest form as three 'Egyptian Eagles' on the ceiling of the lobby. Lying on the chaise lounge, looking at the ceiling, Stirling's cabin-mate, Carol Mather, was certain where Lewes had got the design.[35] Lewes added a touch of dark blue for his alma mater, Oxford, and light blue for Stirling's short time at Cambridge.

It might still be a boat race for Lewes, but the god Ra rises in the east, carried on those wings, crosses the Nile to the west, towards Rommel, and then every night has to descend into the underworld to make it back under the Nile to the new dawn. In Shepheard's, gods – both Christian and Egyptian – were marking a path for Lewes.

The wings were the most prized, but the SAS would come to be defined by its cap badge, the winged dagger. The design for the badge was a competition won by Tait, who thought he had depicted the sword of Excalibur, and Du Vivier, who came a close second with a man diving through flames. The badge looks a bit like a sword, but also could be a dagger, not dissimilar to the Fairbairn–Sykes fighting knife officers carried. The distinctive feature of the badge's 'flames', or wings, is their shape.

The manager of Shepheard's was quite clear when he saw it. The stuffed egret from the foyer was missing, and – adding insult to injury – the commandos, with whom he had had much trouble, had used it as a template for their badge.[36] It had probably been sketched by Stirling – becoming an artist had been one of his pre-war ambitions. The shape of the badge does indeed resemble the arching wings of the bird of the Nile, and lifting a stuffed egret was small fry to men who could persuade a donkey up to their third floor flat. It may have fitted Peter Stirling's eclectic taste, which included Sudanese shields and masks, and an elephant-foot umbrella stand filled with spears.

Stirling had the wings and the cap badge made up at John Jones, tailor, Cairo, and added the moto 'Who Dares Wins', which Randolph Churchill hated. Stirling offered a wager if he could do better, but Churchill lost: his family moto was *Fiel pero desdichado*, 'Faithful though Joyless'.[37]

On 16th October 1941, Fraser drove out to the field with his men, donned his helmet, struggled with his good arm to buckle the chute over his overalls, and stood on Kabrit airfield looking at the Bristol Bombays of 216 Squadron. His arm ached, but he clambered on board, and they lumbered up over the Great Bitter Lake.

Fraser and most 11 Scottish Commando recruits were on the first aircraft. The Bombays circled to gain height, then levelled at 900 feet, throttled back to 70mph, and circled back towards Cairo. The RAF dispatcher shouted get ready. Fraser and the recruits stood and checked that their static lines were attached to the rails bolted to the floor. Their lines were attached by clips, a bit like those on a dog lead – a large hook with spring release. They waddled down the fuselage towards the door, and the roar of the twin Pegasus engines and slipstream outside.

First in the door were 11 Scottish Commando veterans, originally Seaforth Highlanders, Ken Warburton and Joe Duffy. The RAF dispatcher checked their static lines, then stood by the door. 'Get ready watch for the light!' he yelled.[38]

The dispatcher turned to face the stick of recruits. Warburton stood in the door, the roar of wind and engines outside. The dispatcher clenched his fist. They all watched the dispatch light by the door, which would show when they were over the drop zone.

Suddenly the light flickered, and shone a dark ruby red. The dispatcher shouted:

'One!'

Warburton jumped.

'Two!'

Duffy hesitated.

'Two!'

And Duffy followed him.[39]

Then the RAF dispatcher slammed his arm over the opening, stopping the next man, Bill Morris, in his tracks. Duffy and Warburton had left the aircraft with their static lines still attached to their chutes, instead of attached to the rail inside the aircraft.

Far below, on the other side of the canal, one of the SAS men watching the aircraft over the drop zone said, 'I saw something come out.'

'If it had, it would have had a parachute on it.'

Duffy and Warburton spun towards earth. Duffy reaching behind him as he tumbled, desperately trying to pull his chute from its pack, screaming until impact.

It took ten seconds.

The men on the home bank watched the aircraft land. On board, Fraser and the rest of the 11 Commando men were sitting, shocked. At the drop zone, Mayne had heard them screaming the whole way down.

Lewes paraded the men. The practical problem – the clip ring to the rail on the floor had been weak and broken – was easy to rectify. But this was little comfort to the men of L Detachment. Lewes said they would be jumping first thing in the morning. Lewes told them that, 'Anyone that wants to leave the unit is welcome to go.'

No one did. They boarded the transport back to camp, while the two bodies were carried back across Suez. There was another stipulation: officers would be jumping first. Fraser went back to his tent, sat with Withers, and watched the men smoke. They sat up all night, butts glowing in the darkness. Fraser smoked more than two packets. There might not have been a tomorrow.[40]

Fraser was first in the door. Ahead, Lewes had jumped at the head of his men. Fraser looked at the drop light. It was dark. He looked out of the door, Suez was visible, the wide expanse of Bitter Lakes, surrounded by flat desert.[41] It didn't help. He looked back at his men. The lines of faces were all staring at him. That was worse. He looked at the light. It flickered red.

'Ready!'[42]

He barely heard the dispatcher. He felt a hand on his shoulder.

'One!'

He flung himself into the void.

Outside, he span briefly in the roaring air. With no orientation, the earth seemed to be above him, the sky below, then it was all blue. Then the yank as the static line reached its limit, his head went down, and he broke free.

Suddenly a white cloud burst over his head and he looked into a fully formed canopy with relief. Pulsing slightly at the edges, 28 lines reaching down to his four harnesses. He reached up to them to take control of the chute, and looked round.

The view was terrific. He could see right down the Canal to the Gulf of Suez, to his right, Ismailia was visible beside the Great Bitter Lakes.[43]

He floated slowly down to the tiny figures on the drop zone below him. Before experiencing ground rush – the feeling that the ground is accelerating towards you as you approach.

From the ground someone was shouting, 'Feet up, feet up!'

It was terrible advice. You need to be rigid jumping a static-line chute to act as a spring to absorb the shock. Fraser crumpled into the ground. An instructor was shouting something unintelligible. His arm, which he had forgotten about, hurt even worse. He stood and tried to wrestle his chute down with his good arm. Byrne, Tait, Du Vivier and Phillips all landed in one piece. Fraser wanted to get the rest of his jumps over with, and did all his qualifying jumps that day, sewed on his wings and went to Cairo in his kilt to celebrate. He was 'badged'.[44]

The final rehearsal for their attack was on the RAF on Heliopolis airfield, 90 miles from Kabrit. Heliopolis was no stranger to SAS operations, since it was from here K Detachment dummy drops were carried out. Fraser and his men had four water bottles each, a piece of hessian to cover themselves by day, a pound of dates, raisins and army-issue biscuits nicknamed 'Sand Channels', after the steel plates used to drag vehicles stuck in the sand.[45]

RAF patrols flew over the empty desert looking for them. Fraser and his ten men were one of six SAS teams heading to the target. Under their hessian by day the heat climbed to over $35°C$ and they didn't touch their water until nightfall. It took three days to walk into the target. They had just over 2 litres of water per person – half a litre per day – in conditions that demand 4 litres.

Dehydrated and hungry, they made a final approach to the

The class of 1916 – Cadet Clarke, right of frame, wears the dark shirt. (Credit: *Brigadier D.W. Clarke CBE, CB, Courtesy of Imperial War Museum*)

Clarke's Bristol Scout fighter, Egypt 1918. (Credit: *Brigadier D.W. Clarke CBE, CB, Courtesy of Imperial War Museum*)

Going solo – Clarke's pilot's license, 1918. (Credit: *Brigadier D.W. Clarke CBE, CB, Courtesy of Imperial War Museum*)

In influential circles – Clarke skiing at Mürren, Switzerland 1927. (Credit: *Brigadier D.W. Clarke CBE, CB, Courtesy of Imperial War Museum*)

Clarke, at the head of his squadron – Transjordan Frontier Force, 1930. (Credit: *Brigadier D.W. Clarke CBE, CB, Courtesy of Imperial War Museum*)

Incognito – Clarke on the terrace of Hotel Cecil, Athens 1931. (Credit: *Brigadier D.W. Clarke CBE, CB, Courtesy of Imperial War Museum*)

Dressing up – Clarke, on the right, Staff College, Sandhurst 1934. (Credit: *Brigadier D.W. Clarke CBE, CB, Courtesy of Imperial War Museum*)

Clarke in foreground of Junkers 52 airliner, Nürnberg 1934. (Credit: *Brigadier D.W. Clarke CBE, CB, Courtesy of Imperial War Museum*)

Clarke's photograph of British Bren gunners watching Junkers 57s fly over, Norway 1940. (Credit: *Brigadier D.W. Clarke CBE, CB, Courtesy of Imperial War Museum*)

11 SAS train with Whitley bomber. (Credit: *The Airborne Assault Museum*)

B Troop, 11 SAS capturing Shrewton bridge, December 1940. (Credit: © *Illustrated London News Ltd/ Mary Evans*)

Fraser, on the top right, Gordon's depot, June 1936. (Credit: © *The Gordon Highlanders Museum*)

General Erwin Rommel with General Fortune behind him, Saint-Valéry-en-Caux, 12 June 1940. 10,000 Highlanders went into captivity. (Credit: © *Imperial War Museum*)

Fraser joins 11 (Scottish) Commando. The 'Black Hackle' is the feather on their glengarry. (Credit: © *National Museums Scotland*)

SAS fiction – A Cairo laundryman poses as an insurgent ready to descend on Italy, January 1941. (Credit: *The National Archives, ref. WO169/24904*)

The den of intrigue – Shepheard's Hotel terrace. (Credit: *Bob Landry/The LIFE Picture Collection/ Shutterstock*)

General Dill inspects 11 SAS. The pamplona beret is CO Colonel Jackson. The men wear their parachute manufacturers silver wings in absence of a badge, December 1940. (Credit: *The Airborne Assault Museum*)

Clarke holding a map and Jack Evetts obscured by busby. When Clarke and Evetts met in 1941 it created the confluence between the real and fake SAS. Taken during Palestine Intifada, February 1937. (Credit: *Brigadier D.W. Clarke CBE, CB, Courtesy of Imperial War Museum*)

'This should help the Commandos'. The Prime Minster's personal minutes on Benzedrine, March 1941. (Credit: *The National Archives, PREM 3/103/2*)

'Joe-the-Swiss' Scialom at Joe's Parish. (Credit: *Bob Landry/The LIFE Picture Collection/Shutterstock*)

Clarke's fake 1940 passport. (Credit: *Brigadier D. W. Clarke CBE, CB, Courtesy of Imperial War Museum*)

Cairo from the flying boat. Qasr-el-Nil barracks is just above the bridge, below is Semiramis Hotel, then the British Residency, then Qasr-el-Dubara military zone. The Stirling's flat is just off the bottom of the picture. (Credit: *FAY 2018 / Alamy Stock Photo*)

Real and fake – On the left, Clarke's view, 1918. On the right, fake SAS gliders on Helwan airfield, 1941. (Credit: *Brigadier D. W. Clarke CBE, CB, Courtesy of Imperial War Museum*)

Egyptian Disneyland – the foyer at Shepheard's Hotel. The wings are visible behind the foyer. (Credit: *Courtesy of Andrew Humpherys*)

For Whom the Bells Tolls. Lunch at Mena House Hotel, scene of creation of 8th Army and Special Forces operations, July 1941. (Credit: *FAY 2018 / Alamy Stock Photo*)

Clarke, taken by Spanish police, October 1941. (Credit: *The National Archives ref. FO 1093/252*)

The survivors photograph – Stirling, tallest in centre. Mayne directly behind and to his right. Fraser, second man to his left in the back, partially obscured by his shadow, November 1941. (Credit: *Family of the late Lieutenant-Colonel 'Jake' Easonsmith, DSO, MC*)

Phillips on the right. Taken by Doctor Pleydell, who wrote on the back, 'Phillips is great character, very tough little chap +, I fear, a big killer.' The SAS, 1942. (Credit: *Private Papers of Captain M.J. Pleydell MC, Courtesy of Imperial War Museum*)

The SAS, Kufra Oasis 1942. (Credit: *Private Papers of Captain M.J. Pleydell MC, Courtesy of Imperial War Museum*)

Fraser on the left, Pleydell in the centre, Jim Chambers on the right, operating from Sand Sea 1942. Chambers died shortly after this picture. (Credit: *Private Papers of Captain M.J. Pleydell MC, Courtesy of Imperial War Museum*)

Stirling on the right and Mike Sadler on the left, 1942. This is the last picture before Stirling's capture. (Credit: *Private Papers of Captain M.J. Pleydell MC, Courtesy of Imperial War Museum*)

General Bernard Montgomery speaks to the Special Raiding Squadron before the assault on Italy, 1943. (Credit: *Peter Davis thanks to Paul Davis*)

Phillips learning to ski in Lebanon, 1943. Last picture of him with SAS. (Credit: *Private Papers of Captain M.J. Pleydell MC, Courtesy of Imperial War Museum*)

The SRS training on cliffs at Rosh Hanikra for the assault on the gun positions at Capo Murro di Porco, Sicily 1943. (Credit: *Peter Davis thanks to Paul Davis*)

SRS training for Sicily on route march, Palestine 1943. (Credit: *Peter Davis thanks to Paul Davis*)

SRS men on captured Italian gun position, Sicily, July 1943. (Credit: *Peter Davis thanks to Paul Davis*)

Fraser aboard one the SRS' LCI landing craft between operations, Italy 1943. (Credit: *Peter Davis thanks to Paul Davis*)

The afterparty – SRS men, Augusta, July 1943. (Credit: *Peter Davis thanks to Paul Davis*)

Fraser's A Squadron, 1 SAS ready for the assault on France, 1944. (Credit: *Peter Davis thanks to Paul Davis*)

General Montgomery, wearing white gloves, inspects an airborne Jeep, 1944. (Credit: *The Airborne Assault Museum*)

Supreme Allied Commander Eisenhower's message to SAS, Fraser and A Squadron asking if they can drop into Morvan forest to cut off Rommel's panzers, 1 June 1944. (Credit: *The National Archives ref. HS6/604*)

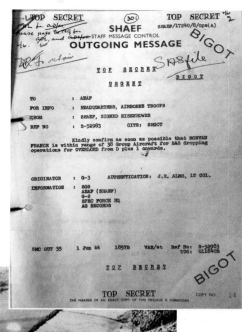

A US Flying Fortress dropping supplies, France 1944. (Credit: *Courtesy of the National Army Museum*)

A jeep and 6 pounder loading into the the belly of a Halifax bomber, 1944. (Credit: *The Airborne Assault Museum*)

Clarke's sketches of women's fashion. (Credit: *Brigadier D.W. Clarke CBE, CB, Courtesy of Imperial War Museum*)

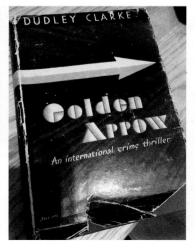

Clarke's novel, published 1955. (Credit: *Tom Petch*)

airfield at night, and lay up by day to observe it. Fraser watched sentries patrol the perimeter road, working out their routine, and then waited till night, when he led his team onto the airfield. They made their way into the RAF aircraft, putting their SAS stickers on the fuselage, sometimes overlapping theirs with other teams who had already visited. And then they left, the RAF none the wiser. Lewes even made it into the canteen. As on the Scottish coast, the takedown of the airfield was complete. And Stirling won a bet with the Wing Commander over it.

Even as they reached their first real operation, Clarke's influence was felt. A camera crew visited them in training, filming them swinging from their harnesses and jumping off trucks, before heading to the airfield for the Auk's inspection. Then the camera crew climbed into the Bombay with them, and shot them throwing themselves out. The cameraman even threw himself out too with the camera strapped to him.

The finished film went out in cinemas on a Pathé newsreel, showing Stirling silhouetted next to the Auk under the wing of a Bombay. In the next shot, three Bombays are lined up as the SAS climb on board. Men pass close to camera, a line behind them boarding another aircraft, yet another walking to a third Bombay, giving the appearance of a much bigger force.[46]

The suspension of disbelief continued, with Bombays flying side by side as the SAS jump. The parachutists pour out, their white canopies appearing, cut with the tumbling footage of the cameraman falling with them.[47] The ruse worked, and the *Abwehr* and Italian *Servizio Informazioni Militare* got the impression the SAS was a brigade of 1,500 men, rather than a detachment of less than 60.

For Clarke, who had no intention of the SAS being kept secret, the film was the icing on his cake. Showing in Cairo, running in cinemas around Britain, visible proof that the British had an airborne brigade in the Middle East. It was impossible for the Germans and Rommel to ignore the fact the British had parachutists ready for operations on the eve of the Auk's coming offensive.

Whatever happened to the real SAS, 'Clarke's burden' was certainly relieved.

Fraser had been doing his best to conceal how bad his arm was, but Lewes wouldn't let him go on the operation. No surprise it wasn't healing, and with training it was getting worse. There's no record of which arm he broke, but most probably it was his right. If he couldn't hold a weapon, and if he injured the arm again, he would become a liability.

When Brigadier Sandy Galloway, from 8th Army, issued Stirling their 'Operation Instruction No 16', on 10 November, Fraser had to page down to serial 13 to find his job. He was ordered to select three men, take two lorries, and join the LRDG operation to pick up the SAS after the drop. The SAS would drop two days before D Day, to be in place to hit the airfields simultaneously, just before 8th Army rolled on Rommel. It was now eight days before D Day. Fraser needed to get moving.[48]

Fraser chose Phillips. Or, more likely, no one wanted Phillips, the Brummie gangster, on their team. He also chose Byrne, one of the youngest of a young unit. But they were all young, Fraser was still only 24. While they loaded their Bedford trucks with rations, tents and water, they enviously watched the rest of the unit get ready for the operation. Though they might have been disappointed, for these young men this was 'Fraser luck'.

Fraser headed east down the highway to Cairo, and for Abbassia barracks, the LRDG base on the outskirts of town. Until recently Chevrolet and Ford trucks had cluttered up the main square and crowded the alleyways, part of the huge 'For Whom the Bells Tolls' operation being launched by the Auk. Few trucks remained, waiting for Fraser, and around them the cannibalised hulks of their predecessors, evidence of weeks of frenetic activity.[49]

After farewell celebrations had been held, and held again, in the morning the LRDG's Ford V8 cylinders roared to life. The LRDG tore into the Cairo morning traffic – armed with Lewis guns, heavy loads – Fraser, Byrne and Phillips hammered their two Bedfords, with only six cylinders and half the engine size, struggling to keep up. The convoy weaved through trams and cabs, onto Gezira island. Giving the Short Range Desert Group, leaving their flats for their offices in Qasr-el-Dubara GHQ, a good view of what real soldiery looked like.

Over Qasr-el-Nil bridge, and the glittering Nile, past Qasr-el-Nil barracks on the left, giving Phillips the opportunity to give the Officer Training Unit the finger. Fraser, riding shotgun, thought it was a lovely early November morning. They hit the road west and sped up. Dust rose and Fraser could see why these LRDG men had wrapped Arab scarfs round their faces and wore goggles. The team sped past the pyramid of Giza to their left, and headed for the desert.

Their route took them north over smooth *serir* (pebble-covered desert) to the arch of the Great Sand Sea, known as the *Garet Khod* route – an easy crossing point known to the LRDG, because the dunes run north and south. The vehicles drove between them like a ship in wide troughs between huge rollers.

For Fraser, Byrne and Phillips, men raised in Aberdeen, London and Birmingham, who had never been further than France, it was an alien landscape. Having crossed the Sand Sea, they reached the *Gardaba track* and turned east, towards Siwa.

If the landscape was extraordinary, their LRDG escort was no less so. Fraser learnt the hard way that beard-growing was more than just a question of saving water: it protected the face, especially when driving 200 miles a day in a truck with no windshield. The LRDG wore nothing but shorts and Kepli sandals by day, but at night donned thick sheepskin coats. On their heads they most often wore caps, though there was no regulation to what type. They sometimes wore the Arab headdress, the *Kaffiyeh*, or the *Agely*, more of a bandana. The only exception were guardsmen, raised on the spit and bull of Whitehall, who, if they wore anything at all on their head, wore a wool stocking cap.[50]

When their convoy bounced down the track into Siwa, Fraser came face to face with ancient civilisation. The Berber town has been consistently inhabited for thousands of years. The buildings of sand and mud grew one upon another, some ruined, others occupied, resembling a human beehive. The only Berber settlement in Egypt, it dates back to before the 11th-century Arab conquest. These people were descended from those of Bagnold's cave paintings.

Fraser climbed down from the Bedford and rubbed the small amount of stubble covering his sunburnt face. He had seen nothing like this in his life. Beyond the village, date palms ran down to a huge, blue lake, and the scale of the LRDG operation became apparent. Their HQ and mess was in a stone Rest House, the hospital and quartermaster stores in abandoned houses, and the workshops in adjoining garages. LRDG troop commanders avoided the official mess in the Rest House, preferring to 'slum it' in two-floor, mud Berber buildings, which they furnished themselves. Chevrolets and Ford trucks lined the shade in trees, or were camouflaged against buildings. And, next to the Rest House, the airfield buzzed with Bombay aircraft, bringing in more supplies, and their own WACOs. Prendergast was flying on liaison trips to 8th Army HQ in the desert to their north, or back east to see the Auk in Cairo.

Fraser had definitely left regular soldiering behind.

The next day, 13 November, Fraser sat with the rest of the LRDG patrol commanders in the Rest House, the sound of aircraft coming and going outside, to listen to Prendergast give his orders for the CRUSADER attack.[51] One of the few houses made of stone, the Rest House was cooler than the Berber huts, but with so many missions to brief it was heating up when Prendergast got to LRDG Troop Leader Jake Easonsmith.

He ordered Easonsmith to leave Siwa in five days with six trucks of the Rhodesian R Patrol, and Fraser and his men in the two Bedfords. He was to set them up in a rendezvous for Stirling's incoming parachutists at the end of Wadi Mara the day after D Day (19 November 1941). He was to leave the Bedfords with Fraser and his men, with the bulk of water and food, then set up a forward rendezvous at Garet Meriem, a hill on the Cyrenaican Plateau. He was to reach this hill no later than 4.30am two days after D Day (three days after the SAS drop), in order to pick up the 55 parachutists who should be waiting for him.[52]

Garet Meriem rises 200 metres above sea level, and is referred to locally as a mountain. The feature provides good vantages onto the Trigh el-Abd track. Fifty miles west of Tobruk, behind Rommel's lines, the feature should have been easy for the SAS to see. But if they missed it they would hit the Trigh el-Abd track, cutting across their path in the desert. Hard to miss, as it was now a seven-lane, mud or dust motorway, having been crossed first by O'Connor's tanks, then Rommel's panzers. Of course, having hit it, they then had to decide to turn either left or right to reach Garet Meriem – a fifty-fifty bet – if you don't know where you are.

Fraser sat in this legendary company, looking at the tough, bearded, special forces troop leaders. Prendergast ordered most of them west, across the Sand Sea, towards Jalo Oasis – over 200 miles due west of Siwa. He explained that moving on the same oasis to their north was another force, which included armoured cars: E Force. This was coming from the Oasis of Jarabub, to their north-west, under command of Brigadier Denys Whitehorn Reid.

Prendergast explained that while the LRDG were under command of 8th Army, they were to contact Brigadier Reid with any information that would affect his operation. His force was very mobile, and once it reached Jalo Oasis, it could potentially strike Agedabia, behind Rommel, threatening to cut his line of communications on the coast road. The familiar theme of Clarke's ANTI-ROMMEL plan.

The LRDG, with E Force, were part of a huge deception. The LRDG had already been out ambushing Rommel's transport in the moonlight, getting into gun battles with infantry, whom they killed, then 'planting' a fake map to give Rommel the idea that a large British force was about to move on Jalo Oasis from the east.[53] They had also been dropping 'Coppers' – Clarke's scheme to plant doctored ammunition which would explode on discharge, bursting the weapon, and injuring the firer. With Rommel's forward troops 800 miles from their base at Tripoli, scrounging ammunition was important. And it gave Clarke the opportunity to plant doubt in the mind of the enemy soldiers about the quality of their ammo.

Easonsmith dropped nine crates of Clarke's dodgy Italian machine-gun ammo on a road leading to a new ammunition dump near Mechili, along the Trigh el-Abd on his last patrol. But the Copper scheme went further than that – by inserting abusive messages inside the cases to Hitler or Mussolini, Clarke hoped to arouse suspicion that factory workers were sabotaging ammo.[54] Given the amount of forced labour the Axis were using, this would be believable.

The deceptive map the LRDG had dropped was their original recce for the Auk's preferred plan for OPERATION CRUSADER. He had wanted to cut 400 miles across the desert into Rommel's rear, and smash into Benghazi, forcing him to fight the battle O'Connor had forced on the Italians. But the Auk did not command 8th Army, General Cunningham did. And the Auk's risk-averse staff, in their Cairo flats, including the newly appointed Freddie De Guingand, had shot the plan down. De Guingand had much to recommend him; from spotting the BEF problems in France, to warning of the Mediterranean Dunkirk, but like most HQ staff he struggled with the logistic demands of lightning war. The result was the better plan was now a fake plan – one that would worry Rommel.

That Fraser followed this, or understood everything that was being said, is unlikely. In the hot room in the Rest House, in the biggest British special forces briefing to date, this was his introduction to being a special forces officer. He was in a room where it was possible to discern not just his immediate commander's intention, but the force commander, the Auk's. Much of what was going on appeared to be fake. Though Fraser did not know about A-Force, and Clarke's operation, he was now part of it.

His ears pricked up when he heard that an 11 Commando team with his old CO, Keyes, were being inserted by submarine. Then Fraser heard that an LRDG patrol had been tasked to insert a

Captain Haselden, three other officers and two Arabs, at Slonta on the Cyrenaican coast to meet them.

The meeting broke up. Troop leaders put away their notebooks, lit cigarettes and compared notes with neighbours before heading out to brief their troops.

Fraser was immediately collared by Easonsmith. Fraser, with his sunburnt face, poor stubble, wool Commando hat and sand-coloured overalls looked ill equipped for the mission. Easonsmith wanted to see his new charges. One look at Fraser's trucks, and he decided the transport supplied by Captain Stirling was inadequate. They were not equipped for the desert, and didn't have enough capacity, so he added an LRDG 3-ton Bedford.

Easonsmith was among the best of the LRDG. He had recently taken out an entire Italian convoy. He had stopped it by pretending to be broken down, shooting it up, then walking along it throwing grenades under their vehicles to flush out a prisoner to capture, to the amazement of his men. For the experienced, 32-year-old Easonsmith, the jury was out on Fraser and the SAS.[55]

Fraser might have quizzed him on the Haselden–11 Commando operation. Easonsmith could have told him that he had picked up the spy, Haselden, after he dropped Clarke's dodgy ammunition and shot up the Italians on his last patrol. But he couldn't tell him what the spy was up to. Nor what 11 Commando were doing.

Captain John Haselden was born in Alexandria, son to a British father and Egyptian mother. Fluent in Arabic, French and Italian, he worked for the Houston-based cotton trading firm Anderson, Clayton & Company. He was married to the beautiful Egyptian Nadia Ida Marie Szymonski-Lubicz in 1931. He was a wealthy cotton broker at the outbreak of war, and the lawn of his house ran down to the Nile. He volunteered for the Libyan Arab Force – and became a spy.

His work was made easy by Marshal Graziani, the man deposed by O'Connor, nicknamed The Butcher by the Senussi. The Italians had turned Cyrenaica into one great big intelligence cell for Haselden.

Haselden's handsome looks from his Coptic Egyptian mother allowed him to move freely through the country. And, after Easonsmith dropped him off, he could pose as Arab or Italian.[56] What few other than Prendergast and Shaw in the Rest House room knew was that the Mudir (Mayor) of the village of Slonta, Hussein Taher, had told Haselden where Rommel's HQ was.

Bob Laycock described the operation as 'almost certain death.'[57] No one thought it would result in Rommel's capture. The order 'kill or capture' is a special forces euphemism – there was no chance of dragging the Desert Fox out of his lair alive.

Assassination, parachute operations, and deception. British special forces had come a long way in two years. Fraser watched the LRDG men prepare for D Day. He was learning fast.

Roulette

Three times Clarke had deceived Rommel they would attack. On the last occasion, 15 September, which Clarke had set up in Lisbon on his way back to Britain, Rommel even sent his panzers into the desert to look for the British.[58] Now the Auk and his intelligence officer, Brigadier E Shearer, needed Clarke to go the other way. With the November D Day approaching they needed to deceive Rommel that there would be no offensive until after Christmas.

This was to be a double bluff. Clarke would feed that they would be attacking after Christmas through his less-reliable channels, while CHEESE, whom the Axis considered their best spy, told them the British would attack before Christmas. Then, just before D Day, CHEESE would 'reveal' there had been another delay – and there would be no attack before Christmas. Hopefully Rommel, lulled by three cries of 'wolf!', would think advancing British tanks were part of a feint. But Clarke knew that could blow CHEESE's cover. Surely the Italians, and Abwehr, would think their spy complicit when real British tanks crashed into Rommel's positions round Tobruk. But for the biggest offensive against Rommel to date, Clarke thought it was worth the risk.

For his final hurrah, Clarke set CHEESE up with a new, fictional spy named Piet. Piet was the clerk to the Director of Operations – the military department for planning and control of operations. Piet, allegedly, was in difficulties over women and money, and a habitual grouser. With CHEESE begging the Abwehr for more cash, Clarke planned to feed the Axis that this new valuable source had told him the attack had been delayed just on the eve of CRUSADER.

Clarke still needed to explain why they hadn't attacked in September. This was his fiction that Churchill had ordered the Auk to send troops to shore up Russian defence of the Caucasus and Stalingrad against the panzer onslaught. This was a very good reason why the Auk couldn't attack Rommel until after Christmas, and one flattering to the Germans. CHEESE would use the same ruse to deceive them that CRUSADER was going to be delayed just before D Day. The good thing about changing dates of an offensive, rather than the location, was it was always possible to explain away why it hadn't happened, and use the same ruse multiple times.

Clarke was recognising the Germans were easier to deceive than the Italians. They liked things in the right place, like a fake Cyprus Army commanded by a fake general, and a fake SAS brigade with its fake badges and letterheads. And they were vainglorious. The Italians were harder to hoodwink – after all, Machiavelli was an Italian.

But the real German advance into Russia continued to cause problems with his deception. German General von Manstein's troops had slogged into Crimea during the summer, and now only Sevastopol held out. With German panzers approaching Stalingrad, Clarke's Turkish conduits felt threatened by Nazi expansion. With his Istanbul spy network closing, he had to rely on Lisbon. But Lisbon wasn't Istanbul, chiefly because there was no equivalent to Commander Wolfson who could keep alive the old channels and substitute new agents when the old ones burnt out.[59]

A month before D Day, Clarke was back in disguise as Wrangel the war correspondent aboard the flying boat out of Poole,

England, heading for the intrigue and roulette wheels of Estoril, to make sure Rommel got the news. A few days later the German Embassy in Lisbon sent a wire saying that there would be 'no desert offensive before Christmas'. This directly contradicted CHEESE, but prepared the audience for his starring role.

Not satisfied with this, Clarke headed into the wolf's lair – Franco's fascist Spain – in an attempt to drop confirmatory evidence on the German military attaché in Madrid. Clarke had good reason to head there. In Madrid, spies were falling over each other, and, unlike Lisbon, it had a first-class British intelligence section. Clarke obviously hoped to repeat the success he had had in Istanbul with Wolfson – which would enable him to run future deceits remotely, without having to go undercover himself. [60]

In Madrid he checked in with the British military attaché and Leonard Hamilton-Stokes of the Secret Intelligence Service (SIS, or MI6) – an 'awkward man' but experienced intelligence officer.[61] This was the proper thing to do, particularly with Hamilton-Stokes, who was not known to extend a warm welcome to others operating on his patch. Clarke seems to have impressed Hamilton-Stokes with his intimate knowledge of military secrets, and the plans of Middle East Naval Intelligence. Running the biggest deception of the war so far, Clarke needed his help. Clarke left the meeting with his blessing.

The signal sent from Madrid at 10 o'clock on the night of 18 October from the British Consul in Madrid, Arthur Ferdinand Yencken, hit the Foreign Office desk in London. Dudley Clarke, a *Times* war correspondent, had been picked up by the Spanish police wearing women's clothes. He had told the police that he was a novelist, and wanted to study the reactions of men to women in the streets of Madrid.

The police had searched his luggage, found another complete set of women's clothes, a war correspondent's uniform and note book, with a number of names of people in London in it. This was probably his Letts appointments diary – he scrawled his immediate contacts with their numbers in the flyleaf.

The Shadow would have been upset. But a name and a phone number is not a major compromise. The police also found papers, which did not turn up anything, and a roll of super-fine toilet paper, about which they got particularly excited, submitting each sheet to chemical tests, only to find out it was toilet paper.

With Clarke in custody, the consul, Yencken, an Australian, and MC-winning member of Clarke's Royal Artillery, hurried to interview him. The consul knew he was a spy and had every reason to be very worried.

In the cell he found Clarke unperturbed. Clarke told him he had been taking the women's clothes to a female friend in Gibraltar, and had tried them on as prank. Yencken thought that hardly squared with the photographs the Spanish police had just shown him. The dress and shoes fitted far too well. What we can deduce is that with two well-fitting sets of women's clothes, it was unlikely this was the first time Clarke had gone undercover as a woman. One has to wonder from Berlin, Lisbon, Cairo to Istanbul where else Ms Clarke may have made an appearance. Clarke certainly had the ability to get better intelligence than most.

Scratching his head, Yencken left Clarke in the cell. The Spanish police were treating Clarke as a homosexual. The Germans thought they had a first-class espionage incident, and Yencken had a problem. Not least the damage being done to *The Times* in the British community, with jokes about their editor masquerading as a woman. But what should he do, when, or if, Clarke was released? Let him proceed to Gibraltar for the Middle East? Or send him back to London?

The reply arrived the following evening. If Clarke was released, get him to Gibraltar, ideally 'accompanied'. The Commander in Chief of Gibraltar was receiving instruction, and Clarke was to be handed over to him on arrival. Find out from Clarke if he had compromised anything that Whitehall or Cairo needed to know about. In no circumstances reveal he is a British officer. Clarke sat in his Spanish cell, looking up at the small window. He was the one spinning many plates in deceiving Rommel but, for once, events were beyond his control.

Then, from Whitehall, his old friend Dill asked that Clarke be sent back to Cairo. Dill said that Clarke had verbal information for the Auk which no one else could give him. The Auk could deal with the 'disciplinary side of the affair' as Clarke was on his staff. Perhaps Clarke did have information. But Dill had saved his bacon twice before, grabbing his ankles to stop him falling out of a biplane, and telling him he was on an insurgents' hit list. The wire sent to Gibraltar was to get Clarke on a plane to Cairo, but keep him under surveillance, and if he shows any sign of 'mental derangement' get him sent home to Britain on the first ship.

Having sent the signal, Dill went to tell Churchill, who ruled that Clarke must be called back to Britain to face the music. A tug of war between Cairo and London started.[62] No less than Sir Miles Lampson, the British Ambassador to Cairo waded in, requesting Clarke's return to Cairo. But Churchill out-ranked Lampson.[63]

The keys to Clarke's cell rattled. The Spanish policeman said he was free to go. Clarke thought it wise to dress in his war correspondent's uniform – a single-breasted pin-stripe suit, bow-tie and stout brogues, finished with a handkerchief in the top pocket. They did not return his 1941 Letts diary.

Yencken sent Clarke escorted to Gibraltar, and his escort handed him over to the authorities. Clarke found himself another sort of prisoner. He now had no way of telling how effective his deception had been. Nor could he tell the Auk what he had done. Clarke must have felt trapped. His deception plan went into action that day. And he had no way of contacting his agents, while waiting to be sent back to England on a ship.

For the last two weeks CHEESE, the fictional Nicossof, had been preparing his Italian masters and the German Abwehr for a massive intelligence scoop. On 20 October, the entirely fictional Piet inside GHQ spilt the beans to CHEESE. And that night the 'excited Syrian', actually the same British operator who tapped all his messages, transmitted:

'Very important news. Piet is desperate for money. He visited us yesterday. According to him Wavell visited Cairo secretly yesterday . . .
Auchinleck under pressure from Churchill has consented against
his better judgement to send one armoured division and three infantry divisions to help the Russians in the defence of the Caucasus.'[64]

Everything Clarke had set up was now in play.

Clarke boarded a ship bound for London to face a potential jail
sentence for being gay, but he was saved by the *Kriegsmarine* when
a U-boat torpedoed his ship. Clarke had been born with a caul over
his face, a piece of amniotic sac still attached when new born,
which, he was convinced (as Vikings had been) meant he could
never drown.[65] It appeared he wouldn't, as he survived the second
U-boat attack of his life. He was rescued and carried back to Gibraltar.
He came ashore with the survivors on 30 October. It appears he did
not immediately advertise his survival to Whitehall: he needed to
get back to Cairo.

There was no flying-boat route from Gibraltar direct to Cairo,
the Mediterranean was closed to sea traffic, and he couldn't cross
back into Spain to get to the flying-boat station in Lisbon. He was
stranded, with no way of assessing the success of his plan while
CHEESE hammered his keypad again, and the wires burnt with
the next part of his deception. Piet outlined the attack on Tripoli
by Commandos and the parachutists of 1 SAS Brigade. Which
dovetailed with the Pathé newsreel of the Auk inspecting his 'sky
troops'.

By now Rommel should have deduced two things. The British
wouldn't attack until after Christmas. And a special forces operation
was going to hit his supply base. But, stuck in Gibraltar, Clarke
could not find out if the German had swallowed any of this.

He waited two weeks.

It wasn't until three days before D Day on 15 November that he
manged to find a lift on a Coastal Command, Catalina flying boat,
bound for Alexandria. But huge storms blew through the

Mediterranean and it wasn't until D Day (18 November) he finally took off to make the dangerous overnight passage through the Mediterranean gauntlet.

He must have been worried. The storm raged, the flying boat crashing through turbulence. And as they approached the Cyrenaican coast that night, he looked out of the right window towards the coast of Africa, where he knew CRUSADER was being launched. He saw the flashes of RAF bombs exploding on German airfields; somewhere in the darkness beyond, the 8th Army's tanks moved forward in the attack.[66] He could only pray that he had deceived Rommel.

In the darkness, far below him, while British tanks rolled on Tobruk, amid those flashes of battle, 11 Commando was trying to kill Rommel and 1 SAS was carrying out its first operation. But things were not going well for his special forces prodigies.

Killing Rommel

Despite the nepotism, Keyes had proved able as the youngest CO of the British Army. Laycock decided to accompany the hit on Rommel, but only as far as the beach. The team ran into the target underwater on submarines HMS *Torbay* and *Talisman,* crammed with their kit, rubber dinghies and folboats. In the red light, to accustom the eyes to darkness, Keyes reread the 'Dear John . . .' from his sweetheart, Pamela. She had met someone else, and was getting engaged. After the numbing shock, he penned her a missive: 'One cannot have everything in life, . . . if you get this letter, it means I have made a bit of a bog, and not got back, as I am leaving it with someone. Only wanted you to know that I got your letter and how I feel.'[67]

A letter that had been written over millennia, in infinite conflicts.

When they surfaced, the gale ripped over the decks of their subs, and from the shore Special Boat Service Troop Leader Tommy Langton's torch stabbed the darkness. To a gasp of amazement from everyone, that part of the plan had worked. It meant Haselden, dropped inland by Easonsmith a few days earlier, had made it to the beach.

The gale was Force 7, with winds reaching 40mph. White breakers piled into the bay, and the landing was chaos. Those who made it ashore – not drowned, or swept off the deck of the sub and spending six hours in the raging foam – made towards a fire they could see. Haselden had lit it, made of driftwood, in a derelict coastal fort. The shivering men huddled together around the bonfire to share any tobacco they had kept dry. The coast road lay 12 miles inland, up on the Cyrenaican escarpment, and the only tracks to this beach were fit for a donkey. They took the chance it was better to stave off hypothermia.

On the day before D Day (17 November), the men who had made it ashore, led by Keyes, lay up in a cave stinking of goat near Rommel's HQ. They ate goat, which local cattlemen brought, cooked by a Slonta village boy. They had to attack that night.

A torrential thunderstorm broke as Keyes took the recce party out, which helped cover their approach. From the escarpment a mile from the target, Keyes could see Rommel's HQ. He persuaded the village boy, Musa, to go into town to walk around. When Musa returned, many hours later, it allowed Keyes to piece together what he could see, with what the boy told him, via his interpreter Drori. He drew up an accurate sketch map to brief the men for assault. Faces blackened, they left the cave at 6pm.

They felt their way – it was so dark they held on to each other – and slipping in mud, slid down the escarpment at 10.30pm. As they started to climb up the rise into the town, a man's Tommy gun clattered against rock, a dog barked, and the team went to ground. A door opened 100 metres to their right. A strip of light. The man called the dog. The door shut. Everyone breathed.

They pressed on until their guides lost their nerve. Keyes handed Drori his Colt.45 revolver and said, 'Tell them to go on until I tell them to stop.'

Drori levelled the pistol at the nervous guides, and reluctantly they moved on. They got into town. Suddenly headlights hit them.

They pressed against the lee of a building in a souk, the water of the deluge still providing some cover. The headlights panned past. Keyes went on with his troop sergeant, 19-year-old Terry, on the final target recce.

It was around midnight when Keyes scoped the approach through Rommel's garden. Somewhere deep in the desert, hundreds of British tanks were moving to their start line. The LRDG would be behind German lines. And L Detachment, SAS should be on Luftwaffe airfields. He was in a hurry.

There were bell tents in the villa garden, but no sign of guards. The weather seemed to be keeping everyone indoors. He rushed back and split the team: one team took the car park; a cut-off team laid in front of the house to shoot anyone reinforcing the HQ; and the assault group, with him.

Keyes led his team as they cut their way through the fence into the back garden. The villa had several floors. The whole ground floor was shuttered with heavy, wood shutters. He tried the back door. It was locked.

They had explosive, but Keyes thought that was probably soaked. They would assault with guns, and use the explosive for demolition. He posted two men at the back door, ordering them to shoot anyone trying to escape.

He led the final assault team of five: Lieutenant Campbell, Sergeant Terry, Commandos Coulthread and Brodie, and his commando interpreter Drori. They swept round the house. A gravel drive led to the front door past the bell tents and the door was set back up a short run of steps, with a balcony overhead, flanked by return walls of the ground floor.

Keyes and Campbell ran up the steps, with the others covering them. Keyes, reunited with his Colt.45, held it at the ready. It was 3am. Campbell banged on the door, and – in German – demanded to be let in.

A pause. Footsteps. And the door was opened by a German, Rifleman Jamatter, in steel helmet and overcoat. Keyes pushed him back inside on the end of his Colt.45, and through a set of internal glass doors.

Jamatter, a big man, grabbed the gun and called out. Behind Keyes, Campbell and Terry's path was blocked by the glass partition either side of him. They couldn't get a clear shot. Keyes, wrestling for his revolver, couldn't draw his fighting knife. Campbell fired repeatedly into the darkened lobby with his Webley.38, thinking it would make less noise than Keyes's Colt 45.

The assault had 'gone noisy'.

Rifleman Jamatter had fled. Campbell thought Keyes was wounded. Keyes said his arm had gone numb.

Then, Germans in room WuG off the lobby, Lieutenant Kaufholz, Sergeants Leutzen, Bartl and Rifleman Koviac, alarmed by the noise, leapt from their beds.

The commandos were in a marble lobby. Stone staircase to the upper floors on the right. One door to the right. Two to the left. Glass doors in front to the shutters leading to the garden. They heard footsteps above. Terry opened up, his Tommy gun splitting the silence. Someone fled.

On the ground floor, German Sergeant Leutzen opened the door to their room a crack, and shone a torch into the entrance hall. He saw Campbell in the lobby, who shot him with his pistol.[68]

Hit, Leutzen leapt to one side, clearing the field of fire for German Lieutenant Kaufholz to open up from behind him from room WuG, with his Luger P08 pistol. He was greeted by a hail of bullets from Terry's Tommy gun.

In the hallway, Keyes was down. Terry had shot 20 rounds and was swapping his magazine. Campbell said he threw one grenade into the room. The Germans said two came in. Inside the room, Leutzen and Lieutenant Kaufholz were both down, hit several times. The grenade(s) detonated, and killed or knocked out everyone except Sergeant Major Bartl, who had dived behind a wooden screen.

Meanwhile, Coulthread, covering the door, and looking out into the garden, saw a torch approaching up the front drive. Brodie and Drori were still outside in the doorway. Drori let the man get close enough to see he was dressed in pyjamas, but armed, before he 'dropped him' with his Lee Enfield rifle.

Inside, on the top floor, German Lieutenant Ampt had been in a conference with Lieutenant Schulz. He went to the balustrade, and shone his torch down the staircase into the lobby. He saw the body of someone lying on the marble lobby outside the door of room WuG. But, hearing shots, drew back. Ampt and Schulz armed themselves, and organised the defence of the stairwell.

Below, in the room adjacent to room WuG, now decimated by the grenades, German Lieutenant Jager jumped out of the window, only to be cut down in a burst of Tommy gun fire from the two commandos waiting outside.

In the lobby, Lieutenant Campbell and Sergeant Terry grabbed Keyes's body, and dragged him outside. From the top of the stairwell, now armed, the German Lieutenants Ampt and Schultz pressed down the stairs. It was clear from the dragging marks of blood on the marble that the body, which had been lying outside room WuG, had been pulled out of the front door.[69]

Outside, Keyes groaned. He was bleeding out from a point-blank, high-calibre shot to the chest. Drori saw him touching the wound. Campbell turned to Terry,

'It's no use worrying about him now, we can't do anything. He's dead.'

Drori asked if they were going to retreat.

'No.'[70]

Campbell ran around the back of the house, to see who had jumped out of the window. They still hadn't found Rommel. But the cut-off group, the two commandos posted to make sure no one escaped, shot him. Campbell was hit in the leg. Sergeant Terry, following him, dived for cover into a bush.

In the chaos, there was one certainty: no one had seen Rommel. With both officers, Keyes and Campbell, down, Terry needed to get out of there. They shoved explosives through the window to

WuG. Others fed the generator outside with hand grenades, and it blew and the lights went out. They propped Campbell up as comfortably as they could, and, before they said goodbye, he took his morphine. Terry blew his whistle; it was time to go.

Inside, German Lieutenant Ampt reached the lobby. The central heating was pouring water into room WuG, the water pooling with blood. Everyone was wounded. Outside he found Keyes, the dead body lying by the door.

The Germans found Lieutenant Jager, shot when he jumped out the window. He showed only slight signs of life. Then Campbell, whom they attempted to interrogate while he was suffering from the shock of his wound. They were unsuccessful. It was impossible to get him to make a statement. All his subsequent interrogations proved to be equally abortive.

While Campbell resisted interrogation, the Germans tried to figure out who had done this. The finger squarely pointed to the SAS deception Clarke had built. Judging by the commandos' clothing, they came to the conclusion that the Englishmen had been dropped from the air and belonged to an airborne unit dropped some time ago. And had chosen this day of particularly heavy rain as favourable for their undertaking.[71]

Rommel may not have been home. But it had been a big success for Clarke's fictional SAS. And for 11 Commando's last mission.

Later, Italian intelligence officer, Major Presti, made a more astute assessment. When he saw this report, and put it together with those coming in from LRDG raids, and Reid's E Force scout cars, he said the enemy is attempting to draw troops from the front and spread panic among the people. By acts of sabotage and terrorism, by means of coast landings, parachutists, and long-range raids by motor vehicles along the southern roads. These are being carried out by the famous 'commandos' instructed and directed by their Intelligence Service.[72] The Machiavellian Italian, Major Presti, had Clarke's number – even if no one else had.

Sergeant Terry got the men back to the beach, good work for a nineteen-year-old who would go on to join the SAS. The Senussi, finding their boats hidden on the beach, had moved them. They couldn't get out to the sub. On the evening of D Day, 18 November, Laycock could see HMS *Torbay* waiting offshore though his binoculars. He signalled her to send boats. But the storm stopped the attempt, she signalled back, 'No more tonight. Too rough. Try again tomorrow. No more from me tonight.'

Laycock replied, 'Thank you. Good night.'[73]

Torbay submerged, and 11 Commando went back to shelter in a cave. From the bench outside Clarke's office in Whitehall, and with help from his nephew David Niven, Bob Laycock's hopes for leading a raiding force floundered on a windswept, rocky Cyrenaican coast, as the submarine's conning tower sank beneath the waves.

In the firefight the following day, 11 Commando, true to their grit, tried to shoot it out. When they ran out of ammunition, Laycock gave an oft-repeated Commando order: 'every man for himself'.

An 11 Commando man, Gornall, was picked up after an abortive attempt to shoot it out from a cave, and was marched into an aircraft hanger in Benghazi by Italians. He found it full of captured Allied servicemen. An RAF man gave him a pack of cigarettes. He climbed onto the top bunk of a bed, lit up, and thought he was hearing things when a familiar voice said, 'Give us a fag, mate.'[74]

It was Bill Morris, who he had fought alongside at the Litani River in Lebanon; the same Morris who had been saved when the RAF dispatcher slammed his arm across the door while Duffy and Warburton plummeted to their deaths. He knew his own Commando, 11, had been wiped out. But if Morris was also in captivity, what had happened to L Detachment, SAS?

9

Agedabia: 1941

The Storm

It was impossible to sleep the night before the offensive. The thunder sounded like artillery fire rumbling across the desert, a prelude to what was to come. Fraser watched vivid flashes tear up the sky to his north and west, then thunder burst overhead with a crack like a bomb and rain hissed into the desert.[1] Far on the horizon, in that maelstrom, his comrades were falling to earth.

He pulled out of Siwa Oasis at 5.30am the next morning, shivering in tropical clothing. It was 17 November 1941, the day before D Day. Eighty miles out of Siwa, the Bedford truck Easonsmith had given him blew a gasket and got dumped. Fraser crossed 'The Wire', the long multi-layer barbed wire frontier that ran hundreds of miles from the coast – it required knowledge of its gaps, and excellent navigation to penetrate. The LRDG led them through a gap and they crossed into Libya, passing huge pools of water from the deluge, and lay up for the night 15 miles beyond.

This was Fraser's, indeed any SAS man's, first view of the LRDG in action. The patrol moved in a box formation, their vehicles dispersed across the desert, meaning if one got hit, the rest could run for cover. Each driver drove on a bearing, the man riding shotgun turning the sun compass on the dashboard every 30 minutes. They were so good that they averaged a 3-mile error in dead reckoning in 150.

At night, they fixed their position using sextants. Fraser watched the laborious and mystical process whereby the patrol's navigator 'shot the stars' to establish their latitude. The technique had been developed by the Arabs a thousand years before, and had fascinated a West Country man the Rhodesians picked up in their bar, Corporal Mike Sadler. Plotting the reading using air almanac and air navigational tables, it could take several hours to fix their position. It took three months for a navigator to learn his craft, and Sadler was almost qualified.

Fraser watched them send their nightly situation report. The operator huddled at the HF set in the side of the vehicle, pressing his earphones to unscramble the traffic from static. Patrols came on air, in turn, according to a schedule. They used civilian frequencies, such as desert mining outfits, to mask their signal, and stop their position being found by the Axis. Called 'direction finding', Axis radio operators could fix an LRDG patrol position in the desert by triangulating the direction from two or more of their receivers. Consequently, their exchanges were fast and concise – Prendergast downloaded the information then issued instruction for the following day. If you missed your slot you had to wait 24 hours. If you missed many, they assumed you were dead.

Each patrol had a cook. Only very close to Axis forces did they go onto 'hard routine' (no fires or cooking) as they closed on the enemy. Most nights they felt safe beside a blazing campfire, sharing their rum ration, the officers their whisky. Both the enemy and locals would assume, at least in 1941, that the fire denoted no more than an Arab camp.[2]

Fraser rose before first light, and the patrol moved out without breakfast, only stopping for a brew later, in case their presence had been picked up during darkness. They headed westward, made a poor day's run – 110 miles – due to minor breakdowns. Fraser saw a lot of aircraft, mostly British. Even with the appearance of Axis aircraft, the LRDG kept going, and acted with confidence. Their best protection was their irregular clothing and non-British vehicles, making pilots unsure whether they were a target. It helped that it was blowing a gale: blown sand and rain covered their journey.

It poured with rain that night. The desert filled with water, wadis becoming rivers as rain hammered on Fraser's flapping 'basher' (tent) tied to the side of his truck. The LRDG came up on the radio to find out three RAF Beaufighters had shot up the other half of their patrol, despite their T-panels being out (the T-panel was a T of cloth laid on the ground to mark they were friendly, since they were behind Rommel's lines). The LRDG troop leader had calmly lit cartridges to illuminate the T-panels in gale-force winds, but the RAF continued to attack until their ammunition was finished. The patrol cannibalised their wrecks and managed to get two of the six running, but had to abandon their mission. Miraculously, no one had been hurt.

Not part of the SAS pick-up plan, this patrol should have been up on the hill at Garet Meriem ahead of them to observe enemy movement on the Trigh el-Abd track. Now they weren't, it ran the risk that any SAS man hitting the Trigh el-Abd and turning in the wrong direction would simply walk into the desert unobserved by anyone. The patrol got replaced by newbie Troop Leader David Lloyd-Owen, on his first mission, but he would arrive after the SAS estimated time of arrival.

Fraser drove into the dried river bed of Fraser's camp at Wadi Mara at eight o'clock the following morning. Fraser, Phillips and Byrne had no experience of setting up camp in the desert, so the LRDG showed them what to do. Fraser set up camp for the 55 incoming SAS men. Called a 'Patrol Harbour', the camp used the wadi, a dip in the ground, to conceal the vehicles from view. They drove trucks into ravines running off the wadi, covered them with camouflage nets, cutting and filling the net with scrub to blend in, and where the soil was a different colour, rubbed the new soil colour over the vehicles. They brushed off muddy tracks leading to their hides, and, once done, the harbour was virtually invisible from the air or ground, unless you walked into it.

Fraser tied the flapping wet canvas of his basher in the lee of his vehicle. Now they had to wait. It had been pouring rain for most of the previous two days. He couldn't imagine how bad this was out on the escarpment for his thinly clothed comrades.

Easonsmith left Fraser and set off towards Garet Meriem to find the SAS. He crossed fresh enemy tracks and hid his vehicles, and then waited until late afternoon before making the final approach. Dusk fell; he drove on. He found the debris of a military exercise: slit trenches and gun pits, freshly dug, he guessed from the Trieste Division, whom he had chucked hand grenades at and had captured a prisoner. They had confirmed Clarke's deceit had worked, because the prisoner revealed his division were headed to attack Tobruk, rather than prepare for a British attack.[3]

Reaching the hill, he bumped into Lloyd-Owen's patrol, who had been tasked to replace the half of their patrol the RAF had wiped out. Lloyd-Owen observed the track junction at Gadd El Ahmar on the Trigh el-Abd from the feature, which was the navigation point the SAS would use to know they had reached the rendezvous. No one knows if his late arrival meant any SAS men went missing.

Easonsmith told him to look out for SAS parachutists, and headed up to the top of Garet Meriem, where, according to his orders, the 55 men of L Detachment, 1 SAS, should have been waiting for him. There was no sign of any of them. He moved back three-quarters of a mile and concealed his vehicles. At 5.20am, his men lit two hurricane lamps on top of the hill, and they settled down to watch.

The Drop

Before dawn on 16 November, two days before D Day, L Detachment, SAS, gathered at Kabrit for Church Parade. From the smell on their breath, it was obvious they had been drinking. Lewes shouted at them that they were either criminals or idiots. They'd stolen some whisky and indulged the British soldier's traditional activity before any operation, of getting impossibly drunk.[4,5]

Full of the not-so-holy spirit, the men clambered into their Bombays, crammed with their parachute containers, containing their weapons and explosive, wedged in by long-range fuel tanks that filled the fuselage. The RAF had fitted the tanks, as they had for 11 SAS, to extend their range. With heads throbbing, they lifted off.[6]

They made the short hop in clear skies west into the desert at Bagush, touching down in the early afternoon. On arrival, the RAF laid on a final meal in their mess. The troops tucked in with a bottle of beer, 'hair of the dog', for most. Then they got news the Force 7 Gale that had kept Clarke in Gibraltar was now washing over 11 Commando and blowing over their Gazala airfields. The RAF advice was to abort. Stirling reckoned they were going to take some casualties. The officers conferred. It was unanimous they go. The officers went to talk to the men.

Lewes gave a motivational speech, and then Stirling one on the importance of their mission. No one wanted out. For Seekings, the Commandos had been cancellation, cancellation, cancellation. If this was cancelled, that was them finished.[7] But no one could envisage what a Force 7 Gale, with winds 30 to 40mph, could do on a drop zone.

They bussed back to their aircraft at 6.30pm, and took off after dark. The Bombays flew north, over the sea, then turned parallel to the Cyrenaican coast, and headed west, towards Rommel. Their targets were five airfields west of Tobruk, and the latest intelligence put around 300 Axis aircraft on them, both new Messerschmitt 109 fighters, and assorted ground attack aircraft, in front of 8th Army's advance.

The men shivered at altitude. The aircraft had no doors, and waist gunner positions were a wind tunnel, filled with nothing more than a Vickers K machine gun.[8] From the cockpit, pilots could see the storm rising ahead of them. Dark clouds reached high above, filled with flashes of lightning, and the old airframes lurched and dropped as they entered the maelstrom.

The SAS men felt their aircraft bank to the left – they were heading south, on the final approach to the target. Peering from the cockpits the pilots could see nothing, forcing them down to sea level to get under the cloud base to orientate themselves. Crossing the coast at little over 500 feet, all hell broke loose.

On Lewes's aircraft, Du Vivier saw 'flaming onions' (37mm exploding tracer) rip past the aircraft, which pointed the way for the searchlights. Six of which immediately converged on them. He watched one tracer round enter through the thin fuselage wall and exit through the roof, just missing the fuel tank. Unknown to him, another round had just wedged under his seat, but not exploded.[9]

Pilots wrenched their Bombays back into the cloud, to escape the flak. Troop Leader Bonnington's aircraft was hit, and Pilot Warrant Officer Charlie West lost his instruments. His port engine failing, he peered out to see fuel pissing from his wing. He aborted. Without instruments he had no way to find the drop zone, and he could only guess which way was east, towards the British front line.

Fighting the gale and a failing aircraft, even his considerable skills couldn't keep them airborne. With spluttering engines, amazingly, he emergency landed the overloaded aircraft, in a gale and torrential rain, on the rocky desert, intact.

On the ground, Bonnington and his men chipped away their containers, which had frozen to the bomb racks. They recovered their Tommy guns, wedged two empty containers under the wheels of the Bombay to stop it blowing away, and set out into the darkness to find out where they were.

Lewes's plane was locked in searchlights and flak. The inside lit up like daylight, and commandos watched in amazement as Lewes got up and walked up and down as though he didn't care. The former coach was using his skills to give them confidence: they thought, if he's not frightened, then why am I?[10]

Lewes told them to 'prepare to jump'.

The red drop light glowed. Lewes threw himself into the gale, and after a final check of the static line, Du Vivier and the others clung on to the rocking fuselage and followed each other out of the door.

Du Vivier went into the blackness, the noise of the plane grew fainter and fainter, and suddenly he felt terribly alone – disorientated, the drop seemed endless.'[11]

Their Bombay was hit in the wing just after he jumped.

*

The desert of the Cyrenaican plateaux is not sand, it is a jumble of rock and wadis covered in thorn. The wind had risen to gusts of more than 50mph. Often on a night drop it is sound, rather than sight, that warns you that you are about to hit the ground. Du Vivier heard the man ahead crunch into a thorn bush.

High wind on the drop zone increases the impact speed, therefore the force and chance of injury. It reduces any realistic chance of achieving a good landing. And, once they are down, it stops the parachutist being able to collapse his chute. The drill was to pull down on one side of the harness, to get the chute down and prevent it becoming a kite.

Those who weren't killed or critically injured on impact needed to release their harness to survive. The four harness straps are clipped into a circular buckle on the chest, which require both rotation and pressure to release the straps. Possible for a parachutist to do on their back, but injured, or being dragged on their front across rock and thorn, impossible.

Du Vivier flew over 100 metres before he got stuck in a thorn bush and released his harness. When he finally freed himself, he was bruised and bleeding, with a sharp pain in his right leg. When he looked back and saw the ground he'd travelled over, he thanked his lucky stars he was alive.[12]

Troop Leader Mayne fell first in his stick. He could see flashes and bangs on the ground, which he thought was enemy small-arms fire. His landing was 'unpleasant', on ground studded with thorny bushes. He broke his foot, probably a metatarsal, one of the most common injuries on a combat drop. He found no enemy, and concluded that the flashes must have been caused by their own detonators exploding in containers whose parachutes had failed to open.[13]

Behind him, Seekings was dragged across the rocks and thorn. He had expected a rough trip, but nothing like this. He managed to get on his back, twist and release his buckle, only to find the harness immediately caught on his entrenching spade, which they carried on their back. He struggled and struggled to turn over, then when he eventually flipped, smashed into a thorn bush face first. He could feel blood pouring down his face, and his hand and arms were completely skinned.[14]

Mayne's team looked for their scattered containers in the gale. At 1.30am, they gave up. They found only four containers, with two Thompson machine guns. He had to leave two men too badly injured to attack the airfield, telling them to remain there that night, and in the morning find and bury any containers they found. They would then have to try and make Easonsmith's rendezvous, which he estimated was 15 miles away.[15] They didn't make it.

Mayne and his team walked north towards the target. It was too late to carry out their plan of getting close to their target airfield to observe it.[16] With only five hours of darkness left, they pressed on trying to get close so they could attack it the following night. Mayne had 8 men, 16 bombs, 14 water bottles, food for 4 men and 4 blankets.[17]

On landing, Lewes, had taken a beating. He reversed the bearing given to him by the dispatcher before he jumped, and struggled back into the storm to find his men, called 'rolling up the stick'. He couldn't find Sergeant Cheyne, who had carried Fraser over the Litani River. In some accounts, they covered him with a blanket and gave him water and a pistol – to use on himself, not the enemy. In others, he wasn't found.

Lewes's team recovered some containers, and Lewes decided to press on to see if they could find their target. They weren't sure where they had been dropped. Dawn broke and Sergeant Pat Riley, one of Lewes's Tobruk team, who was uninjured, went forward to recce the airfield. There was no sign. They pushed further north, in the hope of establishing a landmark, but the storm broke again. Du Vivier watched tortoises swimming about in the puddles. With their explosive soaked, Lewes aborted. No sign of the target, they turned south to look for the rendezvous.

Struggling south, they stopped frequently, lying up shivering under soaked blankets. Lewes went down – injured, suffering from exposure and exhausted after months of single-handedly driving L Detachment into existence. He handed over to Sergeant Riley, who kept them going, because by this stage, they just wanted to fall out, lie down, and die.[18]

Stirling's team were in a terrible state. He was knocked unconscious, and came to being dragged over the ground and hit his release. It took two hours to find everyone in the gale. His men had broken wrists and ankles; only he and Tait were spared, though Tait had injured his ankle. The containers they found contained blankets, food, Lewes bombs, but no fuses. Stirling was so damned angry. Even though they were in a sorry state, if they had had weapons and explosives they could have still achieved something.[19] He decided he and Tait would head north for the coast, and at least carry out a recce. He gave Sergeant Yates the job of getting the rest home.

Stirling and Tait walked north all day, and at dusk looked over the Cyrenaican escarpment to the sea. There were no airfields. They had no real idea where they were. They gave up. And they turned south to find Fraser.

Mayne's team lay up in a wadi that day. Trying to rest, but shivering with cold. Then, at 5.30pm, it chucked it down with rain again. After about half an hour, the wadi became a river, and they had to move to higher ground. It kept on raining, and they huddled, two under a blanket while the rain smashed into them. Mayne handed round some rum, and they shared tobacco that Seekings had managed to keep dry. An hour later, Mayne tried two of the time pencils to detonate their bombs and they didn't work. He tried the instantaneous fuses they carried and they didn't work either.[20, 21]

Despite this, at first light on 19 November, the day after D Day, Mayne determined to do what damage he could. Seekings, his stripped face dripping blood in the rain, watched him rage against the torrent. He had a 'helluva job' talking Mayne out of it – they had no weapons, no explosives, and the team were in pieces. Finally, he persuaded Mayne to turn back. They too slipped their way in the mud, towards the Trigh el-Abd.[22]

Dawn broke on Bonnington's Bombay, which had been brought

down by flak. They'd come down close to the coast road, and in the morning light Pilot Charlie West could see traffic. Then Bonnington appeared from his reconnaissance with an Italian prisoner, meaning he had come down behind enemy lines. West reckoned he could get his kite off the ground, their only option. Quickly they clambered on board and the engines fired, sounding ominous, but powering up.

The aircraft was pointed at the road – not the best trajectory, as it was covered in enemy vehicles, but their best runway option. West and his co-pilot pressed the throttles fully open, and the Bombay bounced towards the enemy. Picking up enough speed, they lifted off just clear of the road – to a hail of Axis gunfire. West banked violently right, east, towards the British front line. He followed the coast, the only navigational feature he could see, nursing his damaged aircraft, when anti-aircraft fire slammed the fuselage. In the back, an SAS man felt something hard hit him, and the Italian prisoner sitting opposite him was blown into his side of the aircraft. In the cockpit, West felt the hit. The co-pilot clambered back to check the damage, while West tried to gain altitude, and the battered airframe clawed upwards.

The co-pilot looked into the fuselage. The long-range fuel tank had blown up and was on fire. The Italian had been burnt, and half the skin was blown off the fuselage.[23] Luckily, they had expended most of the fuel from the tank, otherwise the result would have been fatal. It was no consolation to the SAS men sitting in the back of what looked like a flaming wreck.

West and the co-pilot wrestled with the joysticks. Then the steering went dead. An Axis fighter blasted past their windshield having filled them with rounds. Some survivors thought it was a Messerschmitt Bf 109, but the Italians claimed the kill, meaning it must have been a Caproni Vizzola – the Italian monoplane fighter.

With steering gone, and the aircraft shot to pieces, they plummeted. West and the co-pilot slammed the throttles back and dropped the flaps. The last action of West's co-pilot. They were going in hard; and those who did survive would be captured.

On the ground the injured men from Stirling's team reached the Trigh el-Abd. They looked at the muddy seven-lane path. Which way was the rendezvous – left or right? It was fifty-fifty.

Sergeant Yates was sure they should turn right. They even started in that direction. But others in the patrol persuaded him he was wrong, and they turned round. Yates had been right and they hobbled into captivity.

L Detachment had been decimated.

The Survivors' Photograph

At 9am on 19 November, the day after D Day, Easonsmith's patrol watched as one of the lanterns on top of Garet Meriem, was lifted and swung from side to side. The prearranged signal from the SAS. He replied and went up to find Lewes and nine men.[24] Saved by Sergeant Riley, Lewes and Du Vivier had made it – they had missed the hill and walked into a signpost 3 miles south of it by chance. In spite of their weakness, they had cheered and danced round the post, and kissed it as though it was something sacred. The LRDG gave them a meal of bully and biscuits and tea, which was undoubtedly – in Du Vivier's opinion – the best meal he had eaten in his life.[25]

Easonsmith watched the hill all the next day. His orders were to close this rendezvous at 5.30am the following morning, having dumped 12 gallons of water and some dates for the parachutists, and pull back to Fraser at the wadi. But Easonsmith had seen the state of Lewes's team and he knew how bad it would be for the remaining injured men out on the plateaux in thin clothes, with no cover. He stayed put.

Night fell, and at 1am, the lamp moved again. Easonsmith set off up the hill: it was Stirling and Tait.

Stirling thought he had seen Yates and the rest of his patrol ahead of them. Easonsmith broke the news they hadn't made the rendezvous. Easonsmith had orders to close shop, but this was a disaster. He only had 11 of the 55 men. He decided to remain for another day to give the SAS a chance. It was a risk – he had no idea what was happening in the battle between Rommel and 8th Army, where, if things went according to plan, the area could soon be swamped by Axis forces falling back from Tobruk and he would be overrun.

He moved his team to the better cover of the Italian vehicle pits dug in the wadis, and left a small team atop Garet Meriem, instructing them to light a small fire. At dawn this bought in Mayne, Seekings and their team.[26] But their appearance did not reassure Easonsmith. These men had been lucky to make it. He now had 19 out of 55. He sent his men out into the desert, to spread out and take up vantage points to the north, the direction the SAS should be coming from.

On the other side of the hill, Lloyd-Owen was watching the Trigh el-Abd when he saw two figures walking around in the desert. He could see they were parachutists. He showed himself, standing in front of their well-concealed hide made of scrub, and they came towards him. The tall one said, almost as though they were meeting for the first time outside his club in London, 'My name's Stirling. Have you seen any of my chaps?'

With him was Seekings; Tait with his injured ankle had been taken to Fraser's camp. The LRDG gave the parachutists tea laced with whisky, and they talked about the raid. Lloyd-Owen said, 'I don't see why you don't let us take you there. We can get you with accuracy as near the target as you want to go and will then lie up before coming to pick you up again.'[27]

Stirling quizzed him. It was slow. Surely they would be spotted. What about the loads? Additional men? Explosives? Lloyd-Owen, the new boy, offered him much more than an experienced LRDG troop leader might have. He assured him he could get Stirling's teams within 5 miles of a target. Stirling was sceptical, but a seed had been planted.

By dusk that evening, Easonsmith had overstayed his welcome. He would have to come up on air soon and give their situation report to Prendergast, and explain why he hadn't left. No one else had come in, and his men in their desert vantage points had seen no parachutists in any direction. He contacted Lloyd-Owen to tell him he was pulling out but to keep his eyes peeled. At dusk, he withdrew to Fraser's party, having stayed eight hours over his contracted time at the rendezvous.[28]

Even then Easonsmith didn't give up. The next morning, 21 November, he sent his whole patrol out to form a line across the likely direction of the SAS approach. They kept a lookout all day, with trucks displayed for 8 miles across the SAS approach route. He was taking a huge risk in the face of Axis aircraft.

Nothing.

At daylight the next day, he sent his men out again, and repeated the process until midday. He got a wireless message telling him in no uncertain terms to take the survivors to a neighbouring LRDG patrol, who would ferry them back to Siwa Oasis. It was over. He left the water and dates at Fraser's camp for any survivors who weren't in captivity, or dead.

In the desert, it was always Bagnold's Rules.

Back at his camp, Fraser counted 22 survivors, including himself, Byrne and Phillips. They lined up and Easonsmith snapped their picture. Unbelievably, they were smiling. From the Panzer onslaught in France, the first Channel raid with Clarke, up the Italian Apennine Mountains, onto the beach at Bardia, across the rocky shore of Kastellorizo, into the holocaust of Crete, over the Litani, onto the stormy beach to Rommel's HQ, to this drop – to be in this picture you had to have survived. These men – The Originals – became legend.

Fraser stood at the back of the picture, looking sheepishly over the shoulders of the others, barely visible. Perhaps he didn't feel he had earned a place at the front – the quiet man from Aberdeen would never seek the limelight. But Fraser was the only officer to have worked with the LRDG, seen them in operation navigating and concealing themselves in the desert. Crichton-Stuart had told Stirling about them, but, for Britain's special desert force, seeing was believing. Fraser undoubtedly spoke to Stirling. That night Stirling,

Lewes and Sergeant Riley shared a tent, and Riley heard Stirling and Lewes talk. They had been wiped out without destroying a single aircraft. They needed a different way in, and discussed being inserted on operations by the LRDG. Riley thought – that's when the SAS was born.[29] But to work with the LRDG, the SAS would need an invitation.

The next day Stirling called them together. He started talking about 'the next time' and Du Vivier thought, I don't fancy the next time if this is what it is going to be like. Stirling gave the survivors a choice, of returning to their units, or continuing with L Detachment. Du Vivier thought, this is the lesser of two evils.[30]

That afternoon, Fraser loaded the survivors onto his trucks to follow Easonsmith and hand them over to another LRDG patrol to take them home. They didn't get far. First, a Savoia 79, Italian three-engine bomber, saw them and machine gunned them. They shot back and it scored no hits. When the aircraft ran out of ammunition, they sped on. Reaching hard ground, their tracks disappeared and they dispersed and hid. Then, as feared, the Italian summoned help, and 40 minutes later a German twin-engine Heinkel He 111 bomber appeared.

The Heinkel circled, hunting – its Perspex dome nose sniffing at the country below while it tried to make out their tracks. The bomber made several attack runs, bombing and strafing derelicts – burnt out and destroyed vehicles and tanks, and scrub 3 miles away. Air attacks continued for two days, on both them and the patrol they were supposed to be meeting – who were similarly pinned down. In one day they counted no fewer than 38 aircraft hunting them. The special forces operation – the raid on Rommel, the LRDG, E Force's scout cars, and captured SAS parachutists – had stirred up a hornet's nest.[31]

Since Rommel had arrived, the Heinkel He 111 had been used by the Germans to hunt 'Kommandos gangs' – their generic term for British special forces – both because it could stay airborne longer than any of their other aircraft, and it had great visibility. Two months earlier, LRDG Commander Prendergast had noticed a

Heinkel 111 poking around over Kufra Oasis. It approached from the south (which was odd, as this was the opposite direction from the coast), completed one circuit of the oasis at 4,000ft, then dropped 15 bombs on the aerodrome. Prendergast picked up the pieces and confirmed that the bomb tailfins were German.[32]

In fact, the Germans had set up a battle, or destroyer group, called *Sonderkommando Blaich*, to hunt the commandos. At the outbreak of war, German national, Cameroon landowner, farmer and pre-war explorer Theo Blaich had identified there was a threat to Libya from the south, from neighbouring Chad through the Tibesti mountains to Kufra. The same threat Clarke had identified with Leclerc. Blaich's concern had fallen on deaf ears. But when he went to see Rommel when he touched down in 1941, he got a much more favourable response. Blaich would spend the war hunting irregular units.[33]

During his first air attack, Fraser lay watching the Heinkel He 111 pummel the desert until it ran out of bombs, Lewes beside him. Neither realised the significance of the aircraft.

After two days' bombardment, and failing to make their rendezvous, Easonsmith came on air to get Prendergast's that night, to be told he was to drop the SAS asap. The role of the LRDG was suddenly changed – 8th Army had issued orders that the LRDG was to attack any enemy targets or lines of communications within reach.[34] The LRDG were going on the offensive. From what Easonsmith could deduce, 8th Army had run into serious trouble.

Early in the morning, Fraser reloaded his trucks. His men had to put their foot to the floor to keep up with Easonsmith as he raced to re-join his unit. Even with urgent orders, Easonsmith diverted through Fraser's camp to make sure no more SAS parachutists had come in. The dates and water were untouched.

In Easonsmith's speed, one of the leading LRDG trucks hit a bump and overturned, luckily with no casualties. The LRDG never left vehicles behind if they were salvageable, so they righted the truck, and at 12.30pm on 25 November 1941, Fraser saw Jarabub Oasis in the distance. A low-domed mosque peered over the fortifying walls, surrounded by plaster buildings. The oasis, also called Jagh-bub, and any number of variations, was home to the tomb of the founder of the Senussi, many flies, and HQ 29th Indian Brigade.

Beyond the town Fraser could see dunes stretching as far as the horizon. This was the northern edge of the Great Sand Sea. The usually parched desert around the town was flooded with lakes from the rain. But, Fraser discovered, when he jumped from his truck, the rain had done nothing to dampen the enthusiasm of the flies. In the desert around the oasis was clustered a tank unit. At least that is what they looked like from the distance.

Fraser and Seekings went to take a closer look to find out the tanks were wire, covered with hessian, mounted on trucks. Fraser was face to face with K Detachment, SAS, and the reality they were not alone. Seekings, who had been told by Stirling that they were part of something that didn't exist, now found out what. Apparently, a load of 'boffins' in Cairo had dreamt this up. In reality, K Detachment had been sent there by Clarke to beef up the deception that this 'Oasis Force' had a tank element which could threaten Rommel.[35]

Inside the compound, Fraser and the surviving L Detachment, SAS officers, Stirling, Lewes and Mayne, went to find the oasis commander, Brigadier Patrick Claude Marriott, of 29th Indian Bri-gade, who was almost family to the SAS. Marriott's wife, Maud 'Momo' Marriott, an American debutante, daughter to million-aire philanthropist Otto Kahn, was the centre of the Blue Bloods' Cairo social life. Waugh was in almost permanent residence at her house, she fêted rising stars such as Stirling, and invited them to her glamorous Cairo Salon – and, in Randolph Churchill's case, to her bed.[36]

With Marriott in his fly-infested HQ building, Fraser, Stirling, Lewes and Mayne were offered a drink, and discovered that the Punjabi Infantry of Brigadier Reid's E force had pushed the Italians out of Jalo Oasis. Jalo was the perfect forward operating base to hit Rommel's line of communications.

But Stirling was heading for what the British Army call 'an

interview without coffee' – euphemism for a severe reprimand by a senior officer, in this case General Cunningham of the 8th Army. It was going to take some explaining how he had lost 60 per cent of his team without destroying a single enemy aircraft. Marriott advised him to make himself scarce.

Clarke had also prepared for an awkward interview with the Auk, as his Catalina flying boat taxied to its mooring in Alexandria on D Day. When he reached Grey Pillars, he was surprised by the Auk's cheerful reception. Many commentators now think the Auk may have been gay or bisexual.[37] He clearly loved his young, vivacious American wife, Jessie Stewart. She was 16 years his junior, and he had fallen for her the moment he saw the 21-year-old heiress step foot on a tennis court at a friend's house in Scotland. He carried a photograph of her everywhere.

But the Auk was raised at the Indian frontier, where binary sexualities were considered a British concept. He would eventually eschew British society altogether and retire to Marrakesh. The Auk didn't care if Clarke wanted to wear a dress: he cared about what he did.

And in deceiving Rommel he had been outstanding.

Rommel, shown air photographs of the British extension of the desert railway from El Alamein west, to support the forthcoming offensive, had thrown them on the ground in disgust. Panzergruppe's own Intelligence Section told their Italian intelligence counterparts they were much too nervous, and that they mustn't worry, because the British wouldn't attack. Even after British tanks rolled, for nearly 48 hours Rommel thought that he had to deal only with a reconnaissance force. Clarke heard this, and thought there were some good grounds for claiming that his deception plan had at least made a contribution.[38]

Very good grounds indeed.

Rommel was so confident he had moved all his forces north to prepare for an all-out attack on Tobruk on 20 November, almost on the date of the British offensive. He had allowed himself to become obsessed by Tobruk, sucking in his forces. Rommel had been so confident the British wouldn't attack, he even went to Italy on the eve of his Tobruk offensive to drum up support. He celebrated his birthday with his wife on 15 November (three days before the attack) in Hotel Eden on Monte Pincio, amid the ancient family villas of Medici, Malta and Ludovisi. It was Rommel's chief of staff, General Bayerlein, who reported during the night of 17–18 November that British commandos, in a raid of great audacity, had tried to wipe out what they supposed to be Army Headquarters in Beda Littoria – 200 miles behind the German front – as a prelude to their offensive.

The place they attacked was occupied at the time by their quartermaster, who lost two officers and two other ranks. Bayerlein thought it interesting that Rommel had formerly had his HQ in that house. He himself had had the first floor, and his aides the ground floor. Rommel's chief of staff rightly guessed that the British must have received knowledge of this through their intelligence service. Haselden's intelligence had been good, just out of date. Rommel landed back in Tripoli on the day Keyes knocked on the door of his old HQ.[39]

Clarke's double bluff had worked. The night 11 Commando attacked Rommel's old HQ, the Germans captured a British prisoner close to the front line at Hellfire Pass. He provided them with a detailed account of British forces and plans for the offensive. So detailed, in fact, that at first Rommel's chief of staff doubted its veracity. Clarke had successfully lured them in with his successive 'Cry Wolves' when the prisoner's information on the attack had 'confirmed it in every detail.'

Clarke's subliminal methods had placed some very serious doubts in the minds of German command. On his shifting sand, they were having trouble distinguishing fact from fiction. It was not until operations were already underway that the Panzer Group realised the British had even launched an offensive.[40]

Clarke's deception brought the British within two days and thirty-five miles, of the besieged town of Tobruk. But, as was often the case, the success of Clarke's methods did not lead to success on the battlefield.

Back home, optimism had reigned. On the eve of the offensive, Churchill took Alan Brooke, Monty's commander in France, aside at Chequers to tell him he was sacking 'Dilly Dally' Dill. Alan Brooke was to replace him as head of the Army. With new leadership, the desert offensive would be followed by the invasion of Tripolitania, then Sicily. His message on the eve of the attack was that, 'For the first time British and Empire troops will meet the Germans with an ample supply of equipment in modern weapons of all kinds . . .'[41]

'New' might have been more apt than 'modern'. The mechanics of *Blitzkrieg* were *vorsprung durch technik* – panzers manufactured by Henschel, MAN, Krupp, and Daimler-Benz. And once Rommel realised the British were attacking, he turned his attention from Tobruk to destroy them. After two days' intense fighting, when Cunningham counted his tanks he had 44 left from 450, mostly 'modern' Crusader tanks with which he had crossed The Wire. He had outnumbered the panzers over two to one, but once again British engineering had been left for dead.

The 8th Army had ceased to be a fighting entity.

In the battle, Gatehouse, with Bonner Fellers' in tow, had a fight with General Ludwig Crüwell's panzers. Gatehouse had replaced his old 9mph tanks with new US Stuart Honey light tanks, and with the US still not in the war, Bonner Fellers was interested in the performance of their first tank in combat. The Honey had two Cadillac engines giving it top speed more than 30mph. Gatehouse used them to get round Crüwell's 100 panzers, and in the firefight he drove them off. The next day Crüwell turned up again. The Honey had a gun that didn't penetrate the front of a German tank, and he destroyed Gatehouse's force. Which Bonner Fellers told Washington, and which Rommel would read.[42]

But on the dockside far behind British lines these tanks were just the first of several massive US shipments. Those shipments of vehicles developed from analysing the Germans on the battlefield also included small four-wheel drive prototypes, inspired by German manoeuvrability: the Willie 'Bantam' Jeep.

Convinced he was beaten, General Cunningham decided they should retreat; it was SAS enthusiast Sandy Galloway who prevented it. Given the order to pack up the HQ, he prevaricated – never have HQ tents been lowered, or vehicles loaded, so slowly. The brusque Scotsman Galloway phoned Grey Pillars to demand someone come up urgently.

The following day, German *Totensonntag* (Sunday of the Dead), at 3pm, Rommel tried to destroy the 8th Army. The attack failed. Panzer after panzer split open in the hail of shells.[43] Dorman-Smith might describe Freyberg as 'a bear of very little brain', but in many ways it was lack of imagination kept Allied commanders fighting against the odds. In the chaos, one of the few British disciples of the Indirect Approach, Gatehouse, rode to the rescue in an armchair strapped to the back of a tank. Tartan rug over his knees to keep himself warm he could use the tank's radio. Later, asked why, he replied, 'What else was I supposed to do? I had no headquarters.'[44]

As well as tanks, the main problem with the CRUSADER battle was the plan. Advancing through the desert on Tobruk had not forced any decision on Rommel, he had taken the initiative, and the British paid a high price for their lack of daring. Now the Auk flew up and handed Cunningham his orders, which he read in disbelief. He was to attack, not retreat.

The Auk directed he use his special forces – 'Oasis Force' (Marriott, Reid and the LRDG) – and send them 200 miles into Rommel's rear, to cut the coast road. If possible, capture Agedabia, and use the LRDG offensively, to the limit of their endurance, against every possible objective on the enemy lines of communication. The Auk assessed the advantages to be gained by a determined effort against the enemy lines of communication worth the immense risks which would need to be taken.[45]

The diversion – the Indirect Approach – had now become the

real plan. And one to be carried out by special forces. As the Auk said of this type of operation, there would be 'No written orders!! No ruddy principles of war!!! Except hit and have after him. No Generals!!!'[46]

With the sun over the yardarm, he then went to have a drink with Air Vice Marshal 'Mary' Conningham. Conningham had made himself at home in his trailer, which had a red settee, a desk and a bar.[47] Mary Conningham had been born in Brisbane and raised in New Zealand and was a breath of fresh air for the Army. Unlike his boss, Tedder, he was starting to see the British Army could do with some close air support.

They were sharing a whisky when ex-8 Commando Randolph Churchill walked in, with the writer Ève Denise Curie Labouisse (daughter to Marie Curie) – a war correspondent, who had an appointment to interview Conningham. The Cairo rumour mill was working overtime and Randolph Churchill was here to check on progress – anything the Auk said would go straight to his father, the prime minster.

Curie's interview was going well, though she doubted whether her questions made any sense, as she was terrified by the strong, sunburnt man with light-brown hair and blue eyes, sipping his drink and listening in complete silence. His presence rendered Randolph Churchill absolutely mute and motionless, a remarkable result to anyone who knew the turbulent son of the prime minister. Finally, the Auk had heard enough, and said, 'He is making a desperate effort, but he will not get very far. That column of tanks simply cannot get supplies. I am sure of this.'[48]

He had called the German's bluff before; retaking Narvik in Norway – now he forced Rommel to lay down his cards.

In the darkness, Rommel was only 28 miles from where they sat, but the Auk was right – he was at the end of a wild drive, in complete disregard to the British threat to his flanks.[49] Rommel's distortion field was flickering: his staff car had broken down and he had stood by the road to Egypt shivering with cold. Only by pure luck, as dusk was falling, had the Afrika Korp's Mammoth command vehicle pulled up, containing General Crüwell, Bayerlein, and his battle staff.

When they reached The Wire, they drove up and down the miles of entanglement in the dark, but couldn't get through. Rommel grew impatient. He dismissed his aide de camp, who had been navigating, but even Rommel's legendary sense of direction did not help.[50]

Retreating Allied tanks, lorries and dispatch riders flew past them in the dark, unaware that in their midst was the epicentre of German command in Africa, lost in a four-wheel-drive armoured box.

Rommel needs to take some share in the credit for creating the SAS. Stirling flew up for his 'interview without coffee', and found General Cunningham in a small tent, surrounded by tobacco smoke, and was immediately struck by the strain and fatigue on the general's face.[51] He had prepared a few lines of responses to explain his disastrous operation, which it turned out he didn't need. Cunningham asked him, 'Can you give me any idea of what reinforcements are coming up? I'm particularly interested in the enemy's tank strength.'

Stirling was dumfounded.

'I watched the road for about half an hour, I saw no armour. Only supply trucks.'

He was out in five minutes. Blinking in the sunlight, he put on his sunglasses.

Stirling watched RAF Blenheims buzz in and out of the HQ airfield, trying to cadge a lift to Cairo, when a young staff officer approached him to tell him the commander would like to see him.

'But I've already seen him.'

'No, you haven't, we've got a new one.'

The Auk's consigliere, General Arthur Smith, had been sent up to make sure Cunningham left peaceably. And to tell him he was to check himself into No.64 General Hospital Alexandria 'in the public interest'.[52]

Ritchie had received the promotion of a lifetime and Stirling was overjoyed when he re-entered what was now Ritchie's tent to find his sponsor smiling, oozing confidence.

'I hear you were scuppered by the weather,' Ritchie said. 'Rotten luck. Heavy losses?'

'Not too bad,' Stirling lied.

The SAS had survived. With some thanks to Johannes Erwin Eugen Rommel.[53]

Rommel, Round 2

Fraser landed back in Kabrit camp to be greeted by Withers and a sea of empty tents. Some men refused to pack away comrades' personnel effects, still hoping they might make it. Fraser left his men to mourn Cheyne. He had been a good sergeant.

Far out in the desert, the LRDG went to war with Rommel. First blood went to an LRDG patrol that drove straight into a roadhouse on the coast road; the Via Balbia. The lorry park was full of Rommel's transport, and LRDG gunners shredded the trucks with a mix of armour-piercing and incendiary rounds. Crews threw grenades from their truck as they cruised down the line of parked vehicles.[54]

Over the next week, LRDG patrols laid waste to Rommel's lines of communication. Time and again they hit his convoys, their Standard Operating Procedure for raiding became hitting as late as possible, then running for cover into the dark to evade the omni-present threat of enemy aircraft overhead. Rommel's tankers, caught in the lethal hail of bullets, careered off the road, though the LRDG realised raiding was a murderous game – inspecting the bodies of drivers they discovered many were civilians.[55]

The effect of the firing on coast traffic was that north and south of an ambush, traffic turned round and went in the opposite direction.[56] Local Axis commanders thought the British had a huge force up on the Benghazi escarpment. Night convoys shut down, the Axis scrambled for escort vehicles, and more and more aircraft were diverted from the frontline to hunt Kommandos. Over the next nights, at Agedabia, Slonta and Timini, the LRDG estimated they destroyed 70 vehicles. They sheltered by day within wadis, traded dates from Siwa for 'eggies' (shakshuka: baked egg on a base of tomato and spices) with the friendly Senussi, who also gave them intelligence and warning of Axis patrols.

The big battle with Rommel had become surreal, the opposing armies so entangled there was no front line. Rommel walked into an Allied Field Hospital he had captured, but by this time no one was sure who was captor and who was captive – except Rommel, who was in no doubt. But no force-field could resist this pressure. Rommel summoned General Crüwell to see him on the night of 28 November. Crüwell found him in his Mammoth – the captured British Armoured box on wheels. Rommel sat with his chief of staff, Bayerlein – both of them were unshaven, worn with lack of sleep and caked with dust. In the lorry was a heap of straw for a bed, a can of stale water to drink and a few tins of food. Evidence that perhaps Rommel's reality distortion field had some chemical help from German methamphetamines. Their supply line was continually being molested: fuel tankers going up in flames, vital supplies and ammunition failing to reach their forward troops. The LRDG operation was beginning to bite. The Auk had called his bluff, with a force that Rommel didn't even know he had in his hand.[57]

That day, Britain's nascent special forces stepped up their attack on his lines of communication, with the 8th Army ordering the Auk's attack on Agedabia. Rommel's problems, real and imaginary, were mounting.

LRDG Commander Prendergast climbed into his WACO and took off to dodge through the Luftwaffe, 200 miles forward to Jalo Oasis, to discuss the mission with Reid. Brigadier Reid wanted the LRDG to hit the Axis airfields in front of his advance, to clear out the Luftwaffe that were preventing the RAF operating in his support.

Prendergast knew this wasn't a job for the LRDG. His Ford and Chevrolet trucks were big targets, longer than a tank, and anyone six feet tall standing in front can look straight into the eyes of the driver. Nor were they manoeuvrable. Each only had a three-man crew, and with no Lewes bombs could do little damage to aircraft on an airfield. He thought back to Shepheard's, to the tall persuasive man who he'd got drunk with in the garden, and suggested parachutists were brought in to blow Axis aerodromes.

Fraser and his tiny team, the remnants of his Gordons troop – Byrne, Tait, Du Vivier, along with Phillips, got wheels down in their Douglas DC-3 on the dirt airfield of Jalo on 7 December. The whole L detachment, SAS was now 22 men including 4 officers. The LRDG picked them up and drove them into the oasis. Fraser lit a cigarette, looking at the map to orientate himself, while his men got ready for the operation. They had come a long way from the banks of Galashiels and the rousing pipes and drums of the Highlands.

At seven o'clock the next morning the first teams were ready, and Stirling and Mayne with LRDG Troop Leader Holliman left with orders to hit the airfields at Sirte. It was to be a deep penetration behind enemy lines into Libya, over 300 miles.[58]

Fraser watched the men of Troop Leader Morris's LRDG patrol try to get a captured Italian Lancia running. Everyone stopped work to gather round the radio to listen to President Roosevelt's announcement on the BBC of the Pearl Harbour attack on the USA. The debate around the radio was did this mean the US would also declare war on Germany?

Finally, the Lancia spluttered to life and kept running. Watered, the patrol strapped the fuel into the back of their trucks – they had 14 LRDG men, commanded by Morris, 5 Ford trucks, with 10 SAS, Fraser and Lewes in the Lancia – not a huge force, but one with Lewes bombs that could pack a punch.

Leaving Jalo early on 10 December, they immediately cursed the Lancia, which they damn near had to carry across the desert. Apart from getting stuck, the only way to refuel its small tank was by sucking diesel from a can and syphoning it into the tank. SAS men got mouthfuls of diesel – and hated that perishing Lancia.[59]

*

Three hundred miles ahead of them on the coast, at noon that day, 40 miles south of their target of Sirte airfield, the LRDG patrol carrying Stirling and Mayne broke radio silence to synchronise their raid with Fraser and Lewes. It had taken two days to reach the target area deep inside Tripolitania, and they were concerned Fraser and Lewes were going to hit their field before they could get into position. It was a risk, and nearby Axis radio operators picked up their signal loud and clear, quicky triangulated their position and dispatched their Ghibli aircraft.

The patrol saw the first Ghibli aircraft scouring the country that afternoon, but it failed to see their trucks. The team laid up overnight, but, in the morning, as they approached the road to Sirte, they heard the tell-tale scream of its two Alfa Romeo 6-cylinder engines. The Ghibli dived in to attack. Breda cannon rounds pounded the desert around them, LRDG gunners swung their Lewis guns, the SAS fed their Breda and the dog fight raged over the desert. The Ghibli disappeared, but so had the advantage of surprise.

The LRDG quickly dispersed their vehicles, threw camouflage nets over them and wiped their tracks. Just in time they dived under the nets as two more Ghiblis arrived. The aircraft circled, hammering likely-looking bushes in the surrounding country. Mayne read a paperback during the attack.

At sunset they moved on, crossing some Bedouin, who warned them of Italian troops ahead.[60] They also told them there was a second airfield; a new satellite field had been built to the west of Sirte, at Wadi Tamet.[61] The SAS now had two targets: Stirling would have to take one, Mayne the other.

Finally, they hit a belt of sand and reached the coast road with too little night left for an attack, and had to lay up for the day.[62] Trying to coordinate the attack with Fraser and Lewes, much further east, the team were running so late they decided to drop Stirling just 3 miles from Sirte aerodrome that night at 11pm,[63] then drove on to drop Mayne, Seekings and five men, to take out the other airfield at Wadi Tamet at the same time.

Stirling and his sergeant made it to the airfield perimeter, but they triggered a sentry who fired into the darkness. The two men fled and laid up to watch the airfield from a ridge. Day broke and they could see the village of Sirte, a cluster of whitewashed houses, fishing boats pulled up on the beach. Below them was the airfield, stacked with Italian aircraft, mostly twin-engine Caproni Ca.135 bombers – the bottom of their target list, but a target all the same.

Women from the village came to till the soil a few feet away, so they lay still while the ground became harder and harder, until after several hours the women made back for the village.

Stirling relaxed and with the sun turning pink he prepared to go in. But the Italian aircraft roared to life – and in two's and three's they watched their entire haul fly off over the Mediterranean. Dejectedly they trudged 2 miles up the coast road before tearing some scrub and placing the marker in the middle of the road for the LRDG to pick them up.

Mayne's team made it to their target, the airfield at Wadi Tamet, without a hitch. They walked onto the airfield, single file. It was pitch black – all the raids were timed to coincide with the smallest moon – and from a hut a glimmer of light shone. [64] Someone opened a door to go inside, and Mayne followed him. He kicked the door open. He had a Colt.45 and one of his team had a Tommy gun.

The men inside stared at him.

A young German rose and moved slowly backwards. Mayne shot him. Then fired again. One of his team opened up with the Tommy gun.

Their raid had gone noisy.

The battle quickly centred on the hut, and from across the airfield Italian gunners opened up. Tracer arched across the field; Seekings flung himself to the ground.

Mayne left four men to handle the firefight, while he, Seekings, and another ran onto the airfield. In the light of battle at least it was easier to see the aircraft. The airfield was stacked.

They ran between the planes triggering 30-minute timers,

pressing them into the soft explosive of the bomb, throwing them up onto wings, into any openings. Quickly, they ran out of bombs. Seekings and Mayne had more aircraft, but no bombs. Mayne jumped up onto the wing of the plane. Seekings thought he had lost it. Then he saw him rip the instrument panel out; how he did it he would never know. In the chaos, the huge former rugby international tried to disable Axis aircraft with his bare hands.

Mayne, Seekings, and the other man from this part of the team ran off the airfield. After less than 50 yards the first plane went up. They stopped to look, but a second one went up near them, and they began to run. Once they put some distance between them and the field, they watched as planes exploded all over the place, with the terrific roar of petrol and bombs.[65]

The three men headed for their rendezvous with the LRDG, and Seekings became worried by the glow from the luminous dials on the aircraft panel Mayne was carrying. Pillaging was a legitimate wartime activity, and – as Mayne put it – it had a good clock.

The LRDG should have been flashing lights to indicate their position. But the enemy was also flashing lights. In their haste to get off the airfield they hadn't taken a compass bearing and became lost. This was not an unusual occurrence with Mayne; as one of his men put it, Mayne couldn't navigate, and once he'd got lost he would give a man the compass and say: 'There you are, you've done it again, you've lost us.'[66]

Using the alternative signal they blew a whistle – luckily from the darkness it was answered. They ran up to the LRDG truck; Seekings was gasping for a drink. A big LRDG sergeant from the Rhodesian patrol handed him a water bottle – he took a long chug, gasping for air, but could not get his wind, and, too late, realised he had consumed the best part of a water bottle of neat rum. In a matter of minutes, he was three-parts blind. He passed out in the back of the truck as they bounced across the desert.[67]

Further east, Fraser and their LRDG team's progress to their target was also slow, not helped by the Lancia. It was made worse on 12 December when they found their way blocked by a newly laid German minefield, which meant they wouldn't make the target on time. LRDG Troop Leader Morris' plan had been to drop the SAS about 11 miles south-west of Aghelia, which is on the coast, and let them do the rest in the Lancia, which could pass as Italian, or go in on foot. But now they were too late. They were laid up for the night and Stirling and Mayne were due to hit their airfields at 11pm.

With no chance of coordinating the raids, in the morning a low, steady drizzle covered the patrol's approach to their target. Out of time, they hit the coast road and ran down it in broad daylight. They forked left before they reached the fishing town of Aghelia. Fraser, bouncing in the back of the Lancia between thorn bushes, hoped the journey would finally end. Lewes out-ranked him and rode shotgun. Fraser, Lewes and the SAS, along with two LRDG patrol trucks and personnel stopped about 12 miles south-east of the fishing town. The rest of the LRDG turned round to go and attack their target, another roadhouse.

The SAS drew a blank: when they got onto their airfield that night it was empty, and they hurried back to the rendezvous with Morris's LRDG team hoping they still had enough darkness to do damage elsewhere. Fraser and Lewes similarly found out the LRDG had failed. Morris had tried to walk in to the roadhouse on foot to attack it with Lewes bombs the SAS had given them, but his team found the approach from the desert was blocked by a marsh. But Morris had carried out a detailed recce, and had a plan.[68]

Fraser, Lewes and he gathered round, as he explained that they could use the Lancia in the front of their convoy to drive into the lorry park at the roadhouse, just as the first LRDG patrol had done hitting the coast road. The icing on the cake would be the SAS. Once they parked up, the SAS could bomb the lorry park with Lewes bombs.

Night fell, and the six-vehicle convoy pulled onto the coast road and headed east for the roadhouse with killing on their minds. The Lancia, which had no headlights, was out in front, and they'd taken the dimmers off the LRDG trucks to blind oncoming traffic to make them think their speeding silhouettes were Italian.

They sped past 47 vehicles in the opposite direction: Rommel's traffic retreating in front of the British advance. Fraser gripped his weapon in the back. The road was metalled, and narrow; he was separated from Afrika Korps soldiers by about a couple of metres. He lit a cigarette to act natural. Phillips was enjoying himself, and waving.[69] After 9 miles they slowed, and turned into the roadhouse.

Engines throbbing as they cruised into the lorry park, the team counted 22 vehicles, and around 60 Axis troops milling around. A meal was about to be served.[70] The Lancia parked up between two trucks, engine idling. The LRDG also stopped, waiting for their last two trucks to catch up.

An Italian walked up to Lewes in the Lancia.

'Got a light?'

Lewes gave him one. Lewes had done a lot of rowing in Germany before the war and been in love with a beautiful Nazi debutante – until Kristallnacht had changed all that.

Lewes said, in perfect German, 'You have guessed that we are English.'

The Italian replied, 'You Germans have such a wonderful sense of humour.'

Lewes pointed his revolver at him. For him this war was personal. 'Get in.'[71]

The Italian obliged.

Fraser and the SAS men hauled the man into the back and quicky smothered him. Silently, Fraser and the SAS men dropped from the vehicles – working in teams of three, one bombing, the other two covering. Fraser ran between the trucks, sticking in time pencils, placing the bomb on top of a wheel or chucking them into the back. Byrne, Du Vivier, Tait and Phillips were all enjoying this.

In one of the other SAS teams, a man opened a truck cab to find the driver sleeping. The driver woke up. The SAS man shot him in the face.

The attack had gone noisy.

The LRDG opened up at point-blank range, at less than 20 to 30 paces, and armour-piercing and incendiary rounds tore through the lorry park.[72] In the back of the Lancia the SAS crew found their Breda jammed – the oil had congealed in the cold. They slammed the mechanism, trying to free it.

Fraser and his team sprinted from the shadows and jumped into the Lancia. The Italian prisoner was sobbing like a baby. Around them the park was exploding. Axis troops not cut down fled into the roadhouse, and the gun battle raged between the men sheltering in the roadhouse and the LRDG.

The LRDG weight of fire prevailed. Speed, aggression and surprise had made the difference. They sped out of the lorry park before 38 Lewes bombs did their work. Holding on in the back of the speeding Lancia, Fraser watched the lorry park blow into the night sky.

The patrol sped south out of the target area, putting 24 miles between them and the coast, and camouflaged their trucks before daylight. In the morning they watched a plane circling over their tracks.

LRDG Troop Leader Morris had picked something up on his recce of the roadhouse from the locals. The reason the SAS's target airfields had no aircraft: the Axis had shifted their planes to Agedabia.[73]

After the long haul back in the stuttering Lancia, Fraser rolled into Jalo at 10am on 19 December. The SAS men vowed they would never use the truck again. Stirling and Mayne had got in the previous day. There had been celebration after Mayne's raid. Stirling had seen first a great flash from the coast, then a series of explosions in rapid succession, and he and his sergeant had danced with joy, with the sergeant saying, 'What lovely work. It almost makes the Army worthwhile.'[74]

The LRDG report sent to Jalo said 22 aircraft had been made unserviceable, either burnt out or with instrument panels smashed. Mayne said bombs had been placed on 14 aircraft, because, he,

Seekings, and the other SAS man, carrying 8 apiece, had managed to bomb 14 aircraft, the rest had been used to destroy the hut. He added 10 had had their instrument panels destroyed.[75]

The problem, in the cold light of day of Jalo Oasis, was that Mayne's team, carrying a total of 56 Lewes bombs, on an airfield full of aircraft, had only managed to blow up 14 of them.

Initiative is the cornerstone of special forces operations. The mission had killed Axis personnel, but that had no value to the overall mission to help Reid take Agedabia. 'Compromised' in the military means either the enemy, or you, did something to force you to abandon your operation – Mayne had compromised his. Stirling and Mayne had a row, which Stirling later put down to Mayne overstepping the mark. Lewes may have been frustrated that after his careful training about how to get onto an airfield, and get off undetected, Mayne had blown it. Fraser certainly said nothing. He had enough problems with Mayne already.

There is no record of why they then chose Fraser, the only regular officer among them, to go back in and destroy aircraft at the location they knew the Axis had moved them. But it wasn't the first time Lewes, the coach, had given up his place in the boat.

Agedabia

Save for the throb of their truck's eight cylinders, the desert was silent. Fraser bid LRDG Troop Leader Olivey farewell. Olivey repeated his instructions to be back at the 16km stone by 2am the following night. Fraser looked at this 'road' – it was little more than a track known only to the Bedouin and the LRDG. He was going to have his work cut out on this mission.[76]

His broken arm strapped, he picked up his pack of Lewes bombs and set his prismatic compass to the bearing the LRDG navigator had given him. The navigator had shot the stars and given Fraser his exact position and the bearing for the landing ground.[77] Navigation could have been a good reason Fraser was selected for the mission.

The Rhodesian LRDG patrol sped off, leaving Fraser with Byrne, Phillips, Tait and Du Vivier. For a few moments after the Rhodesians left they stood listening until the sound of the engine faded into the darkness. The desert was empty and quiet. They holstered their pistols, Byrne shouldered the team's Tommy gun and they marched due north – five men, single file, aiming for Agedabia airfield, 16 miles away. Tait was limping on his injured ankle.

The going was soft and the sand muffled their steps. The hours passed and the ground hardened. The men were approaching the coastal region now, clambering over rock scree, through wadis filled with low scrub. With only two hours of darkness remaining, Fraser called a halt. They needed to find somewhere to lay up for the day. The eastern sky was growing lighter when they came across a fairly deep hollow. They were still 8 miles short of the airfield, but it would have to do.[78]

The first Afrika Korps lorry arrived at dawn.

Then another.

Then another.

With his commanders wounded, sick or dead, and LRDG tearing up his supplies Rommel was pulling back.[79] Unloading shovels and picks, 150 of Rommel's retreating soldiers began to dig a defensive line 800 metres to Fraser's front. Rommel had chosen Fraser's target as the place to make his stand against the advancing British. The SAS troopers pressed themselves flatter as yet more Afrika Korps prepared positions to both their flanks. The elite panzer teams had followed Rommel to Africa in the same way Byrne, Phillips, Tait and Du Vivier had followed Fraser. The crucial difference was that there were hundreds more of them.

Rommel arrived at his headquarters close to Agedabia airfield unaware of Fraser's presence. His mobile HQ was a tent, a staff car and his Mammoth. Fraser's advantage was surprise, and the eight Lewes bombs he and each of his men had in their bags. His, Lewes's and Stirling's belief that the SAS's true striking power lay in stealth, not force, was about to be put to the test.

Surrounded by enemy forces, Fraser could have been forgiven

for calling the operation off. Instead, he watched them at work, and, satisfied they were more intent on preparing a defensive position than looking for British soldiers, he led his team quietly away. Crawling back over rock and through scrub they eventually found a fold in the ground about three feet deep, where he decided they would hole up during daylight.

It started to rain. Through a series of squalls passing over the desert, Fraser saw aircraft taking off from below the horizon. He raised himself high enough to get a good fix on them with his prismatic compass, setting the luminous dial for an accurate bearing that would take them to their target after dark. Then he marked the positions the Afrika Korps were digging, and planned how he would get to the airfield undetected.

Satisfied with his reconnaissance, he settled back into cover. Each of them carried a wool blanket, under which they huddled for protection against the rain, leaving one to stand watch at the edge of the hollow.

A couple of hours later, Fraser was woken by a hiss from one of the team and the sound of a bell. He crawled towards his lookout and raised his head far enough to see a herd of goats grazing through the scrub towards them, followed by a young goatherd.[80]

Afrika Korps soldiers were still digging nearby. The herder stopped. And sat. His charges milled around, feeding. Fraser's men gripped their pistols, and Byrne and his Tommy gun. Fraser surveilled the Germans, then the herder, who made no suspicious move. The Senussi were sympathetic to the British, so he indicated that everyone should relax. In fact, the unflustered presence of the herder and the goats feeding around their position might even reassure their enemy that nothing was untoward.

The herder finally stood as dusk fell, called his bellwether then walked away. His goats followed, uncorralled, in their ancient and mysterious fashion. As the tinkling of the bell faded, Fraser and his team checked their time pencils. One of Phillips's was damaged. They were down to 39 bombs.

The Afrika Korps settled down in the moonless night. Fraser and his men applied boot blacking to their faces. At 6.30pm they moved out, creeping through the German lines to the strains of Lili Marlene from German positions. Fraser followed his compass bearing, stopping frequently – he had fixed the enemy positions during the day, and was now zig-zagging between them. Their occupants talking helped; he was using every shred of advantage surprise could afford him. His daytime recce was paying off. This five-man team was no longer a 'bumbling herd' as it threaded its way silently through the German front line.

It was pitch black when they hit the airfield at 9.15pm. The first indication of the enemy tripwires was the slight tension across the front of the leader's shin. The Germans used flares, or worse still, grenades, like the one Lewes's men had triggered at Tobruk, which flew up and detonated in the air. The point-man stepped back, indicated the location of the booby trap to the rest of the patrol, then carefully traced the wire to its end and led the team round it.

The darkness made it impossible to spot their targets from any distance. The team walked straight into a German anti-aircraft gun position, its sandbagged shape surrounding menacing gun barrels pointing to the sky. They backed up, detoured. And went to ground again when two strolling sentries patrolled across the field. It took them two hours to creep onto the runway.

The team reached their first aircraft at 12.05am, then split and spread out across the airfield. Byrne and Du Vivier wasted a few minutes inside a huge transport plane, hunting for souvenirs, but it was too dark to search properly.[81] They placed a bomb in the cavernous interior and jumped out, just in time to stop Fraser also putting a bomb on the wing.

Fraser and Tait found a line of aircraft, placed bombs on them all, and when they could find no more, added a tractor with a trailer for good measure. The men regrouped at the centre of the strip and waited. Fraser's watch ticked down. The first pencil fuse detonated at 12.42am, bang on time.

And all hell broke loose. The big transport blew, then the line of aircraft. German gunners, thinking it was an air raid, leapt into action. Their Flak 30s spat 120 rounds per minute into the air.

In the glow created by the chaos, Fraser spotted a line of eight brand-new Fiat CR.42 biplanes beside the hangars. These fighters were top of the target list. Fraser shouted to Byrne to collect the team's remaining devices. They had only five left. He turned to the others.

'You three make your way back to the rendezvous. Bob, you're in charge.'

Tait spoke for all of them: 'Get on with it. We'll wait here.'[82]

Fraser ran towards the hangars with Byrne alongside him while the airfield blew around them. Byrne vaulted onto the first wing, cracked the pencil and placed the bomb. Fraser, covering him with his pistol, waved for the Tommy gun but his young companion pretended not to notice.

Fraser was cool enough, despite the intense pressure, to recognise that the Fiats were parked sufficiently close to each other for them to be able to place their limited number of charges on every other aircraft. Then they ran back to get the others.

The team only stopped long enough to place their remaining bomb on an ammunition dump on their way out. The whole area was light as day and, once they were beyond the wire, Fraser stopped to try and count the explosions. It became impossible. The whole line of fighters went up, a series of fires took hold. And all the while the German anti-aircraft gunners hammered tracer into the night sky at imaginary aircraft.

A few miles away, Rommel was woken by the explosions. He walked out of his tent to see Agedabia become a raging inferno. Britain's nemesis wrote to his wife, 'Retreat to Agedabia! You can't imagine what it's like. Hoping to get the bulk of my force through and make a stand somewhere. Little ammunition and petrol. No air support.'[83]

But Fraser wasn't out of the woods. Afrika Korps soldiers stood all around him, firing flares into the darkness in the search of their assailants. With his customary understatement, Fraser later recorded that 'slight trouble was encountered crossing the enemy line'.

The guardians of the airfield still believed they'd been hit by the RAF, whose follow-up raid soon arrived. Fraser and his men watched the RAF bombers completely miss the flaming airfield and hit a nearby road.

It took far longer to navigate this hornet's nest on the way back than it had done on the way in. But stealth and good planning won the day and the target was still burning at 4.30am when Fraser finally lost sight of it. From their hide 12 miles away, LRDG Troop Leader Olivey and the Rhodesians watched the fire in the night sky with admiration.

It had been a textbook special forces operation. In 50 minutes Fraser and his team had destroyed 37 aircraft, a tractor and an ammunition dump. This was the sharp end of Clarke's subliminal methods – the unique British response to *Blitzkrieg*. Never had five infantrymen inflicted so much damage, so fast, against such over-whelming opposition. Fraser, Byrne, Tait, Du Vivier and Phillips – the quiet man from Aberdeen, the teenager, the tough Scotsman, the man who said so little he was unknowable, and a Birmingham gangster.

Rather than *Auftragstaktik*, or mission command, this was inde-pendent action. They had planned their own raid and carried it out, each man relying on himself and never in doubt that any one of them screwing up would sacrifice all their lives.

This then, was the SAS.

PART THREE

Wood Chopping

10

Escape and Evasion: 1941

William Fraser

Alternately running, then walking, Fraser led his team for their rendezvous at the 16km post on the Agedabia-Haseiat track. He looked hopefully at each kilometre post sign as he reached it, all while burning aircraft were lighting up the night sky behind him. The track was covered by deep drifts of windblown sand, forcing the team to detour through soft dune. They had been due to meet the LRDG at two o'clock, but by three o'clock they still had a long way to go, and were just about all in.

The first glow of the sun joined the burning airfield when they finally reached the 16km mark at 4.25am. There was no one there. Fraser bent double, hands on his knees, breathing heavily, for just long enough for him to hear one of the team behind him say, 'They've gone.'

Then LRDG Troop Leader Olivey appeared from the gloom, said 'this way', and led them to his truck, concealed a short way from the track. The sun was fully up by the time they reached the other vehicles of the LRDG patrol. Fraser thanked them for waiting, which had been a risk. A Rhodesian soldier told them, 'It was such a fantastic show that we had to stay until the end.'

The SAS had impressed the LRDG.[1]

The LRDG patrol fanned out into box formation and sped south for Wadi Fareuk, and rendezvous with Reid's advancing E Force. An hour later they spotted dust on the horizon, the scout cars of the King's Dragoon vanguard speeding towards them. Their pennants fluttered to a halt alongside them, and crews jumped down excitedly to hear the news. The first Reid knew of their meeting was pandemonium at the front of his column.

Reid could see Very flares fired into the sky; his whole force had ground to a halt, and everyone was milling around in the desert. He smacked on his driver's cupola and sped forward to get a grip on his troops. He pulled up next to the assortment of scout cars and LRDG trucks, forced his way into their midst, to find five dishevelled parachutists being fêted by his men.

Reid singled out Fraser and asked 'How many aircraft did you destroy?'

'All of them.'

Grinning he marched up to Fraser and gave him a great thump on the back. Fraser winced.[2]

Stirling said it was one of the most useful and successful SAS operations, one that delighted Sandy Galloway in 8th Army, even more than Brigadier Reid.[3] It confirmed to Stirling's sponsor, Ritchie, he had made a good bet, and it gave the Auk an additional Special Force in his arsenal. Thanks to Fraser, the SAS were in business. The British press would focus on Mayne's John Wayne-style kicking in of doors and firing of weapons, but Fraser's stealth was far more effective.

Reid's force sped on for its engagement with Erwin Rommel, and LRDG Troop Leader Olivey decided it was time to take a break, get some breakfast on and get the HF antenna up to radio in their Combat Report. They put out their aircraft recognition panels, the cloth marking a T, to let friendly aircraft know they were an Allied patrol, and set up temporary camp. The signaller tapped out: 'parachutists got 37 planes', at the side of the radio truck while the kettle boiled.[4]

In Jalo Oasis, Stirling and Lewes got excited; Mayne, competitive.

In the desert, breakfast was tea and crushed biscuit porridge. The exhausted men were tucking in when there was roar of aircraft engines, and two RAF Blenheims flashed low over their heads, friends from Kabrit airfield.

On seeing the patrol, the two Blenheim fighter bombers stood on their tails and shot up into the air. They made a wide arc, dropped down to the desert, flying head on at the patrol.

No one had time to process their disbelief as they opened fire.

The Blenheim Mark IV had many guns. Rounds from its .303 Browning machine gun in the port wing, along with the Vickers K under the nose, ripped through the patrol. One Rhodesian, Riggs, was killed instantly, the .303 rounds from the guns, designed to go through panzers, tore him to pieces. Du Vivier was sleeping in the shade of a truck, woke, and rolled away just in time, as the man next to him, the ginger-haired Corporal Ashby, got pounded by bullets.

The aircraft banked, turned and came in for another run. Everyone threw themselves for cover.

Except one Rhodesian.

He stood fully upright, coolly facing the attacking aircraft, their bullets striking all around him; his right arm was fully extended, pointing to the air-recognition panels lying in the sand.[5] The lead Blenheim continued firing, missing everyone. The Blenheim zoomed overhead. His wingman, following, seemed to realise the mistake and banked off.

Corporal Ashby bled out in the arms of a friend.

LRDG Troop Leader Olivey loaded the patrol and they sped away from the horrific scene. When he saw a lonely pile of boulders he decided this would be the final resting place for his men – no one returned corpses from Bagnold's desert.

The Rhodesians went and dug the graves in the shadow of a huge boulder and carried up their friends, wrapped in tarpaulins. When they were ready, Olivey walked up to Fraser and explained the SAS weren't welcome at the burial. Nothing personal, Olivey said, 'But the planes were British, and you are British.'[6]

Fraser, Byrne, Tait, Du Vivier and Phillips watched the small congregation gather in the shade of the huge boulder.

It was a hard road.

Christmas celebrations came early in Jalo, muted by the blue-on-blue. The Rhodesians killed an antelope and roasted it on a braai;

men of the LRDG and SAS shared beer. Operationally, it had been a good run.

8th Army SAS-fan Galloway sent commander of the LRDG, Prendergast, new orders to prepare for the advance on Tripoli. They were to operate deep behind the enemy lines, avoid major opposition and carry out 'pin pricks' at Rommel's lines of communication over as wide an area as possible – to pave the way for the British invasion of Libya.[7] Some in British High Command were getting Clarke's concept of operations.

The 8th Army sent the same order to Leclerc in Chad. He was to operate towards Hon, in the desert south of Sirte, also against the enemy lines of communication.[8] His area of operations would be west of the SAS and LRDG. Rommel was going to be hit the whole length of his supply line – from the front, all the way to Tripoli. Five hundred miles of road, which he would be unable to protect.

Prendergast dispatched an LRDG wireless team to meet Leclerc. L Detachment's SAS men rolled more Lewes bombs out of plastic explosive, thermite and engine oil.

In all of this, Prendergast was clear about his problem: close cooperation between ground patrols and fighter aircraft existed only in the imagination of high command. On the ground, more than one patrol had been shot up by the RAF, with causalities to both men and vehicles.[9] The Germans had been coordinating their aircraft from the ground since supporting Franco's forces in Spain in 1937. At some point, the penny had to drop with the RAF.

The LRDG watered, refuelled, rearmed and prepared to head out with the SAS – first out to ruin Rommel's Christmas were Stirling, Mayne and LRDG man Holliman, on Christmas Eve. Their verbal instruction was to attack Sirte and Tamet landing grounds again, the same targets they had struck out on last time. Mayne, having been out-performed by Fraser, determined to even the score.

Fraser got back just in time for Stirling to ask if he minded going straight back out, before he disappeared in a cloud of dust following

Holliman's Fords. Fraser caught up with Lewes. Regardless of injuries or exhaustion they would hit the road on Boxing Day. He went to get some sleep.

There is a feeling, in sleep deprivation and relentless operations, where the mind starts to detach from the body. The face feels hot. The world around becomes surreal, separated by some field. In this focus shifts, to attention to details, of the checking and rechecking weapons and kit, going over plans. It can improve a man's chance of survival, but on the edge of the physical world, and exhaustion, it is the only thing he can control.

Far from the desert, in the snows of Eastern Europe, Christmas wasn't a happy one in the Fuhrer's bunker, a damp concrete structure built in a forest close to the Russian border. While Rommel watched Fraser burn his aircraft, Corporal Hitler's ambitions faltered in sludge 50 miles outside Moscow. The day Fraser walked to Agedabia airfield, Guderian, architect of Blitzkrieg, flew to see Hitler. In the five hours of ranting, then dinner, Hitler was delusional and wouldn't face facts.

His personal physician, Morell, continued to minister steroids to 'Patient A'.[10] German Chief of Staff Halder witnessed Hitler's first breakdown: 'The Fuhrer is in a state of extreme agitation over the situation. . . . pouring out reproaches and abuse, and shouting orders as fast as they came into his head.'[11] The whole rotten structure collapsed as Russians attacked in the snow. In the heavy fighting, in desperate conditions, Guderian fell back. He wanted to resign, but got fired first.

For Rommel, stranded in Africa, the ghost of Kléber stirred in the gardens of Shepheard's, and Rommel's generalship rose to the challenge. On Boxing Day, he'd done it, and opened his Christmas parcel and took the bottle of champagne straight across to his intelligence truck to share with his intelligence chief.[12] He had survived, just, and if the British thought they were on their way to Tripoli, they didn't understand their enemy.

While Rommel sipped champagne, Fraser watched miles of desert disappear under the wheels of his truck as he sped deep behind Rommel's lines. Morris's patrol carried his and Lewes's teams for two days, and 200 miles, and pulled up 12 miles short of Fraser's target, the airfield at Marble Arch.

The arch stood on what had once been the eastern edge of the Carthaginian Empire. Built over the coast road, Via Balbia, it now marked the boundary between Tripolitania and Cyrenaica, and celebrated Mussolini's brutal suppression of the region. The 31-metre-high folly, on billiard-table flat desert, was also a very convenient landmark for a special forces troop leader.

Fraser and his men dropped from their truck and Morris checked he had a bearing for the airfield. At which point, 21 Stukas flew over. Everyone breathed a sigh of relief as they landed on the airfield to their north. Between them and the landing ground were 40 trucks and Axis troops, and the lethal aircraft had assumed, this far behind their lines, that Fraser and this special forces unit were part of the scenery.[13] At least Fraser knew which way to go.

He shouldered his pack – besides Lewes bombs, he had six days' supply of food and a litre of water.[14, 15] By modern standards, enough for two days at most. Lewes said goodbye. He and Morris would be back in six days to pick him up. Fraser, Byrne, Tait, Du Vivier and Phillips watched them disappear from view.

Fraser and his team laid up till dusk, then walked into the target. They skirted the enemy camp, and 2 miles short of the airfield he found a low hill that gave him a good view of the airfield and the coast road. The team pulled some scrub, used hessian to improve their hide, and as a glimmer of light appeared in the east, settled down for the day.

The men took it in turns to watch the field, those resting fending off flies, cramp and the cold. The airfield buzzed with constant activity. Large formations of aircraft landed, and Fraser assessed these were either reinforcements being flown in from Italy, or this airfield was a staging post for refuelling. Disappointingly, as dusk fell, the last of the aircraft took off, leaving them no target for that night.

Day two, they watched the same number of aircraft take off and land, and again, as dusk fell, the Axis left their airfield empty. The patrol used the darkness to stretch limbs, take some exercise and go to the loo. They couldn't move during the day.

Day three, and again huge formations came in and took off. By dusk, they were watching an empty field – and Fraser and his men were beyond frustrated. Fraser decided this was satellite field, they weren't going to have any joy and, rather than compromise their presence by attacking secondary targets like trucks, they should pull back to the rendezvous and get the LRDG to find them another objective.

Lewes's target, Nofila airfield, was 50 miles straight up the coast road west from Fraser. After dropping Fraser, Morris circled inland, the whole area was crawling with Axis troops, and dropped Lewes as close as he dared, then raced 10 miles south to conceal his patrol.

Lewes made it to his target to see 43 aircraft, many Stukas, and thought he was going to have a field day. He pulled back off the airfield and lay up with his team in an underground water cistern, which they shared with the corpse of a desert fox, the animal had fallen in and been unable to get out. Lewes made the mistake of not leaving anyone observing the airfield.

Lewes led his men back onto the airfield that night – the guards were asleep, the moon full, but in the darkness they found only two unserviceable aircraft, ditched when the rest had flown off. They placed Lewes bombs on them and pulled out.[16] Then went to meet up with Morris's LRDG team.

Waiting at the rendezvous, they saw three Axis vehicles following Morris's tracks to their drop-off. The third vehicle was covered; it could have been a radio direction finding truck, or carrying troops.[17] The Axis were out looking for them. The problem was, as with all their raids, it was very hard for the Axis to pick them up on the way in. But having blown two unserviceable aircraft sky high, they'd announced their presence. Fraser had made better calls.

The trucks hunting them disappeared, and at 6pm Morris's patrol sped into view. Lewes warned him of what he'd seen and they found a hide to lay up and camouflage their vehicles. On the morning of New Year's Eve 1941, they headed to pick up Fraser.

They were just 6 miles from him, at 10am, when they were hit by a twin-engine aircraft – half the patrol said it was a Heinkel 111, half a Messerschmitt 110. Judging by how low it attacked (a Heinkel had a gun in the nose that could swivel, a Messerschmitt 110's guns were fixed) and how much damage the aircraft did, and how fast, those on the flank of the attack saying it was a Heinkel may have been right. A Heinkel would have meant the Kommando hunters had caught up with them.

The patrol were in box formation and dispersed. Lewes was driving. The aircraft flew incredibly low, Morris thought 60 feet, taking a good look at them. An LRDG sergeant on the other side of the box watched it circle and dive for another pass.[18] It singled out Lewes's vehicle, the rest of the patrol hammered at it, tracer arching towards it. From the back of Lewes's truck one of his SAS men shouted, 'He's coming back!'[19]

The desert was completely flat. Cannon fire ripped through the truck, and, as the aircraft screamed overhead, its rear gunner emptied on them for good measure. The truck got riddled. In the back, the team grabbed their Bren gun and ran. One recalls seeing Lewes seated, looking down, and thought, *dear God he's fiddling about with some papers*.[20] They fled to a rock, where they were joined by one of the patrol's Kiwis, and played ring-a-ring-a-roses as the aircraft made repeated passes. From the other side of the box, the LRDG sergeant could see the aircraft targeting men who had fled from their vehicles.[21]

Eventually, the aircraft ran out of ammunition, but when the SAS team got back to Lewes's vehicle it was a wreck, the drive shaft shot through, and there was no sign of him.[22]

The whole LRDG patrol was dispersed over the desert. LRDG Troop Leader Morris had done his best to hide his vehicle when the first two Stukas purred into view along with a Fieseler Fi 156 Storch spotter aircraft. Morris's truck was the first to go – the Luftwaffe meant business.[23]

For the rest of the day, aircraft followed the tracks of individual trucks, and then shot and bombed them to pieces. Packed with fuel and explosives, one by one they blew. Men hid in scrub, terrified to move, because any movement drew the attention of the spotter, and a hail of cannon rounds from their attackers. Morris watched two more vehicles burn up, then smoke rising from the third just out of sight.[24] He only had five trucks to start with.

It went on all day, sortie after sortie. When it was all over, some survivors regrouped at the remaining truck. They managed to cannibalise others to get it running. What had happened to Lewes was unclear. Morris's men reported he had been machine-gunned. One SAS man said Lewes had been shot in the leg, then gunned down trying to get to cover, which confirmed what the LRDG sergeant had seen.[25, 26]

They overloaded the vehicle with the men who had come in and set out to put as much distance as they could between themselves and the Luftwaffe. There was no question of rescuing Fraser, even if they had room, which they didn't. Some survivors left behind at the attack site walked two hundred miles to Jalo – but not Lewes.

Later, an SAS man would say he thought Lewes was buried and his grave marked.[27] Stirling would write to Lewes' father that Lewes had attention from a medical orderly, and remained conscious, giving instruction to the men for 15 minutes until he died from a bleeding artery in the leg.[28] They were good men, sparing any more suffering for friends and family. The truth was that Stirling lost his temper with the SAS survivors, though he knew in the desert it was Bagnold's Rules. No one brought back his body, no one buried him, and, somewhere in the desert, sand blew over Lewes.

When Lewes took the design of the winged god Ra from Shepheard's for the emblem of the SAS, he may not have known that although Ra rises in the east on wings, he sets in the Western Desert, in the Land of the Dead. From there he has to travel back through the underworld, to rise again east of Cairo. Lewes never made that journey.

Escape and Evasion

Fraser waited for Lewes at the rendezvous for six days.[29] A few days earlier they had heard the scream of Stukas, seen them diving in the distance, but had hoped it wasn't one of theirs. The team had virtually run out of water, and had food for two more days. This is the moment every special forces soldier prepares for, and dreads – the moment the umbilical cord is cut behind enemy lines and they are on their own.

Clarke's MI9 team had prepared them for this. In total, his team of seven had now trained 17,000 Allied servicemen in escape and evasion techniques, and had helped lift 1,247 from captivity. Several of them had been captured in the process. A-Force's Lieutenant GP Atkinson paid with his life when the Italians executed him.[30] The SAS, and LRDG, were their highest-risk clients. They were issued silk escape maps, which they sewed into their clothing; survival kits; and a way to distil water using a long rubber tube they all carried. They were briefed on what to do: avoid contact with the enemy and head for British lines. The question for Fraser was where was the British front line?

When they had left Jalo, Reid's scout cars had been attacking Agedabia, and British forces advancing, so hopefully they would be around 70 miles east of their position. Fraser didn't know Rommel had celebrated in champagne having routed the British, and the frontline was now over 200 miles away.

The debate – in special forces it is a debate, unlike in the regular Army – between Fraser and Tait, was whether to highjack a truck, as Tait wanted, or to follow the rules, as Fraser wanted. The rules said to make no contact with the enemy, keep the coast road to their left and follow it home. These men had been in continuous operations for seven weeks. Tait and Du Vivier had suffered more than Fraser, Byrne and Phillips, as they had walked out of the first drop. Tait had injured his ankle – it is easy to sympathise with his resistance to a trek of around a hundred miles.

The team buried their explosives and anything they didn't need, and Fraser told Byrne to bury his Tommy gun. He refused. Fraser said he could keep the weapon provided he understood he couldn't ask anyone else to carry it. Byrne agreed immediately, but Fraser was already anticipating how bad this could get.

In a cold dawn, on 2 January 1942, they cleared up any trace of their hideout, tied their blankets to their haversacks, and, with a tiny drop of water sloshing in their water bottles, set out. [31]

It was only iron discipline that prevented them drinking the remains of their water as they marched single file in the blazing sun. They were in agony immediately. The body needs water; without it, it simply cannot burn carbon into fuel. Their mouths parched and muscles aching, they marched, stopping 10 minutes in every hour to give their bodies a break. No one spoke. At midday they sat in a circle facing each other and the look on their faces said it all. One of Fraser's team suggested this would be how it ended. No one disagreed.

They took turns to lead, each new point-man setting a cracking pace to prove to the others he could do it. Their bodies became automata, stamping into the soft desert sand. At this point the mind goes into a different space, every effort seems huge, the limbs like weights.

When the break approached, those behind closed on the leader. They sat in file, the last man moved to the front to take over. After 10 minutes, they were off again. Only once did the rear man fall out, only just re-joining them when the 10 minutes was almost up. The team asked if he was all right.

'Of course I bloody am. I stopped for a crap that's all.'[32]

At dusk, they had covered 15 miles. They dug holes in the sand, moistened their lips and lit cigarettes. Fraser lay looking up at the night sky. It wasn't raining, but it was freezing. He shivered the night away.

Fraser was up before dawn, still shivering with cold, and as soon as it was light they moved out. In late afternoon, exhausted, they stopped and decided to lay up and continue when it got dark. At dusk they drank the last of their water, and started to drink their own urine.

That night they crested a dune to see the lakes of As Sabkah al Kabirah, 25 miles along their route, shimmering in the moonlight. The lakes are deceptive, not because they are a mirage, but because they are salt water, and the men knew it. For two more hours they marched, each man explaining why, for different reasons, the lakes would now be drinkable. Perhaps in the recent rain, they were. The last half hour turned into a 'murderous' speed march. The men dropped into the wadi, ignored its desolate appearance, lack of vegetation, and threw themselves down to drink. And spat it out immediately.

In desperation, they rushed about the lakes, trying different ones, their beards becoming caked in salt. The more they drank, the more difficult it became to decide if it was salt water. Filling water bottles, they drank fast, and vomited just as fast.

On the north shore of the largest lake are caves, and they lay up in the biggest one. Fraser decided they should try and distil water, which everyone apart from Du Vivier thought would never work. But in desperation they ferried salt water and sand for the distillation process through the hottest part of the day. By dusk they had enough to brew some tea, which tasted like their own urine. Byrne, Phillips and Tait spat theirs out, then watched Fraser and Du Vivier grimace to force theirs down.

Tait proposed he, Byrne and Phillips try and find a well, or derelict vehicles, to drain their radiators. Fraser agreed, provided they left their water bottles so he could keep distilling. Du Vivier wasn't sure who had gotten the shorter straw.[33]

Shortly after they left, Fraser felt the first pain in his stomach. Within the hour both he and Du Vivier were doubled up in pain, retching.

Tait did exactly what he'd wanted to do; he headed north and within an hour was watching Rommel's vehicles racing in both directions on the coast road. The three men hit the road only a few miles west of their first target, where they had driven up the coast with Lewes and shot up the roadhouse. They walked alongside the metalled highway, till they reached a parking space for about three vehicles, marked out with large, empty oil barrels. They rearranged the barrels to make space for only one vehicle, and fell back and hid, Byrne nursing his Tommy gun.

An hour later they were rewarded when a lone covered lorry pulled over. It switched off. They checked the back of the lorry to make sure that there were no troops aboard, and moved to surround it. When no one left the cab, they moved. Tait pulled open the driver's side; Phillips pulled open the passenger door for Byrne to point his Tommy gun at the passenger.

Inside, two German soldiers were examining a miniature pistol, some souvenir, by torchlight. Startled, they made no move when greeted by the bearded, emaciated desperados outside their truck. Tait yanked down the man from his side. Byrne pocketed the tiny pistol and pulled out the man on his side. Phillips was aggressive, but too short to reach.

Quickly they searched the back. It was empty except for the thing they wanted: a jerrycan full of water. Marching the Germans south, they made one carry the can. Tait was determined to persuade Fraser to return and take the truck, but within about half a mile of the lakeside and cave, he said, 'Sod it. Let's turn 'em loose. By the time we collect the others and walk back to the lorry – that's if Bill [Fraser] agrees – it will be nearly daylight.'

Fraser was, ultimately, calling the shots. Tait ordered the Germans to put down the jerrycan. Both Germans, thinking they would now be shot, begged that they were actually Austrians. Tait told them that they shoot Austrians.

The German told him, 'I was born in Hamburg.'

'All right. Clear off then.'[34]

Terrified, they vanished into the night.

The team had a long cool drink from the jerrycan and a smoke. When the Germans came back, saying they were lost, Tait gave them the north star, and the team set off again.

Fraser lay looking out of the cave onto the moonlit lake. He had retched, and – when he didn't have anything to throw up – doubled in pain, with nothing to help Du Vivier, who was similarly suffering. The Italians often threw dead animals into the lakes to degrade the water quality, which is a possible explanation for their illness.

Tait, Byrne and Phillips were as independent spirits as he had ever met in the British Army. It must have crossed Fraser's mind in this dark night that they might not return. When Fraser caught a glimpse of his men clambering down to the lakeside, he breathed one big sigh of relief. In an environment where anyone would have understood leaving a comrade behind, where they had actually captured a vehicle and two German uniforms, these men had chosen to come back. Fraser's greeting 'defied description'.[35]

The next days were good ones. They marched for three days and ran into Bedouin, who gave them dates and replenished their water. With fresh water and food, they were making progress when their bag of wind caught up with them.

Reaching the edge of Wadi el Faregh, the sand started to give way to broken rock and deep wadis. Close to Agedabia, the target where they had blown up 37 Axis aircraft, they had hoped to find some sign of the front line, but they were out of water by mid-afternoon when a sand storm blew up. Parched, the sand ripped through the desert, forcing them to carve out hollows in the ground and shelter under their blankets.

In the morning, the storm had subsided, and they emerged from their holes to find an entire Italian motorised unit had taken shelter in the same spot. The closest basher, tied to the side of truck, was just 20 metres away. As one they rose, their overalls caked in grey dust, indistinguishable from the enemy, turned their backs on the Italians, and marched away to the sounds of the Italians shouting to each other as they also emerged from shelter.

The bluff worked and they got clear of the unit and flung themselves into the cover of a wadi 100 metres further on. Then they noticed one truck parked some distance from the others. Tait took a bearing on it, marking it for attack that night.

All day they laid up, one observing while the others rested. The sentry alerted Fraser. Twelve Italians were advancing straight on their position, and they were only 200 metres away. Realising they had to get out now before they got closer, Fraser pulled his team out. They fell back, found another hollow, then at dusk retraced their steps – the Italians had laid a telephone line over their wadi.

The team prepped their weapons, and once it was dark set out after the lone truck. There was a hurricane lamp burning in the back, covered by flapping canvas, which helped, and at 7.30pm they surrounded the truck.

Three of the team covered Fraser and Phillips as they crept forward silently. The cab was empty. They moved to the back, and everyone braced their weapons. Fraser climbed up over the tailgate, pushed the blanket aside and leapt in, leading with his pistol.

In the glow of the lamp, two Italians were sleeping. He kicked them awake, and they immediately became hysterical, assuming Fraser was a German. Repeatedly telling him they weren't 'Ingleesi' (Fraser's spelling). Phillips, who had been too short to follow him and was hanging onto the tailboard by his elbows, now eventually manged to pull himself in. Inside, the Italians realised they were facing Englishmen. Phillips, the short Brummie gangster, in no way resembled a German. At this point, he may have produced a knife, something that he would use mercilessly throughout his career. The Italians fell silent. If these men were dangerous, here, arguably, was the most dangerous of them all.

Fraser and Phillips turfed out the Italians and searched the truck, while Du Vivier interrogated the Italians in French. The Italians were cooks, and unarmed. From the back Fraser and Phillips threw out a large tin of jam, sardines, a petrol stove and what Tait took to be a water bottle, from which he took a heavy draw, only to find it was the petrol for the stove.

Finding no water, they drained the radiator into their bottles, filled their packs with food and told the Italians there were hundreds of British in the area, before tucking them back into bed. Fraser put the bearing on his compass for Agedabia and, hopefully, home.

Like all escape and evasion, survival had become a combination of skill and luck, but ultimately endurance. If there was one thing these SAS men had in common, they were very, very stubborn.

Crossing Wadi el Faregh, the broken ground and deep crevasses made it impossible to continue walking on the compass bearing, and not making much progress they decided to lay up for the day. Tait was still breathing petrol, so they let him have the first spoonful of jam, watching him push a spoonful into his big bushy, black beard with relish. Next was sardines; Phillips didn't hold back, tipping the empty tin full of oil into his mouth. Finally, they rounded the meal off with pears for pudding. When you are hungry as they were, this was a three-star Michelin feast – Du Vivier never recorded if this topped the meal the LRDG gave him after the drop, but you could hazard a guess.

In good spirits they pushed on as darkness fell, both because they were full and because they thought they would reach the front line that night. The only concern in Fraser's mind was why there was no evidence of that line. They had wandered among dispersed enemy units but if they were approaching the front line these units should be tighter, better camouflaged, dug in and more alert.

Progress through the wadi was murder. The ground kept getting worse and in the end Fraser decided the time had come to agree with his sergeant, Tait, and hit the coast road. They swung north.

Fraser stumbled across a track they hadn't expected to be there, and the team dived for cover as the headlights of a car bounced past. It gave them an idea. They would knock off a car and drive up to the coast road, past the roadhouse, and on to Agedabia.

Phillips, because he was the shortest, volunteered to stand in the track, his blanket pulled round him like a shawl, posing as an Arab, while everyone spread themselves for the ambush.

An hour later they were rewarded when headlights hit Phillips. The car sped towards him and he took two paces forward, confusing the driver, who swerved off the road. Within seconds both driver and passenger were on their faces in the dirt, their rifles thrown into the darkness. The team had bagged a small open-top

Mercedes Benz. The men wanted to drive but Fraser insisted they put a German behind the wheel, who would know where the minefields were. Fraser pointed his pistol at the driver and he climbed in beside him, the others crammed into the back. The driver immediately told Fraser he was Austrian, and Tait's thick Scottish voice came from behind.

'Dammit. I didn't want to shoot anyone today.'[36]

Terrified, the driver sped off.

The tiny car hit the coast road and turned right towards the remains of the roadhouse. Axis vehicles flashed past on the narrow road. Like when they had been in the Lancia, the team were confident that their stolen car and dust-covered uniforms gave no cause for suspicion. But when they approached the roadhouse at Mersa-Brega, the driver complained the road ahead was mined, and they forked right into the salt marsh.

The driver complained this area was also mined, and, approaching another junction, instructions were issued to him from both Fraser in the front and those in the back of the vehicle. The terrified driver, in his confusion, drove off the track and into the salt marsh. Despite repeated efforts to free the vehicle, it stuck fast, burying its wheels ever deeper into the mud to the point where five of them couldn't budge it.

Fraser sent the driver and other prisoner back up the track, Du Vivier having pointed out the north star for them. Once they were out of sight, Fraser set his compass for Agedabia again and the patrol turned east, trudging through marsh, which was both noisy and hard work.

When dawn rose, they waded out of the marsh to lie down exhausted on dry ground, fearing to move so close to the front line. They roasted all day like lizards, only without the water retention. Parched, they moved on after dark. Fraser smelt the mass grave before he saw it. The moon hadn't risen and it was pitch dark, the night filled with the sickly sweet, cloying smell of human decomposition, accompanied by the sound of flies. And they walked straight into it.

In the darkness Fraser could see from the uniforms that they were British. They had been buried in a long pit, but the grave had been looted, and now bodies were pulled out and strewn all over the ground, probably by animals. Inside the pit, heads, arms and limbs extended at odd angles from the sand. Their comrades had died *en masse*, wood chopped on a regular battlefield. It was a death Fraser and his men had joined special forces to avoid – they might be alone, behind enemy lines, but they held their fate in their own hands.

They picked their way through the bodies in silence.

After two miles there was a shout from a German sentry, and they went to ground and doubled back. Now they wondered if they were hearing things. Had there really been a shout? Or had they only thought they heard it? They circled round the suspected sentry position and Fraser resumed walking on the same bearing.

Three miles later they hit the German position proper, on a feature running from north to south across their front. This was it. The start of the German line. Fraser walked south, parallel to it, trying to find a way through, but it doubled back, trenches and sentries stretching across their front going to their west. He stopped. They were exhausted. There was no way round.

Close to the end of their journey, Fraser knew this would be the most dangerous part – the density of enemy troops would be highest and the enemy at their most alert.

The team decided to walk through.

The moon was up, and bright, when they walked up the escarpment, German positions all around them. There was a shout. And then the Germans opened fire. Green tracer arched into the night; Fraser and the team dived for cover and crawled forward on their bellies.

As he crawled, Fraser could see the net closing in. The Germans were out of their trenches, looking for them, unsure where they were. The closest was just 20 metres from him. If he was caught lying on the ground in the open, he was dead. He looked around; there were Germans in every direction. He gripped his pistol, looked back at the team, and they rose, crouched with their weapons at the ready.

They were going down with a fight.

But the Germans didn't open fire. Fraser stood upright and started walking. The team stood and followed him. At the appearance of armed men in their midst, the Germans had assumed they were German. And they walked straight through the position.

For two days they picked their way through the German front line, almost walking into German positions, avoiding sentries, laying up by day. On the second night they saw an orange light ahead. It didn't move, so they crept towards it. It was a low, flat-roofed tent, about four feet high. Fraser picked up a pebble and threw it at the tent. Inside, a silhouette sat up. He watched it. The figure lay back down.

He crept to the side of the tent, lifted the flap, and pointed his pistol into the light. The smell of putrefaction hit him immediately. A man and small child crawled towards him. In broken Arabic, Fraser explained they needed water. The man pointed to a British Army petrol can. He drank gratefully, and handed it out to the team. It tasted like death smelled.

The man was Senussi, and gave Fraser dates, and then showed him the bodies of his wife and other child, the source of the smell, lying at the side of the tent. Fraser couldn't understand how they had died. Perhaps something to do with the battle that had raged around them. The man explained that now sometimes the Germans came, sometimes the English, sometimes on the same night.

They had reached the middle of no man's land. Next they would reach the British front line.

He told the patrol and excitedly they marched for the rest of that night. Dawn approached, and the visibility was low, sand blowing through the battlefield. They found themselves among derelicts, shapes of burnt-out armoured cars and tanks looming out of the sand. They scavenged among their remains for food and water, pulling out incinerated cans and finding the middle edible once they had peeled away the charcoal.

The sun rising ahead of them, they dropped down a wadi, following the rock scree, and looked up. There were scout cars on the ridge ahead. Clambering towards them, they saw that these vehicles flew the pennants of the King's Dragoon Guards, hanging limply from their radio antennas, the same unit of Reid's that had greeted them after they had destroyed 37 aircraft.

The Dragoons scrambled down into the ravine to help them. They had made it. Their wings had carried them through the underworld, and Ra rose to meet them, burning orange through the sand.

The King's Dragoon Guards had been decimated by Rommel. But they patted Fraser and his men on the back and packed them on a truck towards the British forward HQ at M'Sus. Fraser climbed in the front, and a short while into the journey, Tait banged on the back of the cab. Fraser turned round.

Tait told him he needed to take a leak.

'Leak over the tailboard,' Fraser replied. 'What the hell's the matter with you?'

The lorry slowed, and Fraser got out to go round to the tailgate to find out the real problem. He was greeted by the grinning, bearded faces of his desperate crew. Without a word, Tait pointed to their cargo: the truck was loaded with rum and cartons of milk. Fraser clambered into the back and hammered on the cab to move. And pulled his mug from his haversack.

Fraser didn't know how long the journey was, but it was long enough. When they fell off the truck at M'sus, they had drunk the lot. He reported at British HQ to a young British major. Fraser did his best to salute, and slurred, 'I'm afraid we owe you for two jars of rum and 24 tins of milk.'

For a moment the major looked serious, then started laughing, claiming that it wasn't possible. He went to the back of his truck, where the evidence was clear to see.

'Forget it.'[37]

Later, Fraser went to Byrne and asked him for the tiny pistol. He wanted to present it to the major in thanks for not reporting them.

Reluctantly, Byrne gave it to him. Fraser came back later with his precious silver hip flask, and handed it to Byrne; 'I'm sure you'll be able to carry that as well as the Tommy gun.'[38]

Fraser said that his men behaved admirably during both this escape and the raid, and had made his task much easier by their cheerfulness and ready obedience to orders. Their determination not to be captured under any circumstances was particularly noticeable.[39]

He flew up to 8th Army HQ and reported to General Ritchie and British Intelligence (which meant Clarke got to hear about it).[40] Ritchie quizzed Fraser on everything, from raiding with the LRDG, to hitting the airfield, to how he managed to escape 200 hundred miles through enemy lines.

Fraser would receive the Military Cross, the first SAS Officer to receive the award.

Hellfire

Shepheard's had been putting up the Christmas tree when Clarke got called to Grey Pillars yet again. When Rommel had fallen back to Agedabia, he had left behind a force in Hellfire Pass with suitably Nazi orders to fight to the last man. They were led by a German, Major Bach, a one-time Lutheran pastor, who, with a strong position in Hellfire, and God on his side, seemed resolved to ignore his hopeless position now Rommel was 300 miles to his rear.

A British Army unit, 30 Corps, was ordered to 'reduce' the garrison in the New Year – reduce being a military euphemism for particularly bloody fighting against determined opposition that is going to take a long time. The unit had already taken heavy losses outside Tobruk; that they didn't fancy this mission was understandable, and they asked Clarke if he could help.

The first thing Clarke did was get an Egyptian film crew to go and record British tanks driving around their barracks in Cairo. This recording was rushed up to Hellfire, given to a British propaganda unit and within 48 hours the German defenders were listening to a large number of British tanks driving around in the dark. It isn't hard to see where Clarke got his idea from – sitting with his younger brother Tibby in the 'talkies', when the British cinema sound company was his client.[41]

Sun Tzu's maxim is 'know your enemy' – what, Clarke wondered, would induce Major Bach to surrender. An order from Rommel should do it. Clarke found out that the redoubtable Bach did not have a radio capable of talking to Rommel (he would have needed a high-frequency set, such as the LRDG used). It had been necessary for him to slip a messenger out and round the coast to the Italians at Bardia, also under siege, to send a message.

By this time, Clarke had a whole cell dedicated to forgery. A-Force Technical Unit reassembled fragments of Axis documents found on dead soldiers and airmen and produced fake ones for Clarke. In this case a letter from Rommel to Bach. The problem was, Rommel had recently been promoted to Field Marshal, and Afrika Korps were now called Panzergruppe Afrika, and Clarke didn't have an updated letterhead to copy. So he chanced using the old Afrika Korps letterhead. In the Castle of String, his noisy air-conditioner for company, Clarke typed out,

> The heroic resistance of the defenders of Halfays [Hellfire] has now achieved its object . . . I have no wish to demand more sacrifices than are necessary . . . I give you formal permission to make an honourable surrender.[42]

Clarke wanted to send over a captured German aircraft by day. This was chancy, as it could have been shot down by Allied aircraft, or caused panic on the ground. Instead, he packaged the letter up and sent the container over on the night of 29 December in a Wellington bomber – because a Wellington has two engines, and is the same size as a Heinkel III.

German defenders saw the silhouette of this aircraft coming in from the sea. Then they saw its rear gunner open fire on something, which Clarke hoped they would assume was a pursuing British fighter, before dropping a container, and disappearing back out to sea.

Clarke sat in Shepheard's watching the New Year's Eve party in full swing, and wondered whether his plot had worked.

He came close. The only reason it didn't work is because Hitler decided to send his own message to the Hellfire defenders at the same time, exhorting them to fight on, and telling them they were doing a valuable job. But he did achieve a massive, unintended, win. One that would colour his future deceptions.

On 30 December, a confused Bach had dispatched his signals officer to Bardia to use the Italian radio. Querying the letter he had received from Rommel ordering the evacuation of Hellfire, Bach said he assumed it was an enemy deception, but he wasn't sure. Rommel replied strongly he never sent it. Too late, the wires had already burnt to Rome, saying Rommel may have ordered his troops to surrender. In the bust-up, Hitler in his faraway, damp bunker, was suspicious.

Clarke's subliminal methods had reached the epicentre. For the first time he had placed doubt in the mind of the sick and paranoid leader of the Nazi project. He called it a near miss as he celebrated with champagne. Outside, in the garden, the ghost of Kléber knew Rommel was going to die. The only question was, by whose hand?

II

Hubris: 1941–1942

The Real SAS

In the early morning, the sun on the Bitter Lake emerging from the haze, Fraser hobbled through the Kabrit camp lines for his tent. Withers greeted him enthusiastically, but when Fraser lifted the flap, he found another officer was unpacking his uniform on the bed. The bearded, wild-looking Fraser said, in no uncertain terms, 'My tent.'[1]

The man stuttered apologies, and said something about being told Fraser was dead. Fitzroy Maclean was good friends with Stirling's brother at the Embassy, and Stirling had just recruited him. Fraser headed for the bed as the officer hurriedly cleared his belongings. The man fled, his belongings in a bundle, taking one shocked look at the state of Fraser's feet, by which time Fraser was most probably asleep, guarded by Withers.

In Grey Pillars that day, the Auk congratulated Stirling on his fine beard, and outlined what he wanted Stirling to do next – stop Rommel's panzers. Clarke's original concept for PLAN ANTI-ROMMEL, that SAS parachutists, trained in demolition, could disable Rommel's striking power, his panzer units, was coming back into play.

Heavily armed panzer units, dispersed in the desert, were an unrealistic target for the SAS, but the Auk had a plan. Italian special forces had, a month earlier, shown what could be achieved. A team of six Italian special forces frogmen rode underwater on three manned torpedoes, nicknamed *maiali* (pigs), followed a British destroyer flotilla, opening the harbour's submarine boom, and placed limpet mines on the fleet's two largest battleships: HMS *Queen*

Elizabeth, and HMS *Valiant*. Both were holed below the waterline, handing the Italians naval supremacy in the eastern Mediterranean. It was the definition of a strategic special forces operation.

The Auk explained that six of Rommel's ships had just arrived in Tripoli from Italy the night before.[2] Churchill had sent a worried telegram from the White House, where he was meeting Roosevelt. Both men feared the worst: Rommel had been sent fresh panzers. Up at the front line, new 8th Army Commander Ritchie was under no illusions: 'We are out gunned in tanks and until this is righted . . . our tactics must be modified accordingly.'[3]

The Auk pointed at the map. He had forced Rommel out of his port of Benghazi, so the nearest deep-water port to his line was Bouerat, 300 miles to his rear. He wanted the SAS to put limpet mines on Axis tankers in the port, and blow up the panzers' fuel.

Stirling went back to the flat to make a plan. But Maclean's recruitment highlighted the SAS's biggest problem: casualties. Stirling had less than 20 men left for the mission. Even if he persuaded the adjutant general to let him recruit from British units, which had been decimated, it still took more than eight weeks to train for the SAS. And there was a high failure rate on Lewes's tough selection course; many regulars just weren't going to cut it.

In 'Joe's Parish', Clarke could help. There was an existing Allied parachute unit in the Middle East; it was French, and under the command of General Catroux. Clarke, with his personal relationship with Catroux and his staff, could get Stirling in to see him. Catroux had been appointed High Commissioner to the Levant, after Fraser had helped liberate it, and the Free French parachute unit was in Syria.

Clarke would also have been able to brief Stirling; Catroux was a precise man – when he first met Catroux in Fez in 1924, Catroux had been wearing patent leather shoes, not ideal footwear for counterinsurgency operations. Clarke had also found out Catroux did not like the English. During Catroux's tour of Syria-Lebanon after the First War he had fought the Arab Druse insurgency, part of the fallout from the betrayal of Lawrence's Arab Revolt. In the newly divided mandate, the British in Palestine may have been helping the insurgents oppose the French, just over the border in Lebanon. Not a popular move with the Frenchman, though he had been far more helpful to Clarke when Clarke was propping up the British against the Arab insurgency in Palestine in 1936.[4]

Stirling headed to Beirut for the interview. On arrival he bumped into fellow aristocrat Viscount Bill Astor, working for Army Intelligence. The two went on a 'zig-zag' – Astor was very good at showing Stirling all the nightspots and Stirling was done in by the time he rolled into bed in the early hours.

Stirling then set out to do his recruiting act with a man he thought was De Gaulle. He had forgotten the interview was with Catroux – it appears he was not sober. In front of the immaculately dressed, highly polished French officer, the hungover Stirling made no headway. Catroux said 'non', and Stirling played his trump card, saying under his breath, 'You're as bad as the bloody English in Middle East HQ.'

Catroux asked, 'You're not an Englishman?'

'No, I'm a Scotsman. I'm surprised at you, General, for not allowing your chaps to join their own unit, as it's going to be.'

French parachutists had been champing to get into the action, and the offer to let them join as an independent French unit seems to have swung it. Catroux relented.[5]

In the continuing chaos in Grey Pillars caused by Churchill's demand that they reform the Commandos, there was a meeting on Boxing Day. Some unit commanders, such as Stirling, wanted to be 'absolutely independent and directly under GHQ'. Others felt it wrong to have 'a number of little private armies'. But the SAS were a demonstrably successful special force. Four days later, the Middle East Parachute Detachment (SAS being too galling a concession on paper) included the Free French. Protected from on high, Stirling got what he wanted.[6]

He set out with one of Courtney's nascent SBS teams, a folboat and limpet mines for Bouerat, to destroy Rommel's tankers. But after their LRDG patrol were caught by an air attack, they ended up with a bundle of broken canvas and wood and no way to paddle out to the targets.[7] In reality Stirling was already too late. The Auk had been right: two weeks earlier Rommel had landed 55 Panzers and 20 armoured cars, which were fuelled, armed, and ready to go.[8]

Rommel's counterattack opened by reducing the threat from British special forces. Kommando Hunter, Theo Blaich bombed Leclerc's French forces to prevent them harassing his lines of communication. Blaich's Heinkel 111 – stripped of everything, including its defensive guns and loaded with extra fuel tanks to fly more than a thousand miles – took off from a remote strip at Hon on 21 January.

The bomber zoomed over the airfield at Fort Lammy, on the banks of Lake Chad, at 2.30pm. Leclerc's airfield had no anti-aircraft guns, thinking it was inconceivable that it could be hit at this range. In a few minutes, 16 German bombs incinerated the fuel dump and all the defender's Hawker Hurricane fighters on the ground.[9]

Blaich barely made it home. Running on vapours, he crash landed, and spent five days in the desert. He was rescued by the Italians direction-finding his weak signal, as he used the last remains of his fuel to power one engine for the radio.

Leclerc lost all his fighter aircraft and half his fuel. For an operation against Rommel already running on a shoestring, it was significant. More importantly, the 'Kommandos' – whether they be Free French, LRDG or SAS, knew the lengths the Germans would go to get to them.

Rommel's fresh panzers attacked the British line, and the British reeled back 'as if stung.'[10] Churchill signalled the Auk, 'Have you really had a heavy defeat . . . has our fresh armour been unable to compete with the resuscitated German tanks?'[11] Rommel had 111 panzers, the British 150, but it was a massacre. British armour got wiped out.

Stirling and his small team made it back to Jalo Oasis, to find the LRDG packing up in a hurry in anticipation of the arrival of the Axis. He flew up to 8th Army HQ, to meet the Auk, who had flown in from Cairo to prop up his puppet, Ritchie. Rommel had just taken Benghazi. Benghazi was a much bigger port than Bouerat, big enough to bring in both panzers and tankers, providing a great target for the SAS to attack Axis ships. The SAS's mission was unchanged: sink ships.

Stirling arrived back in Kabrit to find Mayne had been drinking, and lost his temper with him. Fraser had watched French paratroops, led by their troop leader, Captain Georges Roger Pierre Berge, arrive from Syria, having left in a snowstorm and driven the whole way. Having lost Lewes, and with Fraser unfit, Stirling had left Mayne to put the French through Lewes's selection and parachute course. But the death of Mayne's best friend, Eoin McGonigal, had hit him hard. With the area of the SAS drop liberated by the British, Mayne hitched out into the desert to look for his friend's body. A man wracked by grief, who thought the region's maps hopeless, wandered alone in the hard, rocky, thorn-covered Cyrenaican desert. He took to drinking in the Sergeants' Mess, despite his superior rank, and they felt obliged to stay up. Du Vivier soon realised there was no point trying to go to bed, for by the morning you'd have drunk yourself sober.[12]

On a night in the Officers' Mess, down on the Bitter Lake, the closest Stirling got to understanding Mayne was when Stirling opened up about his experiences as an artist in Paris. His own frustration with being rejected. The look in Mayne's eyes made Stirling realise he had hit a nerve. Stirling felt Mayne had a creative urge, constantly seeking expression. With no outlet, it got bottled up to an intolerable level, which led to his heavy drinking bouts.[13]

Every reference to intoxication also references the destruction of the ego – blasted, waxed, plastered, smashed – even zig-zag, suggests going round an obstacle in order to discover our true path.[14] Frustrated by this closed door, Mayne fell to bullying, homophobia, violent acts and black moods. Its only positive outcome was the instinct it gave him on the battlefield. Sun Tzu called this the 'Art of War.'

The Desert Fox

The Auk landed back from the frontline on a Sunday evening, 1 February 1942, a worried man. Could someone urgently go and find Clarke? At 8pm on a Sunday evening, Clarke was out to dinner, but was picked up on return to Shepheard's. Late that night in the conference room at Grey Pillars, he discovered the situation in the desert was grim. Rommel had advanced 200 miles in the last few days with his seasoned Germans in the vanguard, and there was little to stop him.[15]

The 8th Army were preparing a defensive line between Gazala, the fishing village 50 miles west of Tobruk, and Bir Hacheim, an oasis about the same distance, south-west of Tobruk. But the British needed time to get established before the panzers arrived. Could Clarke convince Rommel he was walking into a trap, forcing him to advance with more caution?

At 6am the following morning, Clarke rubbed his hands to keep warm, waiting for his aircraft at Heliopolis airfield. He bounced through Bagush and touched down at Gazala at 11.30am.[16] It was clear the 8th Army was in full retreat: vehicles streamed back along the Via Balbia, and Clarke reached Ritchie's HQ to find it being packed up in a blinding sandstorm. Ominously, he found some units had been sent back to prepare defences on the Egyptian frontier, behind Tobruk – no one had any faith that the Gazala line would hold.

He found General Ritchie and RAF man Arthur 'Mary' Conningham under flapping canvas. They told him that for the deception plan to work it had to immediately persuade Rommel to halt his advance. Clarke spent the next two days touring British positions, from the front to Tobruk, in his personal liaison aircraft, before landing back in Cairo to present his findings to the Auk.[17]

The plan, BASTION, was immediately approved by the Auk. Clarke was back on the plane at 6.45am to the front to implement it. Troops were used to haulage trucks zooming into the desert, after which previously unknown units appeared, and the airwaves filled with their transmissions, called 36, 37, 101 Royal Tank Regiments, with fake badges to match.

Clarke had to convince Rommel they had 300 tanks, but he only had 150 dummies. The Germans often used Bedouin tents to hide their panzers, so Clarke had 150 canvas tents dyed black like the Senussi's, and shipped up to the desert. Set up overnight, on 15 February, behind the left of the British line, this camp had two fake tanks sticking out of the front of a couple of tents, as if the tents had blown off, surrounded by tracks. It fooled the Luftwaffe – at noon the following day it was hit by three bombers dropping 12 bombs, after which it was strafed continually.

On the north of the line the story was the same: 52 of his dummy tanks were hit by the Luftwaffe. To the rear he deployed dummy tanks inside Tobruk, while his camouflage unit made the Tobruk defences look far more formidable than they were. Tobruk had been stripped after the port was relieved, and now, with Rommel advancing, old Desert Rats were depressed at the prospect of a siege with so little preparation. Clarke's fakery had the effect of boosting Allied morale when they saw things like a new jetty being built – even though on close inspection, the jetty was very temporary.

All the while Clarke's spy network fed the story to the Abwehr in Portugal and Istanbul. CHEESE was blown after the double bluff before the offensive, but Maunsell managed a 'neat leak' to Vichy French diplomats travelling from Cairo to France via Istanbul. All seemed to be going well until Clarke arrived back at 8th Army to the bombshell news that panzers were gathering on the opposite side of the line. Clarke had only had the operation running for three days, far too little time for him to guarantee it was effective. General Ritchie thanked him and Clarke left for Cairo – apparently, he had failed.[18]

Then a strange thing happened. Rommel's armoured columns approached Gazala, but then stopped. They remained stationary all day. Everyone at 8th Army HQ braced themselves; out in the desert gun crews squinted into the west. That night the panzers withdrew. Nobody knew what lay behind the strangely un-German manoeuvre.

On Rommel's side, a few days earlier, the Italians had taken an Army Corps away from him. They were afraid, and wanted to discourage him from advancing any further.[19] He had moved forward for the next couple of days, then stopped. One explanation was he was desperately short of fuel. But he had flung units at the British with insufficient fuel before. Perhaps, with the Luftwaffe reporting large British tank reserves ahead, he had thought the British were far stronger than they were. Had Clarke subliminally planted this idea? He liked to think so.[20]

Fraser sat shotgun in the LRDG truck. He knew this journey, out past the Giza pyramid, the track to the giant dunes, north through the Sand Sea, before sweeping into Siwa. Here the LRDG were as busy as ever, patrols ranging behind Rommel's advance. He went to the stone Rest House for the briefing. The symbol for the LRDG was the scorpion – it could hide in sand and had a lethal sting in the tail. The SAS was a plug-in-and-play for the LRDG – the SAS added more venom, they could get into airfields on foot, blow up Rommel's aircraft, everything they needed was supplied by the scorpion's body, the LRDG.

Fraser's relationship with other troop leaders such as Olivey in the LRDG was based on mutual respect, but Stirling referred to the LRDG as 'Carter Paterson' – after the British road haulage firm.[21] New Zealand and Rhodesian LRDG rank and file referred to the SAS as 'Parashites'. In the end, they were individual commands led by two very different men: Guy Prendergast, and David Stirling.

Stirling prepared to hit Rommel's tankers in Benghazi using a vehicle he had converted by cutting down a Ford, nicknamed the 'Battle Wagon', which resembled a German staff car. He took the SBS folbot team again. But Fraser and the rest of the SAS would hit five of his airfields spread over Cyrenaica; Fraser's target was

Barce, to the east of the port of Benghazi. This was in response to a message from Churchill to the Auk:

> *I have not much troubled you these difficult days, but I must now ask what are your intentions. According to our figures you have substantial superiority in the air, in armour, and in other forces over the enemy. There seems to be danger that he may gain reinforcements . . . faster than you. The supply of Malta is causing us increased anxiety . . . Pray let me hear from you.*[22]

The Auk had given up trying to explain problems in cooling systems and the range of British tank guns – and turned to the SAS to satisfy the insatiable. The Auk's regular forces were unable to attack Rommel – so it fell to the SAS.

Wearing only shorts and sandals in the early summer heat, Fraser and his team sped west, and through The Wire. At night, he and his team huddled in thick coats round campfires. The LRDG rations were better than the regular Army: sardines and tinned fruit, after which they drank issue rum, or, for Fraser and his Highlanders, whisky, a taste the Brummie gangster, Phillips, might have been acquiring. Tuning their radio to the BBC, they listened to the eight o'clock news, then jazz, after which they spun it to Radio Belgrade, to listen to the German soundtrack for the campaign, Lili Marlene.[23]

Somewhere in the darkness to their north, two massive armies eyed each other up – Fraser fell asleep to the German singer's voice – he felt better off out here.

Further behind Rommel's lines their routine changed, no more wake-up calls to bangers and beans, and now they drove at night. Moving up over the Trigh el-Abd track, so familiar to Fraser, camel bones shone in the darkness. They passed derelicts, filled with the charred remains of their crews, scanned the ground ahead for dangerous Italian 'thermos bombs'. Downed bombers loomed out of the darkness, huge shadows of tailfins, like ghosts, far out in the desert.

They reached Jebel Akdar, the 'green mountains', so called because the rains hitting the escarpment above Benghazi turn them lush with vegetation. Driving through miles of greenish-brown moor, it reminded Fraser of the Highlands. The spring flowers had faded, but the air was filled with wild thyme, crushed under their wheels.[24]

The LRDG team pulled up short of the target. Fraser got the bearing and he and his men moved out, silently, in single file. This was getting familiar. The raid was a wash-out; he saw one aircraft on the field, blew it, and pulled back. When they rendezvoused with the other teams, he found a similar story. Stirling had met with a broken canoe and a gale on the dockside at Benghazi. Only Mayne's team had added 17 aircraft to their tally. And it was a tally for Mayne; this was all personal, and he kept a record of all the aircraft he destroyed. But there was bad news: Mayne had taken Byrne in with him as the fourth man of his team, and he was missing.

On Mayne's airfield, their Lewes bombs went off unexpectedly early, and Byrne and an SAS sergeant ran from cover. Disagreeing about what to do next, they split, Byrne hoping to make the rendezvous with the LRDG. But the LRDG weren't there. He waited till midday, but then with memories of how Fraser and he had waited till they were out of water, he set out for the British line 200 miles away. He had with him two pints of water and Fraser's hip flask, full of brandy.[25]

Mayne had got lost leaving the airfield, and wandered with the rest of his team for five and half hours until it became light. Luckily, they were offered shelter by the Senussi. Not only were the Senussi friendly, but they were obliged to offer shelter to anyone lost in the desert. [26] He was rescued by chance when the LRDG turned up in the morning, trading dates for chickens. The LRDG went to the rendezvous but found it empty, with no explanation as to where Byrne had gone.

Byrne trudged on. On the second day the going got hard: it was now summer. With temperatures soaring, he discarded his beloved Tommy gun, scattering the parts in the sand to render it useless.

Vomiting and delirious with heatstroke, he was saved by some Senussi, who took him in and fed and watered him.

The next day he walked into a German position, not seeing the concealed panzers till it was too late. The Germans had seen him miles away, and Byrne was immediately surrounded by German soldiers. A young, and frightened, German officer emerged from a panzer, shouting, 'Give me your arms. Put up your hands.'

The officer had his pistol pointed at Byrne's face. Byrne reached to remove his own pistol from his belt and the officer shot him in the face.

Byrne went down. Blood spurted from his nose.

Around him there was shouting – *so he wasn't dead.*

Arms reached down to pull him up and everyone, including the officer, grasped his hand or thumped him on the back. It appeared the officer had only meant to hit him in the face with his pistol, not shoot him. By some miracle the bullet had only gashed his nose and left eyebrow.

Byrne was marched through what looked like the whole panzer army concealed in the desert. Their general ordered he be shipped to Germany, and when he arrived back in Benghazi, as a guest of the Germans, his interviewer asked him his name and unit. When Byrne didn't reply, the man laughed, told him his CO was David Stirling, of the Scots Guards: 'Do try and remember it.'[27]

The Birth of a Regiment

On 4 May 1942, Clarke and Stirling sat for dinner at Shepheard's. On the menu was: The Future of L Detachment, SAS.[28]

The success of the SAS had raised the spectre of the rapid expansion of parachute operations. The Auk wanted to form two parachute battalions from his Indian troops, and, as per their remit, training them would fall to L Detachment, SAS. With a strength of 3 officers and 13 men, that would spell the end of operations for Stirling, Fraser and Mayne.

The document Stirling submitted to Grey Pillars flattered the Auk's Indian Troops. Clarke knew the Auk's love of India, and Indian troops did have an extremely good war record. But, they asked, why not expand the SAS instead of inventing new forces? The SAS could be doubled without putting the adjutant general's nose out of joint. If the British SAS were raised to 190 men, and the French paratroops did the same, with some additional recruits, they could create a force of more than four hundred.

It was worth setting down the knife and fork in Shepheard's garden that hot summer night to consider this. It definitely caught the ear of Kléber's ghost. More than four hundred soldiers means a regiment, the smallest independent unit of the British Army. The creation of a new regiment was so rare that it hadn't happened for 42 years, since Stirling's uncle had established the Lovat Scouts for the Boer War.

How did Clarke and Stirling plan to do this?

Besides expanding the French contingent, and taking in the folboatists of the SBS, men such as Jellicoe, Clarke and Stirling planned to plunder a very unpopular unit, the new Middle East Commando (more often referred to in Grey Pillars as 1 SS).

After the meeting between the Auk and Churchill in Chequers on 2 August the previous year, the Commandos had been reformed, but Grey Pillars only kept the name 'Commando' because it was the prime minister's wish.[29] The force was an amalgamation of commandos rotting in Genifa camp, along with new units that had been raised in Palestine to operate as guerrillas on the Turkish-Syrian border (in case the Germans came that way from Stalingrad). Much of this was now under command of the (not so secret) office of the Special Operations Executive, from their flat on Gezira island. Of the unit of roughly 140 men, 40 had even done the SAS jumps course. It would be weeks before Grey Pillars found out Stirling had already poached one officer from the unit.

Stirling had his eye on the rest of this unit, particularly their Palestinian recruits in Genifa camp – a unit set up by 26-year-old

Officer Herbert Cecil Buck, a fluent German speaker. After he had escaped captivity by posing as a German officer, Buck realised how easy it was, and recruited 20 German-speaking Jewish soldiers from the Middle East Commando, including one Austrian, one Lithuanian, two Polish, one Czech, and one Hungarian, and had formed them into the 'Special German Group'.[30] They took the cover name the Special Interrogation Group to hide their real activity: posing as Germans. Grey Pillars found a functioning German staff car, and this became a 'Fifth Column', named after Ernest Hemingway's 1938 book.

This was just the sort of subliminal force Clarke and Stirling loved, and definitely a step up from the Battle Wagon. Dressed as Germans and speaking German, they could spread untold amounts of subliminal damage. In the same way as Clarke's dodgy Coppers ammunition, it could lead to the Panzergruppe Afrika looking for saboteurs among their own ranks.

Clarke and Stirling's proposal made the distinction that the only thing in common between special forces and paratroops was the accident of the parachute, and highlighted the need to invest in selection and training. This was the product of the hard years of experience of Clarke, and now Stirling. They knew better than anyone that selection and training were the cornerstone to any special force.

The next bit of their argument was aimed directly at the Auk. That an expanded SAS, of even between 120 and 160, could sabotage 10 airfields in one night. They could take out all the main staging points on Rommel's lines of communication from Tripoli to Benghazi, and the main Axis aerodromes of Crete, Rhodes, Greece and (possibly) Sicily. They stressed how urgent this was, and that L Detachment, SAS could do it long before any Indian troops could be trained.

Stirling finished with a threat. If they did not agree, then, under the terms of service of the Commando under which they had joined – six-month tours while actively employed – then he, Fraser, Mayne and all the men could resign. They were under no obligation to train Indian paratroops. Berge and the French paratroops, not under British command, would threaten the same.

Clarke and Stirling toasted their work. From the same venue as Bagnold had founded the LRDG, Clarke dreamt up the SAS, Lewes and Stirling forged L Detachment, they sent this missive to Director of Military Training in Grey Pillars.[31]

The Director of Military Training passed it to a subordinate, the newly appointed Director of Special Operations, a Colonel, to assess. His response was terse: 'we would be grateful if the suggestions contained in the letter could be firmly supressed'.

He was particularly annoyed that they had sent it over his head, since he would have been able to crush it, and now couldn't. But it was neither Clarke nor Stirling's first rodeo. Director of Special Operations was annoyed that, having taken great pains to train the Fifth Column unit, he was being asked to give them up. He used the word 'mulcted' – which means take possession by fraudulent means.

Being threatened, the Director of Special Operations politely said he was anxious to assist L Detachment in any reasonable way, that manpower could be 'lent' to them from other units, provided the applications were made through proper channels. There spoke a man who does not know his enemy.

He had lost.

Stirling had already written to Middle East Commando asking for men, and now saw the chink in the armour, though it was another 'mulcted' officer, Jellicoe, who signed the application for more forces the following day. The Middle East Commando's Adjutant's rearguard action to losing his men was to scrawl over Stirling's letter: 'At first sight it certainly appears a bad case of body snatching, but I assume this is not so.' Body snatching is exactly what it was.

Sandy Galloway told Ritchie at 8th Army to give a target list for the expanded SAS and Free French paras, while planning got underway for the biggest SAS operation to date. But Stirling wasn't hanging around, and – keen to impress the Auk – wanted to take another run at Rommel's ships. Grey Pillars consigliere Arthur Smith got wind he was planning yet another raid on Benghazi, and was concerned.[32] Stirling had become too valuable to lose.

This time, new boy Maclean sourced two rubber dinghies for Benghazi, wisely rejecting RAF yellow, for Boat, Reconnaissance (Royal Engineers), which was black.[33] Stirling also took Randolph Churchill.

Randolph's father, Winston Churchill, had a suspected heart attack while in Washington. Two battleships had been sunk by Japanese dive bombers, killing 840 sailors, and Singapore had fallen – with his armies either failing to fight, or fighting badly, he returned to a vote of no confidence in the House of Commons. In the midst of this, Randolph had returned to Britain and stayed to support his father. While the prime minister destroyed all opposition in the House of Commons with his oration, Randolph took flak from the back benches, for both his military service and failure to return to Egypt. Randolph's marriage was also failing; as Evelyn Waugh observed, Pamela couldn't stand him, and was having an affair with US attaché Harriman, which had become public. He started to drink at lunchtime and didn't stop.[34]

When Randolph Churchill got back to Cairo his concerned father messaged him: 'Please let me know what your employment is as naturally I like to follow your fortunes.'

To which Randolph replied: 'Am joining detachment of Special Air Services under Major Stirling. Think I will find the work interesting and agreeable.'

The SAS put him through parachuting. Stirling jumped first, to show him how it was done. The larger Randolph Churchill passed him in mid-air, saying 'Thank God the bloody thing opened.'

He never completed the course.

The LRDG officer accompanying that raid to Benghazi said the only damage done was to a nice chair he had in his Berber digs in Siwa, which collapsed under Randolph Churchill. The dinghies got punctures and it was another wash out. But that wasn't the point for Stirling: Randolph had his father's ear.

On the way back, Stirling almost killed Randolph Churchill. Stirling checked in with his sponsor General Ritchie at 8th Army HQ and offered *Daily Telegraph* war correspondent Arthur Morton a lift to Cairo. He turned the Battle Wagon over, killing Morton, putting Maclean in hospital in a three-day coma and almost breaking Randolph Churchill's back. That Stirling took risks helped form the SAS but, sometimes, people got hurt.

Randolph Churchill wrote a ten-page letter to his father, describing the Benghazi raid. Bluffing their way through Axis lines into the port in the Battle Wagon was 'the most exciting half hour of my life'. Stirling placed the SAS subliminally in the mind of the most powerful man in Britain. The prime minister was overjoyed, and terribly proud. He wanted to meet David Stirling.[35]

Stirling had turned pro. He wouldn't need Clarke anymore.

Betrayal

Two staff cars met on the banks of Lake Fayum, known as the 'magic lake', because its waters reflected the colour, and mood, of the sky. To Dorman-Smith it looked sluggish, unhealthy and large, like a tycoon. The sky reflected his mood. Dorman-Smith had finally been brought in from the cold – in an advisory capacity of course. The selection board of 'Bum Warmer' Arthur Smith, 'Bear of little Brain' Ritchie, and 'No Napoleon' Beresford-Peirse, saw to that.[36]

Dorman-Smith had been up to 8th Army to spy on Ritchie for the Auk, and everything he had found was bad. The divisional commanders did not trust him and a general had resigned over his leadership. He needed to go. The Auk and he had renewed their early morning constitutionals, started in India, on Gezira Island, something they named 'Dawn Patrol'. But this lake, man-made thousands of years ago, far from Cairo, wasn't just discreet, it was secret.

Dorman-Smith laid it out: Cunningham had been a mistake, Ritchie was worse. Possibly the most damning indictment was that Ritchie didn't even realise he was spying on him.[37]

Not a recommendation for a man trying to outwit a Desert Fox.

Churchill had asked the Auk to assume command of 8th Army; the Auk refused. He couldn't see how he could function as a commander in chief if he was immersed in a battle with Rommel.[38] The problem was that Ritchie's most obvious replacement, William 'Strafer' Gott, was one of the few really good operational commanders he had. The Auk's fear was a replacement would be flown out from Britain, and that replacement would be Bernard 'Monty' Montgomery.

In 1940, when Monty was under the Auk's command, his constant insubordination and attempts to undermine the Auk had strained their relationship to the point where having both in one command would be a disaster. Monty had gone over the Auk's head to resist the Commando initiative, going to the War Office to prevent men being recruited from his command. The final insult came when it transpired the slighted Monty was poaching personnel for himself.

But the Auk was also wrong not to take Dorman-Smith's advice and to keep Ritchie in the job. And they had other problems, trying to reform an Army in the middle of a battle. Far from the lake, Alan Brooke in Whitehall had become suspicious of some of the messages coming from Cairo. He was concerned that Dorman-Smith was beginning to 'exercise too much influence'.[39]

Brooke dispatched an officer who shared his own conservative views, Richard McCreery, to reign in Dorman-Smith. Dorman-Smith's nickname for McCreery was 'dreary'. Dorman-Smith had two real allies in the world: Ernest Hemingway and Liddell Hart. A man of his era couldn't have asked for better, but his own enemy, his egocentricity, was far stronger. For the SAS it was the first indication, had they known, that the iconoclasts may have had their day.

It was, once again, Rommel, who placed the SAS in pole position. He came through the night of 26 May 1942, his panzers motoring on flare paths dropped by the Luftwaffe through the desert south of the British line. Initially, he was picked up by British scout cars, but British HQs had their radios off and no one heard their signals. At 6.30am the following morning, Rommel swung north, round the south end of the Gazala line in the desert, unopposed. He hit 7th Armoured Division HQ in the rear. Half had gone for a swim in Tobruk. The general commanding the Indian Division only escaped by ripping off his tabs and pretending to be a batman. By mid-morning, 7th Armoured Division had been wiped out, other British tank units shot to pieces as they warmed up their engines. The only thing that stopped Rommel driving on to Tobruk was that he ran out of fuel.[40]

The Auk gave Ritchie the SAS to attack Rommel's airfields. He sent Dorman-Smith up to the front with the instruction that the LRDG and SAS must harass Rommel's lines of communication everywhere possible.[41] And he called in Stirling for his instructions. Not only had Grey Pillars failed to 'suppress' Stirling's letter on the future of L Detachment, the Auk loved it. Here was the solution to his problems. Churchill had messaged him specifically asking the Auk to protect two Malta convoys being run in June.[42] One convoy was coming from the east, and one from the west, and Churchill again wanted him to attack German airfields in Cyrenaica to relieve pressure. This island was the only thorn left in the side of Rommel's supplies from Italy; but of the last convoy to Malta, only three freighters made it, to be sunk in harbour, delivering one-sixth of their tonnage.[43]

The L Detachment pitch provided Auk with the solution: he approved the SAS strikes on airfields, the attachment of the German-speaking Fifth Column, and the allocation of submarines to attack other targets on islands in the Mediterranean. In the subsequent plan the SAS would hit nine airfields across the Mediterranean and North Africa, on the same night, 12 – 13 June – not the 20 targets of the proposal, but a still huge special forces operation. While this plan had been developed to help the Malta convoys, the Auk's more pressing need was to help 8th Army, who were fighting to hold the line against Rommel.

Grey Pillars had just ordered Stirling not to deploy on the operation – they wanted him to train another officer to take his place in case he became a casualty. Stirling took the opportunity to protest to the Auk, who made his staff eat humble pie – that day they cancelled their instruction to Stirling.[44] The Auk wrote to Ritchie up at the frontline, 'I saw Stirling this morning, and I think he has a good show laid on.'[45]

Fraser was back in the stone Rest House at Siwa, this time with an even bigger team. He was detailed to take in the French and the Fifth Column teams. Fraser went to check his charges. The German-speaking Palestinians of the Fifth Column, with a German Kubel-wagen and two trucks painted with Afrika Korps palm trees and swastikas, and the French; this was going to be interesting.[46] What Fraser didn't know was that he was going to need all his luck on this one. The mission was completely compromised. Amid the German speakers were two of Rommel's men, prisoners of war Captain Buck had recruited to his team because he'd thought it would be good to have a couple of German soldiers from Panzer-gruppe Afrika. The Jewish recruits were, understandably, uncom-fortable with the Nazis' presence.

Before the war, both Germans had been members of the *Légion étrangère*, who had been returned to Germany after the fall of France, then conscripted into 361 German Infantry Regiment. Cap-tured by the British in November, they were very willing to share valuable information with their British interrogators – perhaps too willing. Their willingness saw them recruited to Combined Services Detailed Interrogation Centre, which interrogated Axis prisoners of war. The centre was based in Maadi, a leafy suburb south of Cairo popular with the international community, who frequented its many bars, cafes and its yacht club. Which, if you are a spy, is the ideal place to share information at table with the multinational community.

Before the SAS left Cairo, young Captain Buck let slip that there were French paratroops operating in Cyrenaica. Then, with only three days to prepare for the operation, in the rush to get their German pay books, identity discs, and driver's licences made (probably by Clarke's technical outfit), Buck discussed with the German sergeant the best way to approach their target airfields of Derna and Martuba. He did warn him not to discuss it with the rest of the party.

Fraser, with the LRDG, led both teams into the target area; they then split up. In Fraser and Buck's team, Rommel's German sergeant helped them navigate the German positions until they lay up near the Italian fort of Martuba at 3pm on the day before their scheduled attack.[47]

In the other team, Rommel's man drove the French SAS and headed for Derna, where the accompanying Fifth Column would pose as Germans and the French would pose as their prisoners. Once they had inveigled their way onto their airfield, the French would go to work attacking aircraft.

To make matters worse on 11 June from Cairo, US Attaché Bonner Fellers, sent a signal on the compromised cipher to Washington:

NIGHTS OF JUNE 12TH JUNE 13TH BRITISH SABOTAGE UNITS PLAN SIMULTANEOUS STICKER BOMB ATTACKS AGAINST AIRCRAFT ON 9 AXIS AIRDROMES. PLANS TO REACH OBJECTIVES BY PARACHUTES AND LONG RANGE DESERT PATROL.[48]

The only piece of good news was that even Bonner Fellers thought the SAS went by parachute. For the Axis this confirmed what their spies had told them. For Fraser and the SAS it was a disaster, about which Fraser knew nothing.

Rommel's man driving the French team into Derna had constant engine trouble. They dropped half the French team to walk to their target on foot, while the rest of the French climbed into the back of the truck to pose as prisoners and headed on for their airfield.

Still their truck had 'engine trouble'. On reaching the airfield, Rommel's man suggested he 'borrow a spanner' from the Germans.

He went into the guardhouse, saluted and reported he had brought in the saboteurs.

In the ambush, one of the Palestinian German Jews accompanying the patrol detonated the ammunition in the back of the truck, killing himself, to try and give the French a chance to get away.[49] The French team shot it out, but survivors were captured, then executed.

Fraser did not take Rommel's sergeant with him when he went to recce his airfield. In the darkness he could see sentries, roughly two per aircraft. He had a few men, some Lewes bombs, and a Tommy gun. He'd need a battalion to take this out. Silently, Fraser crept back and vanished into the night.

Fraser jumped into the vehicle next to Rommel's sergeant, who appeared completely loyal, and they hit the road. Fraser's luck had held. Perhaps the sergeant *was* loyal. Perhaps he never got the chance to raise the alarm. Perhaps he wanted to keep his cover. The only thing Fraser could be certain of, on the shifting sands of this desert war, was nothing was ever what it appeared.

Buck's explanation, when Haselden debriefed him, was that they had been compromised because there were Middle East Commandos operating in the same area.[50] Haselden made it his business to know about any spy business on his plateaux. And Buck was right: that night the plateaux was a crowded place for private armies. A Squadron, 1 SS (the Middle East Commando) had blundered into a target, lost their transport to an air attack and got heatstroke.[51] But despite Buck's protest, things went wrong throughout the SAS operation. Even in Crete, where Jellicoe and French paratroop Berge managed to destroy the aircraft on their target, the German response was surprisingly swift. Berge was captured, while Jellicoe rowed to safety.

A month later, German Flight Lieutenant Friedrich Korner was shot down over El Alamein. He told his interrogators they knew a group of English saboteurs led by an English colonel (they had promoted Stirling) was going to carry out raids on German aerodromes in Cyrenaica dressed in German uniforms.[52]

Many good men had died, many shot in the head after capture. Stirling was incensed. He asked an SAS sergeant to shoot the double agent. Tait said, 'I'll do it.'

One night, down the road from their Kabrit camp, the Navy from HMS *Saunders* were just coming out of the open-air cinema when a truck pulled up. A man was thrown from the back; there was a single shot. The truck drove off, and the Navy were left staring at a body in the dirt.[53]

Pay Dirt

Fraser and the SAS were still deep in the desert behind Rommel's lines when the British front line collapsed. The British launched a counter attack into the cauldron and lost 218 tanks. Rommel fired the starting pistol to a new race called 'The Gazala Gallop', after its starting gate. Once again British forces streamed east towards Egypt, chased by panzers.

The Auk wanted to keep the 8th Army intact: there was to be no siege of Tobruk. The Auk was still haunted by memories of the horror of the siege of Kut in Iraq in the First War. He and Dorman-Smith planned to develop a mobile counterpunch to Rommel's attack. But no sooner had he given Ritchie permission to withdraw, than a signal arrived from Churchill:

> *Presume there is no question in any case of giving up Tobruk . . . we went through all this in April 1941. Do not understand what you mean by withdrawing to "old frontier".*[54]

Chaos ensued.

Late afternoon on 14 June, the fans turned slowly in the heat of the map-panelled war room in Grey Pillars, while the Auk, Dorman-Smith, De Guingand and the Auk's chief of staff, Thomas Corbett, held a crisis meeting that dragged on to 1.55am. The following morning the Auk's chief of staff, Corbett, flew up to the front to have a blazing row with Ritchie, telling him he had to hold Tobruk. The two men slammed the table, shouting at each other.

This was the Auk's fault. He had not taken over command of 8th Army himself, and instead appointed a puppet who was out of his depth. Again, Clarke had the same sense of foreboding he had when watching the Spanish hold a narrow front against the Berbers in Morocco, with their backs to the sea. The same feeling he had had in Lillehammer in Norway, watching British troops deploy at the start of the war: impending disaster.[55]

At 8am on 19 June 1942 Rommel personally charged the Tobruk ditch and *Blitzkrieg* flooded the breach. Two days later, the Auk's 58th birthday, the white flag was raised. The entire South African division and everyone inside the perimeter, 33,000 people, were taken prisoner.

Rommel issued his next order:

'Now for the complete destruction of the enemy. We will not rest until we have shattered the last remnants of the British 8th Army.'[56]

In Cairo, Dorman-Smith fielded the ensuing press conference, sweating in the oppressive heat, telling the *Times* correspondent, 'Tobruk was practically indefensible . . . the next time the pendulum swings it will go in our favour, and the swing will be deeper.'[57]

Dorman-Smith went back to his room in the Continental. Out in the desert, Rommel filled up with petrol at the railway station 30 miles short of the picturesque seaside town of Mersa Matruh. Mussolini was shipping a white charger for him to ride into Cairo. Behind his bar, Joe-the-Swiss polished glasses, though Rommel's people hadn't yet phoned through a reservation.

Sweat was pouring off Dorman-Smith in his hotel room; the party never stopped in Cairo, and the dance band thumped through the floor below. He wondered how anyone could think straight in this climate. He had decided to write to his wife, Estelle, when at 11.30pm the phone rang – he was to accompany the Auk to the front in the morning. The Auk was taking over. By 6.15am he'd packed his room, and looked round to see Liddell Hart's *The Strategy of the*

Indirect Approach on the bookshelf. He stuffed it in his bag, the door closed softly behind him, and he headed for the airport.[58]

In the desert, Fraser made it back to Siwa Oasis. He had lost 17 Frenchmen, all probably shot dead, and it looked like Rommel was on his way to Cairo. He didn't hang around and sped on for Kabrit camp.

In Cairo, Clarke watched soldiers at the end of his street sandbag the eastern end of the bridge which crossed to Gezira island beside K Detachment's barracks. The Nile had become a last line of defence. He may even have seen Fraser and the SAS speeding east across the bridge to Kabrit.

The British Embassy had been evacuated, and at Clarke's Castle of String HQ, they were burning documents as fast as they could. Clarke had sent his secretaries, Miss Hopkins and Miss Mason, on a train to Jerusalem with anything he didn't want to burn, which included his file for PLAN ABEAM – the creation of the SAS.

He had arranged with Stirling that an SAS team with a radio would take him and A-Force HQ down into the Nile Delta, from where he could coordinate guerrilla operations. There would be few worse places in the world for Rommel's armour and motorised troops to attempt to combat Clarke and the SAS than in the intensely cultivated Nile Delta, with its intricate network of rivers and canals.

Clarke thought they could rapidly augment their delta guerrilla force with Allied troops escaping capture. For Rommel to clear it of well-armed and determined guerrillas in the face of extensive demolitions in that country would be a formidable and lengthy task. And Rommel would have to run supplies right through the inhospitable triangle of the Nile Delta to pursue the British east of Suez.

Clarke set to work. He prepped their first hideout in the over-crowded suburb of Rod-el-Farag, in an old garage near the flying-boat station. He set up a medical station in a school to the north, then recce-ed their main HQ out amid the canals of the delta, with space enough to land a light aircraft. At all three K Detachment buried caches of food, fuel and ammunition. He bought a laundry van to enable them to move incognito through Cairo, and took over a bookshop and scent factory as fronts. He organised a yacht and launches so they could move on the river. And through his network he got cooperation everywhere. The Egyptian Freemasons joined his cause, setting up escape centres in every village; one wonders if Clarke was a member. And the police and smugglers joined forces to open smuggling routes, move escaping personnel over the Red Sea Hills and down into the Gulf of Suez, and move weapons and supplies for guerrilla operations up into the delta.[59]

Satisfied with his work, Clarke sat on the terrace of Shepheard's. He might, finally, after 28 years, have the chance to fight.

The sky filled with the ash of burning paper. In the militarised zone of the Quarter of Palaces, the air was thick with smoke from multiple bonfires. The day was nicknamed 'Ash Wednesday' and a dark cloud hung over Cairo, black embers rolling through the baking hot streets.[60]

Joe-the-Swiss seemed unperturbed, and went on mixing cocktails. Clarke may have ordered a Gibley's and tonic, or something stronger – Joe had mixed a cocktail called the 'Suffering Bastard' to take the edge off defeat. Shepheard's terrace was never dull.

The Auk and Dorman-Smith landed in their twin-engine Boston bomber at 8th Army HQ near the front at Bagush on the afternoon of 25 June 1942. From there the Auk could hear the thump of artillery. He was back in his natural habitat: the battlefield. Rommel was in trouble.

As 8th Army raced back, Siwa Oasis became threatened. The centre of special forces operations was due south of Rommel's advance, and it would be easy for him to take it out. With a large map spread out in the Stone House, Prendergast discussed the new base for the LRDG. One troop leader said Alexandria, another Cairo. One wit suggested getting behind the Nile, for which he was rebuked. Prendergast pointed to a spot on the map nobody had even heard of before: El Alamein.[61]

G Patrol, LRDG sped west, chased by Rommel's armoured cars, but lost them in the heat haze, only to be nearly taken out by a retreating British column. When they reached El Alamein, on 30 June, they found they were not alone. When Dorman-Smith had assessed before the war that El Alamein was bound to be the decisive battleground for Egypt, he had been told not to be so stupid.[62] Now it was to be the decisive battleground.

The Auk had always displayed a personal interest in the LRDG and SAS, and he did not forget them now. A few hours after the LRDG pulled into 8th Army HQ, John Haselden showed up, and, that evening, David Stirling.[63] The Auk was in calm control – and he was grouping all his special forces. They were to prepare immediately to be sent behind Rommel's lines to do their worst.

At Kabrit, Fraser and the men had been working round the clock. And now the SAS's new doctor, Malcolm Pleydell, watched Stirling motivate his battle-weary teams. The doctor thought within five minutes that he could persuade you black is white. His medical opinion was less positive: this man was run down, had a wrist injury from a car crash, was covered in desert sores and wore dark glasses because of trouble with sunlight.

Fraser and his men zeroed weapons on the target range, kicking up puffs of sand over the Bitter Lake. Equipment was issued and checked, and, over in the motor section, there was the constant cursing, swearing and hammering of fitting out vehicles for the trip. The welding went on late into the night, arc lights reflecting shinning sweat, bright white on shirtless fitters in the vehicle pits. They were taking everything with them and may never be coming back. When each vehicle was finished, it was parked up next to a long line of freshly painted Bantam Jeeps.[64]

It had not been the US manufacturer's intention that these would become a weapons platform, but the British knew the potential of a good piece of engineering when they saw it. Seekings had been sent back to Cairo to fit these out while the SAS were on the previous raid.

Seekings, the boxer, arrived at the depot, just outside the Cairo suburb of Heliopolis, with a letter of authority from the quartermaster general at GHQ to set about Jeep-snatching. He played hell round the ordnance depot, demanding two spare wheels per Jeep for the desert. He took 15 vehicles, also Vickers K guns, a weapon more usually used in aircraft, and compasses from another depot. He demanded that fitters weld armoured plate to the Jeep's radiators, and fit condensers.

He spent two weeks in the depot, organising the vehicles. At first the springs broke under the heavy, twin-gun mountings, because the depot had reinforced them the wrong way round. And then they painted the Jeeps brown. Seekings insisted they rectify the springs and repaint the Jeeps LRDG colours. Fed up, the depot commander, an Irish major, finally said, 'Sure and be Christ, here's the tools. Do it yourself.'

When Seekings and his small team had finished, the Irish major took one look at the pink and pastel Jeep and laughed his head off. Seekings drove him out to the tank firing range at Abasir in a Jeep to prove to him that the camouflage worked.

Next, Seekings jumped a tank ditch at 60mph to make sure the Jeep would hold up – the major, sitting in the back, lost all the skin from his armpits to his ribs

'Sure I suspected it. But I know you're mad now. Are there any more like you?' he asked.

'Plenty'[65]

Stirling had left Kabrit to fly up and meet with the Auk, when Fraser drove his Jeep, leading his two trucks, as the huge SAS convoy hit the long, straight, monotonous road west from Kabrit. The French in Fraser's team had already nicknamed 'les petits Jeeps', which wove through the midday Cairo traffic as they hit the suburbs. SAS truck drivers cursed as Egyptian cars cut up the convoy, but the manoeuvrability of the Jeep crews enabled them to veer close to fruit carts at the roadside and grab water melons. Egyptians shouted after them as the convoy kicked up dust and chaos on its wake, crews singing and shouting. Fraser didn't sing, but he didn't admonish his crews either. The men were confident and blowing off steam, but some wouldn't be coming back.

The convoy stopped after Cairo for lunch, then turned right, instead of straight on to Siwa, headed north up the delta towards Alexandria. Camels filed along the canal towpaths, oxen plodded in circles drawing water, children in rags ran shouting after them as they roared through villages. Night fell and the cooks banged for dinner. It was humid; hundreds of frogs clamoured in the darkness, and the mosquitoes attacked. Fraser lay under his blanket, his night made fitful by their bites and what lay ahead.

At sun-up, 3 July, they skirted Alexandria and finally reached lines of trenches, then 20 vehicles spread out under camouflage nets behind a ridge. In the middle of it all sat the Auk's private aircraft. Fraser jumped down; he could hear the thump of artillery and clatter of machine guns beyond the ridge, but to the north it sounded like a maelstrom. The battle with Rommel was reaching its climax. He and Mayne went with the French to find Stirling.[66]

On 1 July Rommel had thrown his exhausted forces, running on vapours and out of food, but powered by methamphetamine, against the British line at El Alamein. From 2.30am they ploughed into a devastating hail of British artillery; his troops were pinned down under exploding shells, the desert raining rock and shrapnel. At 4pm the first of his units sent an SOS: it was no longer battle-worthy. Rommel's halftrack sped across the battlefield to rescue them. Shells screamed in from north, south and east, anti-aircraft guns streaking tracer into Rommel's ranks. The attack stalled for two hours and Rommel and his chief of staff, Bayerlein, lay in the open unable to move. Rommel was saved by his dive bombers quietening the British guns, and escaped.[67]

In briefings Dorman-Smith would tap the map board, using intelligence from ULTRA to decide the location of that night's attacks. He must have seemed like some ancient soothsayer to the bewildered British officers.

The Auk and Dorman-Smith shared a lean-to tent in the sand

beside the Auk's caravan, sleeping on roll-up beds. The Auk confided in Dorman-Smith that Jessie was leaving him – she had fallen for an RAF officer. At night they lay on the sand, guns thundering in the darkness – two men propping up the West's hopes for the war. Dorman-Smith felt him reach for his hand in his sleep. 'I do not think I could have stuck it out anywhere else, or without you.'[68]

For three days Rommel hammered away. He was down to just over 1,200 men, and had conceded his supply situation was 'strained'. The battle Fraser could hear was the New Zealanders hitting Rommel's Italian Ariete Division. Rommel didn't know about ULTRA, or Dorman-Smith, but he knew that he was weak, and the Italians were fleeing in panic.

Fraser had guessed where they were headed and Stirling confirmed it: behind Rommel's lines, where they would set up a forward operating base to raid his rear areas.

With the LRDG Troop Leader Robin Gurdon now leading, the convoy sped on south towards the Depression, and passed through the British front line. Fraser looked at the 8th Army, stripped to the waist, digging trenches to stop Rommel. A cheer went up from the SAS and LRDG men in the convoy. Some of the Desert Rats stopped, wiped their brows, and looked at the noisy, bearded men in vehicles bristling with machine guns. A few gave them V for Victory, before going back to digging.[69] It was a thin, desperate line – Fraser was very clear where he would rather be.

Past the British line they drove towards Rommel, then swung south-west, along the edge of the Depression. Fraser could see the escarpment falling thousands of feet into the giant, salt-baked sinkhole, and there, ahead of them, were the trucks of LRDG's G Patrol.

The position of the new front line, which stretched from the sea to the Depression, meant the only way now to get behind Rommel was through the bottom of the Depression, a route that G Patrol had just spent three days sweating and heaving vehicles through the cracked salt pan to find. Rommel thought the Qattara Depression was impenetrable to vehicles. Now it wasn't.

The men of G Patrol watched in disbelief as the swarms of Jeeps and trucks brazenly pulled up in a huge dust cloud. Their recklessness in driving in daylight so close to Rommel's line deceived the Messerschmitt 110 fighter that screamed over at that moment.

At the conference that evening, Stirling's enthusiasm was infectious. The Auk would launch a counter-offensive, the SAS's job was to attack his airfields. Starting in the east, working west, they would destroy his fighters, or force them out of range. The LRDG patrols divided up their work, deciding who would take which SAS team to each airfield.[70,71]

Fifty minutes to zero hour, close to Fuka, one of Rommel's most eastern airfields, the LRDG dropped Fraser and his team. He briefed the men: he would move first, then the French team, then the third SAS team. It was pitch-black around the trucks. He shouldered his pack of bombs and set off with his team toward their target airfield. He liked working with the French, they were determined, brave – but a law unto themselves.

He was creeping between two sentry posts, Italians off to his left, one to his right, when the night lit up with fireworks from the neighbouring airfield. He cursed, pressed himself to the ground and looked at his watch: the French had gone in early. He listened to the rattle of their firefight, they must have triggered a response from the defenders. They had some of Captain Buck's Fifth Column with them, so he hoped they were OK. This was definitely getting harder. In comparison, the covert operation in Agedabia had been easy. Now Phillips was using his knife with glee, but the risks were increasing all the time.

To the west there was a white flash, then an explosion, then three more in quick succession. The night sky lit up like summer lightning; then there was a long pause, before the slow heavy rumble reached him – one of the far western teams was in business, probably Stirling or Mayne. He had to get out of here. He heard Italian sentries calling to each other, then calling on all the saints to save them. Fraser smiled.

He wriggled back, waving his men off the perimeter. He crawled back up a small rise, and saw, ten metres away, a group of Italians. He hoisted his pack off his back, pulled out a grenade and put his finger through the ring to pull out the pin. Fraser watched as the Italians just stood there, scared, not knowing where the threat was. He could kill them all. Pull the pin, count to the last moment on the fuse, they'd hear the thump, then, probably, nothing.

He took his finger out of the ring pull. And crawled on for the rendezvous.[72]

Fraser was leading his two trucks when the first rays of dawn lit the horizon. One of the trucks seemed to have engine trouble, so he pulled up in his Jeep, when someone yelled, 'Aircraft!'

For one terrifying moment, two Messerschmitt Bf 109s skimmed towards him. He threw himself down, their high-pitched V12 engines screaming past him at 50 feet. He could see the pilots looking from their cockpits.

The French were dodging round their truck to keep out of sight, praying the pilots would think it a derelict. The planes prowled round, pilots craning their necks.

The French circled their truck. Everyone else was lying in the desert motionless. To their relief the planes disappeared east, black specks against the rising sun, leaving only the thin menacing whine in the air behind them.

The team moved on. With little cover they spread the vehicles out and pulled down their tailgates, scattered equipment about to make them look like derelicts, and lay down to rest. Two hours later Fraser watched two Italian CR.42 Falco biplanes circle above him. High up there, two pilots were looking to kill him. The sunlight glinted off their fuselages. Down here he'd blown up a load of those on his first raid. This war was surreal.[73]

Eventually, they hit the track to Siwa and bounced along it till they saw the conical hill, the rendezvous with the rest of the teams, rise up to meet them.

While Fraser and the SAS attacked Rommel's forward airbases, the Auk boxed clever. Rommel attacked towards El Alamein, and took the well-fortified position in the British line of Qaret el Abd. That night Rommel stood looking at the concrete defences and well-prepared minefield, 'at a loss to understand why they had given it up'.

He went to sleep in one of the bunkers, only to be woken at 5am (on 10 July) to the dull sound of British Artillery fire to his north. He 'had an inkling it boded no good'. He had been caught in a trap.

The Auk and Dorman-Smith executed with perfection. The first Italian division was almost completely annihilated and fell back in panic; the second collapsed. Rommel was compelled to order every last German solider out of his tent or rest camp to plug the gap because: 'The situation was beginning to take on crisis proportions.'[74]

Dorman-Smith had minefields laid in the direction of Rommel's advance, rather than blocking it, to channel him into areas to kill him. BBC war correspondent Denis Johnstone described it as the work of a genius, the 'ace German general not only being outfought, but outfoxed'.[75] Rommel realised he had been outfought.

'Things are going downright badly for me at the moment . . . The enemy is using his superiority, especially in infantry, to destroy the Italian formations one by one . . . It's enough to make one weep.'[76]

The Auk knew he had Rommel on the ropes; now to finish him.

That day, Stirling signalled Grey Pillars admitting the first SAS attack had miscarried. He estimated they had only destroyed 40 aircraft, but that the potential of the twin-mounted Bantam Jeeps was so tremendous that they should get 50 more.[77] Stirling and Mayne had used their two to drive onto an airfield during their attack, and destroy it using twin-mounted Vickers K machine guns. The technique the LRDG used in the special forces raid on Murzuq. Mayne suggested they do it again.

What Stirling asked for he got.

Fraser felt awful. He was exhausted as he tucked his Jeep into the overhanging rock formation that was their base. The SAS were using a series of Aeolian caves, scoured by centuries of wind in a rock escarpment. But they were running out of supplies. On the way in they had had to send back three trucks from the Qattara Depression, with much of their supplies, to lighten their loads in the soft sand. Now it was tough for Fraser to make his water ration last a day. All around him lay smashed pottery, perhaps the remains of Cambyses's army, vanished in the sand. Fraser had been through more than most and was suffering.[78]

Stirling decided to take advantage of the lull in the battle and go back to Cairo. He sent two signals in quick succession: he was coming in for supplies and planned to pick up 25 Jeeps. He specified that they should weld the gun mounts, not braze them, and he also needed six new trucks for the increased scale of his planned operation. He wanted it ready for his arrival because it was vital he return to the desert for the Auk without the smallest delay.[79]

Stirling took Fraser and Mayne, but left a small team at the caves, including some of Captain Buck's Fifth Column. Because the Auk wanted him to be able to sabotage Hellfire and Solum passes, to cut Rommel's lines of communication if the Auk attacked while the SAS were re-equipping in Cairo. The doctor watched the party speed away into the morning haze, he was worried about Fraser, who clearly wasn't well.

The following morning, Fraser drove out of the Qattara Depression, following an old Arab track the LRDG had found, marked by the bones of camels so old they crumbled to the touch. On the plain beyond, specks flew fast towards them, and the Luftwaffe hit them. Fraser spun his Jeep into the direction of attack, which made it difficult for the pilots to hit him. As soon as he got the Jeep in some cover, he flung himself to the ground as the menacing aero-engines roared past.

No one was hit in the attack, and on they sped. The first sign of battle was smoke on the horizon, to the north. When Fraser pulled up at the Auk's HQ, he could hear the constant thud of the artillery and distant clatter of heavy machine guns. Aircraft made everyone twitchy, but to their relief all had roundels on their wings.

He smoked and waited while Stirling had his conference with the Auk. When he emerged, the news was they were to coordinate their next attack, with Jeeps, with the Auk's attack on Rommel. The SAS was to be given a direct radio link to 8th Army.[80] From now on, the SAS would be talking directly to the Auk.

Forty-eight hours later Fraser pulled back into Kabrit camp – with the pressure of operations lifted, and adrenaline gone, Fraser collapsed from exhaustion. He wasn't going back out, he wasn't going anywhere. There's only one thing worse than going on operations, and that's being left behind.

The Auk's ambitions for the SAS were bigger than Stirling's. Grey Pillars allocated Stirling 100 Jeeps with twin Vickers K guns, 50 more than he'd asked for, and there was even talk of getting them anti-tank weapons. Stirling had been dreaming about trying to take out panzer laagers at night, and the Auk hadn't given up on the idea of the SAS taking out panzers.[81]

But, in his trailer near the front, the Auk sat rereading the telegram from Churchill. At that moment an enormous German Army, well over ten times the size of the one he faced, was tearing through Ukraine towards Stalingrad. His northern flank looked like it would soon be under attack. Churchill told him, 'The only way in which a sufficient army can be gathered in your northern theatre is by your defeating or destroying General Rommel.'[82]

Dorman-Smith knew they'd worn Rommel down, but 'He [was] a persistent beast.'[83]

Even before the attack, everything went wrong. South Africans had pulled out of the front line of Rommel's assault, their government determined to avoid another Tobruk. They were replaced by Morshead's Australians, who had borne the brunt of the casualties. Now, with only 24 hours to go until the Auk's counterattack, and the Australians ordered to lead the charge, Morshead insisted he refer the matter to his government.

The Auk invited him to his trailer where, over tea, he and Morshead reached a compromise that a British unit would lead. This meant a 48-hour delay, giving Rommel two days to regroup, dig in and lay minefields. Dorman-Smith thought they should cancel. As if on cue, 'Dreary' McCreery arrived from Cairo, having heard they planned to mix up armoured and infantry units like the Germans did. In the row, the Auk completely lost it, and sacked McCreery – this was not politic since McCreery was Brooke's man in Egypt, and Brooke was head of the British Army.

Rommel sensed what was coming, and the attack stalled with heavy casualties. Exhausted, the two sides stopped again. As Rommel put it, the British thought better of it the next day.

Fraser wasn't there when, five nights later, on 26 July 1942, the Auk attacked again, coordinated with the SAS, who drove out of the darkness onto Rommel's airfield of Sidi Haneish. They drove down the field at 2 miles an hour, Vickers K firing 1,000 rounds a minute, devastating everything in their path. Corporal Mike Sadler, the LRDG man who had guided them to the field, watched the airfield getting blown to pieces, tracer cutting into the aircraft.

Once the Jeeps reached the end of the field, they turned round to do it again. Stirling was driving when his Jeep stalled. His SAS gunner lifted the bonnet to see a 15mm German shell had passed through the engine inches from his knees. A troop leader pulled up next to them, 'Come along, we'll give you a lift.'[84]

They jumped in, Stirling's gunner pulling a man off the Vickers to find he was dead with a hole in his head. In the chaos, Mayne decided he had time to run off to put a Lewes bomb on an aircraft to increase his personal scorecard. Then they drove back down the airfield to finish it off.

The SAS and LRDG team suffered what they now referred to as the 'hangover' the next day, as the Luftwaffe sought revenge and the Axis sent ground forces after them. The LRDG knocked out four German trucks, and their attackers seemed to be being guided by a Fieseler Storch aircraft, which kept landing to confer with their pursuers. When it did this in the wrong place, the Kiwis emerged;

one German put on a Red Cross armband, and, it turned out, really was a doctor. But it cut no ice and he was bundled into the wagon while the Kiwis burned his plane.[85]

Sadler had stayed behind to watch the Germans repair their airfield, and was impressed at how fast they cleared the debris and had it operational.[86]

On the frontline, the Australian attack failed, and Rommel held on to the El Alamein line. But far away, on the Russian steppes, Rommel's friend General Paulus closed on Stalingrad. German resources were being sucked dry by Hitler's last desperate roll of the dice to knock Russia out of the war. Here in Africa, the Auk had called Rommel's bluff, and from the garden of Shepheard's, the ghost of Kléber got up and walked out into the desert to meet his successor.

By this time the Axis had worked out where these special forces' attacks were coming from. They were over the Depression every day. German armoured cars patrolled the passes on the north side of the Depression to where the route led up to the 8th Army. Driving into the tiny oasis of Qara, on the west side of the Depression, locals told the LRDG that Axis aircraft had bombed them. Qara was the jumping-off point for SAS operations. The SAS forward operating base in the caves was only 50 miles from here. If they were found, the SAS would be annihilated, trapped the wrong side of Rommel's lines and the Depression.

The relationship between LRDG and SAS was becoming strained. The LRDG and the desert were symbiotic, reflecting their founder – they cached fuel, tyres, food, spares, even whole trucks, around their huge area of operations. They mapped the uncharted, were independent for navigation, and knew every well and water hole. In this environment, the SAS were a bit like a toddler in a china shop. They had no means of resupplying themselves, couldn't navigate and had no communications, but they were very good at smashing things up. And the smashing caused problems, because the more effective the SAS became, the more the Luftwaffe and Regia Aeronautica sought revenge.

Stirling demanded 1500 gallons of petrol, 5,000 rounds of ammunition and 300 Mills bombs in mid-July, followed by 800 gallons of petrol, 160 ration packs, 12 Jeep tyres with inners on 3 August. Getting these loads across the Depression would have been a big job even in peacetime. The LRDG could no longer support the operation. The SAS had to pull out. [87]

But this had been a peak in special forces operations. It proved how much damage the SAS could do working directly for the force commander – and could have been a template for things to come.

Close to the Sun

Churchill had been in a meeting with President Roosevelt in the White House when he was handed a pink slip of paper telling him Tobruk had fallen. Churchill had to send Pug Ismay out to check. It was, personally and politically, the worst moment of his war. He was humiliated in front of his greatest ally. When they had recovered from shock, Roosevelt asked Churchill what he needed. The moment defined the rest of the war for both the Allies and the SAS.

The two nations had not been seeing eye to eye on Churchill's proposal of landing US troops in Vichy French North Africa, or over Churchill's subsequent wish to invade Sicily then Italy. President Roosevelt had other ideas about where to open a second front. Now the British got 300 brand-new Sherman tanks, with their panzer-busting gun on a turret that could fully rotate. At last the British would be able to tackle German armour. At a dinner that went on until 1am, the US had agreed to send forces to North Africa. Brooke thought it might lead to a US front in the Middle East rather than a European front. [88] He was right.

Politically, Churchill faced a bigger problem across the Atlantic, and further south. The abrasive premier Jan Smuts, who had brought South Africa into the war against the resistance of the Afrikaners, and would lead the battle against Hitler if the PM was killed or captured, wanted blood. Churchill needed a head to roll.

When he flew back to Chequers, his frustration at being stuck in Britain while all the action of the war was occurring two thousand miles away became too much. Brooke was flying out to Cairo to get a grip on things that had clearly gone awry. After dinner, over port with his son Randolph Churchill, and Foreign Secretary Eden, Churchill suggested he accompany Brooke. Eden said he would only get in the way. Churchill: 'You mean like a great big bluebottle? Buzzing over a huge cowpat?'[89] But he flew to Cairo anyway, to decapitate his Commander in Chief, North Africa.

'It was,' he said later, 'like killing a magnificent stag.'[90]

To avoid the Luftwaffe, Churchill's four-engine Consolidated LB-30A aircraft (named 'Commando') flew a circuitous route from Gibraltar to approach Cairo from the south, touching down on 3 August 1942.[91]

He discussed the new Commander of 8th Army over a long lunch at the Mohamed Ali Club the following day with the Auk, Brooke, Admiral Cunningham and Air Vice Marshal Tedder (whom Brooke described as a small-brained, pig-headed man). It was probably not the best venue, since the barman was a known spy. The Auk conceded he would take Monty, which surprised Brooke.

Back at the Embassy, Churchill pressed the Auk to attack. The Auk refused, and after he left Churchill turned on Alan Brooke and told him they had to replace the Auk with Strafer Gott because Monty would not get to Africa in time. A party from Moscow was flying in the next day, and it was imperative Churchill offer them the olive branch of an immediate British offensive to take the pressure off Russia. The argument went on till 1am.[92]

The Auk refused to come to town the next day, 5 August, annoying Churchill, who set out with Brooke for the ridge close to the front. Churchill didn't like what he found. The HQ in which the Auk and Dorman-Smith worked was a wire-netted cube, full of flies. In a long briefing, the Auk refused to launch yet another premature offensive, telling Churchill he estimated it would be six weeks until they were ready, while Churchill repeatedly prodded the map. Dorman-Smith found the experience 'like being caged with a gorilla'.

The poor food, a greasy a fry-up, didn't improve Churchill's mood, and he insisted Strafer Gott accompany him to the airfield, against the Auk's protests that he couldn't leave the battlefield. Only after they left did Dorman-Smith wonder how his and the Auk's sleeping arrangements – two roll beds close on the sand – may have looked to Brooke.[93]

As Churchill and Strafer Gott bounced over the rutted track to a waiting aircraft, Churchill asked Gott if he was tired. Gott said he was, he hadn't been to England for years, but was capable of taking on more responsibility if required. From this, Gott knew he was lined up to take over the 8th Army.

Churchill arrived at the RAF HQ to meet Mary Conningham, only to find the food, special dainties they'd ordered from Shepheard's, had got lost. Frantic efforts were made by RAF reconnaissance to find it and, once it had been recovered, Churchill's mood improved, and he ended up having a jolly time with the RAF.[94]

The following morning, Brooke was naked in his air-conditioned room at the Embassy when Churchill burst in, insisting he join him for breakfast. Brooke hadn't even poured his coffee when Churchill told him he wanted him to take over command of the Middle East, and to appoint Monty commander of 8th Army. Brooke's heart raced. He immediately told Churchill he knew nothing of desert warfare. What he didn't say was that he felt he could exercise a limited amount of control over Churchill's activities. He knew any successor would take six months to win his confidence, and in those six months anything might happen.

At the 10.30am conference in the Embassy, Churchill started shouting at the Auk's chief of staff in Cairo, Corbett, calling him 'a blockhead', as he tried to hold the line. Smuts was there, and still wanted blood. Brooke had found it hard to resist Churchill, but doubly difficult to resist Smuts.

Alan Brooke went to take a break on the lawn. The Nile drifted by. Alexander was his choice to take over from the Auk as

Commander in Chief Middle East, but he was worried Strafer Gott was too tired to take over the 8th Army. They needed Monty (his choice for 8th Army) to take over from Alexander on OPERATION TORCH (the US landing in North Africa) so Alexander could take over as Commander in Chief, Cairo. In the finely balanced stack of cards the Auk would be sacked from two jobs, because he was running both the Middle East and 8th Army. Of course, Dorman-Smith would have to go too. He would put Dreary McCreery as his man in Grey Pillars. But the blood-letting wouldn't stop there – it would become known as the 'Cairo Purge'.[95]

That day, the Auk signalled Stirling to report to HQ at the earliest. Stirling had just landed in Cairo, and answered he would fly out in the morning.[96]

Stirling flew to meet the Auk, for what was to be the last strategy meeting in a partnership that had seen the SAS rise from nothing to become the world's most successful special forces unit. It took place a long way from the bars, clubs and politics of Cairo, with only the crackle of high-frequency radios, the occasional thud of a falling shell and the buzzing of flies for company.

While Stirling had been away, Grey Pillars had been wrestling to reorganise special forces operations, with a Commander Special Forces appointed to command all the different elements. The Auk wrote over the proposal: 'Looks like a very large head on a very small body', and, 'where does Stirling's gang come? Who is to be the "Colonel"?'

The colonel they recommended was HJ Cator, MC, commander of 51 Commando who had served with distinction, having been wounded by the Italians in Eritrea, then sent to Haifa Staff College as instructor, where he had done extremely well. He was a good organiser, had personality and drive, and was a strong character. There is no record of their discussion, but the Auk had sent the proposals to Stirling, and undoubtedly discussed the future of the SAS. The Auk was backing Stirling to become CO of a four-squadron regiment. All special forces, apart from the LRDG, would come under his wing. And his 100 Jeeps would be enough to carry that SAS regiment.[97]

There are traces in Dorman-Smith's 'Combat Appreciation' (the formal analysis the British Army used to consider its options) of where the SAS was heading. His plan had two stages: while holding the El Alamein line, Rommel's threat could be mitigated by seaborne attack, and by enterprises against Siwa Oasis and the southern sector of his front. Then he described the Second Battle of El Alamein, which Dorman-Smith would never fight, and left a tantalising alternative: rather than battering their way through Rommel's front, 'we may develop a threat to the enemy's rear via Siwa'.[98] It sounds surprisingly similar to the Auk's first plan to attack Rommel, and one an expanded SAS would likely lead. After Norway, the Auk had seen what sort of soldiers Britain would need, and now he had them.

After Stirling left, the Auk got wind of a gathering in Cairo that night, to which he was not invited. They were having a feast. For the Auk, the writing was on the wall.

Dorman-Smith saw Strafer Gott transformed from his previously weary self.[99] Assuming it was because he was going on leave, he asked if he wanted to drive to Cairo in his car, or wanted a lift on his flight first thing the next morning. Gott refused both and got the RAF passenger flight aboard a Bristol Bombay transport at Burg-el-Arab airfield that afternoon.

Strafer Gott buckled himself in alongside his 17 fellow passengers as Sergeant Pilot Jimmy James prepared for the 40-minute hop to Cairo. But the fixed wheels of the Bombay had barely lifted off the strip when a swarm of four Messerschmitt 109 fighters dived out the sun and their cannon fire ripped past his windshield.

Losing one engine immediately, James looked for an option to land. Then he was raked by a second pass and came down hard on the desert floor. The Messerschmitts pressed home their attack, and as James ran they hit the Bombay's fuel tanks. James watched, aghast, as flames engulfed his passengers, then turned to see the Messerschmitts continue to circle above them. The passenger door was jammed, and the passengers inside incinerated, including Gott.

As the wounded British pilot struggled to get back to his base to break the news, Luftwaffe pilot Emil Clade landed and was greeted by his commander with the news that he had 'just killed General Strafer Gott, the new Commander of 8th Army!'[100]

If this is true, Gott was assassinated. Rommel got most of his intelligence via Bonner Fellers, and with Churchill in town the transatlantic wire was buzzing. But, by chance, the US changed their cipher that month, making Bonner Fellers's missives indecipherable, so loose talk at the Mohamed Ali Club could have been to blame. Whatever happened, Strafer Gott was dead and Churchill had written his break-up letter to the Auk, to be delivered on the morning of 8 August. Smuts was in town, expecting the Auk to have fallen on his sword. The Russians were coming. And Churchill was now in all sorts of trouble. The list of available replacements was one: Monty. For Brooke, 'It seemed almost like the hand of God suddenly appearing to set matters right where we had gone wrong.'[101]

Not, obviously, for veteran fighter Strafer Gott.

In the midst of this chaos, Stirling arrived back to be invited to lunch with the prime minister as one of 'Randolph's friends' where he regaled Churchill with tales of derring-do.[102] The prime minister's secretary in Cairo asked Stirling to send his own proposal for reorganising special forces in the Middle East.

Clarke had been up at the front during the fighting to help the Auk and Dorman-Smith. On the day Rommel attacked,[103] he was narrowly missed by Stukas and watched them hammer Ruweisat Ridge. He devised PLAN RAYON, the fake invasion of Crete by the SAS and Commandos, to stop Rommel pulling any troops off the island to help his attack. But with the Auk away in the desert, Grey Pillars told Clarke to 'damp down' the deception until the Auk had time to consider its implications, just at the moment he might have needed it most.

On 3 August, the Auk had called Clarke back up to his HQ behind the ridge to push the button on this, not just to prevent Rommel reinforcing, but also because another Malta convoy was running through on 9 August. Clarke picked a D Day of 17 August, when it would be good if the Germans were looking to defend Crete rather than attack a convoy.

Clarke flew back to Cairo: the fake invasion force consisted of the SAS Brigade, and K Detachment, SAS started putting out fake gliders on Ismailia airfield, 30 miles north of the real SAS on the Bitter Lake. The fake Commando force was Greek, in the Combined Training Centre at Kabrit, and there was a fake Greek airborne Unit coming from Beirut (though the Greek SAS had just been formed and would in future play into this deception). He pinged his fake army in Cyprus to support it. Kenyon Jones filled the Suez Canal with fake landing craft, all to avoid giving Rommel the impression the Auk was weakening the El Alamein line.[104]

Given the men's relationship, and that Clarke was setting up a fake SAS operation when Stirling arrived back in Cairo, they may have discussed the proposal for Churchill. It echoed the Auk's: 'the scope of "L" Detachment should be extended so as to cover the functions of all existing Special Service Units in the Middle East as well as any other Special Service tasks which may require carrying out'. The big ambition in the letter was to place control of the SAS with the force commander; while its operations would be planned and controlled by the SAS, and no one else.[105]

This would, one day, be the SAS. But Fraser and the SAS's odyssey had a way to go yet.

Monty was shaving at home in Reigate, Surrey, at 7am on 8 August, when the War Office rang. It was two years since he had entrusted his 'rather good lunch basket' to Friar Rafael Hoedt in Belgium, who had bricked it into the walls of his monastery, believing it to be of greater strategic significance than a mere sandwich box.

Safely back in England, serving under the Auk, he started planning the Commando raid on Dieppe. With five thousand men at his disposal, this was a long way from the revolutionary special forces warfare Clarke and Stirling had developed, and which the

Auk was now employing in North Africa. It would be a disaster: over half the force was lost, 800 of them killed in action. Monty was to proceed to Cairo to take over command of the 8th Army. It was an unusually rapid promotion for a man who had not seen combat for two years.[106]

The Auk watched the messenger bounce up the dusty track to his HQ. After dinner he took Freddie De Guingand for a walk on Ruweisat Ridge where they had stopped Rommel. The Auk told him that he was to go.[107] Dorman-Smith was finished too.

Far away in Cuba, Ernest Hemingway penned his introduction to 'Men at War' and remembered the protective talisman from a young British officer, Dorman-Smith, who had written out some Shakespeare for him:

> *By my troth, I care not: a man can die but once; we owe God a death . . .*
> *and let it go which way it will, he that dies this year is quit for the next.*[108]

Hemingway thought it was the best thing written in the book, and with nothing else, a man can get along all right with that.[109] The Auk and Dorman-Smith, two men who stopped Rommel and helped create the SAS – you could get along all right with that.

Hubris

A month later, Fraser led his men west over the glittering Nile on Qasr-el-Nil Bridge, part of a heavily loaded, 70-vehicle convoy, for the biggest SAS raid to date. Ahead, Rommel blocked their path. Siwa Oasis was now occupied by a unit of young Italian fascists, and instead of heading straight on at the Pyramid of Giza, they turned left. Following the banks of the Nile south, dust filled the date palms before they swung west for Kharga Oasis, the jumping-off point for the 450-mile desert crossing to Kufra.

For the first time, he and his men experienced the deep desert. This was a short crossing by LRDG standards; the LRDG travelled for weeks and over thousands of miles. To meet their deadline, Stirling was pushing them over the radio from Cairo; they pushed themselves too, travelling each day into the night, resting in the early hours. Fraser's Jeep burned red hot, his condenser the only thing that saved his engine. He and Seekings' Jeeps patrolled the edge of the convoy, to spot drivers who had fallen asleep. Even then vehicles got lost, rolled, and got stuck when they crossed the dune fields. By Seekings' estimation, it was the toughest job the SAS had ever done – they put out sentries, not for fear of attack, but to make sure they woke up.[110]

At Kufra, Fraser dived into the salt-lake with relief. Fossilised water, preserved from rains thousands of years ago, gushed from the ground down a trough that was soon full of troops soaking themselves and their clothes. The huge oasis lay in the southern end of a long hollow carved below sea level by the wind over thousands of years. At one end stood the Italian fort of Et Tag, which Leclerc had besieged, built over the remains of the Senussi town of Zawia. Climbing above the oasis, Fraser could see the two sapphire-blue salt lakes, at the edge of which donkeys pulled up fresh water for crops, surrounded by thousands of date palms; thick round the salt marshes, scattered on the upper slopes. Amid the single-storey town stood a mosque, the remains of the Italian brothel, and the market of El Giof – opened after the British retook the oasis. Fat-tailed creatures that the Kiwis refused to call sheep were traded, having been walked hundreds of miles across the sands.

With no rain, deep wells fed the fossil water into this fragile eco-system which relied on the palm. It provided dates, timber, fire-wood, thatch, baskets, mats, sandals and even palm wine – an acquired taste. The LRDG's Kiwis had built a reputation on being able to party anywhere, and the SAS's rum ration augmented the wine. Fraser looked down on a piece of pre-history. It was a long way from Aberdeen.[111]

Up here Fraser could smoke, feeling the faintest of breeze. Below, the airfield buzzed with activity; six Bombay aircraft were supporting their mission, ferrying in supplies and men. Under the palms the startling possibility that Clarke had seen with Leclerc's *méharistes*, when he flew out to North Africa in December 1940, had become a reality. Using Kufra as a base, Fraser looked down on every fiction Clarke had written since – a huge Special Force to tear up Rommel's lines of communications from land and sea.

Back in the oasis, Fraser's men stripped down their Vickers guns, and emptied and repacked their magazines. Even covered up, the guns and their magazines filled with fine sand, and they oiled them knowing they would have to do it all again a few days later when they approached the target – attention to detail could save your life.

Stirling touched down from Cairo on 2 September and, unlike the men, Fraser attended the briefing. Benghazi was an open secret, but only Fraser, an officer, would gain the wider understanding of the huge concept of operations. The hundred officers and men of the SAS were part of 'Force X', along with the Rhodesian LRDG troop, 20 Sappers (engineers), 14 Royal Navy, including the former harbour master of Benghazi and an RAF officer. They even had two Stuart Honey tanks, which had crossed from Kharga Oasis with the LRDG's help.

Once in Benghazi, they were to blow up Axis ships in the port. The Royal Navy would take one vessel to sea, and sink it in the harbour mouth as a block ship. They even had a member of the Army Pay Corps who knew the combination of the safe to rob Barclays Bank. The SAS would keep one ship back, in case this all went wrong and they needed to escape. The Sudanese Defence Force at Kufra would take back Jalo Oasis, which lay on the path from Benghazi, and give the SAS and LRDG somewhere to retreat to.

Alongside Fraser was Commando 'Force B': 43 commandos, what was left of 1 SS Regiment; along with 31 assorted gunners; Captain Buck and 20 of his Fifth Column, who were heading for Tobruk. Haselden was already outside Rommel's other supply port, and he would lead the Commando force into the town using Buck's Fifth Column. Once he and the commandos had taken the German's coastal guns, this would allow two huge seaborne forces, A and C, to land.

Far from Kufra, in the port of Haifa, Palestine, seaborne 'Force A' was 436 officers and men of the Royal Marines. In Alexandria, the seaborne 'Force C' was 167 Argylls infantry, along with the SBS's folboats and submarines, enough to overpower the Tobruk garrison.[112]

Clarke provided the operation's icing on the cake, with a plan to terrify the young Italian fascists holding Siwa Oasis. Called 'Saints', fake parachutists, loaded eight to a plane, were to be dropped and then illuminated by flares. The Saints exploded on impact, giving the effect of gunfire as well as destroying the evidence they were fake.[113] The whole operation should get Rommel's attention, and relieve Monty and the 8th Army at El Alamein.

The operation was ambitious, but Stirling was more so. Malta was 270 nautical miles from Benghazi. He had asked that if the SAS capture Benghazi they be reinforced, rather than withdraw. There were more than a thousand Allied prisoners in the town, captured during the retreat, and it was agreed Stirling would radio to Grey Pillars and if General Alexander agreed, the Maltese battalion would be dispatched to reinforce Stirling and the freed prisoners of war. The new Commander in Chief Mediterranean Fleet, Henry Harwood, said there could be no question of naval escort, and Malta would have to provide fighter cover.[114] German airfields in North Africa were, again, on the list; Barce was being hit by the LRDG with a demolitions team commanded by Polish saboteur Vladimir 'Popski' Peniakoff.

With most of the force coming by sea, two days before D Day GHQ would pass control to the Royal Navy in Alexandria, who set up a room for the Army and RAF next door to their operations room. With the LRDG's high-frequency radios on land, and shipborne radios at sea this was a revolutionary special forces Combined Operations centre.

Fraser may have smoked a few cigarettes by the time Stirling read out the orders for officers, emphasising that more than any other operation, this would rely on surprise.[115]

But therein lay the problem.

The plan originally dreamt up by the spy Haselden in June had morphed to Frankenstein proportions. Haselden had been horrified when two LRDG troop leaders he briefed already knew about the raid. The Stuart Honey tank commander, Brian Edevrain Dillon, who Stirling had recruited in Shepheard's, had gone to the briefing room in Grey Pillars and found the secret file on the desk and no one else in the room. Stirling and the other officers had gone to lunch.[116] The 'secret' was common knowledge among the Short Range Desert Group, who had to appoint a staff officer to the SAS because they did not have the infrastructure to plan the logistics for the raid.[117]

Joe's Parish, Mohamed Ali Club, Kit Kat Club, Groppi's and any other bars and nightclubs filled with talk of the raids. Bonner Fellers hadn't got his new cipher from the US before Grey Pillars started planning the mission. And, according to some, he sent the whole operational plan to Washington, which also meant Rommel.[118]

Twenty-five miles from their target, Benghazi, and 600 miles behind Rommel's lines, Fraser watched his men barter Kufra dates with the Senussi for 'eggies', chicken and bread. Camp fires rapidly sprang up as they ate fresh rations. The sight of the doctor sorting out splints, bandages and blood plasma in the shade of his truck's camouflage netting was not reassuring.[119] The SAS staff officer in Grey Pillars had substantially increased the number of morphine tablets they carried.

Fraser and the troop leaders had pored over the latest RAF photographs showing the ships alongside at port. Each team was allocated a ship – once in the port they would race to the dock, get on board their ship, place their limpet mines and destroy Rommel's ability to resupply. The German password for the month was *Autokolonne,* reply *Rosalia* – but they had orders not to wear German or Italian uniforms, after the killing of the French with Buck's men. Fraser's men cleaned their weapons again, and restacked their limpet mines, not the best thing to be carrying into combat in a Jeep already crammed with ammunition.[120]

Troops had been issued Benzedrine because they were exhausted.[121] But the drug has a side effect: it helps combat fear. The gnawing at the pit of the stomach is offset by the euphoria the drug produces.

Fraser was working with Olivey and his Rhodesians again. Fraser had met him at the rendezvous, and Olivey left him the radio truck to set up the SAS's base. Olivey was attacking a nearby airfield as a diversion from the main raid. Like Fraser, Olivey now had a Military Cross for bravery, but the omens for the operation were bad. The two tanks had been written off speeding around Kufra on their twin Cadillac engines. The elderly harbour master had been killed, when his Jeep hit a Thermos bomb when they crossed the Trigh el-Abd. And now, the day before the attack, Haselden's spy network brought news the Germans were expecting them.

Bob Melot, a former World War One fighter ace, turned cotton broker from Alexandria, and Arabist, had been left to spy on the port when the British evacuated. Fraser had met him the night before, starving, so they had fed him bully-beef rissoles fried in oatmeal, which he wolfed down.[122] He had sent one of his Senussi team into Benghazi, and he had just returned with the news the civilian population was being evacuated, a German machine gun battalion had arrived and was camped in the palm trees on the approach to the port. In addition, 70 trucks of Italian infantry had arrived two days earlier, shipping had been moved from the port and a fresh anti-tank ditch had been installed five months previously.[123]

Stirling told everyone to stand down. They would stay at rendezvous and get some rest, not an easy task loaded on a combat dose of Benzedrine.[124] The LRDG signaller radioed the Combined Ops room in Alexandria. Stirling needed an answer by 10am the following morning, D Day.

In the Operations Room in Alexandria, this didn't compute – a huge naval armada was bearing down on Tobruk, forces massing in the desert. This was the turning point in the war, and here was a signal that contradicted everything. Radios burned to 8th Army HQ; they had no intelligence on it. The Operations Room signalled Stirling:

'Intelligence consider almost certain there is no formed body or fighting unit of Germans near Benghazi.'[125]

They suggested the Italians were training in the area, and their photos didn't show the new ditch. This was not the news the SAS needed. Now they had two completely contradictory pieces of intelligence, one from a human source who had just come from the target, the other collated by a distant HQ. Stirling told Fraser and the troop leaders they were being told to ignore bazaar gossip. He had already decided this was going to be a raid – there would be no question of holding the port against these numbers.

Things went wrong fast.

Melot led a four-Jeep team to clear a small fort on the route in. The operation went noisy and he got shrapnel in the gut. The fort almost certainly got a signal off. Melot was supposed to guide them to the target; now one of his men, who was unfamiliar with the route, had to lead. In the dark, Fraser wound round the hills, part of a convoy of 40 Jeeps.

At 11.30pm he saw RAF bombs explode in the port, and searchlights whipped into the sky – they should have been in position to attack straight after the air raid. But this convoy looked suspiciously like it was lost.

Then they drove into a dead end.

Stirling put his headlights on, lighting the steep, rocky terrain, and most followed suit. Eventually, the long convoy turned round, and found a track that led into the right wadi, and dropped down the escarpment. The plan had been to follow the railway line through the minefield and into town. Now they just headed for the closest point, and reached a barrier facing Benghazi at 4.30am.

Engines idling, they stopped on a road with a line of trees. It was getting light to the east; sunrise would be in two hours. The attached engineer officer walked up to the barrier, looked it over for a booby trap, then lifted it up to allow the first Jeep through.

The first two Jeeps raced past the barrier, but were immediately hit by the ambush. Machine guns tore into the first Jeeps and they burst into flames. Tracer ripped from the darkness and mortars exploded among the Jeeps. Fraser grabbed the Vickers in front of his wheel, his gunner had his twin barrels sighted, but their field of fire was blocked by the chaos of vehicles in front of them. He let go of the weapon and jockeyed to get off the track.

Ahead, a burst ripped through Seekings's Jeep. He threw himself to the ground and saw his gunner had been hit. He crawled over; the burst had gone through his groin and shot his penis off. Another man nearby had his arm torn off. Fraser managed to get a shot off and now his gunner ripped into the enemy. Three of the front Jeeps had managed to get out of the killing zone, and were making covering fire.

In the midst stood Stirling, chewing his pipe; Seekings knew he never smoked it, because he smoked all Stirling's tobacco. Seekings piled wounded men into the back of a nearby Jeep. The incoming fire was high, and the covering Jeeps ripping 1,000 rounds a minute were making some impression.

Seekings called out to Stirling,

'What are we going to do?'

Stirling said something short, he was clearly annoyed by the predicament.

Seekings shouted, 'Well I want to know. Are we going through?'

Stirling told him, 'No, get the convoy turned round and we'll have a go another day.'

Old hands like Fraser needed no encouragement. He spun his Jeep, and raced back for the Jebel, desperate to find cover from the Luftwaffe as dawn broke. The first spotter aircraft flew over Fraser as he sped for the Jebel, followed by two fighters, which took out a truck they had just abandoned. Fraser raced his Jeep up into the rocky ravines that scarred the escarpment, as seven fighters closed on the SAS. He made it about halfway up, then tore at bushes, desperate to conceal his vehicle.

Below, Seekings drove into a Senussi camp, and straight into one of their tents, chickens flying everywhere. The man with his groin shot away begged Seekings to kill him; Seekings thought it lucky he had lost his pistol. Everywhere, Jeeps spread to find cover. [126]

*

In the Combined Operations room, Alexandria, the first signs of disaster came. They had no comms with Stirling, but at 5.39am got the message the Royal Marines, Force A, had failed to land. Only two motor torpedo boats had made it into Tobruk; the rest appeared shot to pieces. Then one destroyer was hit and disabled. At 7.40am, the destroyer sent: 'Emergency, must leave you.' It had been hit by aircraft. The cruiser, HMS *Coventry*, was so badly hit by dive bombers, and on fire, she had to be abandoned. They didn't know it but Haselden and his men were surrounded. Buck would see him try to shoot his way out, then fall to the ground, dead.

At 9.45am, LRDG CO Prendergast's signal was blunt, and concerned for his men: report the last time you heard Stirling and the SAS – this is required to show us they are still alive.

There was no news.

At Benghazi, the Luftwaffe had been waiting. This was their chance to pay back a year of burnt aircraft and aircrew littering their Libyan airfields. From the Jebel, Fraser watched the Luftwaffe rising like angry wasps over Benghazi.

Fraser watched a party of two old men on donkeys, followed by women, heading across the plain into Benghazi. A fighter ripped over, leaving them crumpled on the desert. Then by chance a bomber hit an ammunition truck in a nearby wadi, and smoke billowed out across the Jebel. Once they knew where the SAS were hiding, they became methodical, bombing and strafing each wadi in turn.

The Messerschmitt 109, 110 fighters and Italian Macchi C.202 Folgores came straight down the Jebel strafing at the same level as the Jeeps. Meanwhile, the slower Fiat CR42 biplanes hovered, pulling tighter circles to strafe anyone who moved, along with suspected bushes, to drive the SAS out of cover. The old hands stayed put, the inexperienced ran and paid the price.

In twelve and half hours of daylight there were never fewer than twelve aircraft overhead. The pilots took a break for lunch, then came back. Once it was dark Fraser and his crew cleared their Jeep and headed for the rendezvous, 25 miles into the Jebel.

Fraser pulled into the rendezvous in the early hours. Patrols were coming in, there was no sign of the doctor and his team, who were still out on the Jebel. That night Stirling came in, and in the count they had done remarkably well: they had about 10 injured and dead, but had only lost 3 trucks and 7 Jeeps. Stirling sent an optimistic signal at 10am: Benghazi had been a complete failure, but they were reforming and hoped to carry out raids east of Tobruk.

Shortly after he sent this, the Luftwaffe found them out on the Jebel, and were merciless. By that evening they had destroyed another 11 trucks and 6 Jeeps, and wounded 14 men. L Detachment was no longer capable of operations. That night many of the remaining SAS found the rendezvous by the light of the flaming vehicles.[127]

The doctor came in carrying Melot and some of the wounded.

Stirling told him, 'I'm afraid I've got some very bad news for you. We're moving off in two hours' time, but we simply haven't enough room to take back the wounded with us. I'm terribly sorry.'[128]

The doctor tossed a coin for which of his orderlies would remain.

Stirling remained at the rendezvous, but the rest needed to get some distance between them and the Luftwaffe before daybreak. They wouldn't survive another day on the Jebel. Quickly, troops were allocated to overloaded Jeeps and trucks; Fraser took the doctor and left the desolate scene, the black night lit by fires from burning vehicles, the smell of burning rubber and smoke. The SAS split into three convoys. Fraser led the doctor's column, but after 5 miles, with daylight approaching, he did a U turn back into the Jebel to find cover rather than be caught in the open.

With Mike Sadler navigating, they made good speed the next night, but were almost out of fuel. They headed for Jalo Oasis to refuel, only to hear the thump of artillery as they approached. The Sudanese had failed to take the oasis and a battle was going on. When the first team sent to investigate didn't come back, Fraser drove in with his Jeep. The Sudanese were in a gun battle with the Italians inside the oasis but could spare some fuel. Fraser drove back to his convoy, showered them with oasis dates, then drove back with the truck to get the petrol.

Fraser passed through the pink sands at Zighen Oasis, a group of uninhabited wells that marks the narrowest crossing point in the Sand Sea to Kufra. South, after crossing the Sand Sea, and constantly getting stuck in the sand, the following night they were among the black-rock outcrops and pinnacles that mark the approach to Kufra. That night Phillips sang the sad lament of 'Mad Carew' – about an officer who steals the eye of a god to give to his love, the Colonel's daughter, and pays with his life. Phillip's Birmingham accent echoed through the dark desert rocks. The lament ends: she would have loved Carew had he not stolen the eye.[129,130]

When they got to Kufra, a *Kommando*-hunting Heinkel III flew over and bombed the airfield, in case they were in any doubt about how much the Germans knew about the operation. Stirling was ordered back to Cairo on the next Bombay.[131] He left with damage limitation on his mind. Fraser had orders to stay at Kufra: they were going back out. He rinsed himself off in the prehistoric water. His luck had held.

12

The Soft Underbelly: 1942–1943

The Fleshpots

With Rommel attempting to break through the El Alamein line, the missing member of Bagnold's Zerzura Club showed up – the wrong side of the line. Count László Almásy, who had flown with Clayton looking for the mythical Oasis of the Birds, now offered his services to Rommel. He set up shop in Jalo planning to use the old routes he, Bagnold and Clayton had used before the war to do exactly what Bagnold had once feared someone would do.

But instead of leading a battalion to destroy the Aswan Dam, he took two spies to the railway station at Assuit in the Nile Delta south of Cairo, and half way to Aswan. From where they took a train to town.

The spies had bags of sterling. A dancer at the Continental put her flat on the *Agence Immobiliere* on Qasr-el-Nil (street of spies), and was only too happy to get two new tenants who wanted to pay her cash in advance. When she came to check on them, she found they had left, and taken a Dahabiya – a houseboat on the Nile.[1]

The Hungarian Embassy, allies of Germany, had been shut down and the contents of their basement moved to the Swedish Embassy. In that basement were several large cases belonging to a pre-war German archaeological expedition, which were under the care of a Hungarian Carmelite monk. One of the cases appears to have contained a radio.[2] With their radio set up in a houseboat on the Nile, they started transmissions, but the short bursts, at midnight every night, were impossible for the British counter-espionage team to direction-find.[3]

The spies recruited their driver through the doorman of the Kit

Kat, and with him travelled to Qasr-el-Nil to change sterling to Egyptian currency, but, with Rommel advancing, sterling became worthless. The first black-market rate they got 33 per cent of value, the second, 50 per cent, after which they couldn't change the money at any price. The Egyptians were backing Rommel to win. And herein lay the spies' downfall.

The spies liked a good time, and splashed sterling around on wine, women and song. The first Major Sansom heard was a phone call about an odd British Army officer in the Turf Club. It was Major Sansom who had a man permanently stationed watching Joe-the-Swiss. The oddest thing about this British Officer was that he paid with sterling. No one in Cairo used sterling. Sansom went to the British Army Paymaster, where all sterling ended up, and asked a puzzled young Pay Corps officer to find out how much had been coming in.

'As a matter of fact, I think there has been a bit more in the last couple of weeks.'

From where? All the usual suspects got pinned: Shepheard's, Groppi's, the Turf Club and the nightclubs. When they sent a five-pound note to the Bank of England, they discovered it was fake. The spike in fake British currency coincided with the radio transmission emanating from the city.

Sansom's next break came when an officer from the Interrogation Centre at Maadi showed up with a copy of Daphne du Maurier's *Rebecca*, which they had found on a prisoner of war. He had been picked up in a German mobile wireless truck in the middle of the desert by a Kiwi patrol. The price on the book had been rubbed out, but forensics uncovered the stamp – '50 escudos'. The book was from Spain. Sansom thought, Rebecca *is their code – the reason their transmissions are short is because we have their receiving station.*[4]

It isn't clear whether he told Clarke at this moment, but he was on to something. And, as Sansom chased the spies, CHEESE, the double agent Clarke thought they'd blown, was electrified by a special message: 'Be very active these days. Good information will be well rewarded. From now on we are going to listen every day for your signals.'[5]

*

Sansom stuck a map of Cairo in the wall and got the paymaster to give him all the locations of fake bank notes. Then Sansom decided to get out of uniform and spend the evening in the Kit Kat Club. He walked in and there at the bar a man who introduced himself as Hussein was lighting his cigarette with a five-pound note.

The money-burning spy and he struck up a conversation. In the sting, the barman, Mac Mahood, fed him watered-down drinks – Mac was on the British payroll. The club's Hungarian dancers played for the other side. Sansom had to make a pass at one of the dancers in the taxi to the houseboat as cover. Once they were inside, unbelievably, Egyptian Army Officer Muhammad Anwar el-Sadat showed up, saying he had come to fix the radio. Sadat didn't recognise Sansom, but Sansom recognised him as a member of the Muslim Brotherhood. He was on Sansom's list. Sadat went to look at the radio and came back to tell the team there was nothing wrong with it.

Sadat was disgusted by what he saw. The young Nazis looked like they were in something out of Arabian nights – with thousands of pounds and an easy living, they had forgotten their mission, to spin out their stay in Cairo as long as possible. He was half right. In fact they were out of money, and, worried they had got little information, they had faked a diary full of spurious intelligence to hand to Rommel. Sadat was there because they were trying to arrange to fly out with a pilot colleague of his.[6]

Their copy of *Rebecca* was picked up when they threw it over the side during the subsequent bust, and it landed in the Egyptian police boat.

Clarke gave them the codename FLESHPOTS, but didn't use them because news of their bust was all over town. But it meant Rommel's Cairo network had been shut down, which meant the Axis turned to CHEESE. Nicossof transmitted: he was moody and he was broke. Clarke gave him a real girlfriend to help with his money exchanges – an attractive Cretan who carried a gun. Her nickname was 'the Blond Moll with the Gun'. CHEESE got sent his money, but the U-boat was sunk.[7] Clarke's best conduit into the Axis camp was back up and running.

*

Clarke had tracked how successful his schemes were. When Rommel hit the Gazala line, before Ritchie's Gazala Gallop, he found out they estimated the SAS had a battalion in the desert, 400 men, while in reality the SAS could barely muster 40. He also found out that although the Axis understood the difference between the LRDG and SAS, they still thought SAS teams parachuted in, and the LRDG took them out. Clarke's deception had continued to work, even though the SAS hadn't dropped since the first raid. Neither Clarke nor Stirling wanted to disabuse anyone of this.

Members of the SAS often wondered why the Axis didn't do more to protect its airfields. Aircrews sleeping under planes were easy prey for men like Phillips. The reason was the Axis thought it would be impossible to stop the SAS parachuting in and spent its resources on getting them on the way out.

Clarke also found out that the Axis were overestimating British strength at the front by 30 per cent. And Clarke kept inventing new formations to meet British commanders' needs. Once he had invented a unit, if it disappeared the Axis would smell his fake. What had started with the SAS, then the Division in Cyprus, then tank regiments in Syria and Egypt had got so out of hand that Clarke had an army. He had to draw up (secret) Orders of Battle for his fictional forces and distribute them so no one messed up. He had staff cars driving around Cairo with badges for the different units: Black Cats, Hornets, a Fouled Anchor for a fake Royal Marine unit, a Giraffe for a fake Sudanese force. He called the operation CASCADE. Clarke was on his way to the biggest deception of the war.

Boy Stirling

Stirling and the new special forces staff officer from Grey Pillars, John 'Shan' Winthrop Hackett, drove out to Monty's new 8th Army HQ by the sea at Burg-al-Arab. Born in Australia, 31-one-year-old Hackett had recently been injured in a tank, his burns so bad he needed a staff job. But the good news was he was front line enough for the SAS and LRDG.

He and Stirling stood on top of the bluff over the sea and looked down at British staff officers swimming in the Mediterranean in white swimming trunks. Until they realised they weren't wearing trunks.

Led by a mess waiter in white jacket, they were seated in a marquee complete with white cloth and mess silver, fanned by the sea breeze. Gone was the fly-bitten cage just behind the front line. The waiter returned and offered them chilled white wine. But for Stirling, covered with desert sores and wearing dark glasses, this was business. The Auk's vision for a multi-squadron SAS had been depleted by the Benghazi debacle, and the only place he could get suitable recruits was from 8th Army.

Monty kept them waiting, and then told them he didn't have much time. An old play. He heard Stirling out then retorted, 'What makes you think your men will fight better under your command than mine? They won't be ready for the battle.'

His planned battle for El Alamein was now a month away.

Hackett responded, 'Well they may not be, but they'll be trained for the one after that and the battles to follow.'

Monty hammered the table.

'There will be no other battle in Africa! This will be the last battle. I will destroy Rommel and I propose to destroy him here!'

From behind his dark glasses, Stirling couldn't resist.

'Yes. But the last commander told me something like that. And the one before him too.'[8]

It was a catastrophic error of judgement. Monty was not a man to make an enemy of. Monty stormed out. Driving back to Cairo empty-handed, Stirling cursed himself for not doing his homework.[9] It was amateur; Clarke would have done his. Stirling returned to his brother Peter's flat in Cairo and collapsed on the floor. Since Lewes's death, operating in the desert, planning operations and haggling with GHQ in Cairo to keep them in business, he'd driven himself into the ground.

From Kufra Oasis, Mayne and Fraser went into action with what remained of the unit. For A Squadron, SAS, Mayne chose Fraser as his second in command. They made the most unlikely pairing; the huge former Irish second row, and the slim gay man from Aberdeen. Taking the doctor with them, they moved north and set up a patrol base on the edge of the Sand Sea. Learning from experience they cached fuel, ammunition and, most importantly, water. They didn't lack, and their camp among the huge dunes was well concealed. From here they set out over hundreds of miles to hit Rommel's lines of communication.

By natural selection, these men were old hands, like Phillips, led by Fraser, Mayne and other troop leaders. For Fraser this was now his backyard. The Trigh el-Abd track, the escarpment above Benghazi and always the Via Balbia, which they punished. They blew the Tobruk-to-Matruh railway seven times, knocked down telegraph lines and did so many 'jobs' the details started to blur. But this single force was a long way from the Auk's vision, and with no reinforcement the pace was relentless. But even with their small numbers, in the run up to Monty's attack at El Alamein they made an impression.

Rommel recognised Fraser and Mayne were creating havoc.

But their pace had a price. Sitting at the bottom of a dune at base one evening, troop leader Jim Chambers, who was suffering heavily from infected desert sores, confided in the doctor, 'You know doc, I can't make it out at all, but I don't seem to have the same keenness or enthusiasm these days. . . . Now it is so much hard work.'[10]

The doctor had him evacuated. He died of diphtheria in hospital.

Monty took no chances for his battle of El Alamein. Rommel, in his last attempt to break through to Cairo, and first attack on Monty, thought him a very cautious man, who was not prepared to take any sort of risk.[11]

Churchill had been furious the Auk wouldn't attack until 15 September, but now, with Alexander and Brooke's protection, Monty delayed two months to build a massive reserve, both of troops and

US hardware. Outnumbering Rommel 220,000 to 96,000 (of whom only 56,000 were German), a margin of 800 to 60 modern tanks, aircraft 800 to 300,[12] before taking into account the fact that Rommel had virtually no fuel. When Monty had been Dorman-Smith's instructor at Sandhurst, Dorman-Smith said his idea of tactics was to take a sledgehammer to crack a nut – which Monty thought 'preposterous'.[13]

He also powered his troops with a massive shipment of Benzedrine. Monty had taken a personal interest in every innovation that could help defeat Britain's nemesis, and conducted his own drug trials. He had reached the conclusion they worked. A hundred thousand tablets were distributed to combat units for the first day of the attack.[14] (The British would go on to consume 72 million tablets, most consumed by the 8th Army.)[15] He also, cynically, guaranteed the breakthrough would occur within 13 days, the time the US landed in North Africa. It was inevitable Rommel would withdraw then, and raised the question why El Alamein was fought at all.

Clarke, again, deceived Rommel. He built on his fake invasion of Crete by the SAS, and fed that this would lead to the invasion of Greece. The lie was helped by the fact that US attaché William Harriman was in town, hinting at US involvement. In fact, there was a US convoy on its way across the Atlantic to Morocco and Algeria, but Clarke pretended this was heading for Sicily and Italy.

At El Alamein, Kenyon Jones moved all his dummy tanks to the south of the line, a fake oil pipe in the same direction; in reality, Monty would attack in the north. Clarke gave a fake D Day of 6 November, and fed information the new Sherman panzer-busting tank had engine trouble. He organised a fake conference, with real commanders, including new Commander in Chief Middle East, Alexander, and the RAF's Tedder, in Teheran, Iran, to hint they were going north, and booked the 8th Army general's rooms in the Continental and Shepheard's during the attack. CHEESE fed Rommel this load of garbage: it kept his reinforcements in Crete. And Rommel was in a health spa in Semmering, Austria, for his liver and blood pressure, when Monty attacked.[16] The US African landings would be a complete surprise. As Clarke put it, 'a firm lesson . . . lies perhaps in the readiness of an opponent to accept evidence which from a purely British viewpoint may seem implausible'.[17]

Clarke then flew out to Washington to meet US General George Veazey Strong, head of US intelligence, and Colonel Donovan to discuss the US Rangers, who were training in Scotland.

On 23 October 1942, the closest SAS patrol was just 30 miles behind the German line, and Phillips was putting a Lewes bomb on an 88mm gun when flashes started on the horizon. Fraser heard the noise rolling towards them like thunder, the pounding of a thousand artillery pieces that heralded the start of Monty's attack on Rommel. Rommel flew back to Africa, to fight what he called the 'battle without hope'.

Monty's staff also took Benzedrine, but Monty valued his sleep, a practice he had developed in France.[18] After two days 'wood chopping', the attack had completely stalled, the infantry had not been able to breach Rommel's minefields. Monty was woken by De Guingand to be told that the armoured commander, Lumsden, had pulled his tanks back. The tanks should have been breaking through, but were bunched up in narrow funnels in deep minefields, and easy target for Rommel's 88mm guns.[19]

At 3.30am on 25 October, in the naked electric light of the map lorry, Lumsden and Monty had a tense discussion. Back at the front, Lumsden told Gatehouse to send in his tanks. Gatehouse refused. Lumsden warned him Monty had threatened to sack them both. Gatehouse rang Monty, and, faced with mutiny, Monty conceded. Instead of sending in six armoured regiments to get massacred, he sent one, the Staffordshire Yeomanry, who were wiped out, losing all but 15 of their tanks.[20] The only commander Monty seemed to like was Freyberg, who was a 'bit slow up top', but prepared to charge through a minefield in front of his troops.[21]

On 29 October, Lumsden and Monty had a much bigger row

about sending tanks into minefields to be shot to pieces, audible to everyone nearby, after which Lumsden stormed out through the HQ, past a board covered by a rug marked 'Most Secret', and ripped it off. It was the Monty sweepstake the officers were running on Monty's favourites. Lumsden had plummeted to the bottom.[22] By then, in London, Churchill was shouting abuse at Alan Brooke, who had to concede to himself there was the possibility that Monty was beat.[23]

At 11.30am that day, Rommel found that his tanker full of fuel from Italy had been torpedoed. Even in Rome they realised that without fuel they faced annihilation.[24] Monty slogged on for five more days, until 3 November, the battlefield littered with Allied men and tanks. An ANZAC carved an arrow on the station wall of El Alamein, pointing at the sign, under which he wrote 'Heaven'.[25] That day Hitler instructed, 'as to your troops, you can show no other road than to victory or death'.[26] Rommel decided to show them the road back to Libya instead.

It was Monty's moment to put Rommel to the sword, but Fraser watched Rommel's vehicles rush back. Monty had nothing to follow up. His exhausted troops 'mopped up' the Italian infantry, who had no transport and were surrounded by the time Hitler and Mussolini ordered them to withdraw. Rommel shrugged: he had escaped. Fraser watched panzer towing panzer, to reduce their fuel consumption, and everything that could move rushing back from the front to fight another day.

After the battle, Monty offered Freyberg some chocolate; Lumsden didn't get any. Sacked, he would die on the bridge of a British warship in the Pacific, hit by a kamikaze. On that dark night in the desert, he had merely been guilty of speaking truth to power. Stirling had been right: Monty hadn't destroyed Rommel, and this would not be the last battle in Africa. Monty was the latest commander to be outwitted by the Desert Fox.

On 11 November, it was a more humble Stirling that arrived at Monty's HQ. He needed to impress on this new commander the worth of the SAS. He told Monty he was mounting a major expedition into Tripolitania to cut Rommel's lines of communication. Monty said, 'The boy Stirling is mad. Quite, quite mad. However, in war there is often a place for mad people.' Stirling again offered Mather a job: 'You cannot miss this one, of all of them.'[27]

With Rommel retreating it was time to move out of the Sand Sea. Fraser pulled out, leaving the dunes fading into the heat haze behind him. Mushroom-shaped and sugarloaf hills, their bases carved out by the wind, loomed ahead; then, on his next bearing, needle-shaped rocks. About one hundred miles north of Kufra he came across two Blenheim bombers sitting in the desert, the hot wind moaning through their wire struts, the graves of the crew next to them buried by the sole survivor of the lost aircraft.[28] Approaching Bir Zelten, 100 miles inland from the coast, Fraser really was on his turf. Due north was Agedabia; Marble Arch was to their north-west, and in between was the whole terrain he had escaped through.

The Bir, Arabic for well, was on the south side of a hard-packed wadi that led into the Sand Sea north of Kufra. Protected from the north by dunes, entered from the east, it was difficult for anyone tracking them to follow. The nights had turned cold; Fraser needed a greatcoat, fleece and leather jerkin. When they'd first reached the Sand Sea, he had needed just a blanket at night.

Mather had flown back to Cairo for a quick bath at Stirling's flat, then dinner at Shepheard's. At 9pm they left, with two Jeeps in escort, and one backward glance from the Battle Wagon at the familiar outline of Shepheard's Hotel, with its broad veranda on which were seated assorted members of the 'Short Range Shepheard's Group' sipping their John Collinses, and no doubt muttering, 'There but for the grace of God go I.'

In long white galabias, red belt, and red taboosh, the sufragis were dancing attendance. On the pavement at the foot of the steps stood the Turkish-pantalooned grand dragoman, who seemed to control all the taxi and gharry drivers in Cairo. And the gnarled tree of Napoleon's General Kléber.[29]

At the Bir, Fraser listened to Stirling's briefing. Fraser had looked askance at the raw depot recruits. They looked the part, with their new Jeeps and headscarves, but they were raw. He didn't know the officers except for Dillon, the tank man who'd come with them to Benghazi, and Mather. At least those two could navigate. It seemed Stirling had done a lot of his recruiting from his bath, with shades of Old Flamer, which at least had made their interviews memorable.

Fraser and Mayne and the old hands of A Squadron would take the section of road west to Misurata, which took Fraser past the roadhouse, his old target of Sirte, and Lewes's grave. But Stirling was taking the new boys further west, deep into the heartland of the Carthaginian Empire, to Tripoli and beyond. This was unknown territory for the SAS.[30]

Getting ready to head west, Dillon collared Stirling. He thought few of their 150 men were any use, and when he looked at where his target was, a section of railway west of Tripoli, he calculated his fuel and asked Stirling how he was supposed to get back. Stirling told him he had asked Monty the same thing and impersonated Monty's nasal tones: 'When I have captured Tripoli, I shall have no further use for you.'[31]

The two squadrons split: Stirling with the B Squadron teams went west, and Fraser with the A Squadron teams, north. But German intelligence already suspected the main body of the LRDG and some elements of 1 Special Air Service Brigade were in the area of Marada – and they were very close. If they had gone 60 miles further, over the arm of the Sand Sea, they would have hit the SAS base. They also suspected there was an HQ of the LRDG south-west of Sirte.[32] It was the SAS, but they were right.

At Christmas, Rommel paid Fraser and the SAS a compliment: 'They succeeded again and again in shooting up supply lorries behind our lines, laying mines, cutting down telephone poles and similar nefarious activities. Their parties were extremely difficult to catch, for they made only the briefest appearances and then vanished without trace back into the desert.'

But Mayne had a lucky escape: when he didn't make it back to the rendezvous, Dillon, who had navigation skill from yachting, was tasked to look for him. He was given two Senussi tribesmen as guides, who were immediately relieved to find out that they weren't his slaves, a misunderstanding in the negotiation. Dillon knew Mayne should have been near a specific Bir and set out across the desert crust. Navigating off the sun compass and milometer, he was amazed at the accuracy with which the Senussi tapped him on the shoulder at the very moment he calculated they had reached the well.

The Senussi ran off, then indicated the Jeep tracks. Dillon followed the tracks. Mayne had run over some compacted ground in order to lose any followers.

Again, the Senussi got out and walked in front of the Jeep, and led Dillon, spotting every turned stone. Eventually the Senussi led them to a cave, and there was Mayne and his Jeep, lost and out of water.

'About time somebody came along,' he said.[33]

Further west, Stirling and the SAS crossed into ancient Carthage. Another new recruit, the legendary explorer Wilfred Thesiger's navigation was less impressive; he climbed a dune and pointed south, saying, 'There it is Sergeant Cooper, there's Southern Cross.'[34] The good sergeant had to explain it was Capella, and that the Southern Cross isn't visible at a latitude of 30 degrees north.

Mather was one of the first to go. In a firefight, separated from his Jeeps, he and five men fled, their superior marksmanship keeping their pursuers at bay. Their pursuers had an Arab tracker, and in every village they fled past, children screamed and men jumped onto the roofs of their houses to point them out. With two hours before darkness, Mather thought they might make it, but they were surrounded, and then fired off the last of their ammo. When the enemy opened up with a machine gun from an olive tree, and hurled in grenades, Mather knew they were done. Excited Arabs and Italians grabbed them and pushed them against a wall to be shot. A fierce argument ensued between them, which Mather joined, to explain what would happen when the Allies arrived. It was over in minutes. They had been very lucky.[35]

Rommel was personally on the hunt. Rommel, unlike British generals, led from the front with a small combat command unit called his *Kampfstaffel*, which used captured British tanks and could fight and pursue the SAS. He followed some tracks, trying to find his nemesis, only to run into an Italian scout car. But the story repeated throughout B Squadron was that Stirling's gamble had failed. Insufficient experience, tough operating conditions, and too little logistics support had overcome his effort to prove to Monty the worth of the SAS. B Squadron were captured or killed.

Stirling decided to double down. With Monty slogging his way west through a series of costly battles, he closed towards the US Army coming from the west. On 22 December, Stirling went back to Kabrit with Fraser to bring up the remnants of the partially trained B Squadron, and C Squadron, which had just been formed and arrived from training in Syria.[36]

Coming in from ten weeks of operations at Christmas, Fraser let his hair down, along with his guard. He turned up at Kabrit camp with Stirling on Christmas day with two black eyes. He was sheepish about what had happened.[37]

Fraser left for the desert with the new teams on 31 December. Their limit of exploitation – a military term for how far you are allowed to go – was the Gabès Gap. This is a low lying piece of desert deep into Tunisia, often cloaked in sea fret, sandwiched between sea and marsh, that has long been a barrier to invaders on the southern approach to Carthage. Rommel had improved it with pillboxes, and his troops were pouring north to get behind the gap, as Monty closed on him.

Stirling was not supposed to pass Gabès, but navigator Mike Sadler remembers passing a column full of German soldiers looking at them as they ran the narrow gauntlet.[38] Exhausted, on the far side of the gap, the small SAS team pulled off the road and into a wadi to get some rest.

Stirling awoke to a German kicking him.

He had gambled one last time, to prove their worth and be the first British unit to shake hands with US forces in the war. As Rommel put it: 'Thus the British lost the very able and adaptable commander of the desert group which had caused us more damage than any other British unit of equal strength.'[39]

Stirling would have his detractors, but Lewes, who had known the young man better than most, called him a pudding when he wasn't interested, but if he was, he was an all-in fighter who took every advantage and gave none, and pursued victory relentlessly and without pity.[40] When Clarke had met Stirling in Shepheard's, the SAS had been an idea, drifting about like a gas, a vapour. What he may have realised when meeting Stirling was that if you are going to sell fog, you need a very good salesman.

The Mincemeat Problem

Clarke gave Monty a tactical A-Force HQ to travel with his HQ and look after his needs.[41] The only difference now between Rommel and Kléber, was that Rommel would fly out of Africa on a Junkers 52, an option Kléber had not had. Clarke had bigger plans – the invasion of Europe.

Number 6 Sharia Qasr-el-Nil was bursting at the seams at Christmas 1942, with Clarke's A-Force occupying six flats. As confetti was swept from Shepheard's ballroom, on New Year's Day 1943, the Allies dominated the Mediterranean, and spies dropped into Clarke's lap. The FLESHPOTS were followed by THE PYRAMIDS, an Egyptian team planning to set up a wireless transmitter for Rommel, named, presumably, after the location of that transmitter. Then came QUICKSILVER, a Greek Airforce officer the Abwehr inserted into Syria with his girlfriend, who quickly gave himself up. Three PESSIMISTS landed in northern Cyprus – an Italian, an Egyptian singer and a convicted drug smuggler – who were not optimistic Hitler would win the war. DOMINO, a German veteran from 1918, an attendant on the *Taurus Express* between Baghdad and Istanbul, fell over. MISCHIEF, a British agent who had 'been shot while attempting to escape', started transmitting, but the Italians overreached themselves, asking what was going to happen after the fall of Tunisia, making Clarke and Maunsell suspicious. And CAPRICON, a British agent captured in the Peloponnese, whose radio was operated by the Italians, became yet another channel for Clarke. And there was always CHEESE.

Clarke had met with General Alexander in Alexandria at the end of 1942, to discuss the next stages. They agreed to build up Clarke's fake army to reinforce against the German threat from Russia, and beef up his threatened invasion of Greece. Kenyon Jones's SAS alter ego, K Detachment, started filling Benghazi harbour with landing craft, and 1st SAS Brigade's fake parachutists got ready to drop.

At the end of January, Rommel's friend General Paulus, who had once been sent to rein him in, surrendered in Stalingrad. Eight hundred thousand German troops were captured or killed. Hitler was going to lose the war, it was only a matter of how.

The 'soft underbelly of Europe' is a phrase attributed to many, but if Europe is an armadillo, it is lying on its back. The Allied plan to tackle Europe was to invade Sicily, then the south of Italy, Churchill's wish since the Greek Dunkirk derailed everything two long years ago. The advantage, to Clarke, was that while Sicily made military sense – an island to operate over Italy, France, and into Germany – invading the foot of Italy made no military sense whatsoever. As German defender General Fridolin von Senger und Etterlin would later say to the British, 'Next time you invade Italy, do not start at the bottom.'42

A bad Allied plan gave Clarke the opportunity to fake better ones.

On 25 February 1943, Clarke and his team climbed into a Dakota and flew to Algiers, avoiding the rump of Germans still holding out in Tunisia, to sit down with General Eisenhower's US intelligence staff. HQ was in Hotel St George, with its wide verandas and spacious gardens. The problem was, the Germans knew it was there, and bombed it constantly. Clarke set up office in the converted garage of a nearby house. And two days later Colonel Bevan, his opposite number from the 'London controlling section' that Clarke had created in September 1941, arrived. Clarke shut the door and sat down to read his most important document of the war.

The manila envelope from Churchill, stamped 'Top Secret', contained the Allied deception plan for the invasion of Europe. He tore it open eagerly while Bevan talked. At a conference in Casablanca, Morocco, the month before, Churchill had agreed with Roosevelt that the main objective was to take the pressure off Russia. Fake invasions in Norway in the spring of 1943, which would be pushed back to autumn 1943 when it missed its D Day. A fake cross-Channel invasion of France in July 1943, which would be pushed back to September. And in Clarke's area a fake invasion of the South of France to meet the Channel assault, and fake invasion of Greece that year.

Clarke was already up and running. His fake army was already poised to take Greece, in a deception plan he had been building since the day he first offered the fake SAS Brigade to the Auk to drop on Crete.

Then Bevan told him something that really concerned him. There was another plan from London, called OPERATION MINCEMEAT, to drop the body of a Royal Marine officer off the coast of Spain with a fake letter indicating that the Allies would not invade Sicily.

Clarke sat back.

He didn't have a problem with the concept. He had the LRDG drop fake 'going maps' at Jalo to indicate the Auk would attack across the desert in 1941. De Guingand dumped a derelict armoured car west of Alam el Halfa, when Rommel attacked Monty. The armoured car had a going map showing a route through El Alamein as hard desert, when it was very soft sand, and Rommel's panzers then got stuck.[43] But Clarke already had the painful realisation that the enemy could scarcely avoid the conclusion that Sicily must be Monty's next move, regardless of what his ultimate strategic intentions might be.

Like a film, his deceptions had an 'audience'. Like a film, the deception was designed to make the audience feel a certain way to produce a reaction. In Clarke's case, the reaction he wanted was the enemy jumping the wrong way. He knew it was less important whether the enemy swallowed all the 'story', or drew the correct conclusions from the treatment, provided they did what he wanted.

The story was the architecture of the deception – in this case, 'we are going to invade Greece'. The 'treatment' was how that story was treated – which of his infinite deception devices he would use, such as the SAS, fake aircraft, the multitude of K Detachment dummies, fake documents or leaks via his enormous network of agents and spies. His reach was huge, A-Force had 21 offices (confusingly, he called the 'thirty-committee' *XXIII*, a play on London's *XX* 'double cross') which operated from Cairo to Beirut, Baghdad to Cape Town, Lisbon to Rome. The problem with MINCEMEAT was it was part of a treatment, not the story. Put another way, it was icing but the cake was all Clarke's.

Clarke asked London if they would change the letter to indicate a fake date for the invasion of Sicily – which he had used many times. But the man in charge of MINCEMEAT, Lieutenant Commander Ewen Montagu, thought Bevan was vain, incompetent and a liar.[44] Montagu had written an internal briefing document for Naval Intelligence, London, summarising the 'present hopeless position of deception'. Specifically, that Bevan wanted to discuss any future deception with Clarke, then clear it with the supreme commander, Eisenhower. Montagu continued; while Clarke had done brilliant tactical deception, he had done 'rather little successful strategic deception'. He had taken too long to get the cover for the US landings going, and this deception 'was still going strong five months later'.[45]

The problem was Montagu had no idea what he was talking about.

He could not, for example, know that Clarke had nearly blown the North African landings by mistake, just after Eisenhower and Churchill first had discussed them, with a very successful previous deception for the Auk to distract German attention from the region. After this he had been specifically told (by Churchill) not to mention

French North Africa. His subsequent deception for the US landings had worked: the Germans thought they would hit Benghazi, which would have ended German resistance far sooner than the real US landings. Months later, that the Germans still believed Italy and Greece were threatened was Clarke's intention, and a bonus. And Montagu's criticism that Bevan wanted to check in with Clarke to coordinate the biggest deception of the war before taking the plan to the supreme commander, Eisenhower, sounds like a very good idea. Montagu simply lacked knowledge; much of this occurred outside his sphere of influence or above his pay grade.

There was no dice to Clarke's request in London. Montagu had got MINCEMEAT approved, and was now a loose cannon. Clarke moved on to damage limitation.

Clarke solved his first problem in Algiers, their accommodation, when A-Force moved into a pair of newly built villas on a pleasant wooded slope at 20 Rue Mangin. By 1943 Shepheard's had run out of champagne – but French North Africa had plenty of wine, sufficient until the Allies liberated Champagne.

For the forthcoming invasion, over in Egypt, Clarke's entirely fictional 12th Army cascaded. Meaning even though most of the Sicily invasion force was still in the Western Mediterranean, the Axis thought they could still invade Greece from Egypt. Kenyon Jones ran around building landing craft in Tobruk and SAS gliders in the desert, but the Allied command weren't helping Clarke. Eisenhower moved his HQ to Malta to be closer to Sicily; beach reconnaissance parties on Sicily got captured; the last straw for Clarke was when they decided to invade Pantelleria, just one month before Sicily. Churchill was nothing if not consistent – Pantelleria was the operation Fraser had trained for on Arran, and for which the Commandos had first set sail. It was just 70 miles from the Sicilian coast, and, Clarke said, 'It killed the chance of surprise on Sicily.'

Clarke then had to watch the Allies group their landing craft directly south of Sicily in Sousse. Close behind were two airborne divisions. Clarke thought it useless to make any attempt to persuade the enemy they weren't invading Sicily. Clarke's CASCADE became WATERFALL, and MINCEMEAT went into the water. In response to the letter on the dead marine and to Clarke's fakery, the Germans moved two divisions to the Peloponnese and the beaches west of Athens.

The RAF looked on diversion bombing as 'wasted'. RAF fighters were happy to strafe shipping through the Peloponnese, but despite Clarke's best efforts they would not bomb the South of France. They only hit Sardinia, another Clarke diversion, 29 times. The real target, Sicily, they bombed 33 times. And, while Kenyon Jones's fake army filled Egypt radio waves with traffic, in the air overzealous RAF pilots shot down Axis reconnaissance aircraft, when Clarke wanted them to get home safe with some pictures.

Worse was to come. The plans for the whole airborne attack on Sicily were found in Shepheard's Hotel. An investigation showed that in 48 hours they had passed through the hands of an Egyptian servant, Swiss hall porter, the German manager (he had a Uruguayan passport), a Swiss doctor and his Polish secretary, and the aide de camp to a Czech general. But those questioned expressed the opinion the document was probably planted at Shepheard's to deceive! Two days later a laundryman handed in a book from the pocket of a British soldier with the date, times and places of part of the Sicily assault.

Clarke didn't give up. He had Greek interpreters sent to Malta for units bound for Sicily. One would stow away and be surprised to find himself sailing for Sicily, rather than the Peloponnese. Throughout April into May things looked okay. Most enemy intelligence, and world press, thought the invasion would be in Greece, some Sardinia, no one thought it would come in the South of France. Only one New York paper named Sicily. Clarke put in an SAS team into Sardinia in June 1943, who made enough mess, with some captured, to make it look like it would be invaded.[46]

Then the Allied airforces went heavy on Pantellaria and on 11 June the Allies took the island. Everyone guessed Sicily would be next. By 23 June MINCEMEAT was dead in the water – both London and Washington independently signalled Eisenhower their assessment: Axis intelligence judged 'Sicily is considered the most likely first objective.' But to Clarke's relief the US said that the Axis didn't know when, and London that they didn't know where on Sicily the invasion would take place.

Clarke was still in business.

If Clarke saved MINCEMEAT, it was because of WATERFALL. The Allies had so many units that the Axis really thought they could invade anywhere. But MINCEMEAT would still be blown the moment Monty and General Patton's troops waded ashore in Sicily. The real bonus to Clarke's methods was his deceptions relied on the film premise of 'what happens next is more interesting than what is happening now'. It didn't matter if the Axis decided whether Sicily or Sardinia would be taken (they thought both) because in Clarke's narrative, Greece was clearly the main target. MINCEMEAT remained what it was, part of the treatment. The story was Clarke's.

When it was clear to the Axis that the Allies were heading for Sicily, Clarke went for his old play, a last-minute postponement. Fake gliders were dismantled and boxed, fake landing craft hidden and movement restrictions around Palestine and Egypt lifted. Axis defences in Italy stood down. Finally, there was a deception on the west of Sicily, a naval bombardment, followed by 38 dummy exploding parachutists called Pintails. One of Clarke's team, Major Baxter, paid with his life when their aircraft exploded in flight killing the whole crew.

But the Axis had been duped. They estimated Clarke's fake army would take Greece, and stood down defences on Sicily, when they should have been on alert. But when the Allies landed, Hitler's foreign minister, Ribbentrop, was not slow to realise that MINCEMEAT was a sham – the documents were 'consciously misleading and were deliberately allowed to fall into Spanish hands'.[47] The risk was this now jeopardised the whole deception. If the Axis started looking, and the finger directly pointed at CHEESE, the whole Allied deception plan would collapse.

From Spain, the German Ambassador Dieckhoff replied, 'the English and Americans had every intention of acting as laid down in the documents. Only later did they change their minds.'[48]

On 4 August, Ribbentrop remained convinced they had been duped: 'The P.M. therefore concludes once for all that the possibility of forgery exists, it is therefore merely open to question whether all the Spaniards through whose hands the documents passed believed in their authenticity.' Luckily the Nazi prejudices of 'catholic affiliations' saved the day. They thought the Spanish complicit.[49]

MINCEMEAT was at best unnecessary, at worst irresponsible. But Clarke's deception survived and the proof is where the Axis sent their best general. Even after Sicily had been invaded, they sent Rommel to Greece.

The Soft Underbelly

While Clarke was deceiving the Axis, and before the curtain fell on North Africa, Fraser watched 8th Army artillery pound the remnants of Rommel's force. North of Gabès where Stirling was captured, he was on the final approach to the old capital of Carthage: Tunis. Rommel had flown to Ukraine, to beg Hitler to save his army, guaranteeing that with those forces he could beat off any Allied invasion. Hitler told him to go on sick leave, and to prepare to invade Casablanca. Rommel checked into Semmering health spa for more treatment.[50]

Fraser's was one of the last SAS teams in action. When the barrage lifted, he drove towards the beautiful Tunisian coastal city of Sousse. He skirted the salt marsh, but couldn't make any progress into the town as his Jeep was showered with flowers and wine thrust into his hand. Men and women ran out to shake his hand and kiss him. It was all a little embarrassing for the bearded special forces operative. Eventually he broke clear of the crowd, and with his small team of Jeeps headed up the coast towards Enfidaville. German panzer grenadiers were surrendering from pillboxes by the roadside. It was over. On 13 April 1943, Fraser flew back to Cairo, past Tripoli, Benghazi and over the Cyrenaican desert. He had been on continuous operations for eight months.[51]

Landing in Kabrit, Fraser found Colonel Cator, Grey Pillars's original recommendation, was CO of the SAS.[52] He had missed out on much. Mayne's father had died and, refused leave, Mayne had gone on a bender.

The BBC were disliked by the SAS, inaccurate reporting not helped by their recent piece on 'tough' paratroop training in England. Men who could change their shirts and wash every day. Mayne didn't like the correspondent, Richard Dimbleby. Allegedly, Dimbleby would come over, take the lads drinking, get their war stories, then broadcast as if he were at the battle himself. Mayne, bitter he had seen Stirling's aristocratic friends get leave just for getting their wings, went on an alcohol-fuelled hunt through the bars of Cairo to duff up Dimbleby. Residents at Shepheard's watched the final act, when he crashed into the hotel. Several Military Police were called, and he punched one of them.

Seekings and another sergeant had tried to mount a mission to rescue Stirling, but he had the feeling some people were quite happy to leave him where he was. Back in Kabrit, with the writing on the wall, Seekings and another old hand tried to leave. Not wishing to be disloyal to Mayne, but wishing to secure their future, they went to the Special Operations Executive, to be told, 'If Paddy does win out, he'll be needing you two very badly, so give it a bit more time.'[53]

Mayne went to Grey Pillars, then told the SAS to be in the marquee at noon. Most had just returned from preparing for guerilla operations in Syria, and some, like Phillips, a ski course in Lebanon. Mayne stood in the same place Lewes had once faced down a mutiny. The tent was crammed, with men on hard benches, standing or leaning against tent poles. Mayne walked in and, without preliminaries, said, 'As some of you no doubt know, I have been up in Cairo during this past week, at GHQ.'

He paused.

'The war in the desert is over.'

He went on to tell them that he had been given the choice of disbanding or carrying on in a new role. There was the murmur of disappointment, the wind chased across the floor, the canvas billowed, and everyone thought this was it.

'I have agreed to the formation of a Special Raiding Squadron to undertake special assault tasks for the Army. I shall be in command, for, as I think you know, Colonel Stirling is now a prisoner of war.'[54]

There was stunned silence as he read out the list of those who would remain – the three squadrons, A, B, and C, were gone, to be replaced by one. The SAS would become the Special Raiding Squadron, with the new CO Cator in command of them, the SBS, and a Greek Squadron. The vision of Clarke and Stirling, of Dorman-Smith and the Auk, of the hard years to build the SAS, was gone. Mayne took the new squadron to Haifa, Palestine, to start training for its new role.

Fraser got the train to Haifa, and was picked up by a driver he didn't know to join a unit he had never heard of. He was driven 20 miles north, through the Jewish coastal resort of Nahariya. Houses were laid out in a neat street pattern, where Jewish people now safe from Europe walked on a wide sand beach. A few miles on, a track led to a low hill covered with tents. He dropped his kit bag, looked at the sea, the scent of the orange groves wafted through the camp.[55]

At 5am, Fraser awoke to the opening bars of the old jazz standard, Bugle Call Rag. Mayne's presence was immediately felt as they fell in for physical training. Mayne had grouped all his old hands, with Fraser in command, in 1 Troop. Seekings was Fraser's Troop Sergeant. Wherever they were headed, Fraser was in the vanguard.

At night, trucks dropped them at Tiberias, on the shores of the Sea of Galilee, for a 30-mile hike back to camp, with practice ambushes waiting. Navigation training was Fraser's domain. His team also showed the new men how to use German and Italian weapons, and their Bren guns. A new recruit[56] asked if he could have a Bren gun. Seekings replied,

'Sorry son but a Bren gun is for killing, and I just don't think you could handle that particular job at this point in time.'[57]

The young recruit produced a crumpled letter from his pocket. His brother had been killed in action. Seekings handed him the gun.

April turned to May, and they went down to Haifa harbour to look at landing craft, to discover they were fake (they were K Detachment's) – they practised being pulled round the harbour in landing craft with no engines. Fraser was back in the Commandos.[58]

On the blackboard in the camp marquee a piece of coastline was drawn, with X marking a coastal battery – Mayne took Fraser into his confidence, it was Sicily.[59] Just north of the Jewish resort of Nahariya, on the border with Syria, was a point with steep cliffs jutting into the sea – Rosh Hanikra was a perfect double for Capo Murro di Porco. Using aerial photographs, and some taken from submarines, they marked the rocks of Rosh Hanikra with tape to indicate coastal batteries. Fraser pored over the photographs, and with his men scaled the cliffs, first by day, then by night. The only advantages they would have would be speed and surprise – they had to get to the cliff top and take out the battery before the Italians had time to react.

Mortars arrived and Troop Leader Alex Muirhead was put in charge. The call to Kabrit depot produced recruits who thought they were going on a cushy course near the beach and, Muirhead discovered, had little mortar training.[60] With no experience himself, but based on what he'd heard the Germans could achieve, he trained his team to get 13 rounds into the air before the first landed.[61] The eight tubes and 28 men produced the unit's integral firepower.

The night before they were due to move out, on 6 June, Fraser, Mayne and the men had a party and drank every last drop of alcohol in the camp.[62] The train to Suez, in the summer heat, was nauseous. Getting into the dusty port, crammed with trams, civilians and troops thronged the streets, lighters took them out to the *Ulster Monarch*, a ship Fraser had last seen in Arran. He leant on the rail in the Suez Canal, watching the desert drift by, until they entered the Bitter Lake. They dropped anchor off HMS *Saunders*, where they were to train for beach landings. Fraser was back where he'd started.

The ship's black-bearded Irish captain, Lieutenant Commander Kingscote, appeared to be hated by his men, but they stuck with him because he kept them alive. They said he could smell a torpedo.[63]

The ship sailed south, into the Red Sea, for the final rehearsal on Aqaba. On board, Fraser issued the reconnaissance photographs to his troops, though he didn't tell them the target. Fraser hit the beach at night and saw a small party 20 metres away watching; it was the 'head-sheds', including Jumbo Wilson and his staff. The climb was brutal. The slope was convex, so they couldn't see the target and struggled uphill in the dark, slipping, stones clattering into the darkness. The 2 Troop new boys next to Fraser spread below the summit, until an irate Mayne arrived. They had seen him drinking on the ship and feared this would happen, and sprinted to the top. Fraser was already there with 1 Troop, having taken the position with the Indian troops posing as the enemy.

Mayne's drinking onboard would start slowly at around 8pm. By about midnight he would have collected a few stalwarts to drink with, including Fraser, who knew there was no point going to bed. By 3am, if 'aroused', he started to party. He dispatched his henchmen and any officer in bed found himself in Mayne's cabin in pyjamas. Then food appeared, and the officers, and senior non-commissioned officers, knew they were in for the night. Anyone foolish enough to lock their door would have it broken down, and would triumphantly be borne naked to Mayne's cabin.[64]

It was on one of these occasions, at 3am, that Mayne produced the target. Officers who had just been woken up and handed a drink looked on blurrily as Mayne unpacked a relief model for their objective. It was a beautiful job: every rock, the cliffs, every building and the enemy gun emplacements were built exactly to scale. Normally, Mayne's briefings were hardly audible, hesitant and disjointed, but at 3am on the *Monarch*, he was inspired, and ran through the whole operation in textbook style.[65] The officers were dumbfounded. Fraser may have smiled – nothing, in this war, now surprised him. Least of all Mayne.

Fraser's original team were thinning: Byrne had been captured, and Phillips, one of his best men in the field, had been promoted to sergeant. When they arrived back in Suez to join the invasion fleet, Phillip's final offence was redacted from his record. Many said he'd been caught in a homosexual act; the entry for Mayne's sacking on 30 June, was that he was 'severely reprimanded for creating a disturbance'.[66] Whatever he'd done, he was out of the unit, and Fraser lost one of his best operators and oldest comrades.

With the invasion of Sicily imminent, Monty came aboard, doing the rounds of all invasion units in Port Said. But it appears his aide de camp had not briefed him as he climbed from his launch. Fraser and the men were on parade, and came to attention, banging their boots into the sun-bleached deck. Mayne saluted the general, introducing his regimental sergeant major, but Monty walked straight past. Ignoring the senior non-commissioned officer when visiting any regiment is a crime, so Mayne took him by the arm and drew him back. 'General, this is my regimental sergeant major.'[67]

Fraser now wore the unit's grey-blue shirt with baggy khaki pants. Mayne had introduced ties, but the winged dagger was still sewn on their berets and Lewes' wings were sewn on Fraser's breast, and onto the shoulders of the new lads. Halfway through the inspection Monty twigged he was inspecting the SAS.[68]

A short man, he clambered up the ladder to the bridge to make his speech. He told the men he was pleased to meet them again and promised they would be given the chance to chase the Hun still further. He said if it were not for the unit's work behind the lines in the desert, his Army would never have been able to reach Tripoli. Fraser and Seekings may have stiffened at this: a British soldier can smell bullshit a mile off. Monty paused for his customary rousing applause.

There was silence on deck.

He climbed down the ladder and started backing towards the

companionway. Mayne, realising they were offending the general, started clapping on his own.

As his launch pulled away, a cheer went up.

New recruits said they had been told beforehand not to give him the customary cheer, which he was undoubtedly expecting, until he was in the launch. One suspects there are other explanations.

Fraser watched Monty's launch move on to the next ship. Monty was not a man to make an enemy of.

The unit was issued its Benzedrine, and Mayne decided to conduct a personal trial. His methodology was similar to the original Commando trial: as soon as it was dark they marched, Mayne setting a blistering pace, resting ten minutes in the hour. Mayne's enormous stride ate up the miles, and 3 Troop started to tire, so Mayne gave them Benzedrine. The transformation was remarkable; soon they were swinging along together in grand style, singing and cracking jokes. The control group was 2 Troop, who struggled to keep up, though whether this was due to the predominance of 'Benzedrine addicts' in the unit, or Mayne's motivational tactics, they didn't know.

When they turned round to head back to Suez, 2 Troop were put in front. One of the men, a former trade unionist, decided on a go-slow, which was short lived. Mayne arrived like a whirlwind. Once again the trial was conclusive: the drugs worked.[69]

Before they left, they paraded through Port Said along with other units. Crowds filled the palm-lined avenues, and, though they had removed their badges, with the enormous concentration of ships in the port Fraser felt they were advertising the invasion.[70] In the eastern Mediterranean this was part of Clarke's huge deception; the Axis would think Fraser was bound for Greece. At 11am on 5 July they sailed.

Once at sea, the Tannoy echoed through the ship: 'All officers report to the briefing room.'[71]

The ship was rolling in a heavy swell as Mayne distributed the latest target photographs and went over the plan. Fraser would go in first, take a group of farm buildings directly east of the Italian gun battery, with the mortars setting up a base plate behind him. They would provide covering fire as 2 and 3 Troops assaulted the battery.[72] Beyond their battery was a second Italian gun position, and a glider force would be dropped on that at the same time to take it out. With the first glider landings, everything Clarke had imagined was coming true.

Fraser summed up the briefing by telling the other two troop commanders they needn't bother: by the time they had reached the top of the cliff, he would have captured the battery.[73]

They thought he was joking.

The convoy came within aircraft range of Crete, the ship's gunners cleared and test fired their anti-aircraft guns, the bridge doubled the watch. Fraser looked at the horizon. Somewhere just below it, Jellicoe and the SBS were hitting German airfields, doing a job he should also have been doing. The same was true on Sicily. David Stirling's brother, Bill, had been allowed to form 2 SAS Regiment, which had operated in Africa with the Americans, and they had dropped a team to disrupt enemy communications on the island.[74] Instead, Fraser was part of a shock unit spearheading the invasion. It wasn't that he couldn't do it, it was just a waste of his skills and those of his men. He would need his 'Fraser luck' to survive.

On 9 July the ship's White Ensign, which had been hanging limply on the stern, started to flutter. By the afternoon the rising wind had lashed the sea into an angry maelstrom, the enemy of all Commando operations. It was getting dark when the Tannoy announced, 'If you care to look out to the starboard bow, you will just be able to make out the summit of Mount Etna, Sicily's highest mountain.'[75]

Troops stampeded to the decks, and Fraser squinted into the haze. White foaming tops sped towards him from the target. He went to find out if they were going in; it was neither his nor Mayne's first time at this. In the rocking ship it felt exactly the same as it had off Litani River. On the bridge, the bearded Irish, torpedo-sniffer proclaimed, 'Sure and be Christ, Paddy, not only will I land you, if necessary I'll go along the cliffs and jump you off.'[76]

The *Monarch* ploughed into the gale, determined to close onto the target. Fraser went below and they were served their last meal of bacon and eggs, though most were throwing up. The ship's lights switched to red. Fraser had bagged his personal belongings and left a letter for his mum. His pack weighed 36kg, the contents wrapped in oiled silk. He stuffed his watch into a rubber bag, put it in his pocket and did the same with his pistol. Above the roar of the storm, the Tannoy sounded: 'SRS stand by.'[77]

He ricocheted along the corridor lugging his kit to join his troop.

Seekings was at the head of 1 Troop, and the scene on the mess deck appeared satanic. Among the 70 men, long shadows danced and the red lighting made it look like the place was on fire. The dull metal clang told them their landing craft were being smacked against the ship's hull, and water sluiced through open doorways over their feet. There was nothing but darkness outside.

'SRS embark.'

Fraser led his men into the spitting gale. Immediately soaked, he slipped across the companion way. A narrow plank held by sailors led to his landing craft, swinging dangerously on its davits. If he looked down, the rage-foaming sea rose up towards him. He ran and half fell in. Behind him, others took the same dive. The ship lurched and landing craft smashed into the side. Someone else, 'Man overboard!'

The man was fished out and from the darkness a sailor called, 'Lower and cast off.'[78]

With relief, Fraser felt the landing craft whack into the water, and heard its engines roar as they leapt away from the hull into the waves.

Some men were huddled being sick. The Navy had issued cardboard basins, but they had turned to pulp. Fraser needed to focus; everything depended on him getting this done fast. Great sheets of spray came flying over him from the bow as the craft dived into the waves.

In the lee of the cliffs the storm subsided. From the cliff top, a lighthouse's rays swept the bay, each one illuminating their craft. Fraser could see a cluster of flares dropped into the sky ahead. Could have been theirs, or ours. Off the starboard bow he saw a British submarine, the faint glow of her blue lamp guiding their little convoy to the beach, then she was gone.

Ahead, the cliff loomed. Suddenly he heard shouts from the water. A shadow emerged ahead; at first Fraser thought it could be another sub, but it was too close inshore. It was a glider, sinking, five men clinging to the wing. Nearby a landing craft throttled back to pick them up.

In the water around them were dozens of men. The pilots of the aircraft towing the gliders had had too little training and released the gliders too early. The strong headwind meant half of the force of 140 gliders went into the water. Only 88 airborne men made the shore; 252 drowned that night.

Fraser listened to the cries from the darkness. They were heading for an enemy-held shore; they didn't have time to pick these men up. Mayne said, 'It was a terrible thing to do.'[79]

Seekings crouched behind the Vickers K machine guns they'd mounted in the bows of the squadron's landing craft. They had also put on winged dagger plaques. The cockswain was from Wisbech, and they'd named their boat the Isle of Ely. Seekings had a plan to hit the cliff and scale it using a bamboo ladder they'd made. There was a figure at the bottom of the cliff, clinging on. They hauled him in; it was the adjutant of the airborne unit.[80]

The engines went dead slow on Fraser's craft, the ramp dropped and he hurled himself into the water. The drill was: as soon as the craft hits, get moving. This is the most dangerous moment. It was just after 3am, he was on a rocky beach, the lighthouse above the cliff to his right wasn't visible, but the pulse of light showed the direction. The battery would be 600 metres towards him from that light. Around him his men gathered, someone said there were more airborne men on the rocks but he didn't have time to think about that; he needed to get inland to the farm complex. He had the men cache their packs and get up the cliff.

The cliff wasn't steep, which meant they were probably in the wrong place. They seemed too close to the lighthouse. Fraser turned to his radio operator, who could hear nothing but mush on his set, and they bounded up the rock escarpment. At one point, steps had been cut, and they ran past a terrified Italian sentry pressing himself into the rock face.

At the top, Fraser set a bearing, across the fields to where the buildings should be. They were definitely much closer to the battery than they had intended. He ordered his sections forward. The lead men hit the wire and minefield surrounding the farm complex. Seekings and another went in and cut the wire, feeling their way for the tell-tail three-prong trigger of the German S-mine that had once jumped up at Lewes outside Tobruk. Then they held the wire open and 1 Troop rushed through.

Fraser held his breath; there was no response so far. The rest of his men were up against the coils of wire, working their way through. Seekings was almost through the wire when two machine guns opened up, firing high. Tracer ripped over Fraser and his men.

Muirhead's mortars had landed from a different vessel. His men, soaking wet, had lugged the base plates and tubes up the escarpment, and piled the rounds next to them. Sighted, the first mortar man dropped a round down the barrel of the first tube – a mixture of smoke and phosphorus, it would be used to adjust the fire of the rest of the tubes onto the enemy gun battery.

Across the field, Fraser heard the pop.

The first round exploded; the second was right on target, hit the magazine which exploded with a flash setting light to the dry grass over the gun emplacement.

Fraser and his troop rushed the farm complex.

In the buildings one man heard a noise, rushed in and thrust his bayonet into the darkness repeatedly, and came out saying, 'I got him'. (In the cold light of day, it transpired he'd 'got' a donkey.)

A figure, backlit, took multiple rounds, but wouldn't drop. It was a statue of Mussolini. Seekings dodged towards a pillbox and emptied his Tommy gun into the embrasure. Fraser's men ripped through the position; only Italians fast enough to get their hands up survived, as they went from building to building with bayonets fixed.

Fraser looked to his south. The mortars were still hitting the furthest of the guns from him. Resistance was pathetic. He decided to roll on the main position. With the troop reorganised, he pushed south towards the sea and their main objective.

His men rushed forwards, Seekings came on a big bunker, and shouted for anyone to come out. It was the villagers. He realised their blood was up, around him men were throwing charges into bunkers. The villagers were lucky: they could have killed anyone. One, a pretty 13-year-old girl, came out with her head held high. A grenade went off nearby, and she broke down sobbing, which sobered Seekings up.

Beyond the gun position, the first of Fraser's men saw figures advancing towards him, their blue-grey shirts were similar to the Italians and without thinking he fired his Bren from the hip. On the receiving end, an officer from 2 Troop dived for cover behind a rock, and shouted the password, 'Desert Rats!'

Fraser hadn't been joking, he had kept his threat and taken the whole position. The squadron regrouped on the farm. They had captured loads of prisoners, and freed the airborne brigade commander, who the Italians had captured the night before. Mayne discussed the situation while the men ate a hot meal. He offered the mortar commander a medal or a promotion. Muirhead replied, 'I'll take the promotion if you don't mind, sir, as I'm sure my widow could do with the extra money.'

With gliders in the sea, the guns the airborne men should have taken out were still intact, so Mayne decided the squadron would do it. The airborne brigade commander told Fraser's troop they didn't have any boots because the Italians had taken them. 'All right,'

Seekings said, pointing to the Italian prisoners of war, 'there's 700 pairs over there.'

Fraser and his troop moved out while they were debating it.

With the sun up, at 6am they pushed north, tramping swiftly through Sicilian lanes, churning up fine white dust smothering them as they sweated. Fraser's men led, Bren gunners taking out the desultory opposition, one watching an Italian's head explode in his sights. They fought through small towns, picking up wounded airborne on the way. At one point, Fraser's men stopped shooting. The Germans had pushed some Italian women out in front of their position. The women were calling for them to open fire on the Germans.

'The bloody Germans will kill us,' Seekings said. 'Fire.'

The women dived for cover, the Germans got nailed, and three women were shot in the leg. When they mortared a farm which had airborne prisoners in it, the brigadier complained. Fraser didn't know how many they hurt, but this war, on European soil, was taking a different turn from the war in the desert. By the afternoon Fraser was sitting on the other gun position. It had been a good day's work.

There was a huge, dusty column of prisoners, around five hundred. One, coming out of a dugout, smiling with his hands up, at the last moment threw a grenade. It went off, severely wounding one of the men. Mayne happened to be standing nearby, and plugged him with two rounds, almost cutting him in half.

At 4pm they marched to join the rest of the landing forces. As they were crossing a bridge, a German plane flew over and one man dived for cover. Mayne sacked him. On the morning of 12 July, they marched down to Syracuse harbour and climbed up the gangplank to the *Monarch*. Fraser had one corporal who had been killed, the unit had two wounded. Mayne sacked two more straight after the operation, and a total of 17 men during their campaign in Italy. His sacking of popular veterans would always shake the unit.

*

Fraser got back on board, and below decks back on the *Monarch* everyone queued for steam showers. Fraser dumped his kit on his bunk. Then someone burst into the cabin; Mayne wanted him.

In the briefing room with the other two troop leaders, Mayne broke the news they were going straight back in. He pointed to a spot on the unfurled map on the table: Augusta, a naval base just up the coast had been bypassed by the main invasion and they had been asked to 'mop up' – the Army term that has nothing to do with a bucket of water.

Augusta was only 10 miles up the coast. Fraser looked at the land, smoking. It was a lovely evening, the sun setting behind the island, not a breath of a breeze. The *Monarch* felt like a cruise liner gliding into the picturesque Italian port. It seemed strangely quiet when the Tannoy rang out, 'SRS first wave, stand by to embark.'

Fraser went below to the mess deck. Seekings had the men fallen in; they were going in with 3 Troop and they filed out to board their landing craft.

On deck, Fraser saw a British cruiser steaming fast into the bay, her destroyers scurrying around her. There was a sharp exchange of signals with the *Monarch*'s bridge, until the captain told them he was going to land troops.

'In that case what support do you need?'

'All you've got.'

Fraser's landing craft lowered as the Italians opened fire. Fraser's craft splashed into the water, engines revved, the cables freed, while incoming shells screeched overhead. From the stern of the *Monarch*, her 12-pounder gun started pumping rounds. There was a whine, then a crash as the British cruiser opened fire. Fraser saw a section of cliff overlooking the harbour vanish. The Italians hammered back, rounds splashed into the sea – somehow he was embroiled in a sea battle.

A British destroyer swung across their bow, white ensign streaming from its stern. Fraser was looking at the shore, praying they would make it. Ahead the destroyer swung broadside to the port, all its guns hammering the town. From somewhere onshore machine guns had opened up; he could hear rounds cracking over-head, see splashes in the water around them – 500 metres, 450, 400. His heart was racing. Red tracer raced overhead towards the port, smashing into the rocks ahead. It was the *Monarch*'s 20mm cannon opening up; the torpedo-sniffer was determined they get ashore.

The dockside was in range and the gunner in the bow let rip – the whole dockside disintegrated as six twin Vickers K machine guns from their landing craft tore up the town – as effective here as they had been in the desert. There was a bump as they hit land, doors flew open, and Fraser was out and running through knee-high water. No pack on this one, half ammunition scales, he felt light, his signaller breathing hard to keep up.

Bent double, he ran into a narrow street. He looked round, 3 Troop were heading up into the town. He shouted to his men, get-ting Bren guns into position, pushing forward parties to the end of the street. He looked back and one of 3 Troop was dragging a limp body from the water.

Once 3 Troop were clear, he moved after them, up the narrow, dark streets. Ahead he could hear the crack of small arms, the occa-sional thump of a grenade. Silently he padded up the street in his rubber-soled boots, keeping a wary eye at the top windows above him. If it wasn't for another clatter of a Tommy gun ahead, it could have been a ghost town. His men ahead were on both sides of the street, the last man facing backwards. He pulled out his compass and sent a man forward to get word to the point section to adjust the direction.

Ahead was the red glow of a burning building. It was dark now. He reached the main street; there was a public garden on the other side, the building burning was off to the left, he turned right. Ahead, 3 Troop were in contact. He could see tracer – German green and British red – ricocheting down the street. There was no way of knowing what was happening: sea water had done for the radios again.

Then a runner came back; 3 Troop had run into trouble and they were falling back. Mayne wanted Fraser to take up a defensive position to their right. Stay close to the walls; Jerry was pumping rounds down the streets.

Fraser led his sections to defend the edge of town, to occupy buildings that overlooked the outskirts. The buildings had thick walls, part of an old citadel, which was good. With his men in fire positions among the buildings, he settled in for the night. It was freezing cold and they had no rations. Men went scavenging among the buildings, turning up alcohol, among other things. In the early hours he heard the dreaded clank of panzer tracks, which they could not combat, but which faded into the darkness.

Dawn broke and it was quiet. Then the message was passed that the Allied force had reached the edge of town and they were relieved. Fraser led his men back to the town square, and by the time he got there the party had started. Men were wearing assorted hats looted from the houses, someone had dragged a piano out of a café to have a sing-song. They had liberated champagne, and much else; trousers were bulging with loot. Neither Fraser nor Mayne did anything but encourage it. They had eight wounded and two dead.[81]

Born Lucky

Fraser was always afraid, but back on board that night he found out what terrified Mayne. Moored alongside at Syracuse harbour, he awoke to the shattering crash of an explosion. The deck above his head shook as an anti-aircraft gun pounded attacking bombers. He raced up to huddle under the upper deck with other troop leaders. On deck, Mayne paced, shaking his huge fist at the night sky; he had once confessed to a friend he couldn't conceive of how anyone could take this type of soldiering.[82] Like Fraser, he felt that in special forces his fate was in his own hands. Even in an air attack in the desert there was an element of skill: camouflage, evasion, as well as luck – but in regular soldiering, like being stuck on a ship in an air raid – he was trapped.

Every night the Germans attacked, bombs falling continuously alongside anti-aircraft gunners pouring water over red-hot barrels.[83] After three nights of continuous air raids, the Luftwaffe hit one of the neighbouring Commando ships in the magazine, killing 18 and wounding 70. Everyone's nerves were frayed when, with relief, they got an operation.

The Allies wanted to cross the Strait of Messina to the toe of Italy. At 4.45am on 4 September, Fraser stood in the bow of his landing craft. Ahead, the seaside town of Bagnara nestled against the black backdrop of steep mountains, the bay fronted by a sandy beach lit by the moonlight. The landing was two hours late, and the Navy were twitchy. They wanted to get off before daylight and another pummelling from the Luftwaffe. The Allies had landed the day before, and Bagnara, on the east coast of Italy, lay north of their advance. It was Fraser's mission to take and hold a bridge south of the town until 8th Army got to it – which sounded a bit like their Litani River mission.

There were two loud 'booms' from land; it sounded like the Germans had blown their bridge – this *was* just like Litani River.[84] His gunner gripped the twin handles of the Vickers K machine guns. The doors opened, Fraser was out and running, up the beach to a sea wall, above which was a promenade – none of which should have been there. He should be in a dry river bed, looking up towards his target bridge.

He looked round in the darkness, the details of landmarks from the reconnaissance photographs fitting with his surroundings. The town was to his right, it should be to his left – they were 2 miles too far north.[85] His two sections, B and C, crouched up against the sea wall. He had already lost A section when their landing craft broke down.[86] The second wave would be coming in. The plan was blown. He pushed his men out to secure the beach and 3 Troop pushed on into the edge of town. There was no response from the defenders.

The rest of the squadron came in on a huge 'LCI' (Landing Craft Infantry) 30 minutes later, unlike their usual craft, this could land half the squadron of 200 men. The huge vessel stopped just off the beach, its two 20-metre ramps lowered with a deafening clatter of chains. If the Germans hadn't realised they had landed, they would now.

He searched for Mayne's huge figure coming down the ramp, and picked him out. He ran to discuss the situation – they wouldn't make the objective, even if it was intact, before daylight, and they didn't have time to clear the town. In the beach conference, Mayne told Fraser to push through the town, and stop the Germans reinforcing it; 2 Troop would follow to help.

Fraser and his men moved fast down the beach. They were taking chances, to their left was the town: if it was occupied, they would just have to shoot it out. Some of his men were humping a water-cooled Vickers machine gun, a big, lethal beast from the First War. It was broken into parts – barrel, tripod, and belts of ammunition – but if they could get it into position above the town and assemble it before the Germans arrived, they could dominate it. They doubled up the sand.

A mile later and it was getting light. Up to their left was Ponte Di Caravilla, a unique bridge because the road doubles under its arches twice before making its way up into the mountains – a good place to make a stand. Fraser signalled they head left into the town. Dawn broke as they ran up the narrow, confusing streets. They didn't have time to clear any buildings: this was a race against time.

The country beyond the buildings was almost vertical, covered in scrub and trees, and ahead his men were scrambling upwards. Fraser stopped at the end of the last alley, scanning the terrain, looking for the best route. Seekings came running back, calling out he'd seen a German mortar team. At which moment the ground between him and Fraser blew apart with mortar rounds. Seekings vanished in the dust and muck.

Fraser dived against a wall of a house, one of his troop commanders next to him, while the Germans pounded the area.

Fraser said, 'Sergeant Seekings has had it.'

The troop commander: 'We better get our heads down then, if he's had it.'

At which point Seekings appeared round the corner: 'What's the trouble?'[87]

The only way round the German mortar team was up a vertical cliff. Most had belts of 250 rounds of Vickers ammunition draped over them, on top of their own kit. Their pulses racing with adrenaline, they went up the cliff as though it wasn't there.[88] Above the cliff they hit the road, and doubled back towards town. Beyond the corner of the next hairpin was a vineyard, built on a series of terraces, from which they could look down on Ponte Di Caravilla, 600 metres below. Fraser's navigation had been spot on; from here they could stop anything except a tank.

The two sections started improving the stone walls in the vineyard for protection, and set up the Vickers and their Bren guns. Fraser went back between a narrow alley that led from the vineyard to the road with his two signallers to try to raise Mayne on the radio.

Then he decided it was time to get a brew on.

The men of 2 Troop had been slowed down killing a German patrol in town, and were surprised to find Fraser having his 'customary brew' with his two signallers, sitting by the side of the road.[89] They turned down the temptation of Fraser's fried bacon and moved to take positions further up the hill.

No one knows why Fraser got up from his breakfast and walked into the alleyway between the two houses to the vineyard. He heard the first mortar round explode on the mountain above, then the second right behind him. He turned to see a wall of dust fill the alley and went back to the road. The round had hit their breakfast spot and both his signallers were dead.[90]

The Germans tried to take the bridge; mortars exploded around Fraser and his men, and the vineyard tore to pieces. Across the gorge the far hilltop was a thousand metres high, out of range. But below that, a road wound down through some houses, that was in range for their Vickers and Bren guns, and became a shooting gallery. Germans trying to run from building to building were hit by Fraser's men. At one point the firing stopped as blue-shirted men appeared, and a voice called from below, 'Cease fire.'[91]

Everyone assumed the Germans had captured some of their men, but Seekings pointed out the accent was German. They were Gestapo, and Fraser's men opened up, killing three and forcing the rest into a house with a veranda, where they got picked off.

When Fraser heard the whistle and crash of an 88mm gun he knew they were in trouble. He looked through his glasses to see a Tiger tank across the gorge above them. The 50-ton German engineering solution of putting their best weapon in a panzer with impenetrable armour was every British commander's nightmare.

Fraser sent message back to Mayne to call in the Navy.

Fraser watched a destroyer steaming to their rescue across the calm blue sea below. The Tiger opened fire, twice, and two rounds smashed into the destroyer. The destroyer turned and opened fire, nearly taking down their bridge. The Tiger hit it again and the destroyer fled. Round one to the Tiger.

Panzers didn't fight like pillboxes: they fired then moved, only to come up in a different position. A Tiger, in the right hands, could hold up an entire brigade. Fraser called Muirhead and his mortars – mortars were ineffective against tanks, a Tiger's armour is far too thick to penetrate, but Fraser was desperate. However, panzer commanders fought 'head-up' to give them spatial awareness on the battlefield, which they were deprived of when looking through the tank's periscopes. The loader, sweating to push high explosive shells up the breach, left the hatch above him open. Unbelievably, the first of Muirhead's mortar rounds dropped straight into one of these hatches. In a flash, Fraser watched his problem vanish.

The Germans resumed their mortar barrage on their vineyard. Fraser pressed himself to the ground and they fought all day, by which time they had run out of water. Seekings picked grapes off the vine; a bunch was shot from his hand by a sniper. The Germans sent in a two-man demolition team to take down the bridge. Fraser's team's sniper got one in the gut and Seekings claimed his best shot of the war, 500 metres into the thigh of a 'small man'.[92] At night the enemy fell silent, and Fraser could hear the distant crump of artillery to their south, from whatever battle the 8th Army were fighting. At 6am there was a sharp explosion, with a single mortar round the Germans signalled goodbye.[93]

In the morning 8th Army arrived and it was over.

There was a garden between the two houses close to where Fraser's men died, and it seemed a good spot for signallers Richards and Howell.[94] On their way into town they came across a donkey and cart that had been hit by one of their bombers. The whole area was levelled, the cart wrecked, donkey dead, and an old woman's arm with a wedding ring on it lay on the road. It affected Seekings more than anything he had seen in the war.[95] Five men had been killed, seventeen wounded. Everything was affecting Fraser.

Two nights later, he was drinking wine on the wide veranda of the villa they'd taken over in the tiny fishing village of Gallico. On a warm night, he was looking out over the Strait of Messina when church bells started ringing. A crowd filled the street below, women wrapped in the Tricolore, and on the hills bonfires sprung up. Italy had capitulated. Churchill had achieved his aim of knocking them out of the war. Unusually for Mayne, in the high spirits he adopted a policy of live and let live and that night those going to bed early were untroubled.

The next night he went on a complete bender. It was hot, and officers sleeping on the balcony of the villa heard Mayne crashing around. Then he started dropping plant pots on them from his room above. They continued to feign sleep, wondering how long it would go on, till he ran out of ammunition. He came back with immense earthenware bowls full of earth, which burst on the street below them with sickening explosions. The chaos the next morning could easily be explained away as bomb damage.[96]

Fraser and the squadron's role as shock troops continued. At 2.45 am three weeks later, 3 October, Fraser was on the prow of a huge LCI landing craft with half the squadron, and somewhere in the darkness and drizzle ahead was the port of Termoli. The port is on the Adriatic, and 8th Army was advancing from the south. They were landing behind the Germans' line to, again, capture two bridges to help them. Ahead, 3 Commando had just signalled they had taken the beachhead.

The craft edged towards some low cliffs, the Navy gunner scanning them with his Oerlikon 20mm cannon from his cupola in the bow. It was completely black; Fraser tensed for the moment they hit. Suddenly the craft shuddered to a stop.[97] The moment the ramps were down, Fraser was off, down the ramp, into the water, and his feet fell out below him.

There was no beach.

Weighed by his pack, ammunition and kit, he sank fast. His training from Arran kicked in. He was wearing a buoyancy vest, and, shedding his pack, he kicked for the surface. He came up right next to the ramp. Eager hands pulled him out, some of the new men laughing. He panted hard on the metal. The ship was wedged on a sandbank 50 metres from shore.[98] If there had been Germans up on those cliffs, no one would be laughing.

It took ages to ferry the unit from the stranded craft, by which time the narrow beach in front of the town's huge Norman sea walls was chaos. Men from all units muddled up trying to find their section. Fraser was part of a Commando brigade like Layforce, and with 3 Commando, and 41 Commando, who had who landed at the same time. The password was 'Jack Hobbs', reply 'Surrey and England', but not everyone was familiar with the legendary cricketer, and one of the officers trying to find one of their lost sections got the reply, 'He's not in this section. This is the SRS here!'[99]

Fraser gathered his men; he had Bob Melot with him. The man who had been wounded on their way into Benghazi was now their intelligence officer, and, strictly speaking, should have stayed with Mayne's HQ. But a popular man in the unit, Fraser put him with one of his sections. They headed up the treacherous slope above the town, slipping in the mud in their rubber-soled boots, struggling with heavy packs, many losing their footing. It was 5.30am, 30 minutes before dawn, when they hit the road to Campomarino, 3 miles from the bridge.

The ground was flat, so using some ditches in the fields parallel to the road for cover, they set a blistering pace. At the next bend in the road, the lead section went to ground. Fraser moved up. Ahead were some farm buildings, from which came the sound of engines starting and German voices shouting. There was the rattle of gunfire from Termoli behind them. Ahead, German troops were getting ready to reinforce that attack. It was a split-second decision to rush the buildings.

Fraser and his men poured out of the ditch in a line, into the farmyard, where there was a halftrack Kleines Kettenkraftrad HK 101 motorcycle pulling a 10.5cm recoilless gun, on which were crammed German paratroops, all laughing and chatting. Fraser and his men took a moment to process what they were seeing before they let rip.[100] The air was thick with lead and in seconds they were gone. Two could have survived, but ran. One got dropped, the other turned to fire and Seekings shot him.[101]

The Germans in the next farm building opened fire. Fraser's men went to ground. In the battle, they shot it out with the first building till they surrendered. Fraser got two sections round the flank, and by 7am the enemy were dead or outflanked. Melot had been wounded, again, fighting with his lead section, and 14 German paratroopers surrendered, leaving 10 of their number dead. They hadn't been a match for the former SAS men.

At 11 o'clock they reached their bridge, which the Germans had destroyed.[102]

The lead elements of the 8th Army arrived, and Fraser's men headed back to town. He arrived that evening to discover 23 were missing, presumed captured, 3 had been wounded (including Melot), and 1 was dead. The squadron had taken over the ground floor of a monastery on the town square, which had a well-laid-out public garden with views over the sea. They had done their job, and hopefully they would be lifted off.

Worryingly, 3 Troop said they had taken out a Tiger tank, and the 8th Army Infantry Brigade sent three requests to go back out and help hold the line. Both Fraser and Mayne were loathe to do this: they were a unit capable of special forces operations and had taken their fair share of casualties. They also thought the less experienced unit was exaggerating the threat.[103]

By dinner time they couldn't ignore the requests, and Fraser supplied one section, who reluctantly gathered kit to go and join the regular Army. For Fraser's departing C Section, as they said goodbye to their friends, this was the luckiest moment of their war. Fraser walked across the cold, bare stone floors and empty monastic passages to find a place to sleep.

He woke to the steady burst of a Bren gun on the morning air, to which the faster roar of a German machine gun replied. It sounded about half a mile away.[104] The Germans were on the edge of town. Inexperienced British troops were deserting the line; some had already got down to the beach, to persuade the squadron's LCI landing craft to take them off. Its commander was having none of it.

In the monastery, the atmosphere was tense and oppressive. Fraser found an old gramophone and an Italian recording of Lili Marlene. He played it repeatedly during the morning, while outside the German shells fell closer and closer. Another officer wished he could have the same detachment. Fraser was content, and oblivious to the furious battle developing around him.[105]

At 2.30pm came the order to move. Since the Germans had Tigers, Fraser and his men prepped Number 78 anti-tank grenades. These were big cylindrical explosives, into which you stuck a detonator on a handle, about a foot long. When thrown at a tank they could blow off a track, but they were sensitive, so troop sergeants, such as Seekings, carried the detonators, while the men shoved the explosive charges in their packs.[106]

In an alley across the square the squadron had lined up five captured trucks. The town was being bracketed by German artillery: overhead, shells ripped through the air or thudded short of them into the town. Without a word, the men crossed the square, the Adriatic shining in the sun beyond the town, and started climbing up into the trucks that lined the road leading up from the front.

A family who had taken in their washing stood in a doorway opposite to wave them off, a boy of 12 waving at the soldiers. Fraser saw some sort of argument going on at the front of one of his trucks: 2 Troop wanted to ride with the driver, a popular member of the troop. 2 Troop got evicted, and Fraser's men got on. Then it looked like there was going to be another delay; Fraser saw that one of Mayne's messengers was coming. Instead of climbing in, Fraser stood beside the cab, waiting to see if they were going. Frustrated, Seekings kicked the tailgate free to jump down and find out what was going on. They say you never hear the shell that kills you.

Fraser knew nothing, his world was nothing. No memory, no past or future. Seekings stood at the back of the truck trying to comprehend what he was seeing. The back of the truck was gone.

The Italian family were lying in a heap, the woman split open, the man blown apart, disembodied. One of their men was burning. Seekings didn't realise how fast a body could burn.

There was a jug of water in the house. Seekings was stepping over the bodies of the Italians to get water to tip on the burning man, when the young boy, lying on top, jumped up and started screaming, his guts blown out like a huge balloon. Seekings drew his pistol and shot him. He couldn't let anyone suffer like that. He went to the driver's side of the truck; the driver was just sitting there, grinning like a Cheshire cat. Seekings was annoyed the driver wasn't helping so he opened the door, thinking the man's nerve had gone. The driver too was dead.

Another man was holding his face, screaming, 'What about my eyes, what about my eyes.' One eye was hanging out of its socket; blood was streaming down his face. One of Fraser's men had been blown against the wall. He came to and found 'Skin' (Fraser) lying on him. He pushed him off, and saw he was covered in blood, then realised he was uninjured: the blood was all Fraser's. Fraser was limp and motionless, his face ashen grey. Their new doctor rushed to examine him.[107]

On the street was a carcass, that looked like it was from a butcher's shop. Until those arriving found khaki stuck to it. A man lay with half his head missing. A lump of flesh hung from a telegraph pole. There was an arm on the street, some unrecognisable lump of flesh that seconds before had been pulsing with young life.

Seekings was still making his way through the charnel house. One man was hanging upside down from the wreckage, his chest blown open. Seekings could see his heart beating. His Tommy gun was still strapped across his chest. He spoke: 'Take that gun off, it's hurting me.'

Seekings got him onto the deck. The man pulled the gun off his chest, saying, 'It's a bad one this time.'

Seekings told him, 'You'll be all right, we'll get you to hospital.'

Seekings knew he wouldn't be all right. He stepped across another mass of pulp, from which a voice said, 'Sergeant, can you get me a drink please, I'm thirsty.'

When the man dropped his arm to his side, Seekings could see his heart and lungs were also visible. The explosives they had carried had done this. One lived an hour and a quarter, the other an hour and half. There were four 'survivors' from the truck, one of whom suffered a mental breakdown. He couldn't speak, and they found him smashing his head against a brick wall two nights later.[108] Seventeen men died on that street. Mayne couldn't bring himself to make an entry of the event in his war diary.[109] Fraser knew nothing of this as he was stretchered away.

He was fed back through the casualty stations with the maimed coming out of Italy, first on the mainland, then to Sicily, and 97th General Hospital, before being shipped back to Egypt. He was lucky: their new doctor had stemmed his bleeding on the street, and the piece of shrapnel embedded in his shoulder was removed by surgery, but, when he came to, they had to break the news of what had happened to his men.

He was discharged on 8 December and two days later flew to Philippeville, Algeria, where the SAS was reforming.[110]

The rest of Fraser's squadron were visited in Termoli after the battle by Monty, to be given another vainglorious speech.[111] They moved back from the front to the coastal town of Molfetta, where they could swim off the rocks, and the officers messed in an ornamental villa with enormous mirrors round the walls. They were joined by four English nurses, who they invited for a drink. This provoked the worst outburst they ever saw from Mayne. He had sat in a dark corner of the hallway, brooding over a bottle of whisky. Ignored and deserted by his officers, he was unable to exercise his control over them while visitors were present. The other officers could see trouble coming, and reluctantly hurried the women out of the mess. Mayne pushed his officers into the anteroom and tried to make them drink. Infuriated that they didn't want to, Mayne smashed his hand on the table and swept away their glasses onto the floor.

'So you won't drink with me! I know what you are thinking to yourselves "He's a drunk – a disgusting sight isn't it?" '[112] Whereupon he went to find more breakable objects to throw at them.

The officer in charge of the mess, which was borrowed from the Italians, asked him to stop. Mayne went to throw his whisky bottle, realised it was half full, and picked up a decanter, missing his head by inches, and hitting another officer in the chest. The officers fled, but Mayne managed to grab the nearest, the doctor who had saved Fraser's life, and threw him across the room.

Moments later he seemed to calm down, and called for a road map of Italy: he wanted to see Naples. He left the building, jumped into a car, and drove off. There had been 13 officers in the room, none attempted to restrain his 17 stone of muscle and bone, fearing, in the mood he was in, he was capable of killing.

At Philippeville, Fraser and the squadron met up with Bill Stirling's 2 SAS. Bill Stirling had managed to keep his 2 SAS in the strategic special forces role, operating behind Italian lines, and his outfit had had one man killed, and one wounded. In the same period, Fraser's squadron of 280 men had lost 38 killed, 54 wounded and 22 taken prisoner. The difference between wood chopping and rapier play was human life.

Fraser and the other officers thought Bill Stirling a charming and sociable man, unpractical like his brother David, but without the compensating verve, dash and personality which had made David Stirling such an extraordinary leader.[113]

Fraser spent Christmas Eve 1943 in a transit camp in a forest outside Algiers, watching the incessant rain dripping from the trees. He needed to get used to it: that evening trucks arrived and drove them to the ship awaiting them in the port of Algiers. He was back in the SAS, and under no illusion where he was headed.

13

Killing Rommel: 1944–1945

Casting

On 4 January 1944 Clarke was sitting in a darkened cinema in Caseta, just north of Naples.[1] He'd missed the Shepheard's New Year's party, checking out at 1am on 30 December to fly to Italy for an urgent meeting with General Alexander. Having rolled into bed at 1am after 'a very good New Year Night!', he was, three nights later, indulging his passion for film, watching *Five Graves to Cairo* with a bunch of exuberant GIs on a pass from the front line.[2]

Clarke noticed one of the actors bore a striking resemblance to Monty and made a note of his name: Miles Mander.

The invasion of Italy had ground to a halt. In the winter, rain and mud on the narrow corridor north provided for nothing but brutal frontal assaults reminiscent of the First War. Allied command was in disarray. Churchill had flown out in December and got pneumonia; Alan Brooke was depressed, and the relationship between US and British commanders continued to resemble an argument between film stars over whose trailer was bigger.

Clarke was working out of his A-Force Tactical HQ in the Allied HQ in Charles III of Spain's huge palace. The Allied solution to getting Italy done was an amphibious assault at a place called Anzio, and then a short drive to Rome.[3] Clarke's deception centred on two landings much further north, on either side of Italy, one at Pisa on the west, the other at Rimini in the east. German forces sent to defend these locations would have to spend 250 miles on bad roads to get back to Anzio. Rommel went one step further than Clarke, warning Hitler that the logical point was even further north, cutting across the Po Valley.[4] Both men's ideas were more daring than the Allies'.

At the jumping-off point for the fictional western landings, Corsica, Clarke had created a 7,000-bed hospital for casualties, extended airfields, deployed more US fighters, and started building dummy ammunition dumps and landing craft. Clarke pretended the western landing included French forces, based in Algiers, and Polish forces based in Egypt. He printed leaflets on the 'Preservation of Works of Art' in Italy, in Polish and French. He had the US General Patton visit Polish troops in Ismali on Suez. Patton was cooling his heels after Sicily had proved to be too small to contain both him and Monty, not helped by Patton slapping a soldier with shellshock. But the Germans thought him the best Allied general and were watching his moves.

Clarke's deception was helped by an Allied convoy of battleships and aircraft carriers passing through the Mediterranean in January 1944, bound for the war in the Pacific with Japan, which he pretended was part of the invasion force. And there was the very real invasion force gathering in Naples, which no spy could fail to notice, which he pretended was destined for Pisa. Information was all supplied to the Abwehr by his usual suspects, including CHEESE.

Churchill was excited, awaiting the outcome and signalling Stalin, 'I hope to have good news for you before too long.'[5]

Clarke's deception was brilliant, best described by 35-year-old US correspondent Don Whitehead: 'we walked in behind German lines with hardly a shot being fired in a most sensational amphibious operation. It was so easy and so simply done, and caught the Germans completely by surprise, that, as I write this dispatch six hours after landing, American troops are literally standing with their mouths open and shaking their heads in amazement.'[6]

After this the Allies didn't move for two days, allowing the Germans to react. Their lack of daring resulted in appalling carnage on the beachhead that matched everything that happened in Gallipoli in the First War. Churchill was so sick he didn't even paint.

The killing went on for four months. Dorman-Smith was brought in from the cold by Churchill one last time, and the Army sent him to Anzio as a brigade commander. He was too old for the command, and not a field commander. It was a deliberately poisoned chalice.

In April, spring flowers bloomed in the churned earth and a wrecked factory stood in the distance as Dorman-Smith rode to the front line in a Jeep, passing a sign reading, 'DANGER, SHELLING, MAKE NO DUST. NO TRAFFIC PAST THIS POINT IN DAYLIGHT'.[7]

In the three-mile-deep perimeter, 72,000 Allied soldiers clung on, hammered by five and a half German divisions.

Dorman-Smith was haunted by the night on Railway Wood in 1915, when he had earned his MC, ordering his men to leave a dying man in the mud because there was no room for him in their trench. He still suffered nightmares of the man's eyes boring into him. When Dorman-Smith returned to London afterwards with shellshock he went missing. His father found him at night, in the garden of a house in which they used to live, sitting alone.

They sent Dorman-Smith back into the mincing machine, and broke him.

Italy had not been soft, and the Allies now had to grasp the nettle of a cross-Channel invasion into France. Clarke's deception plan to draw German forces away from Normandy was called ZEPPELIN – by now his deception was so full of gas it was likely to explode. In the Berlin publication of the Allies order of battle of 28 May 1944, of Clarke's 26 fictional divisions, 21 appeared. The Germans were particularly nervous of the 5th Airborne Division, and wondered why it had not been used on operations yet. Only two divisions were queried by German intelligence, meaning the Germans thought the Allies had roughly 210,000 more men and 85 per cent more aircraft and ships in the Mediterranean than they really had.

Clarke almost doubled the Allied strength.

With this fictional force, Clarke kept the Greek invasion in play, and also the Balkans – very specifically, landings to capture the port of Pula, in Yugoslavia. This made no military sense, and, at the northern end of the Adriatic, would have invited a massive

German response. However, Pula is only 300 miles from Hitler's alpine holiday home, Berchtesgaden. You cannot get any closer by boat.

Clarke's channels supplied the codeword for this invasion – the BBC would broadcast *'Dragi slušatelju'* (Dear listener) at the start of their Yugoslav broadcast, and 30 days later the invasion would start. However, if the same codeword were broadcast twice, the invasion would be off. The first 'Dear listener' went out on 22 March 1944 – meaning invasion 21st April. Then on 13 and 14 April came 'Dear listener' on two consecutive nights. It was postponed. Then on 21 April, 'Dear listener' again, meaning the invasion would take place on 21 May.

German intelligence didn't know whether it was coming or going. And it was probably no surprise Hitler didn't make his last stand at Berchtesgaden – Clarke may have placed a subliminal fear in his mind.

The other key to ZEPPELIN was a landing in the South of France, to keep German forces in the French Riviera after the Normandy D Day. He still had problems persuading any Allied air-force commander to bomb it – because, Clarke felt, the plan only benefited Supreme Allied Command, and had zero local benefit.

But Clarke did have an enormous number of his 'channels' to supply fake information. So many, he had to start killing some off, as each channel had to draw on A-Force resources to keep functioning. As Clarke put it, his agents 'one and all died hard', albeit mostly fictionally. One that he kept, for the South of France, was GILBERT.

Clarke thought it would have been a fascinating study in psychology to trace the development of GILBERT from a romantic young soldier to a middle-aged double agent. When he first surfaced in June 1943, he seemed a typical, professional French Army officer: greying hair, military moustache, fond of wine, women, horses and shooting.

GILBERT had signed on in 1914, fought, and demobilised in 1919, after which he had several mistresses, and found it hard to live on his Army pay. He fought bravely in 1940, and was given 'armistice leave' after France surrendered. Clarke thought it would be at this point that he suffered a crisis of indecision he shared with most of his compatriots who took up arms to fight for Hitler. He joined the Légion Tricolore, the Vichy French legion in the German Army, but never went to Russia. At the end of 1942, with El Alamein lost and the scales of war tipping against Germany, he was interviewed by Parti Populaire Français, the French fascist and antisemitic organisation, to be inserted into Tunis to operate a sabotage team against the British. A six-month advance of 180,000 francs, and 500,000 for his team's salaries and expenses may have swung it.

He met his team above the Elizabeth Arden beauty parlour on 52 Rue du Faubourg Saint-Honoré, Paris. His second in command was a wealthy playboy in his forties called Le Duc. There was another member of the team, Lieutenant Duteil (alias Joseph Delpiere) who had orders to watch GILBERT, and if he was playing double, kill him. From there the Germans took over the operation and they flew out of Naples on a Junkers 52. When they landed in Tunisia a German Naval officer took them to a Princess's house in Carthage.

At this point Fraser and the Allies were closing on the town. The day Tunis fell, GILBERT walked into the Deuxième Bureau (French intelligence) office, and handed himself in. Luckily, Duteil fled the Allies, was arrested and executed, without carrying out his mission to shoot GILBERT.

Clarke had a goldmine.

Playboy Le Duc was turned and dispatched to Sicily, when it fell, to continue his useful work. GILBERT continued to work out of Carthage, his radio operator none the wiser. Clarke found it necessary to swap out his operator when the Germans planned to parachute in more agents, and he was dispatched to Dakar, where he found his way into a naval prison cell.

The German pilot flying in the new agent missed the British-laid landing lights, and initially they thought the plan had gone wrong. But he arrived at GILBERT's flat under his own steam having been dropped miles from Tunis. The new agent brought much useful information. He had been GILBERT's receiving station, and

GILBERT's work was considered so important it was being transmitted straight to Berlin by teleprinter. Tunis wasn't being bombed because his work was so valuable they didn't want to knock out his electricity. Only his French fascist controllers were not happy, because he was not supplying enough political information.

With GILBERT feeding Berlin daily, Clarke thought back to the cinema and the Monty double. Since Monty had been sent back to Britain to take over the invasion armies, the Germans would certainly be watching his movements. Discreet enquiries revealed the actor he had seen in *Five Graves to Cairo* was far too tall: Monty was a small man.

Clarke got MI5 in Britain casting.

They found a substitute, who, no sooner than he was put in training broke his leg in a car accident. Eventually, the 46-year-old Lieutenant Meyrick Edward Clifton James of the Royal Army Pay Corps, a former actor, got the role of his life. He was rung by Clarke's good friend David Niven, who pretended to be running an Army film unit and invited him to come in for a casting. With one year's difference in age, his physical resemblance to Monty was striking.

Still Clarke had problems with London. He wanted his Monty to be in Gibraltar five days before the Normandy landings, which would have made his first appearance 31 May. London advanced this to 29 May, to give German intelligence more time to digest it. Clarke pointed out you wanted fake-Monty wandering around the Med as close to D Day as possible. In the event, D Day got pushed back by 48 hours, and Clarke's fake-Monty's curtain rose on 27 May, ten days before the actual D Day. Less than ideal.

Clarke's passport, issued in Algeria 18 September 1943, read 'Mr Derek Wilson Carter, profession: Government officer'. We don't know his disguise, but in his passport photograph he is wearing a fine Prince of Wales three-piece suit. Accompanying his protégé, though presumably at the back of the cortège, the new General Montgomery (Clarke got him a general's pay for the role) touched down on 'The Rock'. The instantly recognisable, multi-badge,

Pamplona beret emerged from the brand-new four-engine Avro York airliner, and the Governor of Gibraltar called out from the tarmac, 'Hello, Monty, glad to see you!'

After breakfast at Government House, shortly before 10am, they walked across the courtyard to their cars to coincide with the invitation of a known Spanish spy to visit the Colonial Secretary. He failed to hide his interest in what was happening, and Clarke was very pleased. The Colonial Secretary told him Monty was on his way to Algiers, at which point the Spaniard exited at speed, jumped in his car and drove very fast for the border. James was so good he even hoodwinked Monty's former aide de camp.

In Algiers, they got an American motorcycle escort to clear the traffic. When the female British Army driver, who had driven the real man, and policemen asked him for an autograph, James had to turn them down.

In Cairo he touched down, was taken out of the role and hidden by Clarke until after the real invasion was over. Clarke never knew if it made a difference. But there was one place in which his subliminal methods were measurable. On D Day in Normandy, 6 June, the Germans had 2 Panzer Divisions, 3 Field Divisions, and 5 Reserve Divisions on the French Riviera. But, to quote the Nazi broadcaster Karl Praeger in Berlin, '15 enemy divisions are stationed at present in French North Africa ready for an attack on Europe's southern flank.'

The broadcaster went on to describe how Corsica had been converted into a springboard for this operation, landing craft had been seen in North African ports, and commented that the fighting in Italy was just to tie down German forces, to allow this huge North African army to support the Normandy landings by landing in the South of France.

He was describing a huge army that did not exist – had never existed – but that had taken years to create. Clarke's biggest deceit was what he had started out with. Sketching the idea of a fake SAS brigade of parachutists in a converted bathroom, after receiving a captured Italian diary, had led to him pinning entire divisions of thousands of men in useless defence from the French Riviera to the Peloponnese.

Clarke and Fraser may have met in the bar at Shepheard's, the Kit Kat, Mohamed Ali, or at a party, but as ships passing in the night. They were opposite ends of a spectrum: Clarke, the master of his subliminal methods, and Fraser, the very sharp end of those methods. In this case it was not until nine days after the Allies landed, on 15 June, that the Germans realised that they may have been duped, and 2nd SS Panzer division abandoned its positions and started to move north. When it did, it moved into the welcoming arms of Major William Fraser and A Squadron, 1 SAS.

The Last Round: France 1944

Fraser looked down through the coffin-shaped opening in the belly of the four-engine Stirling bomber. Rain streaked through the darkness, nothing else was visible. The drop light flickered red above him; the pilot was saying something over the intercom. They had a really bad crossing, flak, night fighters, and now the pilot couldn't find the drop zone. He looked at his eight-man team, huddled in the cramped fuselage behind him. If they kept flying around they'd run out of fuel, but he wasn't going to abort. Fraser told the pilot they were going to drop. On the ground at least navigation would be in his hands.

Fraser had a 40kg pack strapped to his leg, and his weapon, to prevent the mistake, made by L Detachment years ago, of becoming separated from your kit. He heard the inboard engines of the Stirling bomber cut, the aircraft dipped into a shallow dive designed to reduce buffeting when he jumped.[8] The dispatcher gave him the thumbs-up, the green light flicked on, he leaned forward, and dropped into the night.

Ripped into the slipstream, he spun in the black vortex, then with relief felt the wrench of the static line and looked up to see the faint glow of the silk canopy above his head. He'd jumped at 1,000 feet, but in the darkness and rain couldn't see a thing. It was impossible to judge how far he had travelled. If he released the pack too early it would hang on the line below him, and spin dangerously in the storm, and if too late, he would hit the ground with it still attached to his body, which could seriously injure him.

Dark smudges, indistinguishable as fields, forest or lakes, swept beneath him in the rain-soaked night. He pulled the quick release on his leg and the kit bag dropped 3 metres into the darkness below him, and pulled up short on the rope to his harness. He looked up at his chute. He seemed to be going fast, but he had no idea of the wind direction to turn into and use as a brake. The ground rushed towards him, and he realised with horror that he was going into a forest. He covered his face, then his kitbag snagged, the rope tied to his harness pulled taught, and he smashed through the forest canopy. He rushed down, crashing through leaves and branches, and came to an abrupt halt on the lines of the snagged parachute, hanging in his harness.

He did a quick inventory of his body: it hurt, but nothing seemed broken. From the darkness around, heavy drops of water smacked into the forest floor. He wasn't on the ground, but when he looked he couldn't see the treetops either. He appeared to be in the thickest forest in the world. He would not be able to release the harness with it holding his weight. He could cut himself free with his knife, but how far would he fall?

He decided to light a cigarette. He cupped his zippo lighter and in the glow found he was almost on the ground. On tiptoes he pushed himself up, twisted the harness buckle and hit it, and stepped back onto French soil for the first time since 1939.

Fraser searched the forest for his team, eventually finding only his Eureka man, the one who carried the set to identify the aircraft drop zones. But he had had a worse landing than Fraser, his kitbag rope had broken. They searched for the vital Eureka set and the man's carbine, to no avail. Also missing was the most vital part of the mission, his five-man Phantom team. Phantom was a long-range communications device that could reach Britain. After Clarke left for Africa, David Niven had trained a Phantom Squadron, and their operators were dispersed among frontline units. Without Phantom, the whole mission was over. Fraser settled down in the dripping forest for the night.[9]

Four days earlier, on Tuesday, 6 June 1944, the Allies had landed at Normandy. Lord Lovat, who commanded the SAS's forerunner the Lovat Scouts, was now commander of a Commando brigade. Byrne, who had escaped captivity but decided the SAS was more cloak than dagger had re-joined the Commandos. They had waded ashore, led by a piper waist-deep in water playing 'Blue Bonnets are Over the Border', to be knocked down like ninepins, with 209 killed in a morning.[10] Byrne needed all his skills to make it off the beach, dodging two Germans who sprang back to life behind him.[11]

Hobo Hobart had prepared the best division to hit the beaches, 11th Armoured, but was sent ashore as an armoured observer having been removed on 'medical grounds'. Not even Churchill was able to rehabilitate him. O'Connor had escaped captivity on an Italian trawler, sailing past the fighting at Termoli, and, it was hoped, would reproduce his North African magic. For Monty there could only be one man waiting beyond the sand dunes, his nemesis, Rommel. As Rommel himself put it; for 'The most decisive battle of the war.'[12]

As D Day approached, Monty planned once again to use the SAS as shock troops, deploying all three SAS Regiments on the day before D Day in a 40 mile corridor running parallel to the coast stretching from Brussels all the way to Brittany. Small teams, scattered about like confetti, would hit Rommel's lines of communication immediately behind the front. Once they had completed this, the draft operation order stated 'it is recognised that many of them, for various reasons, will not be able to reach Regimental concentration areas'[13] to which could be added: because they will be dead.

This order was written on 1 May, but on 9 May it was scrapped when 'representations' were made by HQ airborne forces to Monty's HQ. One whistle blower appears to have been Bill Stirling, CO of 2 SAS, because later he either resigned or was sacked. But the Americans got wind of the fact that the whole Allied special forces component could be wiped out on D Day, rather than employed strategically. The US were parachuting in large numbers of OSS men (the nascent CIA) to help the French resistance, and it had been hoped the SAS would support this operation.[14]

No lesser man than Eisenhower's Chief Planning Officer, General Bull, went to see Monty's right-hand man, De Guingand. After the meeting there was still a question mark about who controlled the SAS: Monty or Eisenhower. Eisenhower by now had the measure of the man to put it in writing – 'SAS troops are expected to be used mainly strategically, their strategic employment will be controlled by SHAEF'[15] – Eisenhower's HQ. When he realised Clarke's panzer divisions were still on the French Riviera, he was very specific: was the forest of Morvan, which lay across the route they would have to take to Normandy, in range of the SAS's aircraft?[16]

Fraser's mission would become a special forces playbook. As commander of A Squadron, 1 SAS he was to drop into the forest of Morvan, 100 miles south-east of Paris. The deep forest, with few roads, and dense foliage made the ideal base for special forces' operations, and here he was to link up with the Maquis (French resistance). Just 40 miles west of Dijon, the 1,000 square miles of forest and isolated villages lay next to the major rail route, and across the route nationale road, that ran from Marseille to Paris. It was up this route that the two panzer divisions and troops on the French Riviera must eventually travel to reinforce Rommel.

It was Fraser's job to stop them – to cut those lines of communication, and keep cutting them.[17] For this he needed both his Phantom team to talk to London, to bring in his squadron and supplies, and also to task aircraft to bomb those panzers in their railheads. The SAS was making its last developmental leap of the war: working with local forces and calling in airstrikes.

At daybreak, Fraser found a town and worked out their location, and he and his Eureka operator set off for the two-day trek to where they should have been dropped. Eventually, a woodcutter gave them directions for Maquis Jean, their French counterparts, and they arrived at their camp deep in the forest. Wearily, Fraser sat at one of the trestle tables, near a stream, in a clearing surrounded by huts, tents and a cookhouse. The French force numbered about 200, made up of all ages and dressed in assorted garb, from smocks parachuted by the British to clogs. A whole gendarme team had recently come in and were wearing police uniform. Part of his mission was to make them more effective by supplying arms and support.

A good meal was being prepared. Fraser had his first glass of French wine, and the food was excellent, finished off with cherries, which were in season.[18] The troop leader from his SAS reconnaissance party, dropped a few days earlier, arrived to find him asleep.

Fraser waited for the rest of the squadron to drop. The weather was awful, rain incessant and cloud cover too low, and for three nights they listened to aircraft droning around above them unable to see their lights. The Maquis were ambushed, some wearing loose-fitting Denison parachute smocks the SAS had given them. Two had been killed, two wounded then beaten to death, indicating the Germans thought they were British paratroops, killed on Hitler's orders. Fraser knew they had been compromised at a time he didn't have enough troops on the ground. When a woman showed up from a local village complaining to the Maquis, who were mostly communists, that they had stolen her tarpaulins to give to the SAS for tents, his concerns grew that too many people knew where they were.

Finally, the Phantom team were brought into camp and Fraser contacted London. Without the Eureka beacon he could not move the whole squadron to attack Rommel's lines of communication, because he wouldn't be able to mark a drop zone for resupply. Those lines of communication were too far for foot patrols, so he needed their Jeeps, Bren guns, mortars and 6-pounder towed guns to be dropped as soon as possible for him to go on the offence. He did not get an encouraging reply.

Finally, on the fourth night, the noise of the first Stirling bomber swept towards the drop zone, and a Maquis shouted, 'Allumez!'

The lights played on the belly of the lead aircraft. From above came the roar of Stirlings' engines, the rustle of chutes, then the soft thud of containers. There was a crash, as one that had twisted into a roman candle landed. Then, from the darkness, came the voices of men floating above them. The squadron had arrived.[19]

A Squadron was full of old hands. Seekings had come on the other aircraft with Fraser, but this night the mortar officer, Muirhead, was dropped, and they found Du Vivier hugging the top of a tall tree like a bear. A padre was parachuted, but the pilot had decided to go the wrong way up the drop zone, and the padre was hung upside-down in a tree. He had cut himself free and concussed himself on landing. Others were more seriously injured; they picked up one old hand with a badly injured back, and one with a broken leg. Then Fraser sped with the team in the Maquis' small convoy to camp.

On Sunday, 25 June, the padre held a service. In the green earth that was their bed for the night, in the tall trees that lifted their eyes to the heavens, in the clear waters that supplied their needs, in the loyalty of friends, he commended their enterprise to God. The smell of pine and of logs burning on a fire was the incense that rose with his prayers. No man-made house of God could compare to the tracery of leaves that was their roof, and the boughs and branches their walls. Fraser bowed his head, and around him men who in normal circumstances would never set foot in a church did the same.

Then the Germans hit them. Bullets cracked through the forest, to the inevitable comment from an SAS man running with his weapon, 'This is what comes of having a service, Padre!'[20]

Fraser had detached 2 Troop to a Maquis camp east of the forest, and they were first in contact. They ambushed a German patrol, and sporadic fighting continued over the following day, until, on 26 June, it was clear the Germans were going to mount a major attack to clear out the forest.

The first indication was when the Germans attacked the Maquis hospital at Château de Vermont, in a small hamlet nearby. The SAS men injured on the drop and wounded Maquis fled for the trees. The Maquis and Germans ended up in a standoff, 250 heavily armed

Germans unwilling to go into a forest after the Maquis, and the Maquis unable to combat this force equipped with mortars and heavy machine guns. They asked the SAS to help, and to cut off the Germans' escape.[21]

Fraser ran through the forest. Ahead he could hear the crack and thump of small arms, the rattle of machine guns, the thud of heavier explosions. He reached the edge of the forest, and ahead the Germans were dropping fast under French fire. He left some of his men to help hold off the Germans, and took the rest of his men and as much firepower as they could muster to hit them in the rear.[22]

Working round to the left of the Germans, he reached the top of the hill above a valley, and Seekings called out that he could see German trucks on the far side. He left Seekings to deal with them and pressed on, keen to get behind the German attack.

Everyone in Seekings's section was new, bar one man, so he didn't tell them he could also see a German gunner by the trucks. If they were fast, there was a good chance of catching all the German transport. But if he told the green recruits they might have baulked at a speedy advance across open country in the middle of a battle.

Seekings dropped down into the valley, but came out of the dip much closer to the trucks and gunner than he'd expected. The German dropped to the ground, and Seekings turned his head to shout a warning:

'Look! Germans!'[23]

The German fired. Seekings tried to raise his rifle, but couldn't move his arm and fell to the ground. The German threw two grenades, which exploded either side of him without hitting him.

The first man to reach Seekings grabbed him, and started trying to patch up his head. Seekings told him, 'Leave my head, get a tourniquet on my arm, it's my arm, you stupid bastard, not my head.'[24]

He was wrong, it *was* his head. A bullet had gone into the base of his skull and lodged against his spine.

Fraser pressed on, leading two SAS men with Bren guns. An enormous thunderstorm broke, rain and sweat poured down his face, the thunder and lightning drowning the battle. He reached the far side of the tiny hamlet on the brow of a low hill looking down onto the road that led back to Dun-les-Places, the nearby village which the Germans had occupied as their base. On the verge of the single-lane road that led to that village, a small group of Germans sat. Fraser thought they looked like they were waiting for something.[25]

Fraser quickly set up the snap ambush. At 200 metres range he placed a Bren gun to each side, and settled down to wait. He didn't have to wait long; the Germans were withdrawing. First a couple came, then more. In one's and two's they drifted in. With an open field of fire, his Bren gunners rocked their bipods slowly back and forwards to bed them in, adjusted their sights to the range, and put their fingers on their triggers. When there was a platoon of 50 in their sights, with a mortar, at last an officer appeared and ordered them to fall in. The ranks filed into order on the road, Fraser put his hands on the Bren gunners shoulders and they opened fire.

The two Bren guns ripped through the German ranks, the racket overwhelming the noise of the dying. Both Bren gunners swiftly replaced their magazines and went on firing, and when it was done, just as swiftly, Fraser led his team and vanished back into the forest.

When Fraser reported their success in seeing off the threat on the Phantom set that night, SAS Brigade HQ replied, 'Well done, but refrain from engaging in Maquis battles get on with cutting railways.'[26]

Fraser was talking to people who had never operated behind enemy lines.

That night the SAS didn't get much sleep, while both the French and Germans expended ammunition. But the Germans were reluctant to go any deeper after what had happened. In the morning, Fraser decided it was time to move. In the pouring rain they set out with Seekings and another casualty, and the following day reached a valley Fraser had reconnoitred after landing. It became known as Bill's Camp, and the centre of operations.

The padre nursed Seekings, thinking a shave would make him

feel better. Afterwards he confessed he had never shaved a man in his life. He also confessed he would be changing his sermon, having watched the men sacrifice their lives for one another.

When the Maquis asked for help again, Fraser sent a man back to the main camp to find they had gone.

The Germans pushed forwards into the forest, but not as far as the SAS. Fraser had put out patrols to watch them, one of which had a noisy firefight at the smouldering château hospital. Outwitted and frustrated, the German column burnt Vermot to the ground, gang-raping several women and a fourteen-year-old girl. Then they returned to Dun-les-Places and forced captives from Vermot and Dun-les-Places, 17 able-bodied men they suspected of helping the Maquis, into the church.

The carnage continued into the night. There was a huge thunderstorm and a power cut. The Maquis often knocked out their power, and in the darkness and flashes of lightning the Germans raped several women. During the looting and drinking they decided to hang the curate from his bell tower by a bell rope. Then they forced the men out of the church, where they were waiting for them in front of the steps and gunned them down. Then they threw hand grenades to mutilate the bodies. Drunk in the square, they tried to shoot the curate down from his belltower until he too landed on the steps.

This was not Fraser's fault. However, for the commander whose actions produce a reprisal of such ferocity this was no comfort. It appears Fraser found this one of the most traumatic moments of his war. Soldiers are, in many ways, inoculated against suffering among their own ranks. They expect it. But the suffering of non-combatants, of the innocent, who suffer on a far greater scale than soldiers, is hard to process when faced for the first time.

Fraser took another blow when two of their aircraft bringing in more of the squadron and supplies crashed overhead in bad weather. In the morning wreckage was everywhere, there were no survivors. Fifteen men died.

Fraser stood on the edge of the drop zone. They were short of food, always soaked by weather, but the biggest threat to morale was the lack of cigarettes and tea, though Fraser found that in Burgundy there was no shortage of wine. The air drops were always cancelled at the last minute, meaning a stressful night out of camp with every possibility of discovery. That night, Fraser had a wind-up ground-to-air walkie-talkie with him, because Mayne was going to be in one of the three planes, and he wanted to talk with him.

With relief, at 2am, came the roar of approaching aero-engines. The Eureka operator heard the screech in his headphones, indicating the aircraft were friendly, and tapped out the recognition code letter in morse on his set.[27] The drop was on. Men lit drums full of oil and sand and headlights lit the drop zone.

Along with the supplies, three Jeeps appeared out of the sky, floating down on four parachutes each. One landed in the field, one crashed into the forest, one flew dangerously close to the road, where it hung upside down from the trees. The men ran to extract the Jeeps.[28] It took all night, and 40 trees were felled, but they were operational. Rommel's lines of communication were now in easy reach, and they could go to work.[29] Fraser couldn't hear a word Mayne had tried to say to him, and could guess how angry that would have made the man.

People started fleeing south from Paris to the forest, thinking that once the Allies broke out of Normandy the Germans would make a stand there. They provided great intelligence and the Phantom team radioed back locations of flying-bomb dumps and assembly points around Paris. Then, on 14 July, the Maquis brought Fraser a landowner from near Mantes, outside Paris, who revealed the location of Rommel's headquarters – on the banks of the Seine, in Château La Roche-Guyon.

Everyone at camp was excited. It wasn't going to be easy, a 300-mile drive through enemy territory, but Fraser had the advantage of local knowledge, contacts en route and, of course, he'd done this type of journey many times.

One of Fraser's Phantom operators heard Fraser and his team

discussing a plan to send two or three Jeeps to the château, they would call in an airstrike, then in the confusion the two Jeeps would go in and capture Rommel. Fraser said they would all get a medal if they survived.[30] But that's not the plan Fraser settled on, his terse signal read:

Rommel crosses the River Seine by motor launch and walks and shoots in Forêt de Moisson on the left bank.[31]

He asked permission to carry out the kill or capture operation. Fraser did not intend to drive into the châteaux in an air raid. He planned to wait till Rommel crossed the Seine in his motor launch, where, in the unpopulated Forêt de Moison, Rommel, busy stalking deer, was the perfect target. He was unlikely to risk upsetting his prey by surrounding himself with bodyguards. Though it made it no less likely, that any medals awarded on the mission would be posthumous.

Opportunities like this had been anticipated.

There was an opportunity to kill Hitler, passed up, because, as Pug Ismay put it, it was 'an advantage that Hitler should remain in control of German strategy, having regard to the blunders that he has made, but that on the wider point of view, the sooner he was got out of the way the better.'[32]

Some of Fraser's team actually baulked at killing Rommel, to whom the British had attributed chivalric values. Fraser had no such qualms. This man was a Nazi, and from 1940 he had had him in his sights.

The problem was the signal never reached Mike Sadler, the LRDG navigator, now promoted to 1 SAS intelligence officer.[33] The Phantom net fed it into the SAS Brigade Commander, who commanded not only Mayne's 1 SAS (with Fraser's A Squadron in France), but 2 SAS, to whom he decided to pass the OPERATION GAFF. The operation order was issued on 20 July 1944, six days after Fraser's signal, its intention 'to kill, or kidnap and remove to England, Field Marshal ROMMEL or any senior members of his staff'.[34]

The 2 SAS troop leader and his team hit the drop zone 11 days after Fraser's signal. They reached a forest outside Versailles, Paris, three days later, on 28 July. They were still 46 miles from the target 14 days after Fraser's signal when they discovered Rommel had been strafed and badly injured by an Allied fighter sortie on 17 July. Eight Allied pilots subsequently claimed the 'kill'.

Two weeks is long time in war. Fraser had the shot, but they didn't let him take it.

Four days after Fraser found Rommel, Monty launched OPER-ATION GOODWOOD, his breakout from the Normandy beach-head. On the eve, Monty signalled Churchill, 'Am determined to loose the armoured divisions to-morrow if in any way possible.'[35] Those armoured divisions were led by O'Connor, who had once sliced across Cyrenaica. Tedder had bought in, diverting bombers to lay a carpet ahead of the attack. It was a complete disaster, suffering tank losses far in excess of El Alamein. All the Allies' problems reared their heads, but the one which derailed O'Connor was Monty's personal letter to him, contradicting the published order, that he protect his flank at the expense of advancing. Monty, always risk-averse, tied his commander's hands, focusing on not failing, rather than success.

Both the British press and the Supreme Commander had expected better. Fraser knew nothing of this. Operating from a soggy forest, he was tearing up the lines of communication, doing his best to derail the German defence.

Fraser split his force over three bases: Bill's Camp in the forest, Château-Chinon in the west, to strike out of the forest in that direction, and another towards Dijon to take out supply routes there. They cut Rommel's rail link 22 times – derailing 6 trains, destroying 2 engines and 40 trucks. They blew a synthetic fuel plant twice, destroying it with mortars. They killed 220 men, shot up convoys, burnt 23 trucks. The padre, driving Fraser, pulled off a road at his instruction and watched him gun down a staff car full of German

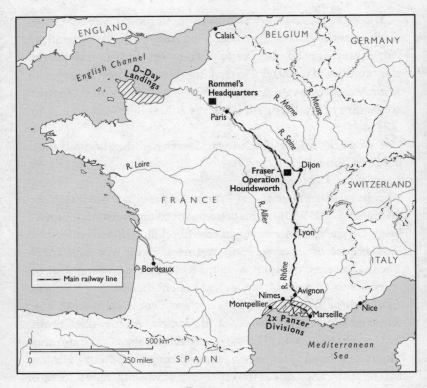

France, 1944.

officers. Fraser personally led patrols, towing their 6-pounder guns, waging a private war over a thousand miles of country. But perhaps the real damage was done via their Phantom team. Working 16 hours a day, they constantly encoded targets given to them by the SAS. And night after night the RAF visited, bombs falling on panzers stuck in sidings, on trains unable to move on destroyed railways and on Rommel's vital fuel tankers blown up or immobilised. They lost 2 killed, 5 wounded, 17 missing.[36] For a squadron of men that often numbered just over 40, it was an extraordinary feat of arms.

The SAS became French heroes, these bearded, hard-fighting men, who the French assumed must have come from the slums of British cities. One of their troop leaders tried to curry favour with farmers' daughters with his K-rations, and their padre washed his dirty feet in their streams, though this was their drinking water.[37]

Fraser became a local hero. Always proud of his roots, he had his Gordons uniform dropped. The squadron pulled into the little village of Anost, in the middle of their area of operations, riding in seven Jeeps pulling their 6-pounder gun. Dressed in nothing approaching regulation uniform, what really interested the village was their handsome commander in a kilt. The mayor was delighted, and asked would 'Monsieur le Commandant' make a short speech, in French!

Fraser, a man of few words in his own language, rose to the occasion, preparing to walk onto the balcony of the Hotel de Ville to an expectant crowd. He stepped out, dressed in kilt and glengarry, rendering anything he had to say, in poor French with a heavy Scots accent, quite superfluous as the crowd went wild with cheers of 'L'Anglais' and their older ally 'L'Ecossais'.[38] Fraser had won their hearts and minds.

He needed to. In that village, the reprisals took the form of German patrols grabbing the young men of the village, including the youngest son of the local judge, lining them against the wall and shooting them.

But no one ever betrayed Fraser and his men.

Mayne jumped in with Mike Sadler on 7 August, and the padre got the chance to watch both him and Mayne work, thinking great soldiers are born, not made. He noticed both had the same instinctive knowledge of what to do when there was trouble, both appeared careless at times, both reached the necessary decision straight away, and both inspired complete confidence. Though Mayne was a great deal older than Fraser, when it came to soldiering in their own type of warfare, they had a great deal in common.[39]

But the padre made another observation – that the cumulative effect of the strain of previous similar operations was obvious. Fraser, and other old hands, had been behind enemy lines too long, and though not conscious of the fact, they could never relax. The constant tension left its mark. That tension had now reached danger point – their soldiering qualities were not in question, but he observed carelessness, impatience, edginess, and depression.[40]

The French surgeon who operated on their wounded, ran into Fraser's bivouac under parachute silk one day during one of their 'flaps' to tell him the English were under attack. Fraser was asleep on a mattress of bottles; his aspect clearly indicated that several of them were empty.

Fraser asked which camp. When the doctor told him it was one of the others, he demanded that he let him sleep. The doctor was indignant, and waited outside for him to wake up to reproach him for his behaviour. Even so, the French doctor was not immune from Fraser's celebrity, thinking he was handsome, very handsome, in his impeccable uniform.[41]

By September, with the Germans in full retreat, it was time to get out. Fraser's squadron was being relieved, and he prepared to take them out, through the American lines, to Paris.

Rommel had time to think, recovering in his hospital bed. He thought that between the wars, while the ideas of *Blitzkrieg* crystallised around Guderian, the British remained conservative, and almost entirely rejected the doctrine that had been so brilliantly proposed by their countrymen. Once the war started, that terribly cumbersome structure the British Army was unable to adapt, and, in Africa, specifically, they continually replaced their commander in chief, having to learn the same bitter lessons all over again – something Fraser and the SAS could certainly identify with.[42]

On 20 July, Hitler was almost killed by a briefcase bomb in a conference and started hanging his generals on meathooks while still alive. Rommel had had nothing to do with the plot, but he had lost faith in the war. He had been loyal up to the last, even believing Hitler's reassurance on miracle weapons, as he had in Africa about more panzers and troops. But when his son was drafted, aged 14, he banned him from joining the SS, saying he said he didn't want his son joining an organisation that was carrying out mass killings.

That he went on fighting to defend the Reich with the knowledge of what Himmler was doing is extraordinary. But he also wrote to his son, 'Often there'll be orders of your superior you don't like . . . Obey without question.'[43]

Cynically, many thought that German generals fighting at the end of the war were fighting to keep the noose from their neck. But by now Rommel had lost faith in winning. While Fraser was trying to get permission to kill him, on 15 July 1944, he wrote to Hitler, 'The troops are everywhere fighting heroically, but the unequal struggle is approaching the end. It is urgently necessary for the proper conclusion to be drawn from the situation.'[44]

Rommel was sent on sick leave from France, and his son, who was an anti-aircraft gunner near Munster, Germany, came home to be by his side. Rommel told his son the war was lost. His son replied, 'Perhaps there are new weapons that will turn things in our favour?'

Rommel said, 'Rubbish, nobody has such weapons. The only purpose of these rumours is to make the ordinary soldier hang on a bit longer. We're finished.'[45]

His son noticed shadowy Gestapo hanging round the village. Rommel gave him an 8mm pistol and the advice that the Gestapo were terrible shots, and would miss first time, shoot back and it would ruin their aim.

His son came home again on 14 October, in time for breakfast and a walk. Rommel said some Generals were coming to see him later. At noon he saw his father change into his favourite uniform, his Africa tunic. A green car pulled up outside with a Berlin number plate. His father took his son into his bedroom. Rommel said, 'I have just had to tell your mother, that I shall be dead in a quarter of an hour . . . I must go, they've only given me ten minutes.'

They walked out of the house together. Two generals were standing by the gate, who raised their right hands in salute. The crunch of the gravel underfoot sounded unusually loud. A knot of villagers stood outside the drive. The SS driver swung the door open. Rommel pushed his Field Marshal's baton under his arm. And he was gone. Not by a bullet from Fraser, but, as Kléber had died outside Shepheard's: betrayed.

Fraser's war ended on the Rhine. In March 1945, A Squadron was back in action in their Jeeps as reconnaissance for the advancing Allies, and to get in behind German lines and shoot them up. Fraser's Jeep was carried across the deep, swift, muddy Rhine in a Buffalo amphibious vehicle, operating ahead of 18 Allied Airborne Corps. He sped up the bank and into Germany. Ahead, Canadian paratroopers had become pinned down by heavy fire from Germans in a copse.[46]

Fraser lined up his Jeeps and charged the wood, with Seekings and others on the Vickers K's firing. A Spandau, a German machine gun, opened up from a hedge on the flank. Fraser's Jeep was riddled, span out of control and crashed. Fraser had been shot in the hand. It was a miracle that he had survived. His luck had held, but his war was over.[47]

It was 28 March 1945.[48] Six weeks later, Germany surrendered.

Epilogue

A Great Man

At the end of the war the SAS disbanded, the last brigade commander, 'Mad' Mike Calvert, took their final parade on 1 October 1945. At the end of hostilities, High Command could see no further use for them. They had no chance of surviving the cuts without a general in their ranks to fight their corner.

Fraser was posted back to the Gordon Highlanders, finally joining his family's regiment as an officer. On 20 November 1945, he shipped out to Tripoli, where they were stationed.[1] His arrival was a homecoming, both to his regiment and to North Africa, but Fraser cut an awkward figure in the Officers' Mess. An unmarried, highly decorated officer, MC and bar, he was sharing the mess with young bachelors almost eight years his junior.

He had his tunes of glory: he had survived a war in which by any measure he should have been killed. But his drinking finally caught up with him and, after only six months with the regiment, he was arrested for being drunk in charge of his men.

He was immediately demoted to captain. Ironically, his court martial took place in Tripoli on 4 June, 1946, the place through which he had chased Rommel. The board of three senior officers was as lenient as possible in the light of his war record, but drunk in charge of soldiers was a serious offence.[2] He pleaded guilty and was given a severe reprimand. He returned to the depot in Aberdeen, where he was invalided out of the Army. This preserved his rank of captain, and he picked up his demob issue: one worsted grey suit, one brown homburg, two poplin shirts, one striped tie and one pair of shoes. The problem was, as Seekings said, he was Army born and bred.[3] Fraser was cut loose from all he knew, and was now in freefall.

Seekings described Fraser as a fine officer, but also as 'a junkie'.[4] Like many servicemen, he took amphetamine addiction into civilian life. Benzedrine, or 'Bennies', brought home by returning servicemen on both sides of the Atlantic would fuel the beat generation, and put Jack Kerouac on the road. Fraser resurfaced in 1950 having put his SAS skills to good effect. Charged with 30 burglaries, he lost his Army rank and tried to keep it quiet. But Mayne found out he'd been arrested, writing to a friend, 'Poor Bill.'

This may have been a turning point.

Always a man to avoid the limelight, he got a job at a bakery in Warwick. Perhaps some sort of parole deal, as he does not appear to have done any time in prison. He was reunited with Phillips, who continued to serve with Warwickshire Regiment – Phillips's Regiment before the Commando, as well as Fraser's stepfather's regiment. Phillips married, but continued to do what he did best, and on 5 November 1951, his position was overrun by Chinese troops in Korea.[5] Missing in action, it can be assured he went down fighting. Mayne's past caught up with him when he died, drunk, at the wheel of his red Riley sports car on a wet night in Ireland in 1955. Such was his reputation, people were too afraid to help him.

Fraser managed to get a job as a clerk at an engineering firm in Warwick. A former officer from the Gordons spotted him on the street, and they went home for a drink, where Fraser's relationship with his stepfather was strained. He passed away in 1975 at the King Edward VII Memorial Hospital, Warwick at the age of 58. He died of congestive heart failure, often caused by heavy smoking; cardiomyopathy, often caused by amphetamine use; and renal failure, a symptom of alcohol addiction.[6]

The war killed Fraser; just not with a bullet.

The Film Business

Clarke's war finished in Florence in 1945, not a bad place to celebrate. He retired as brigadier in 1947 with two mentions in dispatches, Companion of the Bath (CB), CBE, and a Legion of Merit, pinned on him by a US general in Cairo in 1945. No one really knew what he'd done during the war. He offered his services to the Conservative Party. Churchill had been annihilated in the 1945 election by a Labour landslide, after which Clarke got a job as a director at Night Watch Services, a company that would become better known as Securicor.

Seven Assignments, published by Jonathan Cape in 1948, rectified his wartime anonymity, but his book starts in 1939 and ends in 1940, with his summons from Wavell to Cairo, just when the story gets really interesting. He also referred to his visit to Dublin only as a 'neutral country', which many assumed was Spain.

This led to him being asked to do a 15-minute talk on the 'Birth of the Commandos' on the BBC for the price of 20 guineas. He engaged an agent (Curtis Brown), delivered 20 minutes and his agent got him 25 guineas.

He personally sent 38 copies of his biography to his friends, which he paid Jonathan Cape for, and Hermione Ranfurly loved it, telling him it was exactly like listening to Clarke tell a story in his own, quiet way – with a bit of humour and a bit of suspense. She also said Jonathan Cape had rung her to tell her how pleased he was, and how many reprints he was doing.

With a hit on his hands, Clarke also sent the book to people he wanted to connect with, like the head of Ealing Studios, Sir Michael Balcon. What Clarke really wanted in life was to be a writer, ideally a film writer. His brother Tibby had been discharged from the police force (his wartime profession) with asthma in 1943 and worked as a staff writer at Ealing. A string of hit movies followed, including *Passport to Pimlico* in 1949, and *The Lavender Hill Mob* in 1951, for which he was awarded an Oscar.

In 1953 Ewen Montagu spilt the beans, publishing *The Man Who Never Was* about OPERATION MINCEMEAT. Clarke felt he had every right to write the full story, and he completed his proposal for *The Secret War* in July 1953. Clarke wrote, 'these pages tell of a battle of wits – of fantasy and imagination – fought out on an almost private basis between the supreme heads of Hitler's intelligence (and Mussolini's) and a small band of men and women'. It was enough to get any publisher or film producer salivating.

But he needed to clear it with the Ministry of Defence, and took one of the Army's Director of Public Relations out for lunch at the Dorchester before sending him the submission. The answer was a firm no. The Cold War was ramping up, and the ministry didn't want to reveal any of Clarke's tricks of the trade. Those tricks were filed in triplicated Top Secret files. Clarke had, before he left the military, transcribed all he knew and could remember into hundreds of pages of the 'A' Force Diary. The trouble was, few knew it existed.

Clarke may have baulked when Clifton James, the man he and Niven had cast as Monty, published his successful *I was Monty's Double* in 1954, while Clarke was being prevented from telling his story. James Bond had just landed in *Casino Royale*, written by his good friend Peter's brother, Ian Fleming, and Clarke, unable to publish fact, turned to fiction. Curtis Brown landed him a deal with Hodder and Stoughton for what, everyone hoped, would be a spy thriller.

Published in 1955, Clarke's *Golden Arrow* was a complete flop. His writing, honed in trying to influence his enemy, was too nuanced. He needed a much bigger brush for this canvas. The hero was a thinly veiled Dudley Clarke, the plot featured a train and counterfeit money, but the heroine's escape from a houseboat was predicated on her footwear.

With this setback Clarke appears to have destroyed everything: the original manuscript, reviews, letters, and his publisher's and agent's correspondence. But he didn't give up. He went back to the drawing board and started again with short stories.

Film producers liked the real spy stories, and *I was Monty's Double* was optioned for film. In 1957, Clarke was approached for film rights for *The Cheese Story*. He wanted an advance of £5,000, and 5 per cent of gross profits – enough to make any producer flinch. Clarke suggested that rather than whittle away bits of that story, piece by piece, in offerings such as *The Man Who Never Was* and *I was Monty's Double*, and this 'irresponsible Yankee movie' about CHEESE, why didn't he write the whole story – he would even do it without signing a contract.

No dice. *I was Monty's Double* was released the following year.

Then people started approaching him, writers who had found part of his story, for example his part in the cover for the Normandy landings, to which he replied, 'I find I am still completely barred from giving any information about the cover plan.' In 1959, Lord Keyes claimed he founded the Commandos, and Clarke was unable to defend his reputation. He was rescued by Alan Bourne, who had been posted over him by Churchill back in 1940. Alan Bourne wrote to *The Times* that Clarke 'not only originated the name but the idea'.

Then at the Odeon Leicester Square, on 6 October 1960, one of the FLESHPOTS posed with former counter intelligence officer, Sansom: the man who had caught him burning a fiver in a Cairo nightclub, in the fictional depiction of their story – *Foxhole in Cairo*.

In 1960 Clarke decided to start serious research for his story, looking for documents relating to the German end of CHEESE. He found Ribbentrop's discovery that MINCEMEAT was a sham, and that the Italians hadn't believed a word and were listening to CHEESE.[7] He didn't find the intelligence Montagu had used to support MINCEMEAT's success – which included the Axis assessment that Tobruk (where Kenyon Jones had built landing craft) and Alexandria would be jumping off points for Greece, and that they thought the Allies would land at the wrong end of Sicily.[8] All of which point directly to Clarke's work. To be charitable, perhaps Montagu didn't know about Clarke's wider deception.

It appears the Ministry of Defence continued to prevent him from publishing, and his replies to approaches became terse. But it also appears the Ministry of Defence had no knowledge of the treasure trove on which they sat. A member of Sandhurst contacted Clarke in 1969 because he was looking into the means of deception that may be available within the corps area. A contact had tipped him off that Clarke was his man. The British Army had lost all knowledge of Clarke's subliminal methods, and, by 1969, the record of his initiative in deception was gathering dust somewhere in its archives. Clarke replied there was no book – only his files – and the man from Sandhurst said he would spend the next day in the ministry looking for them.

Clarke never married, nor had the children he had wanted to make proud when they asked him what he did in the war. He was an old man in his seventies when he made his last foray into writing. His biography, *A Quarter of My Century*, covered a lost era – when the First War had passed and another was not yet on the horizon. It told of the formative experiences of his youth that led him, with his unique personality, to achieve so much. He submitted the draft to his agent in 1973, but they were not optimistic. Rejection letters piled up and it was never published.

By now a sick man, one of his old team went to see him. He was clearly dying, but Clarke was always his old self, and waved for him to have a drink.

After his death the following year, his sister tried to publish *A Quarter of My Century*, to no avail. She also tried to track down the record of his war years, believing he had written a draft. In correspondence with the Cabinet Office Historical Section, she conceded that what they held was written while he was a serving officer, and therefore couldn't be published as a book. They also concluded that he had not written a private history of A-Force – his book proposal for *The Secret War*.

History is not written by the victors, but by those who write. Perhaps there was no manuscript. But Clarke's loss was a loss for all. As he himself said, the greatest benefit of deception is saving lives.

The Wings

The SAS burst, live and kicking, onto the world's TV screens as B Squadron assaulted the Iranian Embassy on 5 May 1980 – and everyone wondered where on earth this capability came from. The SAS had been an idea, created by men like Clarke and Fraser, it had floated like vapour after being disbanded, and its kingdom had lived on in the minds of men.

After Orde Wingate handed his paper 'guerrilla-force theory' to Clarke at Shepheard's in 1941, he had tried to take his own life. Having survived, he went east, to the war with Japan. Other men, such as 'Mad' Mike Calvert and Chapman from Lochailort training wing, went east too. The idea grew there, a parallel branch of the same tree, while they fought in the jungles and sweated and died, and finally won, as Fraser and his men did.

After the war the idea lived on in other men's minds. Men such as John Harding, who had stood alongside O'Connor in the first British *Blitzkrieg*, and whom Dorman-Smith had flown in to see in Tobruk, as Rommel advanced on the port. And even though Orde Wingate died in a plane crash in 1944, the idea could never die nor be disbanded. When John Harding was struggling with Chinese insurgents in Malaya in 1950, he thought of the idea, and some men who might help.

That is, as they say, another story.

So the SAS was reborn – and, through the years, members of the SAS would rely on their wings to carry them through the dark night of the underworld, and lift them safely to meet the dawn.

Acknowledgements

I would like to thank my gorgeous wife, Alexia, both for her support and telling me this was a book – for the sake of argument, my wife is always right. Roland White for suggesting it could be a book, to my agent, Mark Lucas, without whom it would never have been a book and my publisher, Jamie Joseph at WH Allen for believing it was a book even if it didn't look like it at times. I would like to thank Rob Pinchbeck for his help proofing the final draft. Finally, I would like to thank my children, Lula, Minty, Sam and Max, since I have been an absent father much of the time writing this book.

Researching the book, I would like to thank Mike Sadler, last survivor of the early SAS, whose sparkling eyes didn't look a day older than the young man looking out of the photographs in the 1940s. To Alan Orton, whose father John Orton was a member of 11 Scottish Commando and jumped with L Detachment as part of Stirling's team into Cyrenaica in 1941 and was captured. To Paul Davis, whose father Peter Davis was a Troop Leader with the SRS and then Fraser's A Squadron SAS in France, who edited his father's two excellent books and supplied photographs for this book. To Gavin Mortimer for the letters relating to Fraser's later life. To Stewart Mitchell and the Gordon Highlanders' museum. To David Baynham and the Fusilier Museum, Warwick. To Tarek Ibrahim, who wrote *Shepheard's of Cairo,* for his time, and help sourcing the original wings. To Marina Waugh and the staff at the Army Records Office. To the staff at National Archives, Imperial War Museum, Liddell Hart Centre for Military Archives, and the Kings College London Archive, and to many others who took the time to respond to my enquiries.

This book is dedicated to my friend David Abbott, who died tragically and suddenly of Covid as I was finishing this manuscript. He would never have joined the British Army, nor could any institution have contained him. To paraphrase another writer, he was one of God's own prototypes, never even considered for mass production and was too rare to die. He lived by the motto: 'You've got a brain, use it.'

Bibliography

Alanbrooke, Field Marshall Lord *War Diaries 1939–1945* (Weidenfeld & Nicolson, 2001).

Almonds-Windmill, Lorna *Gentleman Jim. The Wartime story of a founder of the SAS and Special Forces* (Constable & Robinson Ltd, 2001).

Arthur, Max *Men of the Red Beret* (Hutchinson, 1990).

Avery, Julian *Approach March* (Hutchinson & Co., 1973).

Badoglio, Pietro *Italy in the Second World War. Memories and documents* (Oxford University Press, 1948).

Barnett, Correlli *The Desert Generals* (Castle Books, 2004).

Bagnold, Ralph A., *Sand, Wind and War. Memoirs of a Desert Explorer* (University of Arizona Press, 1990).

Baynes, John *The Forgotten Victor* (Brassey's, 1989).

Bird, Michael *Samuel Shepherd of Cairo* (Michael Joseph, 1957).

Byrne, J W *The General Salutes a Soldier* (Robert Hale, 1986).

Carroll, Joseph T, *Ireland in the War Years 1939 – 1945* (David and Charles, 1975).

Chapman, F. Spencer *The Jungle is Neutral* (Chatto and Windus, 1949).

Churchill, Winston *Painting as a Pastime* (Odhams, 1948).

Churchill, Winston, *The Second World War. Vols I-V* (Cassell, 1949).

Clark, Lloyd *Anzio* (Headline Review, 2006).

Clarke, Dudley *Golden Arrow* (Hodder and Stoughton, 1955).

Clarke, Dudley *Seven Assignments* (Jonathan Cape, 1948).

Clarke, TEB *This is Where I Came In* (Michael Joseph, 1974).

Combined Operations 1940-1942 (HMSO, 1943).

Connell, John *Wavell, Scholar and Soldier* (Collins, 1964).

Connell, John, *Auchinleck,* (Cassell, 1959).

Cooper, Johnny *One of the Originals* (Pan Books, 1991).

Crichton-Stuart, Michael *G Patrol* (William Kimber, 1958).

Currie, Eve *Journey Among Warriors* (William Heineman Ltd, 1943).

Davis, Peter *SAS Men in the Making* (Pen & Sword Military, 2015).

De Guigand, Freddie *Generals at War* (Hodder and Stoughton, 1964).

De Guingand, Freddie *Operation Victory* (Hodder and Stoughton, 1947).

Dillon, Martin and Bradford, Roy *Rogue Warrior of the SAS* (John Murray, 1987).

Dixon, Norman F. *On the Psychology of Military Incompetence* (Basic Books, 1976).

Dunning, J. *The British Commando: The origins and special training of an elite unit* (Paladin, 2000).

Fleming, Peter *Invasion 1940* (Rupert Hart-Davis, 1957).

Gilbert, Martin *Winston Churchill: Road to Victory, 1941-1945* (Rosetta Books 2015).

Greacen, Lavinia *Chink. A Biography* (MacMillan, 1989).

Guderian, Heinz *Achtung-Panzer!* (Cassel Military 1999, first published in Germany 1937).

Guderian, Heinz *Panzer Leader* (Penguin 2000, Dutton, 1952).

Halder, Franz, *The Halder War Diary 1939–1942*, edited by Charles Burdick and Hans-Adolf Jacobsen (Presido, 1988).

Harrison, D.I. *These Men Are Dangerous* (Cassell & Company Ltd, 1957).

Hart, Liddell *The Strategy of the Indirect Approach* (Faber and Faber, 1967, 1941).

Hemingway, Ernest *A Moveable Feast* (Arrow Books, 2004, Jonathan Cape, 1936).

Hemingway, Ernest *For Whom the Bell Tolls* (Jonathan Cape, 1941).

Hemingway, Ernest *In Our Time* (Scribner Paperback Fiction 1996, Charles Scribner, 1925).

Holt, Thaddeus *The Deceivers* (Orion Books, 2004).

Humphreys, Andrew, *Grand Hotels of Egypt: In the Golden Age of Travel* (American University in Cairo Press, 2015).

Hyam, Ronald *Empire and Sexuality* (Manchester University Press, 1990).

Ibrahim, Tarek *Shepheard's of Cairo* (Reichert Verlag Wiesbaden, 2019).

Ireland, Josh *Churchill & Son* (John Murray, 2021).

James, Malcolm *Born of the Desert* (Collins, 1945).

John, Evan *Time in the East* (Heineman, 1946).

Keyes, Elizabeth *Geoffrey Keyes V.C. of the Rommel Raid* (George Newnes, 1956).

Lawrence, T.E. *Seven Pillars of Wisdom. A Triumph. Volume 1.* (Jonathan Cape, 1939 reprint).

Lewes, John *Jock Lewes. Co-founder of the SAS* (Pen & Sword, 2000).

Lloyd-Owen, David *The Desert my Dwelling Place* (Cassell, 1957).

Longden, Sean *Dunkirk, the Men They Left Behind* (Constable, 2008).

Lovat, Lord *A March Past. A memoir by Lord Lovat* (Weidenfeld and Nicolson, 1979).

Macintyre, Ben *SAS: Rogue Heroes. The Authorized Wartime History* (Viking, 2016).

Macksey, Kenneth *Armoured Crusader: Major Gen. Percy Hobart* (Hutchinson and Co., 1967).

Maclean, Fitzroy *Eastern Approaches* (Jonathan Cape, 1949).

Maclean, Stewart *SAS. The History of the Special Raiding Squadron* (Spellmount, 2006).

Manstein, Field Marshal Erich von *Lost Victories* (Zenith Press, 1982).

Mather, Carol *When the Grass Stops Growing* (Leo Cooper, 1997).

McHarg, Ian *Litani River* (SHM, 2011).

McLuskey, J.Fraser *Parachute Padre* (Spa Books, 1985).

Mitchell, Stewart *St Valery and its Aftermath. The Gordon Highlanders captured in France 1940* (Pen and Sword, 2017).

Montgomery of Alamein, *The Memoirs of Field-Marshall the Viscount Montgomery of Alamein, K.G.* (Collins, 1958).

Mortimer, Gavin *Stirling's Men* (Weidenfeld and Nicolson, 2004).

Neave, Airey *They Have Their Exits* (Leo Cooper, 1953; Pen and Sword, 2013).

Neillands, Robin *The Raiders: Army Commandos, 1940–46* (Weidenfield & Nicolson, 1989).

Nelson, Nina *Shepheard's Hotel* (Barrie and Rockliff, 1960).

Nicolson, Nigel *Alex. The Life of Field Marshal Earl Alexander of Tunis* (Weidenfeld and Nicolson, 1973).

Niven, David *The Moon's a Balloon* (Hamish Hamilton, 1971).

Ohler, Norman *Blitzed: Drugs in Nazi Germany* (Penguin, 2017).

Oliver, David *Airborne Espionage: International special duty operations in the world wars* (The History Press, 2005).

Parkinson, Roger *The Auk, Auchinleck, Victor at Alamein* (Granada, 1977).

Peniakoff, Vladimir 'Popski' *Private Army* (Jonathan Cape, 1950).

Pressfield, Steven *The War of Art* (Black Irish Entertainment, 2002).

Prochiantz, Alec *Promenons-nous dans les bois* (Société des Écrivains, 2011).

Ranfurly, Hermione *To War with Whitaker* (William Heinemann, 1994).

Rankin, Nicholas *Churchill's Wizards. The British Genius for Deception* (Faber and Faber, 2008).

Rasmussen, Nicolas *On Speed; From Benzedrine to Adderall* (New York University Press, 2009).

Roberts, Andrew *The Storm of War* (Penguin, 2010).

Rommel, Erwin *The Rommel Papers* (Collins, 1953).

Ross, Hamish *Paddy Mayne* (Sutton 2003).

Sansom, A.W. *I Spied Spies* (George G. Harrap & Co, 1965).

Shaw, Bill Kennedy *Long Range Desert Group* (Collins, 1945).

Smith, Peter C. *Close Air Support* (Orion Books, 1990).

Tedder, Lord *With Prejudice* (Cassell, 1966).

Timpson, Alistair *In Rommel's Backyard: A memoir of the Long Range Desert Group* (Pen & Sword, 2000).

Troy, Thomas F. *Donovan and the CIA. A history of the establishment of the Central Intelligence Agency* (University Publications of America, 1981).

Ward, Arthur *Resisting the Nazi Invader* (Constable and Company Ltd, 1997).

Warner, Philip *The SAS. The official history* (Time Warner Books, 1988).

Waugh, Evelyn *Officers and Gentlemen* (Penguin Classics, 2001).

Waugh, Evelyn *The Diaries of Evelyn Waugh*, edited by Michael Davie (Weidenfeld and Nicolson, 1976).

Wellstead, Ian *SAS with the Maquis* (Frontline, 2016).

Welstead, Ian *With the SAS across the Rhine* (Frontline Books, 2020).

Woodman, Richard *Malta Convoys 1940–1943* (John Murray, 2003).

Endnotes

HMSO His/ Her Majesty's Stationery Office
IWM Imperial War Museum
NA National Archives

To make the references as helpful as possible, repeated references have been consolidated and moved to the end of the relevant section.

Chapter 1

1 Dudley Clarke, *Seven Assignments* (Jonathan Cape, 1948), p. 13.
2 IWM 8080, 'Private Papers of Brigadier DW Clarke CBE CB.' Unless otherwise stated, details about Clarke's life are from either Clarke, *Seven Assignments*, or IWM 8080.
3 IWM 8080, letter, 'Dear Dad', 10 Sept 1916.
4 Nina Nelson, *Shepheard's Hotel* (Barrie and Rockliff, 1960), p. 88; IWM 8080, 'A Quarter of my Century.'
5 IWM 8080, Clarke's passport issued 14th November 1940.
6 Kenyon Jones, 'The Road Uphill: episodes in a long life' (Oxuniprint, Oxford University Press 1997) cited by Nicholas Rankin, *Churchill's Wizards. The British Genius for deception* (Faber and Faber, 2008), p. 478; Dudley Clarke, *Golden Arrow* (Hodder and Stoughton, 1955), p. 10. Clarke's description of his fictional creation in the novel, Colonel Giles Wreford.
7 Most Cairo premises of the time used Serbo-Croat speaking staff to provide security.
8 Ralph A. Bagnold, *Sand, Wind and War. Memoirs of a Desert Explorer* (University of Arizona Press, 1990), p. 120.

9 Bagnold, *Sand, Wind and War*, p. 8.

10 Bagnold, *Sand, Wind and War*, p. 30, p. 54.

11 Bagnold, *Sand, Wind and War*, p. 65.

12 IWM 9862, Bagnold, Ralph Alger, oral history.

13 Bagnold, *Sand, Wind and War*, p. 87.

14 Kenneth Macksey, *Armoured Crusader: Major Gen. Percy Hobart* (Hutchinson and Co., 1967), Part 2, Development, Ch.s 6 – 8.

15 Bagnold, *Sand, Wind and War*, p. 121.

16 IWM 8080, The 8th Battalion The Sherwood Foresters Campaign in Norway 1940. Colonel E.G.C Beckwith, 1958.

17 Airey Neave, *They Have Their Exits.'* (Leo Cooper, 1953; Pen and Sword, 2013), p. 8.

18 Neave, *They Have Their Exits,* p. 10.

Chapter 2

1 Joseph T. Carroll, *Ireland in the War Years 1939 – 1945* (David and Charles, 1975), p. 41.

2 IWM 8080, letter Joe Carroll to Clarke, 27 October 1972.

3 Carroll, *Ireland in the War Years*, p. 43.

4 NA DO 121/83, 'Records of talks with Mr de Valera, Head of Eire Government, and Mr Malcolm Macdonald' Declassified Feb 15, 2001.

5 University College Dublin Archive. 'Proposals by the British Government presented to de Valera by Malcolm MacDonald [Minister for Health] on 26 June 1940.'

6 Winston Churchill, *The Second World War. Vol 2. Their Finest Hour* (Cassell, 1949), p. 73.

7 IWM 8080, 'We Call them Commandos' Radio Broadcast transcript; Clarke, *Seven Assignments*, p. 205.

8 IWM 8080, 'We Call them Commandos'; Clarke, *Seven Assignments*, p. 206.

9 Clarke, *Seven Assignments*. There is no record of the original pitch in Clarke's papers. The record is from Clarke's radio broadcast and *Seven Assignments*, pp. 206 – 207.

10 IWM 8080, 'We Call them Commandos'; Clarke, *Seven Assignments*, p. 208.

11 IWM 8080, letter Gen. Sir Alan Bourne to Clarke, 24 January 1959.

12 IWM 8080, 'A Quarter of my Century'.

13 IWM 8080, 'We Call them Commandos'.

14 John Connell, *Auchinleck*, (Cassell, 1959), p. 141.

15 NA DEFE 2/699, 'Operations in Northern Norway: 13 May 1940 to 8 June 1940.'

16 Parsons, Second World War Experience Centre (SWWEC) https://war-experience.org.

17 IWM 8080, 'A Quarter of my Century'; NA CAB/24/240/11, 'Recent persecution in Germany of Jews and other persons. Despatch from His Majesty's Ambassador in Berlin to Sec of State for foreign affairs.'

18 See David Niven, *The Moon's a Balloon* (Hamish Hamilton, 1971) for all details of Niven's involvement unless otherwise stated.

19 Women's Auxiliary Air Force.

20 IWM 8080, *Herald Tribune* cutting, Paris, 19 October 1945.

21 IWM 8080, Press cutting of Hilary St George Sanders, *The Green Beret* (Michael Joseph), filed 3 December 1949.

22 'Combined Operations 1940-1942' (HMSO, 1943), p. 25.

23 *The Times*, 27 June 1940.

24 Stirling family 8mm film footage courtesy of Adam Curtiss.

25 F. Spencer Chapman, *The Jungle is Neutral* (Chatto and Windus, 1949), p. 7. Only the 1949 edition carries the description of special forces. It was redacted from subsequent editions.

26 Lord Lovat, *A March Past. A memoir by Lord Lovat* (Weidenfeld and Nicolson, 1979), p. 178.

27 Chapman, *The Jungle is Neutral*, p. 6.

28 Lovat, *A March Past*, p. 180.

29 Chapman, *The Jungle is Neutral*, p. 6.

30 J. Dunning, *The British Commando: The origins and special training of an elite unit* (Paladin, 2000), p. 21.

31 Chapman, *The Jungle is Neutral*, p. 6.

32 Lieutenant Tony Deane-Drummond in Max Arthur, *Men of the Red Beret* (Hutchinson, 1990), p. 14.

33 IWM 8080, letter Gen. Sir Alan Bourne to Clarke, 24 January 1959.

34 NA DEFE 2/1, 'War diary of the Independent Companies', memo by the Director of Combined Operations, 23 June 1940.

35 NA WO 193/405, 'Combined Operations' Memo - Winston Churchill to General Ismay, 2 July 1940.

36 NA WO 218/3, 'War Diary No.3 Commando. Plymouth.'

37 NA WO 218/3, 'War Diary No.3 Commando. Plymouth.'

38 NA PREM 3/330/9, 'Letter to Sec. State for War.'

39 NA PREM 3/330/9, Ismay, Nov 1940.

40 NA PREM 3/330/1, 'Appointment of Roger Keyes as Director Combined Operations.'

41 NA DEFE 2/1.

42 Major Tony Hibbert in Arthur, *Men of the Red Beret*, p. 2.

43 British Parachute Regiment Archive.

44 NA DEFE 2/1, Air needs of irregular forces, 2 August 1940.

45 NA DEFE 2/1, Air needs of irregular forces, 2 August 1940.

46 NA DEFE 2/1, memo for the Chiefs of Staff, 12 October 1940.

47 Clarke, *Seven Assignments*, p. 219.

48 Roger Parkinson, *The Auk, Auchinleck, Victor at Alamein* (Granada, 1977), p. 71. Auchinleck and Ritchie left for India 27 Dec 1940.

49 *Pegasus Journal of the Parachute Regiment and Airborne Forces* 1 (4) January 1947.

50 *Pegasus Journal of the Parachute Regiment and Airborne Forces* 1 (4) January 1947, Sketch by Bryan de Grineau.

51 IWM 8080, Passport 1940.

Chapter 3

1 This and further details of his service come from Fraser's Army Record, Army Personnel Centre, Historical Disclosures.

2 Gordon Highlanders Museum, *The Tiger and Sphinx* (March 1937).

3 Stewart Mitchell, *St Valery and its Aftermath. The Gordon Highlanders captured in France 1940* (Pen and Sword, 2017), p. 42; NA WO 167-744/1, 1st Bn Gordon Highlanders War Diary 1940.

4 NA WO 167-744/1; JW Byrne, *The General Salutes a Soldier* (Robert Hale, 1986), p. 10.

5 Gordon Barber, RHA, 51st Highland Div, in Sean Longden, *Dunkirk, the Men They Left Behind* (Constable, 2008), p. 125.

6 51st Highland Division, Tom Gardside, RASC, written account by his son, Jim Gardside.

7 Captain Rhoderick Macleod, https://eastlothianatwar.co.uk, 165 Officer Cadet Training Unit, Dunbar.

8 Liddell Hart Centre for Military Archives, LAYCOCK 1/3, The War Office, 9 June 1940, letter addressed to officers commanding all battalions.

9 Alan Orton, *Bill Fraser L Detachment's Forgotten Hero*. Unpublished paper.

10 Ian McHarg, *Litani River* (SHM, 2011), p. 27.

11 This and subsequent details about Keyes taken from Elizabeth Keyes, *Geoffrey Keyes V.C. Of the Rommel Raid* (George Newnes, 1956); McHarg, *Litani River*; Keyes, *Geoffrey Keyes*, pp. 22 – 6.

12 Sir Thomas Macpherson quoted in Hamish Ross, *Paddy Mayne* (Sutton, 2003), p. 46.

13 Reg Harmer interview; AG Lappin, *Black Hackle: The Story of the 11th (Scottish Commando)*, unpublished, cited Ian McHarg, *Litani River*, p. 22 – 26.

14 Arran is Waugh's fictional 'Isle of Mugg' in Evelyn Waugh, *Officers and Gentlemen* (Penguin Classics, 2001), pp. 46 – 47.

15 Lappin, *Black Hackle*, cited Ian McHarg, *Litani River*, p. 43.

16 NA DEFE 2/1.

17 NA DEFE 2/699, Brig. Layock 'Early History: The Origin and Work of the commandos.'

18 Evelyn Waugh, *The Diaries of Evelyn Waugh*, edited by Michael Davie (Weidenfeld and Nicolson, 1976), p. 493.

19 Kings College London Archive, LAYCOCK, Maj Gen Sir Robert Edward (1907-1968) papers – box 2/5.

20 IWM 8080, letter Gen. Sir Alan Bourne to Clarke, 24 January 1959.

21 Waugh, *Diaries*, p. 493.

22 NA WO 218/166, 'War Diary Z Force HQ Layforce 28th Jan 41- 24th Feb 41.'

Chapter 4

1 Michael Crichton-Stuart, *G Patrol* (William Kimber, 1958), p. 54.

2 NA CAB 154/1, 'A Force Narrative War Diary.'

3 Evan Jones, *Time in the East* (William Heinemann, 1946), p. 25.

4 WB Kennedy Shaw, *Long Range Desert Group* (Collins, 1945), p. 16; Pietro Badoglio, *Italy in the Second World War. Memories and documents* (Oxford University Press, 1948), p. 14.

5 Bagnold, *Sand, Wind and War*, p. 128.

6 Shaw, *Long Range Desert Group*, p. 45.

7 Bagnold, *Sand, Wind and War*, p. 67.

8 Bagnold, *Sand, Wind and War*, p. 131.

9 Correlli Barnett, *The Desert Generals* (Castle Books, 2004), p. 37.

10 John Connell, *Wavell. Scholar and Soldier* (Collins, 1964), pp 164 – 165.

11 See Lavinia Greacen, *Chink. A Biography* (MacMillan, 1989), p. 95.

12 John Baynes, *The Forgotten Victor* (Brassey's, 1989), p. 22.

13 Lavinia Greacen, *Chink*, p. 163.

14 NA CAB 154/1, 13 November 1940 to 31 December 1941.

15 This and further details from NA WO 169/24904, 'Plan "ABEAM"' unless otherwise stated

16 NA CAB 154/1, 13 November 1940 to 31 December 1941.

17 NA DEFE 2/152, 'Operation Colossus.'

18 NA DEFE 2/152.

19 NA CAB 154/1, 13 November 1940 to 31 December 1941.

20 IWM 8080, letters, 'Dear Mum', 6 September 1918, 17 September 1918, 1 October 1918.

21 NA CAB 154/1, 13 November 1940 to 31 December 1941.

22 IWM 8179, Ritchie, Neil Methuen, oral history.

23 TE Lawrence, *Seven Pillars of Wisdom. A Triumph*. Volume 1 (Jonathan Cape, 1939 reprint), Akaba deception and capture, Book IV; shooting camel, p. 310.

24 Crichton-Stuart, *G Patrol*, p. 27.

25 Shaw, *Long Range Desert Group*, p. 61.

26 Crichton-Stuart, *G Patrol*, p. 50.

27 Crichton-Stuart, *G Patrol*, p 63.

28 Connell, *Wavell*, p. 321.

29 Greacen, *Chink*, p. 169.

30 NA DEFE 2/152, 'Operation Colossus.'

31 This and following details from Arthur, *Men of the Red Beret*, Ch. 2, and NA DEFE 2/152, 'Operation Colossus.'

32 NA PREM 3/100, 'Operation COLOSSUS in Italy' - *PM's enquiry*.

33 Lawrence, *Seven Pillars*. Volume 1, p. 198.

Chapter 5

1 NA WO 218/166.

2 NA WO 218/166.

3 Greacen, *Chink*, p. 169 – 170.

4 Greacen, *Chink*, p. 170.

5 Winston Churchill, *Painting as a Pastime* (Odhams, 1948), p. 37.

6 NA CAB 154/1, 13 November 1940 to 31 December 1941.

7 Erwin Rommel, *The Rommel Papers* (Collins, 1953), p. 100.

8 Rommel, *Papers*, p. 101.

9 Connell, *Wavell*, p. 334.

10 NA WO 201/713.

11 NA WO 201/713.

12 Waugh, *Diaries*, p. 494.

13 John Lewes, *Jock Lewes. Co-founder of the SAS* (Pen & Sword, 2000), Ch.s 5 – 7.

14 NA WO 218/166.

15 NA PREM 3/103/2, 'Use of Benzedrine'. PM personal minute 29.3.41.

16 Norman Ohler, *Blitzed: Drugs in Nazi Germany* (Penguin, 2017), Ch.s 1, 2; Nicolas Rasmussen, *On Speed: From Benzedrine to Adderall* (New York University Press, 2009), Ch.s 1–3.

17 NA PREM 3/103/2, 'Use of Benzedrine'.

18 TEB Clarke, *This is Where I Came In* (Michael Joseph, 1974), p. 113.

19 NA WO 201/713 'Operations Abstention and Blunt.' Feb/March 1941; NA CAB 154/1. ' "A" Force Narrative War Diary', 13 November 1940 to 31 December 1941.

20 Unless annotated Clarke's narrative from NA CAB 154/1.

21 IWM 8080, 'A Quarter of my Century'.

22 Unless annotated Clarke's narrative from NA CAB 154/1.

23 Evan John, *Time in the East* (Heineman, 1946), pp. 24 – 25.

24 Jones, *The Road Uphill* (1997), cited in Rankin, *Churchill's Wizards*, p. 478.

25 IWM 8080, The Origin of 'Cheese' Kenyon Jones.

26 Rommel, *Papers*, p. 102.

27 Baynes, *The Forgotten Victor*, p. 133.

28 Connell, *Wavell*, p. 393.

29 NA CAB 154/1.

30 NA CAB 154/1.

31 Rommel, *Papers*, p. 111.

32 NA WO 218/166.

33 Greacen, *Chink*, p. 173.

34 NA WO 218/166.

35 NA CAB 154/1.

36 NA CAB 154/1.

37 Navy, Army and Air Force Institutes.

38 NA CAB 154/1.

39 National Archive WO 218/171 '11 Commando ("C" Bn. Layforce) War Diary.'

40 NA WO 218/166.

41 NA WO 218/166.

42 NA WO 218/171.

43 NA WO 218/171.

Chapter 6

1 NA CAB 154/1. The Ambassador; Sir Hughe Knatchbull-Hugessen.

2 NA CAB 154/1.

3 NA CAB 154/1.

4 NA CAB 154/1.

5 NA CAB 154/1; NA WO 169/24904 'Plan "ABEAM"', letter to De Guingand 26 May 1941.

6 NA WO 169/24904 'Plan "ABEAM"', letter to De Guingand, 26 May 1941.

7 NA WO 169/24904 'Plan "ABEAM"', letter to De Guingand, 26 May 1941.

8 Robert Ruark *One for the World* (Collier's magazine, 4 September 1953), cited Andrew Humphreys, http://grandhotelsegypt.com, joescialom.

9 AW Sansom, *I Spied Spies* (George G. Harrap & Co, 1965). *Spies*, p. 89.

10 Sansom, *I Spied Spies*, p. 89.

11 NA CAB 154/1.

12 NA CAB 154/1.

13 NA WO 218/171.

14 HH Butler quoted in Michael Asher, *Get Rommel*, Ch. 6.

15 Robin Neillands, *The Raiders: Army commandos, 1940–46* (Weidenfield & Nicolson, 1989), p. 85.

16 NA WO 218/171.

17 Neillands, *Raiders*, p. 86.

18 Neillands, *Raiders*, pp. 87 – 88.

19 NA WO 218/171. Tevendale's account is missing from the archive.

20 NA WO 218/171.

21 Gerald Bryan collection, McHarg, *Litani River*, p. 118.

22 Neillands, *Raiders*.

23 NA WO 218/171. Fraser's sketch map of the action is missing from the archive.

24 Letter to his brother, 15 July 1941, cited in Martin Dillon, *Rogue Warrior to the SAS* (John Murray, 1987), p. 23, and Ross, *Paddy Mayne. SAS*, pp. 41 – 42.

25 Byrne, *The General Salutes a Soldier*, p. 12.

26 NA WO 218/171.

27 Humpheries collection in McHarg, *Litani River*, p. 156

28 NA CAB 154/1.

29 NA CAB 154/1.

30 Geoffrey Keyes personal diary, cited in Asher, *Get Rommel*, Ch. 12.

31 Ohler, *Blitzed*, Ch. 3.

32 Geoffrey Keyes personal diary, cited in Asher, *Get Rommel*, Ch. 12.

33 NA WO 218/171.

34 NA WO 201/716. Layforce. Keyes letter to Laycock, 14 July 1941.

Chapter 7

1 Franz Halder, *The Halder War Diary 1939–1942*, edited by Charles Burdick and Hans-Adolf Jacobsen (Presido, 1988), entries for 11 May p. 385, and 25 April, p. 374.

2 Barnett, *The Desert Generals*, p. 72.

3 NA CAB 154/1.

4 Churchill, *The Second World War. Volume III*, p. 277.

5 NA CAB 154/1.

6 Rommel, *Papers*, p. 141.

7 Bagnold, *Sand, Wind and War*, p. 134.

8 Weaver Aircraft Company of Ohio.

9 WO 169/24882, 'A Force use of deception', handwritten on request to de Guingand, 'arranged verbally . . . First day probably 6 June.'

10 NA WO 218/166.

11 NA WO 218/166, letter, Laycock to Smith 6 May 1941.

12 NA WO 218/166.

13 Waugh, *Diaries*, p. 497.

14 NA WO 201/731 'Special Forces. Operational Questions.'

15 Carol Mather, *When the Grass Stops Growing* (Leo Cooper, 1997), Ch. 8.

16 IWM 21759, TVS, SAS Interviews, Box No 62/137/1.

17 IWM 8080. See Clarke's appointment diary, 4 May 1942, Stirling 9.0.

18 21 May, Clarke arrives back from Lebanon. 15 June, Stirling admitted with parachute injury.

19 IWM 21759, Stirling.

20 IWM 8179, Ritchie, Neil Methuen (Oral history), tape cassette 8179/21/01-02.

21 IWM 8179.

22 NA WO 218/173, 'L Detachment SAS Brigade (later 1 SAS Regt): formation, training and report of operations.' Guardsman D'Arcy Irish Guards July 1941 report; Virgina Cowles, *The Phantom Major* (Collins, 1958), p. 20.

23 NA CAB 154/1, 13 November 1940 to 31 December 1941.

24 NA WO 218/173.

25 NA CAB 154/1.

26 NA WO 218/173.

27 John Lewes, *Jock Lewes*, Ch. 8.

28 NA WO 218/173.

29 NA WO 218/173.

30 NA WO 218/173.

31 Barnett, *The Desert Generals*, p. 75.

32 Analysis, Norman F Dixon, *On the Psychology of Military Incompetence* (Basic Books, 1976), pp. 152 – 153.

33 Connell, *Auchinleck*, p. 233.

34 Rommel, *Papers*, p. 141.

35 Hermoine Ranfurly, *To War with Whitaker* (William Heinemann, 1994), Ch. 4, 22 June 1941 Cairo, Egypt.

36 Crichton-Stuart, *G Patrol*, p. 94.

37 IWM 21759, Stirling.

38 Mather, *When the Grass Stops Growing*, Ch. 8.

39 IWM 21759, Stirling.

40 NA CAB 154/1.

41 NA CAB 154/1.

42 NA CAB 154/1.

43 Greacen, *Chink*, p. 182. See also Dorman-Smith's use of 'our new Fords . . . I'd been a fast driver once.', p. 183.

44 Halder, *Diary*, p. 515.

45 Parkinson, *The Auk*, p. 29.

46 Cowles, *The Phantom Major*, p. 23.

Chapter 8

1 From minutes of conference unless annotated, NA WO 169/24904 'Plan "ABEAM"', 1000hrs on 27 Jul 41.

2 Hoe, *David Stirling*, p. 71.

3 NA WO 201/716 'Layforce – A.G. – Questions Feb/July 1941.'

4 NA WO 218/171.

5 NA PREM 3/330/9.

6 NA WO 201/716.

7 NA WO 218/171.

8 Keyes, *Geoffrey Keyes*, p. 192.

9 Arthur Phillips Army Record, Army Personnel Centre, Support Division, Historical Disclosures.

10 Commander Philip Noel, VRD RNR, Combined Operations, combinedops.com.

11 NA CAB 154/1, 13 November 1940 to 31 December 1941.

12 Gavin Mortimer, *Stirling's Men* (Weidenfeld and Nicolson, 2004), p. 19.

13 Lewes, *Jock Lewes*, Ch. 8.

14 Lewes, *Jock Lewes*, Ch. 9.

15 Hoe, *David Stirling*, p. 60.

16 Lewes, *Jock Lewes*, Ch. 10.

17 Jeremiah 45:5, cited in Lewes, *Jock Lewes*, Ch. 11.

18 Lewes, *Jock Lewes*, Ch. 11.

19 IWM 21759, Bennett.

20 IWM 21759, Seekings.

21 IWM 21759, Seekings.

22 Malcom James, *Born of the Desert* (Collins, 1945). James is pseudonym for Pleydell, p. 41.

23 NA CAB 154/1.

24 NA WO 193/405.

25 IWM 8080.

26 Thomas F Troy, *Donovan and the CIA. A history of the establishment of the Central Intelligence Agency* (University Publications of America, 1981).

27 Alastair Timpson, *In Rommel's Backyard: A memoir of the Long Range Desert Group* (Pen & Sword, 2000), p. 37.

28 Timpson, *In Rommel's Backyard*, p. 40.

29 Timpson, *In Rommel's Backyard*, p. 40.

30 NA WO 201/731 'Special Forces: operational questions. 1941 Mar 15-1942 Mar 29'.

31 Lewes, *Jock Lewes*, Ch. 2.

32 IWM 21759, Seekings.

33 IWM 21759, Bennet.

34 Tarek Ibrahim, *Shepheard's of Cairo* (Reichert Verlag Wiesbaden, 2019).

35 Mather, *When the Grass Stops Growing*, Ch. 8.

36 Commander D.F. Bird RN to author.

37 IWM 21759, Bennet.

38 James, *Born of the Desert*, p. 57; *Mars & Minerva: The Journal of the Special Air Service* (2) December 1996. Malcom James's [Pledyell's] account

of contemporary parachute training says 'One', not the modern instruction, 'Go'.

39 James, *Born of the Desert*; *Mars & Minerva*, p. 57: *The Journal of the Special Air Service* (2) December 1996.

40 IWM 21759, Bennet.

41 Johnny Cooper, *One of the Originals* (Pan Books, 1991), p. 20.

42 Du Vivier's account, Mortimer, *Stirling's Men*, p. 19.

43 Cooper, *One of the Originals*, p. 20.

44 Mortimer, *Stirling's Men*, p. 31.

45 IWM 21759, Bennet.

46 Pathe Gazette, *The Voice of Britain, Paratroops In The Middle East* (1941).

47 Pathe Gazette, *The Voice of Britain*.

48 NA WO 201/811 'Prendergast's LRDG file Nov 41 – Feb 42'.

49 Timpson, *In Rommel's Backyard*, p. 53.

50 For descriptions of Sand Sea and LRDG see Shaw, *Long Range Desert Group*, Ch. 3; Crichton-Stuart, *G Patrol*, Ch. 2.

51 Timpson, *In Rommel's Backyard*, p. 56.

52 NA WO 218/89, LRDG War Diary, Jul–Dec 1941.

53 NA WO 218/89.

54 NA CAB 154/1.

55 NA WO 218/89.

56 Keyes, *Geoffrey Keyes*, p. 198.

57 Laycock's citation to Keyes's VC.

58 NA CAB 154/1; Fritz Bayerlin, Rommel, *Papers*, p. 158.

59 NA CAB 154/1.

60 NA CAB 154/1.

61 Kenneth Benton, 'The ISOS Years: Madrid 1941-3', *Journal of Contemporary History* (30) 3 (1995), p. 377.

62 NA FO 1093/252. Handwritten on Secret and Personal, 19 October 1941.

63 NA FO 1093/252. Handwritten on Secret and Personal, 19 October 1941.

64 NA CAB 154/1.

65 IWM 8080.

66 NA FO 1093/252.

67 Account of raid in Keyes, *Geoffrey Keyes;* Panzergruppe Afrika report 18/11/41. Appendix to Keyes, *Geoffrey Keyes,* unless annotated.

68 Panzergruppe Afrika report 18/11/41. Appendix to Keyes, *Geoffrey Keyes.* Campbell and Keyes had pistols. Terry and Coulthard had Tommy guns. This assumes Keyes was wounded.

69 Panzergruppe Afrika report 18/11/41. Appendix to Keyes, *Geoffrey Keyes.*

70 Asher, *Get Rommel*, Ch. 28.

71 Panzergruppe Afrika report 18/11/41. Appendix to Keyes, *Geoffrey Keyes.*

72 BL Add MS 82529 'Lord Roger Keyes files'.

73 BL Add MS 82529 'Lord Roger Keyes files'.

74 Asher, *Get Rommel*, Ch. 30.

Chapter 9

1 Connell, *Auchinleck*, pp. 336 – 337.

2 Timpson, *In Rommel's Backyard*, p. 65.

3 NA WO 218/89.

4 IWM 21759, Seekings.

5 Lewes, *Jock Lewes*. Ch. 11.

6 IWM 21759, Seekings.

7 Stevens, *The Originals*, p. 63.

8 IWM 21759, Seekings.

9 Mortimer, *Stirling's Men*, p. 23.

10 Stevens, *The Originals*, p. 65.

11 Mortimer, *Stirling's Men*, p. 23.

12 Mortimer, *Stirling's Men*, p. 24.

13 Ross, *Paddy Mayne*, p. 64.

14 IWM 21759, Seekings.

15 Ross, *Paddy Mayne*, p. 64.

16 Timini Airfield.

17 Ross, *Paddy Mayne*, p. 64.

18 Du Vivier, Mortimer, *Stirling's Men*, p. 26.

19 Hoe, *David Stirling*, p. 101.

20 Ross, *Paddy Mayne*, p. 65.

21 IWM 21759, Seekings.

22 IWM 21759, Seekings.

23 Philip Warner, *The SAS. The official history* (Time Warner Books, 1988), p. 14 – 15.

24 NA WO 218/89.

25 Mortimer, *Stirling's Men*, p. 27.

26 NA WO 218/89.

27 Lloyd-Owen, *The Desert my Dwelling Place* (Cassell, 1957), p. 113.

28 NA WO 218/89.

29 Stevens, *The Originals*, p. 75.

30 Mortimer, *Stirling's Men*, p. 28.

31 NA WO 218/89.

32 WO 218/99 'LRDG War Diary Jul –Dec 1941.'

33 Wolgang Erdmann, 'Suggestion for preferential promotion of the Hauptmann and Group Commander of Nachtschl.Gr. 7 Theodor Blaich', 15 March 1944. This relates to Blaich's operations against Tito's partisans.

34 NA WO 218/89.

35 IWM 21759, Seekings; NA CAB 154/1.

36 Julian Avery, *Approach March* (Hutchinson & Co., 1973), p. 286.

37 Ronal Hyam, *Empire and Sexuality* (Manchester University Press, 1990), p. 5.

38 Connell, *Auchinleck*, p. 333; NA CAB 154/1.

39 Fritz Bayerlin, Rommel, *Papers*, p. 158.

40 Fritz Bayerlin, Rommel, *Papers*, p. 158.

41 Churchill, *The Second World War. Volume III*, p. 434.

42 Fellers cable, no. 279 Milid, Washington from Duke, 30 November 1941.

43 Fritz Bayerlin, Rommel, *Papers,* p. 161.

44 Barnett, *The Desert Generals*, p. 117.

45 Connell, *Auchinleck*, p 365.

46 Letter, General Auchinleck to General Smith, 5 December 1941; Connell, *Auchinleck*, p. 393.

47 Eve Currie, *Journey Among Warriors* (William Heineman Ltd, 1943), p. 51.

48 Currie, *Journey Among Warriors*, p. 52.

49 Fritz Bayerlin, Rommel, *Papers*, p. 164.

50 Fritz Bayerlin, Rommel, *Papers*, p. 164.

51 Cowles, *The Phantom Major*, p. 50.

52 Barnett, *The Desert Generals*, p. 120.

53 Cowles, *The Phantom Major*, p. 50.

54 Crichton-Stuart, *G Patrol*, p. 104.

55 NA WO 218/89; Crichton-Stuart, *G Patrol*, Ch. 7; Timpson, *In Rommel's Backyard*, Ch. 2.

56 NA WO 218/89.

57 Fritz Bayerlin, Rommel, *Papers*, pp. 168 – 169.

58 NA WO 201/811.

59 Cowles, *The Phantom Major*, p. 68.

60 NA WO 201/811.

61 IWM 21759, Seekings.

62 NA WO 201/811.

63 11 December 1941. NA WO 201/811.

64 Cowles, *The Phantom Major*, p. 66.

65 Cowles, *The Phantom Major*, p. 66.

66 Stevens, *The Originals*, p. 80.

67 Cowles, *The Phantom Major*, p. 67.

68 NA WO 201/811.

69 Lewes, *Jock Lewes*, Ch. 12.

70 NA WO 201/811.

71 Lewes, *Jock Lewes*, Ch. 12.

72 NA WO 281/94, 'A Squadron LRDG War Diary Apr – Dec 41'.

73 NA WO 281/94.

74 Cowles, *The Phantom Major*, p. 64

75 NA WO 281/94.

76 Unless annotated narrative by Fraser, NA CAB 106/5 Report on operations of the Air Service at Agedabia and Arae Philenorum, 1941 Dec. 19-1942 Jan. 11, by Lieutenant W. Fraser, Gordon Highlanders.

77 NA WO 218/89, LRDG patrol S2 diary of events.

78 Byrne, *The General Salutes a Soldier*, p. 15.

79 Rommel, *Papers*, p. 175.

80 Du Vivier, Mortimer, *Stirling's Men*, p. 32.

81 Byrne, *The General Salutes a Soldier*, p. 15.

82 Byrne, *The General Salutes a Soldier*, p. 16.

83 Erwin Rommel to his wife, 22 December 1941, cited in Rommel, *Papers*, p. 175.

Chapter 10

1 Byrne, *The General Salutes a Soldier*, p. 18.

2 Byrne, *The General Salutes a Soldier*, p. 19.

3 IWM 21759, Stirling.

4 NA WO 281/94.

5 Byrne, *The General Salutes a Soldier*, p. 19.

6 Du Vivier, Mortimer, *Stirling's Men*, p. 33

7 NA WO 201/811.

8 NA WO 201/811.

9 NA WO 201/811.

10 Ohler, *Blitzed*, Ch. 3.

11 Halder, *Diary*, 30 Nov 1941, p. 571.

12 Rommel, *Papers*, 25 Dec 1941, p. 176.

13 NA WO 201/811.

14 NA CAB 106/5.

15 Byrne, *The General Salutes a Soldier*, p. 21.

16 Lorna Almonds-Windmill, *Gentleman Jim. The Wartime story of a founder of the SAS and Special Forces* (Constable & Robinson Ltd, 2001), p. 133.

17 NA WO 201/811.

18 NA WO 201/811.

19 Almonds-Windmill, *Gentleman Jim*, p. 134.

20 Almonds-Windmill, *Gentleman Jim*, p. 135.

21 NA WO 201/811 – Sergeant J. Fair's report.

22 Almonds-Windmill, *Gentleman Jim*, p. 136.

23 NA WO 201/811.

24 NA WO 201/811.

25 Jim Storie, in Almonds-Windmill, *Gentleman Jim*, p. 138.

26 NA WO 201/811 – Sergeant J. Fair's report.

27 Almonds-Windmill, *Gentleman Jim*, p. 141.

28 Lewes, *Jock Lewes*, Stirling's letter, Appendix.

29 NA CAB 106/5; Byrne, *The General Salutes a Soldier*, p. 22.

30 NA CAB 154/1.

31 Unless annotated account of their escape; NA CAB 106/5; Byrne, *The General Salutes a Soldier*.

32 Byrne, *The General Salutes a Soldier*, p. 23.

33 Mortimer, *Stirling's Men*, p. 37.

34 Byrne, *The General Salutes a Soldier*, p. 27.

35 Byrne, *The General Salutes a Soldier*, p. 27.

36 Byrne, *The General Salutes a Soldier*, p. 30.

37 Byrne, *The General Salutes a Soldier*, p. 33.

38 Byrne, *The General Salutes a Soldier*, p. 34.

39 NA CAB 106/5.

40 NA CAB 106/5.

41 NA CAB 154/1.

42 NA CAB 154/1.

Chapter 11

1 Fitzroy Maclean, *Eastern Approaches* (Jonathan Cape, 1949), p. 192.

2 Prime Minister to Auchinleck, 11 Jan 1942, Connell, *Auchinleck*, p. 423.

3 General Ritchie to Auchinleck, 'Armoured engagement south of Agedabia' 30 Dec 1941; Connell, *Auchinleck*, p. 419.

4 IWM 8080, 'A Quarter of my Century'.

5 IWM 21759, Stirling.

6 NA WO 201/731.

7 NA WO 201/811.

8 Rommel, *Papers*, p. 180.

9 David Oliver, *Airborne Espionage: International special duty operations in the world wars* (The History Press, 2005), pp. 63 – 65.

10 Rommel, *Papers*, p. 181.

11 Connell, *Auchinleck*, p. 438.

12 Mortimer, *Stirling's Men*, p. 43.

13 David Stirling's Preface to Roy Bradford and Martin Dillon, *Rogue Warrior of the SAS* (John Murray, 1987).

14 Steven Pressfield, *The War of Art* (Black Irish Entertainment, 2002), p. 139.

15 NA CAB 154/2, '"A" Force Narrative War Diary (1st Jan, 1942, to 31st Dec 1942).'

16 IWM 8080, Clarke's 1942 appointments diary.

17 NA CAB 154/2; IWM 8080, Clarke's 1942 appointments diary, 5 February 1942.

18 NA CAB 154/2.

19 Rommel, 'The Italians have taken an Army Corps off me . . .', 23 Feb 42, Rommel, *Papers*, p. 182.

20 NA CAB 154/2.

21 Ranfurly, *To War with Whitaker*, Ch. 5, 19 Oct 41, Jerusalem.

22 Winston Churchill, *The Second World War. Volume IV* (Cassell and Co, 1951), p. 245.

23 Description of LRDG patrol, Maclean, *Eastern Approaches*, p. 208.

24 Description of Jebel, Maclean, *Eastern Approaches*, p. 212.

25 Byrne, *The General Salutes a Soldier*, p. 38.

26 Dillon, *Rogue Warrior*, p. 41.

27 Byrne, *The General Salutes a Soldier*. Ch. 3.

28 IWM 8080, Clarke's 1942 appointments diary; NA WO 201/732 'Special Forces in Middle East', 'The Future of "L" Det.' David Stirling 3 May 1942.

29 WO 201/732 Special Forces in Middle East, 21 April 1942

30 WO 201/732 Special Forces in Middle East, 1 April 1942.

31 NA WO 201/732 'Special Forces in Middle East', 'The Future of "L" Det.' David Stirling, 3 May 1942.

32 NA WO 201/731.

33 Maclean, *Eastern Approaches*, p. 200.

34 Josh Ireland, *Churchill & Son* (John Murray, 2021), p. 261.

35 Ireland, *Churchill & Son*, p. 260.

36 Greacen, *Chink*, p. 192.

37 IWM 8179, Ritchie, Neil Methuen, oral history.

38 Auchinleck to Churchill, 22 May 1942, cited in Churchill, *The Second World War. Volume IV*, p. 259.

39 Greacen, *Chink*, pp. 193–194.

40 Barnett, *The Desert Generals*, p. 149.

41 Connell, *Auchinleck*. p. 526.

42 Churchill to Auchinleck 2 June 1942, cited in Churchill, *The Second World War. Volume IV*, p. 296.

43 Richard Woodman, *Malta Convoys 1940–1943* (John Murray, 2003), pp. 306 – 316.

44 NA WO 201/732 'Special Forces in Middle East'.

45 Connell, *Auchinleck*, p. 537.

46 Cowles, *The Phantom Major,* p. 139.

47 WO201/727 Haseldene's File.

48 Friends of the Intelligence Corps Museum https://friendsintelligencemuseum.org/

49 Cowles, *The Phantom Major,* p. 145.

50 WO201/727 Haseldene's File.

51 NA WO 201/732 'Special Forces in Middle East', 'A Sqn, 1st SS Regt 20.6.42' and 'A Sqn ME Commando War Diary June 1942.'

52 WO201/727 Haseldene's File. Supplementary report on Lieutenant Friedrich Korner.

53 IWM 21759, Bennet.

54 Churchill to Auchinleck 14 June 1942, cited in Churchill, *The Second World War. Volume IV*, p. 303.

55 IWM 8080, 'A Quarter of my Century'.

56 Rommel, *Papers*, p. 232.

57 Greacen, *Chink*, p. 201.

58 Greacen, *Chink*, p. 203.

59 NA CAB 154/2 (1st Jan, 1942, to 31st Dec 1942.)'

60 IWM 337, Pleydell's diary, 1 July 1942.

61 Crichton-Stuart, *G Patrol*, p. 152.

62 'He was told not to be stupid and made to apologise . . .', Greacen, *Chink*, p. 133.

63 Crichton-Stuart, *G Patrol*, p. 153.

64 James, *Born of the Desert*, p. 86.

65 IWM 21759, Seekings.

66 James, *Born of the Desert*, p. 93.

67 Rommel, *Papers*, '90th Light Division', p. 246.

68 Greacen, *Chink*, pp. 208 – 209.

69 James, *Born of the Desert*, pp. 96 – 97.

70 Crichton-Stuart, *G Patrol*, pp. 155 – 156.

71 Timpson, *In Rommel's Backyard*, p. 168.

72 James, *Born of the Desert*, p. 115.

73 James, *Born of the Desert*, pp. 117 – 118.

74 Rommel, *Papers*, p. 253.

75 Greacen, *Chink*, pp. 219 – 220.

76 Rommel, *Papers*, p. 257.

77 NA WO 201/732 'Special Forces in Middle East', signal, 10 July 1942.

78 James, *Born of the Desert*, p. 144, 156.

79 NA WO 201/732 'Special Forces in Middle East', signal, 13 July 1942.

80 NA WO 201/732 'Special Forces in Middle East' 'Operations – Major Stirling,' signal 17 July 1942.

81 NA WO 201/732 'Special Forces in Middle East' 21 July 1942.

82 Barnett, *The Desert Generals*, p. 219.

83 Greacen, *Chink*, p. 222.

84 Cooper, *One of the Originals*, p. 64.

85 James, *Born of the Desert*, pp. 160 – 164.

86 Mike Sadler to author; description, Shaw, *Long Range Desert Group*, p. 161.

87 Shaw, *Long Range Desert Group*, Ch. 11; NA WO 201/732 'Special Forces in Middle East', 3 August 1942.

88 Field Marshall Lord Alanbrooke, *War Diaries 1939–1945* (Weidenfeld & Nicolson, 2001), p. 270.

89 Nigel Nicolson, *Alex. The Life of Field Marshall Earl Alexander of Tunis* (Weidenfeld and Nicolson, 1973), p. 153.

90 Nicolson, *Alex*, p. 155.

91 Churchill, *The Second World War. Volume IV*, p. 373.

92 Alanbrooke, *War Diaries*, p. 270.

93 Churchill, *The Second World War. Volume IV*, p. 376; John Keegan, *Churchill's Generals* (Weidenfeld & Nicolson, 1991), p. 140; Brooke, 'Their caravans were even now pitched close together'; Greacen, *Chink*, pp. 236 – 238.

94 Churchill, *The Second World War. Volume IV*, p. 377.

95 Alanbrooke, *War Diaries*, pp. 293 – 294.

96 NAs WO 201/732, signal, 6 August 1942.

97 NA WO 201/732 'Special Forces in Middle East'.

98 Barnett, *The Desert Generals*, Dorman-Smith's Appreciation in full, Appendix B, p. 331, Siwa, p. 335.

99 Greacen, *Chink*, p. 239.

100 Hugh 'Jimmy' James, *216 Squadron Association*. http://www.216squadronassociation.org.uk/pages/flt_lineBook/Death%20of%20General%20Gott.html

101 Alanbrooke, *War Diaries*, p. 295.

102 Churchill, letter to his wife 9 August 1942, Martin Gilbert *Winston Churchill: Road to Victory, 1941-1945* (Rosetta Books, 2015) p. 169.

103 IWM 8080, Appointments diary, 18 July 1942.

104 NA CAB 154/1 (1st Jan, 1942, to 31st Dec 1942.)'

105 NA WO 201/732 'Special Forces in Middle East' 'Most Secret. Prime Minister.' 10 August 1942.

106 Montgomery of Alamein, *The Memoirs of Field-Marshal the Viscount Montgomery of Alamein, K.G.* (Collins, 1958), Ch.s 4, 5.

107 Barnett, *The Desert Generals*, p. 237.

108 William Shakespeare, *Henry IV, Part II*, Act 3, Scene 2.

109 Greacen, *Chink*, p. 247.

110 IWM 21759, Seekings.

111 Description of Kufra, Shaw, *Long Range Desert Group*, pp. 78 – 84.

112 WO 201/751 Operation Bigamy.

113 NA CAB 154/1 (1st Jan, 1942, to 31st Dec 1942.)'

114 WO 201/751, Operation Bigamy, Conference notes, 28 August 1942.

115 WO 201/751, Operation Bigamy.

116 IWM 23787, audio, Brian Edevrain Dillon interview.

117 WO201/751 Operation Bigamy, 13 September 1942. Major JAR Freeland attached.

118 IWM 23787, audio, Brian Edevrain Dillon interview.

119 Maclean, *Eastern Approaches*, p. 237.

120 WO 201/751 Operation Bigamy.

121 IWM 23787, audio, Brian Edevrain Dillon interview.

122 Maclean, *Eastern Approaches*, p. 234.

123 WO 201/748 Report on Combined Operations Sept 42 – Oct 42.

124 IWM 23787, audio, Brian Edevrain Dillon interview.

125 WO 201/750 Bigamy Signals.

126 WO 201/748 Report on Combined Operations Sept 42 – Oct 42; IWM 21759, Seekings.

127 Report on Combined Operations Sept 42 – Oct 42; WO 201/750 Bigamy Signals; Maclean, *Eastern Approaches*, Ch. 5.

128 James, *Born of the Desert*, p. 265.

129 Maclean, *Eastern Approaches*, p. 259; J Milton-Haye 'The Green Eye of The Little Yellow God.'

130 James, *Born of the Desert*, Ch. 17; Report on Combined Operations Sept 42 – Oct 42.

131 WO 201/748 Report on Combined Operations Sept 42 – Oct 42.

Chapter 12

1 NA KV 2/1467- Johannes Willi EPPLER, alias Husein Gafaar.

2 NA KV 2/1467- Johannes Willi EPPLER, alias Husein Gafaar.

3 Sansom, *I Spied Spies*, p. 112.

4 Details, including dialogue, from Sansom, *I Spied Spies*, Ch.s 8, 9.

5 NA CAB 154/2 (1 Jan 1942 to 31 Dec 1942).

6 Spies capture, Sansom, *I Spied Spies*, Ch. 9.

7 NA CAB 154/2 (1 Jan 1942 to 31 Dec 1942).

8 IWM 12022, oral history, John Winthrop Hackett.

9 IWM 21759, Stirling.

10 James, *Born of the Desert*, p. 286.

11 Rommel, *Papers*, p. 280.

12 Barnett, *The Desert Generals*, p. 273.

13 Greacen, *Chink*, p. 100.

14 Rasmussen, *On Speed*, p. 68.

15 Rasmussen, *On Speed*, p. 71 (details in note), p. 284.

16 Rommel, *Papers*, p. 295.

17 NA CAB 154/2 (1 Jan 1942 to 31 Dec 1942)

18 'I developed a habit of going to bed early . . . and was never to be disturbed except in crisis', Montgomery, *Memoirs*, p. 61.

19 Mather, *When the Grass Stops Growing*, Ch. 23; De Guingand, *Operation Victory* (Hodder and Stoughton, 1947), pp. 199 – 200.

20 Barnett, *The Desert Generals*, p. 280.

21 Mather, *When the Grass Stops Growing*, Ch. 23.

22 Mather, *When the Grass Stops Growing*, Ch. 23.

23 Alanbrooke, *War Diaries*, p. 336.

24 Rommel, *The Rommel Papers*, p. 313.

25 The Eighth Army, September 1941 to January 1943 (HMSO, 1943).

26 Rommel, *The Rommel Papers*, p. 321.

27 Mather, *When the Grass Stops Growing*, Ch. 26.

28 James, *Born of the Desert*, p. 302.

29 Mather, *When the Grass Stops Growing*, Ch. 26.

30 James, *Born of the Desert*, p. 303.

31 IWM 23787, audio, Brian Edevrain Dillon interview.

32 NA ULTRA intercept A.C.C. in C south IC to Fliegerfuehrer Afrika 1C with copy to panzer army Africa on 26/12.

33 IWM 23787, audio, Brian Edevrain Dillon interview.

34 Cooper, *One of the Originals*, p. 67.

35 Mather, *When the Grass Stops Growing*, Ch. 27.

36 NA WO 218/96 'SAS War Diary Oct, Nov 42'.

37 Peter Davis, *SAS Men in the Making* (Pen & Sword Military, 2015), p. 33.

38 Mike Sadler to author.

39 Rommel, *Papers,* p. 393.

40 Lewes, *Jock Lewes*, Ch. 11.

41 'Mincemeat Problem' references NA CAB 154/2; CAB 154/3 (1st Jan, 1943, to 31st Dec 1943) unless otherwise indicated.

42 Andrew Roberts, *The Storm of War* (Penguin, 2010), p. 405.

43 Guingand, *Operation Victory*, p. 144 – 146, Maps 16, 17.

44 Thaddeus Holt, *The Deceivers* (Orion Books, 2004), p. 373.

45 NA ADM 223/794 Deception DNI, see 'Appendix A, Example of Present Hopeless Position.'

46 J. Keith Killby, 'Memoirs', quoted by *Monte San Martino Trust*. https://msmtrust.org.uk/escape-stories/in-combat-unarmed/

47 IWM 8080, 'The Epilogue of Operation Mincemeat.'

48 IWM 8080, 'The Epilogue of Operation Mincemeat.'

49 IWM 8080, 'The Epilogue of Operation Mincemeat.'

50 Rommel, *Papers,* p. 419.

51 NA WO 218/98, HQ Raiding Force. 1 SAS Regiment 1943.

52 NA WO 218/97, 1 SAS War Diary. 1943.

53 IWM 21759, Seekings.

54 DI Harrison, *These Men Are Dangerous* (Cassell & Company Ltd, 1957), p. 15.

55 Harrison, *These Men are Dangerous*, p. 17.

56 Titch Davidson.

57 Stewart Maclean, *SAS. The history of the Special Raiding Squadron* (Spellmount, 2006), p. 18.

58 Harrison, *These Men are Dangerous*, p. 23.

59 Harrison, *These Men are Dangerous*, p. 23.

60 Davis, *SAS Men*, p. 100.

61 Maclean, *SAS*, p. 19.

62 Davis, *SAS Men*, p. 101.

63 IWM 25504, Mayne's SRS War Diary; IWM 21759, Seekings.

64 Davis, *SAS Men*, p. 115.

65 Davis, *SAS Men*, p. 116.

66 Army Personnel Centre Historical Disclosures, Phillips, Service and Casualty form.

67 IWM 21759, Seekings.

68 Davis, *SAS Men*, p. 110.

69 Davis, *SAS Men*, p. 114.

70 Davis, *SAS Men*, p. 119.

71 Harrison, *These Men are Dangerous*, p. 26.

72 Harrison, *These Men are Dangerous*, p. 27.

73 Davis, *SAS Men*, p. 131.

74 NA WO 218/98 HQ Raiding Forces 1 SAS Regiment 1943.

75 Harrison, *These Men are Dangerous*, p. 28; Davis, *SAS Men*, p. 123.

76 IWM 21759, Seekings.

77 Harrison, *These Men are Dangerous*, p. 29.

78 Harrison, *These Men are Dangerous*, p. 31.

79 Maclean, *SAS*, p. 32.

80 IWM 21759, Seekings.

81 Details of this mission from Maclean, *SAS*, pp. 35, 36, 39, 41, 46; Davis, *SAS Men*, p. 146, 184; IWM 21759, Seekings; IWM 25504, Mayne's SRS War Diary; Harrison, *These Men are Dangerous*, pp. 34, 44, 45, 48, 49.

82 Maclean, *SAS*, p. 47.

83 Harrison, *These Men are Dangerous*, p. 53.

84 Harrison, *These Men are Dangerous*, p. 57.

85 Davis, *SAS Men*, p. 197.

86 IWM 25504, Mayne's SRS War Diary.

87 IWM 21759, Seekings.

88 IWM 21759, Seekings.

89 Davis, *SAS Men*, p. 202.

90 Davis, *SAS Men*, p. 228.

91 IWM 21759, Seekings.

92 IWM 21759, Seekings.

93 Davis, *SAS Men*, p. 230.

94 IWM 25504, Mayne's SRS War Diary.

95 IWM 21759, Seekings.

96 Davis, *SAS Men*, p. 253.

97 Davis, *SAS Men*, p. 258.

98 IWM 25504, Mayne's SRS War Diary.

99 Davis, *SAS Men*, p. 259.

100 IWM 25504, Mayne's SRS War Diary.

101 IWM 21759, Seekings.

102 IWM 25504, Mayne's SRS War Diary.

103 Davis, *SAS Men*, p. 276.

104 Davis, *SAS Men*, p. 277.

105 Davis, *SAS Men*, p. 279.

106 IWM 21759, Seekings.

107 Maclean, *SAS*, p. 100; Davis, *SAS Men*, p. 282.

108 IWM 21759, Seekings.

109 IWM 25504, Mayne's SRS War Diary.

110 Army Personnel Centre Historical Disclosures, Fraser, Army form B199A.

111 Davis, *SAS Men*, p. 317.

112 Davis, *SAS Men*, p. 334.

113 Davis, *SAS Men*, p. 341.

Chapter 13

1 Unless otherwise stated reference for 'Casting' is 'NA CAB 154/4, (1st Jan, 1944, to 31st Dec 1944.)'

2 IWM 8080, Appointments diary 1943 & 1944.

3 Lloyd Clark, *Anzio* (Headline Review, 2006), Ch.s 1, 2.

4 Rommel, *The Rommel Papers*, p. 446.

5 Winston Churchill, *The Second World War, Volume V* (Reprint Society, 1954), p. 374.

6 NA CAB 154/4, 1 January 1944 to 31 December 1944.

7 Greacen, *Chink*. p. 271.

8 IWM 21759, Seekings.

9 Ian Wellsted, *SAS with the Maquis* (Frontline, 2016), p. 66.

10 Lovat, *A March Past*, p. 130.

11 Byrne, *The General Salutes a Soldier*, p. 156.

12 Rommel, *Papers*, p. 470.

13 NA HS6/604 SAS Operations France.

14 NA HS6/604 SAS Operations France.

15 Supreme Headquarters Allied Expeditionary Force.

16 NA HS6/604 SAS Operations France.

17 NA Wo218/192, OPERATION HOUNDSWORTH 6 June–6 September 1944.

18 J.Fraser McLuskey, *Parachute Padre* (Spa Books, 1985), p. 75.

19 Wellsted, *SAS*, pp. 70, 73, 77, 78.

20 McLuskey, *Parachute Padre*, p. 80.

21 NA. Wo218/192, OPERATION HOUNDSWORTH 6 June–6 September 1944.

22 Wellsted, *SAS*, p. 112.

23 IWM 21759, Seekings.

24 IWM 21759, Seekings.

25 Wellsted, *SAS*, p. 112.

26 Wellsted, *SAS*, p. 116.

27 IWM 20936, Wood, Arthur Leonard Edward, oral history.

28 McLuskey, *Parachute Padre*, p. 84.

29 NA WO 218/192 Narrative here from OPERATION HOUNDSWORTH 6 June – 6 September 1944.

30 IWM 20936, Wood, Arthur Leonard Edward, oral history.

31 NA WO 218/191 'Reports on operations Normandy to Paris: Operations Titanic, Haft, Defoe, Gaff, Chaucer, Shakespeare, Dunhill, Bunyan, Trueform. 1944 June-Aug.'

32 NA FO 1093/292 'War: general; assassination priorities for OVERLORD'.

33 Mike Sadler to author.

34 NA WO 218/191 'Reports on operations Normandy to Paris: Operations Titanic, Haft, Defoe, Gaff, Chaucer, Shakespeare, Dunhill, Bunyan, Trueform. 1944 June-Aug.'

35 Winston Churchill, *The Second World War. Volume VI* (The Reprint Society, 1956).

36 NA WO218/192, OPERATION HOUNDSWORTH 6 June–6 September 1944.

37 Alec Prochiantz, *Promenons-nous dans les bois* (Société des Écrivains, 2011), p. 71.

38 McLuskey, *Parachute Padre* (Spa Books, 1985), p. 128.

39 McLuskey, *Parachute Padre*, p. 151.

40 NA WO218/192, OPERATION HOUNDSWORTH 6 June–6 September 1944.

41 Prochiantz, *Promenons-nous dans les bois*, p. 76.

42 Rommel, *Papers*, p. 520.

43 Rommel, *Papers*, p. 428.

44 Rommel, *Papers*, p. 487.

45 Rommel, *Papers*, p. 496.

46 IWM 21759, Seekings.

47 Ian Wellstead, *With the SAS across the Rhine* (Frontline Books, 2020), p. 66.

48 Army Personnel Centre Historical Disclosures, Fraser, Army form B199A.

Epilogue

1 Army Personnel Centre Historical Disclosures, Fraser, Army form B199A.

2 NA WO 90/9 'Judge Advocate General's Office: general courts martial registers, abroad. 1943–1960'.

3 IWM 21759, Seekings.

4 IWM 21759, Seekings.

5 Army Personnel Centre Historical Disclosures, Phillips, Army form B220AB.

6 William Fraser death certificate.

7 IWM 8080, 'The Epilogue of Operation Mincemeat.'

8 NA ADM 223/794 Deception DNI, see appendix 'proof of success of Mincemeat.'

Index

Note: page numbers in **bold** refer to maps.